Workbook for
Administrative
Medical Assisting
4th Edition

Marilyn Takahashi Fordney, CMA-AC, CMT
formerly, Instructor of Medical Insurance,
Medical Terminology, Medical Machine Transcription,
and Medical Office Procedures
Ventura College
Ventura, California

Joan Johnson Follis, BS
formerly, Instructor of Business Education and
Medical Office Procedures
Ventura College
Ventura, California

Contributor:
Linda French, CMA-C
Instructor and Business Consultant
Simi Valley Adult School and Career Institute
Simi Valley, California

Delmar Publishers

an International Thomson Publishing company

Albany • Bonn • Boston • Cincinnati • Detroit • London • Madrid
Melbourne • Mexico City • New York • Pacific Grove • Paris • San Francisco
Singapore • Tokyo • Toronto • Washington

COPYRIGHT © 1998
Delmar is a division of Thomson Learning. The Thomson Learning logo is a registered trademark used herein under license.

Printed in the United States of America
7 8 9 10 XXX 05 04 03 02

For more information, contact Delmar Learning, Executive Woods, 5 Maxwell Dr. Clifton Park, NY 12065; or find us on the World Wide Web at http://www.delmar.com

International Division List

Japan:
Thomson Learning
Palaceside Building 5F
1-1-1 Hitotsubashi, Chiyoda-ku
Tokyo 100 0003 Japan
Tel: 813 5218 6544
Fax: 813 5218 6551

UK/Europe/Middle East:
Thomson Learning
Berkshire House
168-173 High Holborn
London
WC1V 7AA United Kingdom
Tel: 44 171 497 1422
Fax: 44 171 497 1426

Canada:
Nelson/Thomson Learning
1120 Birchmount Road
Scarborough, Ontario
Canada M1K 5G4
Tel: 416-752-9100
Fax: 416-752-8102

Australia/New Zealand
Nelson/Thomson Learning
102 Dodds Street
South Melbourne, Victoria
3205
Australia
Tel: 61 39 685 4111
Fax: 61 39 685 4199

Latin America:
Thomson Learning
Seneca, 53
Colonia Polanco
11560 Mexico D.F. Mexico
Tel: 525-281-2906
Fax: 525-281-2656

Asia:
Thomson Learning
60 Albert Street, #15-01
Albert Complex
Singapore 189969
Tel: 65 336 6411
Fax: 65 336 7411

Library of Congress Cataloging-in-Publication Data:

ISBN 0-8273-7895-5

Library of Congress Catalog Card Number: 97-33446

Contents

Acknowledgments

We wish to express our deepest gratitude to the people and organizations who so willingly and enthusiastically contributed to the contents of this book.

Our thanks are due especially to the following people who acted as consultants and assisted in reviewing various parts of the manuscript. Without their expertise, comments, and suggestions, our work would not be as complete as it is.

CYNTHIA L. HOTTA
Pharmaceutical Representative
Burroughs Wellcome Company
Los, Angeles, California

JOANNE KENNEDY, MSLS
Health Sciences Librarian
St. John's Regional Medical Center
Oxnard, California

SUE STRATTON
Vice President, Health Care Services
Medical Administrative Consultants, Inc.
Agoura Hills, California

JANET LA MACCHIA
Love to Travel
Oxnard, California

JANE E. McCAW
Product Specialist
SYCOM
Madison, Wisconsin

CAROLYN TALESFORE
Ad and Promo Manager
Bibbero Systems, Inc.
Petaluma, California

Other authors, publishers, and manufacturers of equipment have been generous in granting permission to reproduce illustrations, and to them we extend our sincere thanks. We are especially grateful to M and W Printing Company, Waukegan, Illinois, for permission to use order forms, letterheads, and envelope sheets; to Medical Arts Press, Minneapolis, Minnesota, for permission to use hospital log forms; to St. Anthony Publishing, Alexandria, Virginia, for permission to use the Physician checklist for E/M code selection; and to Bibbero Systems, Inc., Petaluma, California for permission to use telephone, filing medical record, appointment, and encounter forms.

We wish to express our gratitude for the help and encouragement provided by our friends, colleagues, families, and the staff of Delmar Publishers.

Introduction to the Workbook

LEARNING OBJECTIVES

The medical assistant should be able to:

1. Perform duties as a receptionist and use professional techniques.
2. Handle patient referrals to hospitals and physician specialists.
3. Triage patient medical complaints, and phone calls.
4. Schedule appointments.
5. Compile and prepare patient medical records.
6. File records appropriately.
7. Replenish office supplies and manage inventory.
8. Process mail.
9. Communicate with travel agency to make travel arrangements.
10. Read a prescription.
11. Follow up on collection of accounts.
12. Make deposits and perform other banking procedures.
13. Perform bookkeeping procedures.
14. Perform payroll procedures.
15. Complete insurance claim forms.
16. Keyboard computer data and generate accounting reports.
17. Compose and prepare a resumé and cover letter when seeking employment.

INSTRUCTIONS TO THE STUDENT

This workbook has been prepared for those who use *Administrative Medical Assisting* as a text. Learning and performance objectives are presented for each exercise. Easily removable letterheads, forms, and patient records are presented as they might appear in a physician's practice. These are included for keyboarding practice. If you are working on a computer when beginning the course, the forms can be scanned by machine and put into the computer memory for completion. You will experience abstracting from patient records to complete some exercises.

Learning Objectives are given for each chapter. *Performance objectives* are stated for each exercise. Your instructor will indicate which standards are expected, the time frame that each exercise should be completed, and the accuracy required for each exercise.

Review Questions are presented to help you prepare for a multiple-choice theory test on each chapter studied.

Performance evaluation checklists for each exercise are located in Part III. These forms should be completed with your name and date and attached to each exercise so your instructor can evaluate and comment on your performance in completing the exercise.

The workbook exercises combined with the theory learned in the textbook meet the educational components of the American Association of Medical Assistants Role Delineation Study of 1997.

The workbook is divided into four parts. Part I presents exercises chapter by chapter, Part II includes blank forms and letterheads needed to complete each project, and Part III contains the Performance Evaluation Checklists corresponding to the Exercises in Part I, and Part IV is the Appendix. If you do not have a background in medical terminology, you need to obtain and use a good medical dictionary.

In addition to the blank forms included in this workbook, you will need:

50 sheets of 8 1/2" by 11" white typing paper

60 3" by 5" white file cards

3-ring binder with indexes

rubber bands, paper clips, pens, highlighter, pencils, transparent tape

correction fluid, typing eraser or correction sheets

2 white Number 10 envelopes (9 1/2" by 4")

1 folder with pockets to hand in assignments

3 manila file folders

3 labels for manila folders

colored felt-tip markers or crayons in red, orange, green, blue, and violet (optional)

optional: 7 white Number 10 envelopes
        7 white Number 6 envelopes
        pin-fed plain computer paper

Part I Chapter Exercises

Read through each exercise entirely before attempting to begin the assignment. Follow guidelines provided by your instructor to complete each exercise.

Part II Forms

The workbook pages have been perforated and punched so you can remove the blank forms found in Part II for handwritten or typed exercises. In some instances, you will be required to cut apart some forms.

Part III Performance Evaluation Checklists

After each exercise has been completed, complete the corresponding checklist in this section. Once the exercise has been graded by your instructor and returned to you, save it in your Student Reference Notebook (described later) for future reference or for your job portfolio.

Part IV Appendix

Before beginning the exercises, tear out the Appendix and place it in a three-ring binder with chapter indexes so you can access information quickly to help you complete the workbook exercises. This will become your **Student Reference Notebook**. This appendix includes the policies, guidelines, and mock fee schedule while working as a medical assistant for the Practon Medical Group, Inc., a simulation for hands on experience. You may wish to either tear out to make photocopies of other sections of the textbook for your personal use. In addition, your instructor may give you handouts pertaining to local office or hospital guidelines to place in your notebook.

Notebook Content Suggestions

From Workbook:

Part II, Blank forms   for possible photocopy use
Part IV, Appendix

From Textbook:

Patients Care Abbreviations	Table 8-1
Common Prescription Abbreviations and Symbols	Table 9-3
Evaluation and Management CPT Codes	Tables 16-6 and 16-7
Insurance form templates	Figures 16-2, 16-5 and 16-6
HCFA-1500 Claim Form instructions	pp. 335-345
Glossary	end of textbook

Medical Assistant Role Delineation Chart

The competencies required to practice medical assisting were first analyzed by the American Association of Medical Assistants in Chicago, Illinois and published as a list in the 1979 **D**eveloping **A** curricul**UM** (DACUM). This was updated in 1984 and 1990. A subsequent study in 1996 has produced the Role Delineation Study listing areas of competence for entry-level medical assistants. A specific list of competencies has been developed by the Curriculum Review Board in another document. The following chart illustrates the areas of competence required for an entry-level medical assistant performing administrative procedures and general or transdisciplinary skills correlated with the corresponding text and workbook chapters. Since this workbook does not address clinical training, those procedures are not included in the following chart.

AMERICAN ASSOCIATION OF MEDICAL ASSISTANTS
MEDICAL ASSISTANT ROLE DELINEATION CHART

AREAS OF COMPETENCE	TEXT/WORKBOOK CHAPTER
ADMINISTRATIVE PROCEDURES	
■ Perform basic clerical functions	1 through 20
■ Schedule, coordinate, and monitor appointments	6
■ Schedule inpatient/outpatient admissions and procedures	6
■ Understand and apply third-party guidelines	16
■ Obtain reimbursement through accurate claims submission	16
■ Monitor third-party reimbursement	15
■ Perform medical transcription	12
■ Understand and adhere to managed care policies and procedures	2, 3, 4, 5, 6, 15, 16
PRACTICE FINANCES	
■ Perform procedural and diagnostic coding	16
■ Apply bookkeeping principles	18
■ Document and maintain accounting and banking records	17
■ Manage accounts receivable	15, 18
■ Manage accounts payable	18
■ Process payroll	19
GENERAL (TRANSDISCIPLINARY)	
PROFESSIONALISM	
■ Project a professional manner and image	1
■ Adhere to ethical principles	3
■ Demonstrate initiative and responsibility	2
■ Work as a team member	2
■ Manage time effectively	5, 13
■ Prioritize and perform multiple tasks	5, 13
■ Adapt to change	2
■ Promote the CMA credential	1
■ Enhance skills through continuing education	1

COMMUNICATION SKILLS

- Treat all patients with compassion and empathy — 2, 4
- Recognize and respect cultural diversity — 4
- Adapt communications to individual's ability to understand — 4
- Use professional telephone technique — 5
- Use effective and correct verbal and written communications — 5, 12, 14
- Recognize and respond to verbal and nonverbal communications — 4
- Use medical terminology appropriately — 1 through 20
- Receive, organize, prioritize, and transmit information — 13
- Serve as liaison — 2
- Promote the practice through positive public relations — 4

LEGAL CONCEPTS

- Maintain confidentiality — 3
- Practice within the scope of education, training, and personal capabilities — 3
- Prepare and maintain medical records — 8, 9, 10
- Document accurately — 8, 9
- Use appropriately guidelines when releasing information — 3
- Follow employer's established policies dealing with the health care contact — 2, 16
- Follow federal, state, and local legal guidelines — 3
- Maintain awareness of federal and state health care legislation and regulations — 3, 9
- Maintain and dispose of regulated substances in compliance with government guidelines
- Comply with established risk management safety procedures — 11
- Recognize professional credentialing criteria — 1, 2
- Participate in the development and maintenance of personnel, policy, and procedure manuals — 11, 20

OPERATIONAL FUNCTIONS

- Maintain supply inventory — 11
- Evaluate and recommend equipment and supplies — 7
- Apply computer techniques to support office operations — 7

Part I

Chapter Exercises

CHAPTER 1

A Career as an Administrative Medical Assistant

OBJECTIVES

After completing the exercises, the student will be able to:

1. Write meanings for chart note abbreviations.
2. Enhance spelling skills by learning new medical words.
3. List the duties of an administrative medical assistant.
4. State important personality characteristics for medical assistants.
5. List ways for understanding human behavior.
6. List attributes for good team interaction.
7. Name the stages of dying.
8. Identify strengths and weaknesses to improve.

AREAS OF COMPETENCE

Administrative Procedures
■ Perform basic clerical functions

General (Transdisciplinary)

Professionalism
■ Project a professional manner and image
■ Promote the Certified Medical Assistant (CMA) credential

■ Enhance skills through continuing education

Communication Skills
■ Use medical terminology appropriately

Legal Concepts
■ Recognize professional credentialing criteria

ABBREVIATION AND SPELLING REVIEW LESSON

Read the following patient's chart note and write the meanings for the abbreviations listed below the note. To decode any abbreviations you do not understand or that appear unfamiliar to you, refer to text Tables 8-1 and 9-3. Medical terms in the chart note are italicized; study them for spelling. Use your medical dictionary to look up their definitions. Your instructor may give a test for the spelling and definition of the words and abbreviations.

Bart J. Stephens

September 15, 199X Routine PE. Ht 6 ft. Wt 163 lbs. P 70. BP 130/70. Pt s̄ complaints. *Systemic* Ex neg. except for Grade I *pulmonic murmur.* EKG, CBC, UA, & chest x-ray films neg. IMP: No disease. Rx: *Tetanus toxoid* booster, 0.5 cc. DC. Ret p.r.n.

Fran Practon, MD

Fran Practon, MD

PE	_____	EKG	_____
ht	_____	CBC	_____
ft	_____	UA	_____
wt	_____	neg.	_____
lbs	_____	IMP	_____
P	_____	Rx	_____
BP	_____	cc	_____
pt	_____	DC	_____
s̄	_____	ret	_____
Ex	_____	p.r.n.	_____
neg	_____		

REVIEW QUESTIONS

Review the objectives, glossary, and chapter information before completing the following review questions.

1. Briefly describe the contribution of each of the following:

   a. Imhotep _____
   _____

   b. Edward Jenner _____
   _____

   c. Fredrick Banting _____
   _____

   d. Anton van Leeuwenhoek _____
   _____

   e. Pierre and Marie Curie _____
   _____

   f. Paul Ehrlich _____
   _____

2. Match the pioneer in medicine in the left column with the appropriate item in the right column by writing the letters in the blanks.

Ignaz Phillip Semmelweis _____   a. father of modern anatomy
Joseph Lister   _____   b. father of medicine
Louis Pasteur   _____   c. founder of nursing
Jonas Edward Salk   _____   d. discovered the x-ray
Clara Barton   _____   e. developed the first lens strong enough
Aesculapius   _____   to see bacteria
Ambroise Pare   _____   f. conquered yellow fever
Walter Reed   _____   g. father of bacteriology
William Harvey   _____   h. discovered the vaccine against polio
Wilhem K. Roentgen   _____   i. Greek God of healing
Hippocrates   _____   j. founded the American Red Cross
Vesalius   _____   k. father of sterile surgery
James Marion Sims   _____   l. father of modern surgery
Florence Nightingale   _____   m. fought against puerperal fever
Alexander Fleming   _____   n. demonstrated circulation of blood
                                      o. invented the vaginal speculum
                                      p. discovered insulin
                                      q. discovered penicillin

3. List the duties an administrative medical assistant might perform.
   a. _____
   b. _____
   c. _____
   d. _____
   e. _____
   f. _____
   g. _____
   h. _____
   i. _____
   j. _____
   k. _____
   l. _____
   m. _____
   n. _____
   o. _____
   p. _____
   q. _____
   r. _____
   s. _____

4. Name three resources a medical assistant can use to keep knowledge of research and new techniques current.
   a. _____
   b. _____
   c. _____

5. Give the names of two national organizations that represent medical assistants.

   a. _____

   b. _____

6. How does a medical assistant's excellent grooming reflect the management and image of the medical office?

   _____

   _____

7. In addition to the many skills that are required to be an administrative medical assistant, there are many important personality characteristics required. Name eight of them.

   a. _____

   b. _____

   c. _____

   d. _____

   e. _____

   f. _____

   g. _____

   h. _____

8. To understand human behavior, list ways you can better orient yourself to the patient.

   a. _____

   b. _____

   c. _____

   d. _____

   e. _____

   f. _____

   g. _____

   h. _____

   i. _____

9. An emergency has occurred in Dr. Practon's office. Name the behavior the medical assistant must exhibit to patients.

   a. _____

   b. _____

   c. _____

10. List some attributes an employee needs for good team interaction.

   a. _____

   b. _____

   c. _____

   d. _____

   e. _____

   f. _____

11. List the stages of dying.

a. _____

b. _____

c. _____

d. _____

e. _____

EXERCISE 1-1   SELF-ASSESSMENT

PERFORMANCE OBJECTIVE

TASK: Answer questions and identify strengths and weaknesses.

CONDITIONS: Use one sheet of white typing paper and pen or pencil.

STANDARDS: Time: _____ minutes
Accuracy: _____
(NOTE: The time element and accuracy criteria may be given by your instructor.)

DIRECTIONS: Following are some questions that will help you do a self-assessment. Read each of them carefully and try to answer them honestly. After you have completed them, try to identify your strengths with an *S* and weaknesses with a *W*. This will not only help you to know what areas you need to work on but will help you determine in which type of job you may be best suited.

a. Are you considerate of others? _____

b. Do you treat people with respect? _____

c. Do you have a kind, friendly, and good-natured manner? _____

d. Do you have the ability to be discreet and keep information confidential? _____

e. Do you have a positive attitude? _____

f. Can you smile easily? _____

g. Can you listen instead of talking all the time? _____

h. Are you polite? _____

i. Can you be sympathetic and empathetic and discern the difference? _____

j. Are you reliable and dependable? _____

k. Are you honest and trustworthy? _____

l. Can you accept responsibility? _____

m. Can you remain calm during an emergency? _____

n. Are you well groomed, with a neat appearance? _____

o. Are you a team player? _____

p. Are you patient? _____

q. Do you reserve judgement of others? _____

r. Do you have good judgement? _____

s. Are you willing to learn? _____

t. Do you accept criticism?   _____

u. Are you sensitive to the feelings of others?   _____

v. Do you have good communication skills?   _____

w. Can you remain free from bias?   _____

TOTAL: Strengths _____   Weaknesses _____

Now that you are aware of the strengths and weaknesses, this information can be a guide to help you work to improve during the course as you interact with individuals.

NOTE: A Performance Evaluation Checklist for this exercise can be found at the back of the workbook.

COMPUTER EXERCISES

Before proceeding, you may want to do more exercises or review the concepts you have learned. Additional practice material is provided on your computer disk.

DIRECTIONS: Install the software into the computer following the instructions on the disk label. Complete the computer exercises for Chapter 1.

CHAPTER 2

Medical Practice Settings: Traditional and Managed Care

OBJECTIVES

After completing the exercises, the student will be able to:

1. List the benefits of using a health maintenance organization (HMO) and a traditional health care system.

2. Differentiate the types of health care settings.

3. Respond to patient calls and make referral decisions regarding appropriate hospital departments.

4. Respond to patient calls regarding specific problems and refer them to the correct specialist.

5. Decode abbreviations for medical health care professionals and apply them in a realistic text.

6. Catalog skills needed by the administrative medical assistant.

AREAS OF COMPETENCE

Administrative Procedures
- Perform basic clerical functions
- Understand and adhere to managed care policies and procedures

General (Transdisciplinary)

Professionalism
- Demonstrate initiative and responsibility
- Work as a team member
- Adapt to change

Communication Skills
- Use medical terminology appropriately
- Treat all patients with compassion and empathy
- Serve as liason

Legal Concepts
- Follow employer's established policies dealing with the health care contract
- Recognize professional credentialing criteria

ABBREVIATION AND SPELLING REVIEW LESSON

Read the following patient's chart note and write the meanings for the abbreviations listed below the note. To decode any abbreviations you do not understand or that appear unfamiliar to you, refer to text Tables 8-1 and 9-3. Medical terms in the chart note are italicized; study them for spelling. Use your medical dictionary to look up their definitions. Your instructor may give a test for the spelling and definition of the words and abbreviations.

Troy Wenzlau

36-year-old W male seen as E for Fx L *humerus*. Pt DNS for re-exam last month as scheduled. Pt has been on SD X 3 mo for back pain and was determined P&S from a previous back injury last yr. Given I of *Demerol* 50 mg IM for pain, x-ray L arm ordered. Cast and return to ofc in 2 wks.

Gerald Practon MD

Gerald Practon, MD

W	white	X	multiplied by
E	emergency	P&S	permanent + stationary
Fx	fracture	yr	year
L	left	I	injection
Pt	patient	mg	milligrams
DNS	did not show	IM	intramuscular
re-exam		ofc	office
SD	state disability	wks	weeks

REVIEW QUESTIONS

Review the objectives, glossary, and chapter information before completing the following review questions.

1. In a health maintenance organization (HMO), what is a treating physician called?

   PCP or Gate Keeper

2. In a preferred provider organization (PPO), what is the health care provider called and what incentive is there for the patient to use this provider?

   a. preferred provider
   b. lower co-pay's and deductibles

3. In an independent practice association (IPA), how is the physician paid?

   Capitation or fee for service

4. Why is an exclusive provider organization (EPO) called exclusive?

   subscribers must utilize providers offered in a limited network

5. What choice of care do patients have when belonging to a point-of-service plan?

   can go in or out-of-network

6. Name several contributing factors to the rise of health care costs.

advanced life expectancy, better life support measures new drugs, more sophisticated tests & procedures/equip.

7. List the benefits of using a health maintenance organization (HMO) and a traditional health care system as you compare and contrast their similarities and differences.

	HMO		Traditional
a.	med coverage	a.	PCP choice
b.	no deductible	b.	choice of specialists
c.	small co-pay	c.	hospital choice
d.	100% coverage	d.	facility choice
e.	preventative svs	e.	no auth process
f.	med supply coverage	f.	immediate testing + referrals

8. When several physicians with different specialties practice medicine together, what is their practice called?

multi specialty practice

9. List three services urgent care centers provide that most other practices do not offer.

a. extended hours

b. walk-in capability

c. one-stop-shopping (lab, x-ray, pt)

10. Why should the medical assistant meet the hospital personnel where his or her physician is on staff?

to develop a relationship for better communication

11. Name several types of nonprofit hospitals.

a. general

b. community

c. industry owned

d. union owned

e. religious

12. Name three important factors in choosing a reliable laboratory.

a. quality-control standards

b. turn-around time -

c. cost to the patient

13. Choose the type of health care *setting* you would like to work in and list the reasons for your choice.

Setting: _____

Reasons: _____

_____

_____

HOSPITAL REFERRALS

PERFORMANCE OBJECTIVE

TASK: Make determinations regarding transferring patient calls to specific hospital departments.

CONDITIONS: Use pen or pencil.

STANDARDS: Time: _____ minutes
Accuracy: _____

DIRECTIONS: You are the receptionist in Dr. Gerald Practon's office. A patient, Reiko Dimon, telephones. She was discharged from the hospital last week and has various questions. List the correct hospital department you would refer the patient to. (NOTE: Refer to Figure 2-2 in the text.)

a. _MR_ — Where does she go to pick up a copy of her operative report?

b. _dietetic_ — Where can she attend a nutritional education class?

c. _lab_ — Where does she go for a urinalysis?

d. _pharmacy_ — She has a question about the medication that was given to her when she left the hospital.

e. _Respiratory_ — Should she use a bronchodilator before she goes to have a pulmonary function test?

f. _administration_ — She would like to personally tell the hospital president how wonderfully she was cared for during her hospital stay.

g. _ER_ — She would like to speak to the physician who admitted her when she first arrived by ambulance at the hospital.

h. _Social Svs_ — She would like to know whether anyone has found a convalescent hospital for her mother, who is an inpatient.

i. _PT_ — She would like to schedule occupational therapy.

j. _business_ — She does not understand a hospital bill and would like it explained.

k. _medical Staff_ — She would like the name of the new OB-GYN doctor from San Francisco who is performing deliveries at the hospital.

l. _nuclear med_ — She has a question regarding the contrast media that will be given to her before a bone scan.

m. _X Radiology_ — She would like to pick up a preparation kit for a barium enema.

n. _financial_ — She has a question regarding an old refund that should have been sent to her by now.

o. _nursing admin_ — She would like to speak to the utilization review nurse who was assigned to her case.

p. _MRF magnetic resonance imaging_ She would like to know if she can wear her wedding ring in the MRI machine.

q. _Physiology / cardiology_ She would like to know how to dress for the treadmill test.

r. _GI_ She would like to know the preparation for a sigmoidoscopy that is scheduled.

s. _ODS_ She would like to know what time to arrive for a blood transfusion.

NOTE: A Performance Evaluation Checklist for this exercise can be found at the back of the workbook.

EXERCISE 2-2

REFER PATIENTS TO THE CORRECT PHYSICIAN SPECIALIST

PERFORMANCE OBJECTIVE

TASK: Match the correct specialist with the patient's complaints.

CONDITIONS: Use pen or pencil.

STANDARDS: Time: _____ minutes

Accuracy: _____

DIRECTIONS: In many situations the administrative medical assistant will be dealing with the authorization referral process. They may also deal with patients being referred by specialists to the practice where they are working. To enhance this understanding, consider the patients' problems and match their complaints with the correct specialist.

	Patient Complaint	Specialist
1. _F_	Pregnant	A. Allergist
2. _P_	Operation	B. Dermatologist
3. _J_	Autopsy report	C. Neonatologist
4. _Q_	Bladder problem	D. Neurologist
5. _A_	Chronic runny nose from dust	E. Nuclear Medicine
6. _N_	Severe depression	F. Obstetrician
7. _M_	Face lift	G. Ophthalmologist
8. _C_	Premature infant	H. Orthopedic Surgeon
9. _K_	Infant DPT injection	I. Otolaryngologist
10. _I_	Ear discharge	J. Pathologist
11. _O_	X-rays	K. Pediatrics
12. _H_	Fractured bone	L. Physiatrist
13. _L_	Rehabilitation for chronic back pain	M. Plastic Surgeon
		N. Psychiatrist
14. _D_	Multiple sclerosis	O. Radiologist
15. _G_	Glaucoma	P. Surgeon
16. _B_	Severe case of psoriasis	Q. Urologist
17. _E_	Bone scan	

NOTE: A Performance Evaluation Checklist for this exercise can be found at the back of the workbook.

| EXERCISE 2-3 | ABBREVIATIONS FOR HEALTH CARE PROFESSIONALS |

PERFORMANCE OBJECTIVE

TASK: Match the correct terms with the abbreviations.

CONDITIONS: Use pen or pencil.

STANDARDS: Time: _____ minutes
Accuracy: _____

DIRECTIONS: Read the following scenario and decode the abbreviations for the appropriate health care professional using the correct terms.

Laverne M. Stinowski   May 15, 199X

Mrs. Stinowski was brought by ambulance to the hospital and was cared for by an EMT. In the emergency room she was treated by a DEM. During her hospital stay she was seen daily by the MD, who was also a FACS. After discharge, Mrs. Stinowski visited the physician's private office and was processed in by a CMA. An LVN drew her blood and escorted her to the treatment room. The physician was out of the office, so an RNP saw Mrs. Stinowski. An order was given for her to see an RPT. The blood test was read in the laboratory by an MT(ASCP). The patient's record was typed by a CMT, and her insurance claim was processed by a CPC. The patient went home, and the PA-C was in charge of ordering the patient a VN for the following day.

Gerald M. Practon MD

Gerald M. Practon, MD

EMT *Emerg Med Tech*   DEM *doctor of emerg med*

MD *doctor medical*   FACS *fellow of the american college of surgeons*

CMA *certified med asst*   LVN *licensed vocational nurse*

RNP *registered nurse pra*   RPT *registered phys therapist*

MT(ASCP) *medical tech*   CMT *cert med tran*

CPC *cert procedural coder*   PA-C *phys. asst – cert*

VN *visiting nurse*

NOTE: A Performance Evaluation Checklist for this exercise can be found at the back of the workbook.

**EXERCISE
2-4** **ADMINISTRATIVE JOB REQUIREMENTS**

PERFORMANCE OBJECTIVE

TASK: Itemize job requirements and determine *basic skills* necessary for the administrative medical assistant.

CONDITIONS: Use pen or pencil.

STANDARDS: Time: _____ minutes
Accuracy: _____

DIRECTIONS: Review the list of job requirements and record some basic skills the administrative medical assistant needs. You will see these skills occurring repetitiously in the different specialties listed.

a. _scheduling tests/appts_   e. _telephone calls_

b. _med term_   f. _mature, calm, diplomatic_

c. _typing skills_   g. _A+P knowledge_

d. _book keeping_   h. _transcribing_

NOTE: A Performance Evaluation Checklist for this exercise can be found at the back of the workbook.

COMPUTER EXERCISES

Before proceeding, you may want to do more exercises or review the concepts you have learned. Complete the computer exercises on the software for Chapter 2.

CHAPTER 3

Medicolegal and Ethical Responsibilities

OBJECTIVES

After completing the exercises, the student will be able to:

1. Write meanings for chart note abbreviations.

2. Enhance spelling skills by learning new medical words.

3. Prepare a legally correct medicolegal letter using letterhead.

AREAS OF COMPETENCE

Administrative Procedures
■ Perform basic clerical functions
■ Understand and adhere to managed care policies and procedures

General (Transdisciplinary)

Professionalism
■ Adhere to ethical principles

Communication Skills
■ Use medical terminology appropriately

Legal Concepts
■ Maintain confidentiality
■ Practice within the scope of education, training, and personal capabilities
■ Use appropriate guidelines when releasing information
■ Follow federal, state, and local guidelines
■ Maintain awareness of federal and state health care legislation and regulations

ABBREVIATION AND SPELLING REVIEW LESSON

Read the following patient's chart note and write the meanings for the abbreviations listed below the note. To decode any abbreviations you do not understand or that appear unfamiliar to you, refer to text Tables 8-1 and 9-3. Medical terms in the chart note are italicized; study them for spelling. Use your medical dictionary to look up their definitions. Your instructor may give a test for the spelling and definition of the words and abbreviations.

David K. Chung

September 20, 199X HX: *Diarrhea* 3 days. T 99°F. No A. Cough producing yellow *sputum*. *Wheezing* in lt base. Moderate PND. Rec *vaporizer* and *amoxicillin* 250 mg p.o. q.8h. Diag URI. Etiol. unknown. Ordered CXR, CBC, & UA. Retn 2 wks.

Gerald Practon MD
Gerald Practon, MD

HX _____	diag _____
T _____	URI _____
F _____	etiol. _____
A _____	CXR _____
lt _____	CBC _____
PND _____	UA _____
mg _____	retn _____
p.o. _____	wks _____
rec _____	

REVIEW QUESTIONS

Review the objectives, glossary, and chapter information before completing the following review questions.

1. Match the terms in the left column with the definitions in the right column by writing the letters in the blanks.

   medical ethics _____ b

   medical professional liability _____ c

   medical etiquette _____ a

   a. code of conduct, courtesy, and manners customary in the medical profession
   b. moral principles and standards in the medical profession
   c. malpractice; any professional misconduct or unreasonable lack of skill or fidelity in professional or fiduciary duties

2. A sales representative from the Hope Surgical Company brings a case of bourbon for your physician. Can your physician ethically accept this gift?

   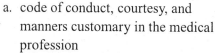 No

3. Betty Harper is given a booklet on the office policies that explains charges for missed appointments, telephone calls, and insurance form completion. She brings two insurance forms, and you bill her for this service. Is this ethical?

   ~~No~~ yes _____

   _____

4. Linda Mason tells another patient in the reception room that another physician is treating her for her stomach ulcer. You overhear this conversation and know Dr. Practon is also treating her for this same condition in addition to her high blood pressure. What should you do?

   ~~Yes~~ Tell Dr. Practon of _____

   conversation immediately

5. Name two types of medical professional liability insurance.

   a. _Claims made by ins._____

   b. _____

6. A physician is legally responsible for any act you perform while in his employ. The legal phrase used to describe this responsibility is _____ , and it means _____ .

7. Name three alternatives to the litigation process.

   a. _____

   b. _____

   c. _____

8. Martin P. Finley is examined, and the physician discovers a wart recurring on the patient's thumb. Mr. Finley asks the physician to remove it. In this instance, what kind of contract exists?

   _____

9. Dr. Rodriguez examines Mr. Garcia and diagnoses a gallstone. He reports this to the patient and recommends surgery. The patient says he agrees to the surgery. Are all conditions of informed consent present in this case?

   _____

   If not, name any that might be missing. _____

   _____

10. A tow truck has a head-on collision on a rural highway 25 miles out of town. Dr. O'Halloran is driving along and notices the accident. He stops, finds a victim of the accident bleeding profusely, and renders first aid. Will he be held liable for any medical complication in aiding this victim? _____

    Name the law that governs this situation.

    _____

11. Candice Goodson, a divorced 14-year-old, comes into the office and requests an examination to ascertain pregnancy. Can the physician care for her without parental consent? _____ Name the type of minor she is. _____

12. Kathy Hornsby does not show up for her 10:30 A.M. appointment. Describe the documentation that is necessary. _____

_____

13. A subpoena is served on Dr. Bradley in regard to patient Teri Sanchez. In this instance, is a patient release-of-information form necessary? _____

14. Gary Ryan has an outstanding bill of $200. You receive a signed release-of-information form from Dr. Homer's office for a copy of his progress notes since surgery. Can you ethically withhold this information until Mr. Ryan pays his bill?

_____

15. Anthony Munroe, aged 10, has had a tonsillectomy. In your state, the laws require you to retain his medical records for how long? _____

_____

16. Mrs. Marinacci states she wishes to donate her kidneys for transplant when she dies. What legal document is required for her wishes to be followed?

_____

17. Match the words in the left column with the definitions in the right column by writing the letters in the blanks.

   malfeasance   _____   a. lawful treatment done in the wrong way

   misfeasance   _____   b. failure of the physician to do anything

   nonfeasance   _____   c. wrongful treatment of the patient

18. Name the three principal defenses in a malpractice lawsuit.

   a. _____

   b. _____

   c. _____

19. What kind of liability are negligence, battery, false imprisonment, libel, fraud, and invasion of privacy?_____

_____

_____

20. Mrs. Williams calls and asks you for her x-rays. She says, "I paid for them, therefore they belong to me." What response would you offer?

_____

_____

_____

<table>
<tr><td>EXERCISE
3-1</td><td>**RELEASE OF INFORMATION**</td></tr>
</table>

PERFORMANCE OBJECTIVE

TASK: Answer multiple choice questions.

CONDITIONS: Use pen or pencil.

STANDARDS: Time: _____ minutes
Accuracy: _____

DIRECTIONS: Each of the questions or incomplete statements is followed by suggested answers or completions. Select the *one* best answer in each case.

1. A minor child has fathered a child and signed for release of his newborn's record. The authorization is:
   a. Valid. The boy has now become an emancipated minor by fathering a child.
   b. Invalid. The boy is not emancipated because he fathered a child. However, a minor child who is pregnant or has been pregnant is considered an emancipated minor.

2. Dr. Fran Practon receives a subpoena served by an attorney requesting the obstetrical records for a mother and the sealed records of an adoptive baby. You should
   a. release the mother's record.
   b. honor the subpoena for both mother and baby.
   c. ask for a court order for both the mother's and baby's records.

3. An insurance company sends Dr. Practon a request for the records of Jerry Osborne. A signed authorization accompanies the request. The face sheet of the medical record indicates that the physician discussed HIV testing, and the patient refused the test. You would:
   a. require a special consent because an HIV test was offered and documentation appears in the medical record.
   b. release the record because the signed authorization is valid.

4. Dr. Fran Practon has been treating a child for influenza and the chart note states, "six-year-old autistic, white female. . . ." The family attorney sends a request for medical records with an authorization signed by the parents. You should
   a. release copies since no mental health services were given and this is not a protected record by law.
   b. ask for a special release-of-records form because of the reference to the diagnosis of autism, since this is classified as a mental health record.

5. Dr. Gerald Practon receives a request from a social worker for medical records on a minor who is a ward of the court. The minor has signed a release. You would:
   a. release the records and send them to the social worker because the child is a ward of the court and he or she has rights to these records.
   b. tell the social worker that the child's parents must sign the release before records may be released.
   c. inform the social worker that since the child is a ward of the court, the child's guardian must sign the release because the child's signature is not valid.

NOTE: A Performance Evaluation Checklist for this exercise can be found at the back of the workbook.

COMPUTER EXERCISES

Before proceeding, you may want to do more exercises or review the concepts you have learned. Complete the computer exercises on the software for Chapter 3.

CHAPTER 4

The Receptionist

OBJECTIVES

After completing the exercises, the student will be able to:

1. Write meanings for chart note abbreviations.

2. Enhance spelling skills by learning new medical words.

3. Respond to situations in a medical office.

4. Supervise filling in a patient information form and a disabled person placard.

AREAS OF COMPETENCE

Administrative Procedures
- Perform basic clerical functions
- Understand and adhere to managed care policies and procedures

General (Transdisciplinary)

Communication Skills
- Treat all patients with compassion and empathy

- Recognize and respect cultural diversity
- Adapt communications to individual's ability to understand
- Recognize and respond to verbal and nonverbal communications
- Use medical terminology appropriately
- Promote the practice through positive public relations

ABBREVIATION AND SPELLING REVIEW LESSON

Read the following patients' chart notes and write the meanings for the abbreviations listed below the note. To decode any abbreviations you do not understand or that appear unfamiliar to you, refer to text Tables 8-1 and 9-3. Medical terms in the chart note are italicized; study them for spelling. Use your medical dictionary to look up their definitions. Your instructor may give a test for the spelling and definition of the words and abbreviations.

DATE	PROGRESS
10/1/9X	Maria D. Gomez, well-developed Hispanic ♀ fell on sharp object at
	9 a.m. Laceration of L lower lip 0.5 cm. Tr.: cleaned, sutured, &
	drained. DPT inj. Retn in 5 days Fran Practon, MD

♀ _____   Tr. _____

a.m. _____   DPT _____

L _____   inj. _____

cm _____   retn _____

DATE	PROGRESS
10/1/9X	Barry K. Wesson This white ♂ had severe pain Ⓛ sternoclavicular
	area. Chest clear to P&A, EKG ō AP&L chest XR–N. Demerol
	75mg for pain Dx neuralgia Fran Practon, MD

♂ _____   AP&L _____

Ⓛ _____   XR _____

P&A _____   N _____

EKG _____   mg _____

ō _____   Dx _____

REVIEW QUESTIONS

Review the objectives, glossary, and chapter information before completing the following review questions.

1. List two reasons for developing an information brochure and presenting it to the patient:

   a. _____

   b. _____

2. Distinguish between stress and burnout.

   _____

   _____

   _____

   _____

3. What safeguard can be taken against the mispronunciation of a patient's name?

_____

_____

4. List five positive personality traits the physician seeks when hiring a medical assistant.

   a. _____

   b. _____

   c. _____

   d. _____

   e. _____

5. How can you use empathy in your patient relations? _____

   _____

6. Give two reasons for having staff conferences.

   a. _____

   b. _____

7. State the difference between verbal and nonverbal communication.

   _____

   _____

8. Describe four actions a staff member can take to counteract stress.

   a. _____

   b. _____

   c. _____

   d. _____

9. List six special considerations that the office staff can provide a developmentally disabled or geriatric patient.

   a. _____

   b. _____

   c. _____

   d. _____

   e. _____

   f. _____

10. Name four types of special needs patients.

    a. _____

    b. _____

    c. _____

    d. _____

EXERCISE 4-1# RESPONSES TO OFFICE SITUATIONS

PERFORMANCE OBJECTIVE

TASK: Study the situations, determine your responses, and key or handwrite them with tact and consideration for the patient's medical problem.

CONDITIONS: Use one or two sheets of white typing paper and a red pen.

STANDARDS: Time: _____ minutes
Accuracy: _____

DIRECTIONS: Consider the following situations that might commonly occur in a physician's office and key your best response. Indicate the situations you have difficulty handling by circling the introductory number in red and bringing them to class for discussion.

1. Another medical assistant in the office criticizes a patient behind his or her back for wearing bizarre clothes. What would your response be?

2. Dr. Practon reproaches you for having forgotten to make a telephone call he asked you to make. What would you say?

3. Mrs. Bettle, who has arrived for her appointment an hour early, is sure that she has come at the right time. What would you say to her?

4. A querulous patient, Mr. Griffin, complains about being kept waiting. How would you respond?

5. A patient, Mr. Avery, invites you to have lunch with him. What would you do?

6. In spite of a "No Smoking" sign, a patient in the waiting room, Mrs. Wilson, lights a cigarette. What would you do or say?

7. An overtalkative patient, Mrs. Crowe, is bothering you while you are trying to complete a number of tasks before the next patient arrives. What would you do?

8. A patient, Mrs. Braun, wishes to use the physician's telephone; you know she is a talkative person. How would you handle this situation?

9. A patient, Mr. Mendez, comes into the reception room, arrives at your desk or window, and asks your advice about some medication he has seen advertised. What would be your response?

10. Mr. Hernandez starts an argument with you about the physician's fee. What would be your response?

11. A patient, Mrs. Jeffers, asks you when she will be through with her treatment. She has just finished seeing the physician and comes to your desk to make her return appointment. What would be your response?

12. Mrs. Bowman asks you for information about hospitalization insurance and medical care plans. What would be your response?

13. Mrs. Jones comes up to your desk and asks you if you think cigarette smoking is harmful. What would you say?

14. A patient, Mrs. Takuchi, stops at your desk on the way out, complaining that the physician wanted to give her an injection but she will not let anybody jab a needle into her and put something into her body. What would you say?

15. The office nurse, Ms. Owens, complains that you did not order the supplies she had requested in time. What would your response be?

16. A friend of yours stops in to see you at the office and wants to "visit." She remains at your desk for 15 minutes talking. The reception room is full of patients. What would you say?

17. A patient, Mrs. James, asks what the fee for a certain operation is, and you quote her the physician's fee, which is $150. She thinks it is too high. What would you say?

18. Mr. Carson, a blind patient, comes to your office for medical care. How would you handle this patient during his visit?

19. A patient, Mrs. Jesse Bacon, has just had an appointment and thinks that the physician is withholding information from her. She stops by your desk and inquires, "What do you think the chances are of my returning to work on Monday?" How would you respond?

20. Dr. Practon expects you to ask patients to pay at the time of their visits. Mr. Owen passes your desk without stopping after seeing the doctor. What would you say?

21. After seeing the physician, Mrs. Hall stops at your desk for a new appointment. What do you say to her?

22. An eldery female patient, accompanied by her husband, has arrived for an emergency appointment. She seems to be in pain and is barely able to walk. What should be your immediate response?

NOTE: A Performance Evaluation Checklist for this exercise can be found at the back of the workbook.

EXERCISE 4-2

PREPARE A PATIENT REGISTRATION FORM

PERFORMANCE OBJECTIVE

TASK: Become familiar with questions on a patient registration form; ask a student (classmate) to write the information requested on the form as one would if visiting the medical office for the first time. Ask the student for insurance cards. Write N/A in areas that do not apply to insure all sections have been read. Refer to Figure 4-3 in the textbook.

CONDITIONS: Use form 1 and a pen.

STANDARDS: Time: _____ minutes
Accuracy: _____
(NOTE: The time element and accuracy criteria may be given by your instructor.)

DIRECTIONS: After your partner has filled in the registration form, read it for legibility and verify that all applicable sections are completed. Note that it has been signed and insurance cards have been presented. If a copier is available for use, photocopy insurance cards.

NOTE: A Performance Evaluation Checklist for this exercise can be found at the back of the workbook.

EXERCISE 4-3   PREPARE AN APPLICATION FORM FOR A DISABLED PERSON PLACARD

PERFORMANCE OBJECTIVE

TASK: Supervise completion of a sample disabled person placard form filled in by a patient checking to see that sections A–E have been completed properly so certification section can be read and signed by the physician.

CONDITIONS: Use form 2, pen, and workbook introduction page for reference to physician license number.

STANDARDS: Time: _____ minutes

Accuracy: _____

(NOTE: The time element and accuracy criteria may be given by your instructor.)

DIRECTIONS: Ask a student or friend to write in ink the information requested to apply for a Department of Motor Vehicles placard, assuming the patient has lost the use of one hand and will be disabled for a period of five months from the current date. Fill in sections F, G, and H for Dr. Fran Practon so that you will become familiar with the form. Refer to Figure 4-1 in the textbook. Note: in an office setting, a photocopy of the form would be retained in the patient's record.

NOTE: A Performance Evaluation Checklist for this exercise can be found at the back of the workbook.

COMPUTER EXERCISES

Before proceeding, you may want to do more exercises or review the concepts you have learned. Complete the computer exercises on the software for Chapter 4.

CHAPTER 5

Telephone Procedures

OBJECTIVES

After completing the exercises, the student will be able to:

1. Write meanings for chart note abbreviations.
2. Enhance spelling skills by learning new medical words.
3. Ask pertinent questions of callers in an emergency situation.
4. Screen telephone calls and apply patient screening techniques in appointment scheduling.
5. Develop and manage a telephone reference log.
6. Prepare a telephone reference directory.
7. Triage patient medical complaints.
8. Fill in telephone message slips.

AREAS OF COMPETENCE

Administrative Procedures
- Perform basic clerical functions
- Understand and adhere to managed care policies and procedures

General (Transdisciplinary)

Professionalism
- Prioritize and perform multiple tasks

Communication Skills
- Use professional telephone technique
- Use effective and correct verbal and written communications
- Use medical terminology appropriately

ABBREVIATION AND SPELLING REVIEW LESSON

Read the following patient's chart note and write the meanings for the abbreviations listed below the note. To decode any abbreviations you do not understand or that appear unfamiliar to you, refer to text Tables 8-1 and 9-3. Medical terms in the chart note are italicized; study them for spelling. Use your medical dictionary to look up their definitions. Your instructor may give a test for the spelling and definition of the words and abbreviations.

John F. Mason

October 15, 199X Pt comes in PO complaining of *anorexia, nausea, & stomatitis.*
CBC reveals RBC 80–90, WBC 60–80, Hgb 17 g/100ml. Applied AgNO₃. Wound
healing well. Cont. med. Ordered BUN. Retn 3 days. RO *uremia.*

Gerald Practon MD

Gerald Practon, MD

Pt _____	ml _____
PO _____	AgNO₃ _____
CBC _____	Cont. _____
RBC _____	med. _____
WBC _____	BUN _____
Hgb _____	retn _____
g _____	RO _____

REVIEW QUESTIONS

Review the objectives, glossary, and chapter information before completing the following review questions.

1. List three telephone procedures that might be discussed in an information booklet
   presented to a patient on his or her first visit to the office.

   a. _____

   b. _____

   c. _____

2. Name four emergency situations that would demand the immediate attention of the
   physician.

   a. _____

   b. _____

   c. _____

   d. _____

3. Why is the multiline telephone usually the one chosen for use in the medical
   office?

   _____

   _____

4. What would be your response to a patient who has missed two appointments and
   who has just called to cancel again?

   _____

   _____

5. Define a conference call and discuss the procedures for setting up this type of call.

    _____

    _____

6. Describe some attitudes that should be reflected in your voice when you are speaking to a patient over the telephone.

    _____

    _____

7. If no action has been taken on a patient call during the day, what should you do so that the call will not be overlooked the next day?

    _____

    _____

8. Name two ways to assure confidentiality when using voice mail regarding a patient's laboratory test results.

    a. _____

    b. _____

9. How does an answering service assist the medical office?

    _____

    _____

10. Give three reasons the physician might choose to install a cellular telephone.

    a. _____

    b. _____

    c. _____

EXERCISE 5-1   SCREEN TELEPHONE CALLS

PERFORMANCE OBJECTIVE

TASK: To screen incoming telephone calls to determine the person or persons who could take the calls.

CONDITIONS: Use pen.

STANDARDS: Time: _____ minutes
Accuracy: _____
(NOTE: The time element and accuracy criteria may be given by your instructor.)

DIRECTIONS: Refer to Table 5-1 in the textbook to aid in determining how the receptionist would screen and transfer incoming telephone calls. Members of the staff are doctor (MD), nurse (RN), certified medical assistant (CMA), insurance supervisor (INS), and bookkeeper (BK). Write the abbreviations of all those who might be able to take each telephone call in the space provided. If a message slip would be appropriate, place a check mark on the line.

Telephone Call Description	Transfer Call to
1. Daughter wants to talk to her father, the physician, and he is with a patient.	_____
2. Doctor is on another telephone and nurse at hospital telephones regarding a patient. After determining urgency, call could be directed to whom?	_____
3. New patient, ill, wants to speak to physician about recently prescribed medication.	_____
4. Patient requests laboratory test results.	_____
5. Insurance carrier requests patient information.	_____
6. Doctor's wife calls to inquire about time of medical association dinner and doctor is involved with an emergency situation.	_____
7. Patient telephones about a recent bill.	_____
8. Pharmacy telephones regarding a new prescription.	_____
9. Attorney telephones doctor regarding malpractice matter.	_____
10. Professional society member calls for physician.	_____
11. A mother calls about a child who has sunburn.	_____
12. Pharmacy requests Rx refill for patient.	_____
13. Family member asks for information about a child who is under the doctor's care.	_____
14. Patient requests telephone consultation with physician, who is out of the office.	_____
15. Pharmaceutical representative asks to make an appointment with physician for sales presentation.	_____
16. Another doctor desires to talk to physician, who is available.	_____
17. OSHA representative calls about making visit to do yearly inspection.	_____
18. Established patient asks to talk to physician, who is unable to take the call.	_____
19. Accountant telephones regarding tax records.	_____
20. Established patient requests Rx refill.	_____
21. Established patient calls to report chest pain.	_____
22. Nurse at convalescent home calls regarding a patient refusing all medication.	_____
23. Telephone referral request is received from another physician, and doctor is with a patient.	_____
24. Dentist calls to ask if doctor's patient is taking a new drug.	_____
25. Former office employee telephones to request a recommendation for a job.	_____

NOTE: A Performance Evaluation Checklist for this exercise can be found at the back of the workbook.

| EXERCISE 5-2 | **TRIAGE APPOINTMENT SITUATIONS FOR APPROPRIATE SCHEDULING** |

PERFORMANCE OBJECTIVE

TASK: Determine how soon a patient should be seen by the physician before making notations in the appointment book.

CONDITIONS: Use pen.

STANDARDS: Time: _____ minutes
Accuracy: _____
(NOTE: The time element and accuracy criteria may be given by your instructor.)

DIRECTIONS: Assume you are the telephone receptionist and the protocol manual states to triage patient appointments into these five choices: those to be seen immediately (stat), those to be seen within 4 hours, those to be seen sometime today, those to be scheduled this week, and those who most likely will not need an appointment after relating their symptoms to the nurse. Write the number of your choice in the space provided. In some situations, two choices might be appropriate.

1. stat **2.** 4 hours **3.** today **4.** this week **5.** no appt. required

1. Foreign body in the eye _____
2. Suture removal _____
3. School team PX _____
4. Child with earache, no fever _____
5. Routine female PX _____
6. Child, 103°F fever and croup _____
7. Diarrhea, adult, every hour for 2 days _____
8. Routine dressing change _____
9. Lower abdominal pain _____
10. Persistent sore throat _____
11. Swollen feet and ankles for one week _____
12. MMR inj _____
13. Cyst in nose _____
14. Menstrual cramps _____
15. Chest pain _____
16. Vomiting, fever 101°F for 3 days, adult _____
17. Pap _____
18. Annual mammogram _____
19. Fainting spell, adult _____
20. Second degree sunburn on upper back _____
21. Headache, tension _____
22. Pain, rt. side, vomiting _____
23. Child drank mouthwash _____
24. Malaise, loss of appetite _____
25. No bowel movement for 5 days _____
26. LBP with abd pain _____
27. Possible FX ankle _____
28. Lac of head by tree branch _____
29. Ingrown toenail _____
30. Skin rash due to allergy medication _____
31. Head cold with sore throat _____
32. Rectal bleeding _____
33. Weak, sore thumb _____
34. Shortness of breath _____
35. Hemorrhoid pain _____
36. OB exam _____

37. Knee pain, swollen	_____	41. Golf ball hit above eye	_____
38. Lac of arm	_____	42. CPX, first visit	_____
39. Toenail fungus	_____	43. Routine well-baby ck	_____
40. Vertigo	_____	44. Frequent urination with pain	_____

NOTE: A Performance Evaluation Checklist for this exercise can be found at the back of the workbook.

EXERCISE 5-3 — PREPARE MESSAGE FORMS

PERFORMANCE OBJECTIVE

TASK: Study the following incoming calls; determine the calls that require the transfer of information to message forms; complete the forms.

CONDITIONS: Use message slips (forms 3-5), and pen or pencil.

STANDARDS: Time: _____ minutes
Accuracy: _____
(NOTE: The time element and accuracy criteria may be given by your instructor.)

DIRECTIONS: It is the morning of Tuesday, November 6, and both physicians are at the hospital and will not be in the office until 1 p.m. Some calls will require transfer to message forms.

9:15 Marguerite Houston [Mrs. C.F.] (678-7892) calls and is upset and excited. She wants to ask Dr. G. P. if she can discontinue the medication he prescribed because she thinks she is allergic to it; she now has a rash on her face. You have told her that the doctor is not in the office and that you will ask him to call her as soon as he comes in.

9:35 Donald Eggert (765-3145) asks to speak to Dr. F. P. He wants to make an appointment for an injection next week.

9:40 A person calls and refuses to identify himself. He requests information on a patient, Marilyn Turner.

9:55 A patient, Bruce Jeffers (486-2468), calls to cancel his appointment with Dr. G. P. that is scheduled for this afternoon because he has to leave on a flight to New York at noon. He will make another appointment upon his return late next week. He would like to know what to do about the series of daily injections he has been receiving from Dr. Practon.

9:58 Phyllis Sperry (678-1162) wants to know the results of the test taken last week by Dr. F. P. (You can find these results in the file.)

10:15 Mr. G.W. Witte (678-5478) represents the General Surgical Supply Company and wants to show the doctors a new instrument. You have suggested he call the next day when you will let him know whether either of the physicians will be able to talk to him.

10:20 Midway Pharmacy (649-3762) calls Dr. F. P. and wants to know if there can be a refill on Philip Stevenson Jr.'s prescription, No. 8711342.

10:25 Sylvia Cone (411-8215) calls and asks to speak to Dr. G. P. She refuses to leave a message and says that it is urgent.

10:55 Charles Jones (487-6650) calls to ask if the Practons can recommend an eye, ear, and nose specialist. (There is a reference sheet near the telephone.)

11:00 Mary Lu Practon, the Practons' 14-year-old daughter, calls to report that she is going to Disneyland with the Cone family for the day. She will return home about 9:00 P.M.

11:05 Betty Knott (678-0076) calls to ask if Dr. G. P. will donate time to give flu injections next Sunday from either 9 to 12 or 1 to 3. She needs to know as soon as possible. She is calling from the Reseda Red Cross office on Sepulveda Boulevard, where the injections are to be given.

11:18 Alan Becker (486-9993) calls and is upset about the bill he received today from Dr. F. P. He thinks the amount is exorbitant, and he asks to speak to Dr. Practon or someone in authority.

11:20 Patricia Papakostikus (687-4512) telephones the office to make an appointment. She is having daily headaches.

11:30 Dr. Martin Laird (643-1108) calls to ask if Dr. G. P. would like a ride to the AMA meeting tonight. Dr. Practon should let Dr. Laird know before 4:00 p.m.

11:45 Elizabeth Montague (411-0068) calls to ask if she should continue her medication. She feels fine now. Dr. G. P. is her physician.

11:50 Alyson Pierce [Mrs. D. M.] (765-9077) calls to ask if Dr. F. P. can stop by on her way home tonight at 562 Lynnbrook Avenue, Agoura, to look at her little girl, Courtney, aged 3, who has a high fever. Alyson has no means of transportation. You tell her you will check with the doctor as soon as possible and will let her know if this home visit can be worked out.

NOTE: A Performance Evaluation Checklist for this exercise can be found at the back of the workbook.

COMPUTER EXERCISES

Before proceeding, you may want to do more exercises or review the concepts you have learned. Complete the computer exercises on the software for Chapter 5.

CHAPTER 6

Appointments

OBJECTIVES

After completing the exercises, the student will be able to:

1. Write meanings for chart note abbreviations.

2. Enhance spelling skills by learning new medical words.

3. Record the physician's personal appointments, meetings, and hospital visits on an appointment sheet.

4. Schedule appointments using abbreviations and coordinating physician and patient availability.

5. Adjust an appointment schedule to accommodate an emergency.

6. Prepare a daily appointment sheet for the physician.

7. Reserve medical facilities and complete procedures to schedule surgery.

8. Refer patients for outside services.

AREAS OF COMPETENCE

Administrative Procedures
- Perform basic clerical functions
- Schedule, coordinate, and monitor appointments
- Schedule inpatient/outpatient admissions and procedures
- Understand and adhere to managed care policies and procedures

General (Transdisciplinary)
Communication Skills
- Use medical terminology appropriately

ABBREVIATION AND SPELLING REVIEW LESSON

Read the following patient's chart note and write the meanings for the abbreviations listed below the note. To decode any abbreviations you do not understand or that appear unfamiliar to you, refer to text Tables 8-1 and 9-3. Medical terms in the chart note are italicized; study them for spelling. Use your medical dictionary to look up their definitions. Your instructor may give a test for the spelling and definition of the words and abbreviations.

Dan F. Goodson

September 3, 199X IV *chemotherapy* started in hospital. Daily hosp PO exams. See op. report giving dx: *superficially infiltrating transitional* cell Ca Class III. Pt DC from hosp 11-1-9X. Retn for OV 3 P.M. Friday. PT to be started in 1 mo.

Gerald Practon MD
Gerald Practon, MD

IV	_____	retn	_____
hosp	_____	OV	_____
PO	_____	p.m.	_____
op.	_____	PT	_____
dx	_____	mo	_____
Ca	_____	Pt	_____
DC	_____		

REVIEW QUESTIONS

Review the objectives, glossary, and chapter information before completing the following review questions.

1. List four columnar headings that are appropriate for the appointment sheet.
   a. _____
   b. _____
   c. _____
   d. _____

2. When might an appointment be scheduled for a patient who is habitually late?

   _____

3. List four ways to enhance patient flow in the appointment book.
   a. _____
   b. _____
   c. _____
   d. _____

4. Describe one modified wave method of scheduling.

   _____

   _____

5. Who determines the symptoms that constitute a real emergency situation for a triage system? _____

   _____

6. List four items of patient information that must be secured before the hospital is called to make arrangements for admission of a patient.

   a. _____

   b. _____

   c. _____

   d. _____

7. What three factors should be taken into consideration when an appointment book is being selected?

   a. _____

   b. _____

   c. _____

8. The most important step the medical assistant takes after the date and time have been determined for a patient's next appointment is to

   _____

   _____

9. Besides having a written record of all appointments, why is it important to keep the information accurate and current?

   _____

   _____

10. List three actions the medical assistant might take when an emergency telephone call indicates an immediate response.

    a. _____

    b. _____

    c. _____

EXERCISE 6-1   SCHEDULE APPOINTMENTS

PERFORMANCE OBJECTIVE

TASK: Record patient appointments accurately using acceptable abbreviations on an appointment sheet adjusting to individual patient preferences and medical needs; adjust to unexpected changes, write legible appointment cards, and make a photocopy for physician reference. Refer to Figure 6-2 in the textbook.

CONDITIONS: Use three appointment record forms 6, 7, and 8, appointment card form 9, and pen or pencil.

STANDARDS: Time: _____ minutes
Accuracy: _____
(NOTE: The time element and accuracy criteria may be given by your instructor.)

DIRECTIONS: You are to schedule appointments for Dr. Gerald Practon (left column) and Dr. Fran Practon (right column) for three days: Monday, October

27; Tuesday, October 28; and Wednesday, October 29. Refer to the office policies at the beginning of this workbook to determine the amount of time for each appointment. If you are unfamiliar with the patient care abbreviations used in column 3 of Table 6-1 in the workbook, then refer to Table 8-1 in the textbook. This column contains all the information you need to complete an appointment record. Block off any time periods when the physicians are not in the office and any scheduled appointments or hospital visits. An asterisk (*) by a patient's name indicates a patient of Dr. Fran Practon; all others are patients of Dr. Gerald Practon. Your instructor may add emergency calls and appointment changes after you have completed the appointment sheets for the three days.

Dr. G. P. plans to visit Donald Pierce at the hospital on Tuesday morning and at noon on Wednesday. Dr. F. P. has a one-hour dental appointment with Dr. Bryce Crowe at 2:30 P.M. on Wednesday.

Table 6-1. Information Necessary for the Student to Prepare Appointment Schedules for Drs. Fran T. Practon and Gerald M. Practon

Name	Phone Number	Complaint or Procedure	Appointment Preference
*Melissa Jones	487-6650	Pap, estrogen inj.	Tues., P.M.
*Marsha MacFadden	487-0027	ECG	Tues., A.M.
Wendy Snow	765-6626	Cast ck, leg	Mon.
Phyllis Dayton	411-2244	Pap, limited exam	Mon.
*Rebecca Martinez	765-0008	Measles inj.	Wed.
Jane Call	678-0134	Smallpox inj.	Wed.
*Mary Fay Jeffers	486-2468	MMR	Mon. after school
*Philip Stevenson Jr.	457-1133	BP, UA	Mon.
*Shirley Van Alystine (husband is an MD)	678-4421	IUD, BP	Tues.
Courtney Pierce	765-9077	OV, E/P, cough, fever	Tues. P.M.
Paul Stone	411-7206	VDRL	Late Tues.
*Alan Becker	486-9993	Face infection, ltd. exam	Mon.
*Marguerite Houston	678-7892	Inj. for allergy	Tues., P.M.
*Paul Frenzel	765-8897	Dressing change	Early Wed., A.M.
Elizabeth Montgomery, RN	411-0068	Sinus condition, brief OV	Tues. A.M.
Lu Chung	678-4455	Allergy complaint	Mon.
Jerry Calhoun	678-8771	CBC, N/P, CPX	Late Tues.
Cathy Martinez	765-0008	Excise lesion on back	Wed.
Lloyd Wix	678-5529	Consult (disc.)	Tues. A.M.—must see G. P. (Wed.?)
Bruce Jeffers	486-2468	Remove glass from eye	Early Wed.
*Ashley Jones	487-6650	SR	Mon. after 2:30 P.M.
David Martinez	765-0008	Remove splinter from leg	Wed. A.M. to see either Dr.
Carl Freeburg	486-0011	Aspirate left elbow	Late Wed.
*Anne Rule	457-9001	N/P, Inter. PX	Mon. A.M.
Charles Jones	487-6650	Audiogram, ear lavage	Mon. P.M.
Robert LaRue	487-3355	VDRL, syphilis	Must have Tues. A.M. (see F. P.?)
*Phyllis Sperry	678-1162	N/P, CPX	Tues. P.M.
Sylvia Cone	411-8215	Hdak, N/P, ltd. exam	Wed. P.M.
*Pat Wochesky	765-3446	New OB	Wed. A.M.
Sheila Haley	678-6669	Tetanus	Wed. A.M.
Frank Elder	486-0918	Pain in side, N/P, BUN, CBC	Mon.
*Donald Eggert	765-3145	Sore elbow, ltd. exam	Early Mon. P.M.

*Asterisks indicate Dr. Fran T. Practon's patients.

Complete the appointment cards for Charles Jones, Wednesday, October 29, at 2 P.M.; *Marguerite Houston, Tuesday, November 12, at 3 P.M.; Carl Freeburg, Wednesday, November 6, at 2:45 P.M.; and *Pat Wochesky, Monday, December 2, at 9 A.M.

NOTE: A Performance Evaluation Checklist for this exercise can be found at the back of the workbook.

EXERCISE 6-2 PREPARE AN APPOINTMENT REFERENCE SHEET

PERFORMANCE OBJECTIVE

TASK: Prepare a keyed or typed appointment reference sheet of names of patients who are to be seen by the physician on a given day; make a photocopy of the appointment sheet to show an alternative reference. Refer to Figure 6-4 in the textbook.

CONDITIONS: Use one sheet of white typing paper.

STANDARDS: Time: _____ minutes
Accuracy: _____
(NOTE: The time element and accuracy criteria may be given by your instructor.)

DIRECTIONS: Key a double-spaced daily appointment reference sheet for Dr. Gerald Practon's reference to let him know who is expected in the morning on Wednesday, October 29. Take your information from Exercises 6-1. Make a photocopy of the Wednesday, October 29 appointment sheet if a copier is available. Additional copies would generally be made for the reference of the office staff. (Reminder: Emergency appointments would not appear on the appointment sheet.) Use an *N* after the patient's name if the patient is being seen for the first time.

NOTE: A Performance Evaluation Checklist for this exercise can be found at the back of the workbook.

EXERCISE 6-3 ABSTRACT INFORMATION FOR A HOSPITAL/SURGERY SCHEDULING FORM

PERFORMANCE OBJECTIVE

TASK: Review a patient's medical record and then abstract and type or key the required information on the hospital/surgery scheduling form.

CONDITIONS: Use Wayne G. Weather's patient information for medical records (Figure 6-1), one hospital/surgery scheduling form 10, and pen.

STANDARDS: Time: _____ minutes
Accuracy: _____
(NOTE: The time element and accuracy criteria may be given by your instructor.)

DIRECTIONS: Using Mr. Wayne Weather's patient information for medical records form (Figure 6-1), abstract data to complete the hospital/surgical scheduling form 10. Additional information should include the follow-

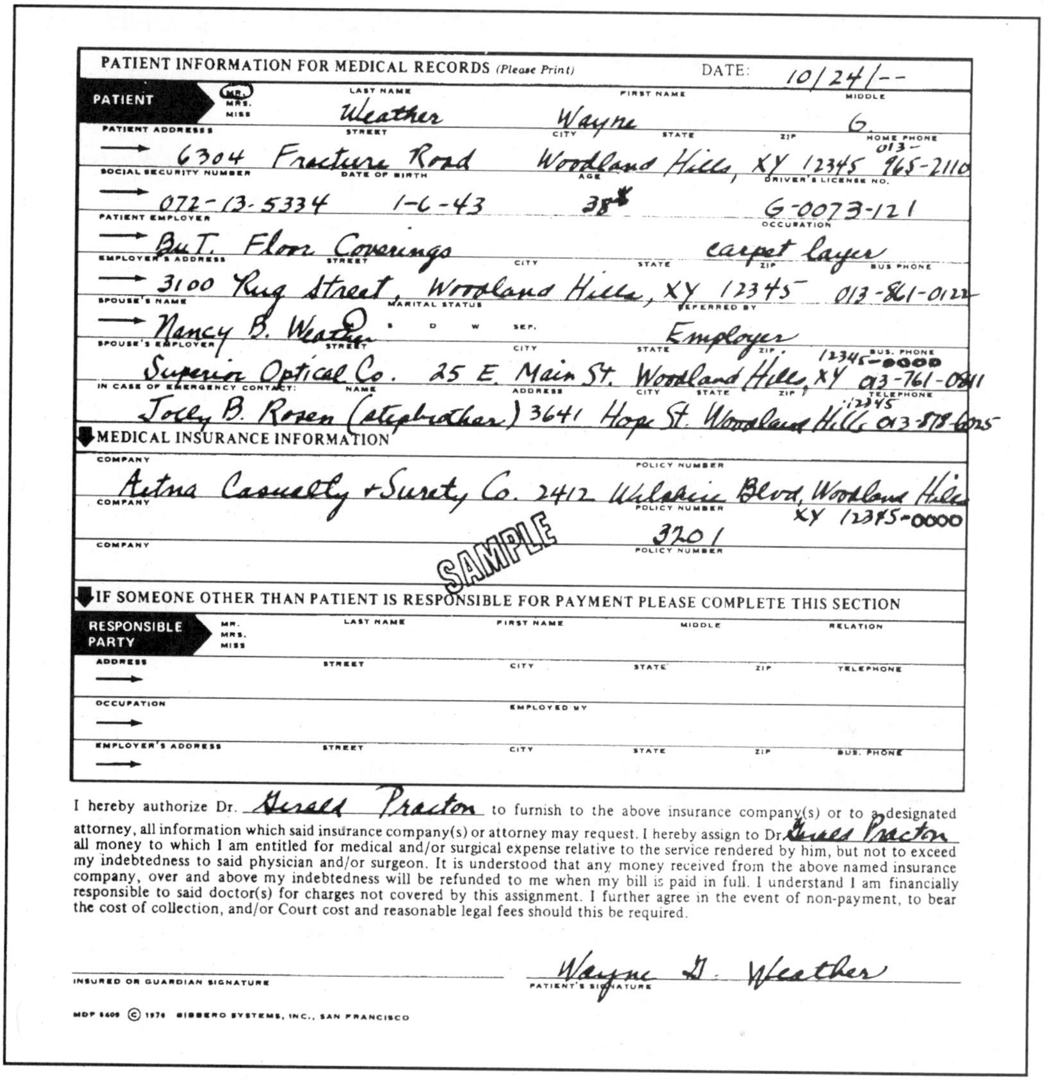

PATIENT INFORMATION FOR MEDICAL RECORDS (Please Print) DATE: 10/24/--

PATIENT — MR. MRS. MISS — LAST NAME: Weather — FIRST NAME: Wayne — MIDDLE: G.

PATIENT ADDRESS — STREET: 6304 Fracture Road — CITY: Woodland Hills, STATE: XY ZIP: 12345 — HOME PHONE: 013-965-2110

SOCIAL SECURITY NUMBER: 072-13-5334 — DATE OF BIRTH: 1-6-43 — AGE: 38 — DRIVER'S LICENSE NO.: G-0073-121

PATIENT EMPLOYER: B.T. Floor Coverings — OCCUPATION: carpet layer

EMPLOYER'S ADDRESS — STREET: 3100 Rug Street, CITY: Woodland Hills, STATE: XY ZIP: 12345 — BUS PHONE: 013-861-0122

SPOUSE'S NAME: Nancy B. Weather — MARITAL STATUS: S D W SEP. — REFERRED BY: Employer

SPOUSE'S EMPLOYER: Superior Optical Co. — STREET: 25 E. Main St. — CITY: Woodland Hills, STATE: XY ZIP: 12345-0000 — BUS. PHONE: 013-761-0811

IN CASE OF EMERGENCY CONTACT: NAME: Jolly B. Rosen (stepbrother) — ADDRESS: 3641 Hope St. — CITY: Woodland Hills — STATE — ZIP: 12345 — TELEPHONE: 013-578-6025

MEDICAL INSURANCE INFORMATION

COMPANY: Aetna Casualty + Surety Co. 2412 Wilshire Blvd, Woodland Hills XY 12345-0000 — POLICY NUMBER: 3201

COMPANY — POLICY NUMBER

COMPANY — POLICY NUMBER

SAMPLE

IF SOMEONE OTHER THAN PATIENT IS RESPONSIBLE FOR PAYMENT PLEASE COMPLETE THIS SECTION

RESPONSIBLE PARTY — MR. MRS. MISS — LAST NAME — FIRST NAME — MIDDLE — RELATION

ADDRESS — STREET — CITY — STATE — ZIP — TELEPHONE

OCCUPATION — EMPLOYED BY

EMPLOYER'S ADDRESS — STREET — CITY — STATE — ZIP — BUS. PHONE

I hereby authorize Dr. Gerald Practon to furnish to the above insurance company(s) or to a designated attorney, all information which said insurance company(s) or attorney may request. I hereby assign to Dr. Gerald Practon all money to which I am entitled for medical and/or surgical expense relative to the service rendered by him, but not to exceed my indebtedness to said physician and/or surgeon. It is understood that any money received from the above named insurance company, over and above my indebtedness will be refunded to me when my bill is paid in full. I understand I am financially responsible to said doctor(s) for charges not covered by this assignment. I further agree in the event of non-payment, to bear the cost of collection, and/or Court cost and reasonable legal fees should this be required.

INSURED OR GUARDIAN SIGNATURE — PATIENT'S SIGNATURE: Wayne G. Weather

MDP 8409 © 1976 BIBBERO SYSTEMS, INC., SAN FRANCISCO

Figure 6-1

ing: Mr. Weather is to be hospitalized at the College Hospital on Tuesday, October 28 at 5:30 A.M. His diagnosis is lumbar herniated nucleus pulposus, and a second opinion is not required. His preadmission testing of CBC, EKG, and chest x-ray was performed on October 21. He has not been previously hospitalized. Mr. Weather is a smoker and prefers a ward room. The lumbar (L4-5) laminectomy is scheduled for Tuesday, October 28, at 7:30 A.M. Operation instructions and insurance arrangements have been discussed.

Dr. Harold Barker, 621 W. Elm Street, Woodland Hills, will give general anesthesia, and Dr. Clarence Cutler, 55011 Paxton Blvd., Woodland Hills, will be the assistant surgeon. The surgery scheduled by Robert Slye should take approximately one hour to complete. Kevin Raye provided the authorization number, 8036981. The scheduling was completed on October 24; be sure to post the arrangements in the appointment book.

NOTE: A Performance Evaluation Checklist for this exercise can be found at the back of the workbook.

<table>
<tr><td>**EXERCISE 6-4**</td><td>**TRANSFER SURGERY SCHEDULING INFORMATION TO A LETTER**</td></tr>
</table>

PERFORMANCE OBJECTIVE

TASK: Key surgery information to a scheduling letter to be mailed to persons involved in the procedure.

CONDITIONS: Use hospital/surgery scheduling form 10 for reference, duplicate form 11 using a photocopy machine for one additional copy, pen, and correction fluid.

STANDARDS: Time: _____ minutes

Accuracy: _____

(NOTE: The time element and accuracy criteria may be given by your instructor.)

DIRECTIONS: After completing the hospital/surgery scheduling form 10, refer to it to determine information to be transferred to the hospital admission letter. You will need to send a letter to the patient and retain a copy for Dr. Practon's files.

NOTE: A Performance Evaluation Checklist for this exercise can be found at the back of the workbook.

<table>
<tr><td>**EXERCISE 6-5**</td><td>**REFER PATIENT FOR OUTSIDE SERVICES**</td></tr>
</table>

PERFORMANCE OBJECTIVE

TASK: Handwrite information on forms to be given to patient for outside services.

CONDITIONS: Use Forms 12 and 13 and pen.

STANDARDS: Time: _____ minutes

Accuracy: _____

(NOTE: The time element and accuracy criteria may be given by your instructor.)

DIRECTIONS: Read the information given for the patient and enter it onto the appropriate forms.

CASE: An HMO patient, Ted N. Thatcher comes to the office complaining of neck pain. After an examination, Dr. Fran Practon orders fasting laboratory tests (arthritis profile, uric acid, and urinalysis) and comprehensive cervical spine x-rays to be done on March 4, 199X. Diagnosis is acute cervical arthritis (ICD-9-CM Code No. 716.98). Patient to return in one week. Mr. Thatcher's social security number is 450-87-9509; birthdate 5/8/42; address 870 N. Seacrest St., Woodland Hills, XY 12345-9087, phone 013-897-4589; insurance: HMO Net, 4390 Main Street, Woodland Hills, XY 12345-0846, policy no. 459-0987-0. For this particular managed care plan, the outside services that Dr. Practon ordered do not require preauthorization.

NOTE: A Performance Evaluation Checklist for this exercise can be found at the back of the workbook.

COMPUTER EXERCISES

Before proceeding, you may want to do more exercises or review the concepts you have learned. Complete the computer exercises on the software for Chapter 6.

CHAPTER 7

Computers and Information Processing

OBJECTIVES

After completing the exercises, the student will be able to:

1. Write meanings for chart note abbreviations.

2. Enhance spelling skills by learning new medical words.

3. List computer functions for health care professionals.

4. Define computer terminology.

5. Key documents and make corrections using the word processing program, spell-check, and search mode.

AREAS OF COMPETENCE

Administrative Procedures
■ Perform basic clerical functions

General (Transdisciplinary)

Communication Skills
■ Use medical terminology appropriately

Operational Functions
■ Evaluate and recommend equipment and supplies
■ Apply computer techniques to support office operations

ABBREVIATION AND SPELLING REVIEW LESSON

Read the following patient's chart note and write the meanings for the abbreviations listed below the note. To decode any abbreviations you do not understand or that appear unfamiliar to you, refer to text Tables 8-1 and 9-3. Medical terms in the chart note are italicized; study them for spelling. Use your medical dictionary to look up their definitions. Your instructor may give a test for the spelling and definition of the words and abbreviations.

Joe Gardena

September 3, 199X General: *Obese* black male. LAB data normal. HEENT: PERRLA, normal *fundi*. TMs normal. Neck without JVD. *Tongue* shows *mucous* patches seen in *syphilis*. Enlarged *submandibular* nodes. Otherwise exam WNL. Dx: No evidence of AIDS or a pre-AIDS-type illness. Ordered a VDRL.

Gerald Practon MD

Gerald Practon, MD

LAB _____	WNL _____
HEENT _____	Dx _____
PERRLA _____	AIDS _____
TMs _____	VDRL _____
JVD _____	

REVIEW QUESTIONS

Review the objectives, glossary, and chapter information before completing the following review questions.

1. A/an _____ is a device that can perform arithmetic and logical operations without human intervention. It is also called a/n _____ .

2. Permanent physical components of computer and word processing equipment, such as a printer and keyboard, are known as _____ .

3. When help is needed to install or use a computer system, who would you call upon? _____

4. Computer data that can be stored and read, but not changed, are called

_____ .

5. Computer data stored randomly and retrieved directly by specifying the address location are called _____ .

6. Name several ways to prolong the life of a monitor.

   a. _____

   b. _____

   c. _____

7. The device that produces a hard copy (machine output) is a/an _____ . List three types.

   a. _____

   b. _____

   c. _____

8. A computer can be linked to another computer via telephone lines by using a/an
   _____ .

9. When computers are interconnected to share data and information, this is called
   a/an _____ .

10. Name four functions of a computerized appointment system.
    a. _____
    b. _____
    c. _____
    d. _____

11. Computer files composed of categories such as patients, drugs, diagnoses, proce-
    dures, diseases, and surgeries are known as _____
    and are used for monitoring of information.

12. To maintain security, _____ , also called
    _____ , are given to employees to limit their
    entry and functions within the computer systems.

13. To avoid losing data, the most important procedure is to periodically
    _____ .

14. A computerized medical records system that manages the retrieval and storage of
    records is called a/an _____ .

15. Working at a computer hour after hour in the same position can cause
    _____ , also called _____ .
    The science that deals with these physical needs is called
    _____ .

16. Name four basic disk operating systems and circle the system that you will be
    working on.
    a. _____
    b. _____
    c. _____
    d. _____

ORDERING INFORMATION FOR COMPUTER SOFTWARE MEDICAL DEMONSTRATION PACKAGES

IBM or IBM-Compatible Software

MEDASSIST Medical Office Management Demonstration Software: This package consists of a 116-page instruction manual and four 3 1/2" or six 5 1/4" diskettes. This demonstration has a limited number of patients on the system and guides you through the day-to-day activities performed in a medical office. Order from Medical Office

Solutions, 2520 N.W. 39th Street, Suite 113, Oklahoma City, OK 73112, telephone 405-949-1200 or 800-637-2251. Technical support is available to students using the demonstration package via the toll-free number. There is a $25.00 charge for the demonstration package.

Macintosh Software Video

MediMac Video: This video demonstration walks you through a day in a medical office using the MediMac computer program. Order from Health Care Communications, 210 Gateway, Suite 200, Lincoln, NE 68505, telephone 402-466-8100 or 800-888-4344. Approximate price $9.95.

EXERCISE 7-1 **COMPUTER FUNCTIONS**

PERFORMANCE OBJECTIVE

TASK: Determine various functions the computer provides for health care professionals working in different positions.

CONDITIONS: Use pen and pencil.

STANDARDS: Time: _____ minutes
Accuracy: _____
(NOTE: The time element and accuracy criteria may be given by your instructor.)

DIRECTIONS: This exercise requires critical thinking. Read the headings that list different types of health care professionals. List several functions the computer provides for each.

1. Receptionist

    a. _____

    b. _____

2. Transcriptionist/medical records clerk

    a. _____

    b. _____

3. Clinical assistant

    a. _____

    b. _____

    c. _____

    d. _____

4. Insurance specialist

    a. _____

    b. _____

    c. _____

5. Bookkeeper

   a. _____

   b. _____

   c. _____

6. All employees

   a. _____

   b. _____

7. Office manager

   a. _____

NOTE: A Performance Evaluation Checklist for this exercise can be found at the back of the workbook.

| EXERCISE 7-2 | **COMPUTER TERMINOLOGY** |

PERFORMANCE OBJECTIVE

TASK: After reading Chapter 7 and studying the glossary terms, determine the correct computer terminology from the clues listed.

CONDITIONS: Use pen or pencil.

STANDARDS: Time: _____ minutes
Accuracy: _____
(NOTE: The time element and accuracy criteria may be given by your instructor.)

DIRECTIONS: Read the clues, determine the word or words being described, and write the answer. Refer to the text and the glossary terms in the beginning of Chapter 7 for additional help.

CLUE 1   a. I am a piece of hardware.

b. I have letters, numbers, and symbols.

c. I am used to enter information and instructions into the computer.

I am a/an _____ .

CLUE 2   a. I control internal memory.
b. I direct the flow and processing of information.
c. I am the "brain" of the computer.

I am a/an _____ .

CLUE 3   a. I appear on the screen.
b. I blink.
c. I show the current position of data entry.

I am a/an _____ .

CLUE 4   a. I hide in a program in the computer.
          b. I can be harmless or harmful.
          c. I infect software or disks.

          I am a/an _____.

CLUE 5   a. I am a magnetic storage device.
          b. I can be made of rigid material.
          c. I can be made of flexible plastic.

          I am a/an _____.

CLUE 6   a. I display text and graphics.
          b. I am connected to the computer as an output device.
          c. I can be monochromatic or color.

          I am a/an _____.

CLUE 7   a. I am an output device.
          b. I create text and graphic images on paper.
          c. I come in three types: dot matrix, laser, and ink jet.

          I am a/an _____.

CLUE 8   a. I store the instructions the computer needs to run.
          b. My information cannot be changed by the user.
          c. The manufacturer determines my permanent program.

          I am a/an _____.

CLUE 9   a. I am a unit of measurement.
          b. I am equal to 1,000.
          c. My abbreviation is K.

          I am a/an _____.

CLUE 10   a. I am a special word, code, or symbol.
          b. I am used to gain access to the computer.
          c. I am used for security purposes.

          I am a/an _____.

CLUE 11   a. I am an input device.
          b. I control the cursor.
          c. I am used to select items on the screen.

          I am a/an _____.

CLUE 12   a. I temporarily store data that the computer needs to operate a program.
          b. I allow data to be stored randomly and retrieved directly.
          c. I lose information when the computer is turned off.

          I am a/an _____.

CLUE 13   a. I am a piece of hardware.
          b. I convert data into signals for telephone transmission.
          c. I can reside within or external to the computer.

          I am a/an _____.

CLUE 14   a. I interconnect personal computers.
           b. I allow data to be shared.
           c. I allow software to be shared.

           I am a/an _____ .

CLUE 15   a. I am a type of optical disk.
           b. I am an audio disk.
           c. I hold text, graphics, and hi-fi sound.

           I am a/an _____ .

CLUE 16   a. I am an input device.
           b. I have special function keys.
           c. I am either separate or sit to the right of the keyboard.

           I am a/an _____ .

NOTE: A Performance Evaluation Checklist for this exercise can be found at the back of the workbook.

EXERCISE 7-3

CHANGE DOCUMENTS: SPELLING ERRORS

PERFORMANCE OBJECTIVE

TASK: Make necessary changes to correct the documents.

CONDITIONS: Use pen and white typing or computer paper. If you have access to a computer, use the word processing program and the printer to make two corrected copies of the document. If you do not have access to a computer, use a typewriter and carbon paper or a photocopy machine to make two corrected copies. One copy will be handed in to your instructor and the other placed in your file.

STANDARDS: Time: _____ minutes
Accuracy: _____
(NOTE: The time element and accuracy criteria may be given by your instructor.)

DIRECTIONS: The following is an example from a document that requires certain changes. Read the document through first, then circle in red all errors. Key the paragraph, correcting all spelling errors. If you have access to a computer, key the documents as they appear in the book, then correct them using the spell-check and search mode. If you do not have access to a computer, use a typewriter and carbon paper or be prepared to copy the final documents using a photocopy machine.

PHYSICAL EXAMINATION: Head, eyes, ears, nose and throat are within normal limits. Neck is supple, with no masses. Lungs clear billaterally. Heart rate and rhythmm regular with no murmers. Breasts symmetrical and nontender, with no masses or discharge. Adomen soft and nontender. Rectal examinatio nontender. Pelviv examination to be reschedul as patient is on menses. Extremities: normal refex and reactions.

NOTE: A Performance Evaluation Checklist for this exercise can be found at the back of the workbook.

| EXERCISE 7-4 | CHANGE DOCUMENTS: NAME |

PERFORMANCE OBJECTIVE

TASK: Make necessary changes to correct the documents.

CONDITIONS: Use pen and white typing or computer paper. If you have access to a computer, use the word processing program and the printer to make two corrected copies of the document. If you do not have access to a computer, use a typewriter and carbon paper or a photocopy machine to make two corrected copies. One copy will be handed in to your instructor and the other placed in your file.

STANDARDS: Time: _____ minutes
Accuracy: _____
(NOTE: The time element and accuracy criteria may be given by your instructor.)

DIRECTIONS: The following is an example from a document that requires certain changes. Read the document through first, then circle in red all errors. Change the patient's name from Thompsett to Tompsett in the following letter. If you have access to a computer, key the documents as they appear in the book, then correct them using the spell-check and search mode. If you do not have access to a computer, use a typewriter and carbon paper or be prepared to copy the final documents using a photocopy machine.

Dr. Richard Thompsett
32 Beverly Court
Anytown, USA 12345

Dear Dr. Thompsett:

I am honored to hear that you and Mrs. Thompsett will be coming to our annual hospital fund-raiser on the 24th of October. I understand that your brother, Dr. Blake Thompsett, will also be attending. In fact it appears that the whole Thompsett family will be well represented this year. I am sure that your grandfather, Dr. Samuel Thompsett, the founder of Mercy Hospital's Cardiac Care Unit, would be very happy indeed to know that his family continues to take such an interest in the hospital. I look forward to seeing you and all the Thompsett clan again.

NOTE: A Performance Evaluation Checklist for this exercise can be found at the back of the workbook.

EXERCISE
7-5

CHANGE DOCUMENTS: PUNCTUATION

PERFORMANCE OBJECTIVE

TASK: Make necessary changes to correct the documents.

CONDITIONS: Use pen and white typing or computer paper. If you have access to a computer, use the word processing program and the printer to make two corrected copies of the document. If you do not have access to a computer, use a typewriter and carbon paper or a photocopy machine to make two corrected copies. One copy will be handed in to your instructor and the other placed in your file.

STANDARDS: Time: _____ minutes
Accuracy: _____
(NOTE: The time element and accuracy criteria may be given by your instructor.)

DIRECTIONS: The following is an example from a document that requires certain changes. Read the document through first, then circle in red all errors. Change all the semicolons to periods in the following excerpt from a patient representative training manual, making all changes in capitalization. If you have access to a computer, key the documents as they appear in the book, then correct them using the spell-check and search mode. If you do not have access to a computer, use a typewriter and carbon paper or be prepared to copy the final documents using a photocopy machine.

If you have not heard from a patient in over a year, do not wait for the patient to call you; call the patient. Keeping in touch with a patient is one sure way of indicating that you think he or she is important, and that you value and are concerned about the patient's health. It is an excellent way to stay on top of the situation; it puts you in a position to know at once if something is wrong with your practice; it affords you an inside track.

NOTE: A Performance Evaluation Checklist for this exercise can be found at the back of the workbook.

EXERCISE
7-6

CHANGE DOCUMENTS: CAPITALIZATION

PERFORMANCE OBJECTIVE

TASK: Make necessary changes to correct the documents.

CONDITIONS: Use pen and white typing or computer paper. If you have access to a computer, use the word processing program and the printer to make two corrected copies of the document. If you do not have access to a computer, use a typewriter and carbon paper or a photocopy machine to make two corrected copies. One copy will be handed in to your instructor and the other placed in your file.

STANDARDS: Time: _____ minutes

Accuracy: _____

(NOTE: The time element and accuracy criteria may be given by your instructor.)

DIRECTIONS: The following is an example from a document that requires certain changes. Read the document through first, then circle in red all errors. Capitalize the initial letters in the words *Patient Service* in the following memo. If you have access to a computer, key the documents as they appear in the book, then correct them using the spell-check and search mode. If you do not have access to a computer, use a typewriter and carbon paper or be prepared to copy the final documents using a photocopy machine.

TO: All patient service reps

FROM: LeRoy Bail, Administrator

Effective immediately, the patient service department will accept only calls that have been previously screened by the patient service operator. The purpose of this new policy is to make the patient service department more efficient. We will no longer be accepting incoming patient service calls directly. Instead of any patient service employee handling a call, calls will be directed to the patient service representative who handles the particular account.

NOTE: A Performance Evaluation Checklist for this exercise can be found at the back of the workbook.

COMPUTER EXERCISES

Before proceeding, you may want to do more exercises or review the concepts you have learned. Complete the computer exercises on the software for Chapter 7.

CHAPTER 8

Patients' Medical Records

OBJECTIVES

After completing the exercises, the student will be able to:

1. Write meanings for chart note abbreviations.

2. Enhance spelling skills by learning new medical words.

3. Prepare a patient record from a patient information form.

4. Prepare a patient record from an interview.

5. Prepare telephone messages.

6. Properly make correction entries in chart notes.

7. Abstract information from a patient medical record.

8. Organize the contents of a history and physical examination report.

9. Use patient care abbreviations in medical records with knowledge of what they mean.

AREAS OF COMPETENCE

Administrative Procedures
■ Perform basic clerical functions

General (Transdisciplinary)

Communication Skills
■ Use medical terminology appropriately

Legal Concepts
■ Prepare and maintain medical records
■ Document accurately

ABBREVIATION AND SPELLING REVIEW LESSON

Read the following patient's chart note and write the meanings for the abbreviations listed below the note. To decode any abbreviations you do not understand or that appear unfamiliar to you, refer to text Tables 8-1 and 9-3. Medical terms in the chart note are italicized; study them for spelling. Use your medical dictionary to look up their definitions. Your instructor may give a test for the spelling and definition of the words and abbreviations.

Elizabeth A. Warner

November 16, 199X CC: *constipation, rectal* bleeding & pain after BM. CPX reveals int & ext *hemorrhoids*. BP 150/95. *Sigmoidoscopy* to 15 cm. Rx: adv hospitalization for removal of hemorrhoids. Dg: bleeding hemorrhoids, int & ext; anal *fistula*; HBP.

Gerald Practon MD

Gerald Practon, MD

CC	_____	cm	_____
BM	_____	Rx	_____
CPX	_____	adv	_____
int	_____	Dg	_____
ext	_____	HBP	_____
BP	_____		

REVIEW QUESTIONS

Review the objectives, glossary, and chapter information before completing the following review questions.

1. Give five reasons for keeping medical records.

   a. _____

   b. _____

   c. _____

   d. _____

   e. _____

2. List 12 items of basic information that should be included on the registration form for a new patient.

   a. _____

   b. _____

   c. _____

   d. _____

   e. _____

   f. _____

   g. _____

   h. _____

   i. _____

   j. _____

   k. _____

   l. _____

3. The following phrases appeared on a history and physical. Place an *S* after those that are subjective and an *O* after those considered objective.

   a. Patient complains of having fainting spells for the past 4 months _____

   b. BP 120/80 _____

   c. Headache _____

   d. Skin shows no rashes _____

   e. Patient denies chest pain _____

   f. Mother L&W _____

   g. There is no inguinal hernia _____

   h. Heart tones are normal _____

   i No masses palpable _____

   j. Patient had a herniorrhaphy 2 years ago _____

4. Name the four basic procedures the physician goes through during the physical examination.

   a. _____

   b. _____

   c. _____

   d. _____

5. Is there a difference between a chart note and a progress note? If yes, state the difference.

   _____

   _____

6. State common medical events that call for chart notes on a medical record.

   a. _____

   b. _____

   c. _____

   d. _____

   e. _____

   f. _____

   g. _____

   h. _____

7. Name five advantages of using a medical record system, such as the problem-oriented record (POR).

   a. _____

   b. _____

   c. _____

   d. _____

   e. _____

8. By this time, you should know over 80 symbols and abbreviations related to patient care. Test yourself by defining the following without referring back to the abbreviation key.

PND _____

CBC _____

URI _____

$\bar{s}$ _____

$\bar{o}$ _____

PO _____

AP & L _____

Dx _____

DC _____

HX _____

DPT _____

Hgb _____

EXERCISE 8-1   PREPARE A PATIENT RECORD

PERFORMANCE OBJECTIVE

TASK: Key a patient record form, label a file folder, and key a 3" by 5" file card.

CONDITIONS: Use an electronic typewriter or computer, one file folder, one label for file folder, one patient record form (form 14), and one file card (3" by 5").

STANDARDS: Time: _____ minutes
Accuracy: _____
(NOTE: The time element and accuracy criteria may be given by your instructor.)

DIRECTIONS: A new patient, Wayne G. Weather, has come in as an emergency case; he was hurt on the job. He completed the patient information form (again, see Figure 6-1) as shown in workbook exercise 6-3. Use those data to complete a patient record, file folder, and file card. The patient record number is 1180 and is keyed in the right corner of the record, file card, and file label. (In routine office procedure, this step would have been done before you scheduled the patient's surgery.) For further information, Mr. Weather's wife, Nancy Weather, is a receptionist.

NOTE: A Performance Evaluation Checklist for this exercise can be found at the back of the workbook.

EXERCISE 8-2 — PREPARE A PATIENT RECORD FROM AN INTERVIEW

PERFORMANCE OBJECTIVE

TASK: Key a patient record form, label a file folder, and type a 3" by 5" file card from an interview and from an October 25 office visit.

CONDITIONS: Use an electronic typewriter or computer, one file folder, one label for file folder, one patient record form (form 15) and one file card (3" by 5").

STANDARDS: Time: _____ minutes
Accuracy: _____
(NOTE: The time element and accuracy criteria may be given by your instructor.)

DIRECTIONS: To complete this assignment, assume you are Krista Lee Carlisle, or interview a person in class or someone at home. The patient record number is 1181 and is keyed in the right corner of the record, file card, and file label. Dr. Fran Practon saw this patient on October 25 in the office and has dictated the note shown in Figure 8-1 for you to record in the patient's record. You will use this record and folder in exercises 8-3 through 8-5.

CC: Pt complained of listlessness, lack of appetite, headache since Oct. 1. Took aspirin & "tonic" several times s̄ results. Does not smoke; drinks 2 beers q night, 6 pack on weekends. On exam liver margins appeared enlarged c̄ tenderness on palpation. All other organs, reflexes & physical functions WNL. Lab: UA dark amber, bile present STAT blood sent to lab for hepatitis panel. Dx: hepatitis. Tx: admit pt to College Hospital and Clinic, Woodland Hills, XY. Light diet ordered, complete bed rest, push fluids. Quarantine to be established for 2 wks. Disability: x 8 weeks. Pt seen in hosp. on Nov. 23 and 24. Pt discharged on Nov. 25, to be seen in office in 1 week. On Nov. 30 at 3 P.M. pt calls in to cancel appt for Dec 1, staying in bed with flu.

Figure 8-1

NOTE: A Performance Evaluation Checklist for this exercise can be found at the back of the workbook.

EXERCISE 8-3 — PREPARE TELEPHONE MESSAGES

PERFORMANCE OBJECTIVE

TASK: Prepare telephone messages for a patient's medical record.

CONDITIONS: Use patient record no. 1181, one sheet of colored paper, one sheet of telephone messages (Form 16), cellophane adhesive tape, scissors, and pen or pencil.

STANDARDS: Time: _____ minutes
Accuracy: _____
(NOTE: The time element and accuracy criteria may be given by your instructor.)

DIRECTIONS: This exercise is prepared for patient record no. 1181. On your sheet of colored paper, type the patient's name and file number in the upper right corner. In the upper left corner, type "Telephone messages." Insert this data on the telephone message slips.

1. On November 30, Dr. Practon telephoned Mrs. Carlisle to recommend that Krista Lee drink plenty of fluids; he will send out a prescription for flu symptoms if it becomes necessary.

2. On March 2, 199X at 3:10 P.M. Robyn Carlisle called Dr. Gerald Practon about her daughter, Krista Lee, aged 17, who has a temperature of 100.2° F. She said Krista is having chest congestion and a persistent dry cough. She asked for a prescription of cough syrup. Robyn's phone number is 849-7730, and her pharmacy is Long's Drug Store (telephone 849-2221). You contact Dr. Practon, and he says to call the pharmacy and order Robitussin-PE, 2 teaspoons, every 4 hours. You called the patient back at 4:05 P.M. to give her the information.

3. On March 3, 199X, at 9 A.M. you receive another call from Robyn Carlisle about Krista Lee. She says she thinks Krista has a possible allergy to the medication because she has a rash on her chest and is continuing to cough. Her temperature is 100°F. Dr. Practon returns the call at 11:15 A.M., tells Robyn to discontinue the Robitussin, and suggests an appointment be made for the next day, March 4.

4. After seeing Dr. Practon, Robyn Carlisle calls on March 6, 199X, at 3:30 P.M. saying Krista's rash has disappeared but she still has a cough, which is now producing discolored phlegm, and a temperature of 100.3°F. Dr. Practon returns her call at 4:15 P.M. orders a chest x-ray and return appt. on March 7.

Glue or tape the messages to the sheet of colored paper and place it in the patient's medical record.

NOTE: A Performance Evaluation Checklist for this exercise can be found at the back of the workbook.

EXERCISE 8-4 — CORRECT A PATIENT RECORD

PERFORMANCE OBJECTIVE

TASK: Make a correction on a patient record.

CONDITIONS: Use patient record no. 1181 from exercise 8-2 and pen.

STANDARDS: Time: _____ minutes
Accuracy: _____
(NOTE: The time element and accuracy criteria may be given by your instructor.)

DIRECTIONS: Previously, Dr. Fran Practon indicated disability as "undetermined." On November 22, she wants it to read "Disability: 4 weeks." Make the necessary change on patient record no. 1181 by handwriting in ink the corrected entry above the word "undetermined," which should be crossed out. Then, in the margin, write the word "correction," your initials, and the date you are making the corrected entry.

NOTE: A Performance Evaluation Checklist for this exercise can be found at the back of the workbook.

EXERCISE 8-5 — ABSTRACT FROM MEDICAL RECORDS

PERFORMANCE OBJECTIVE

TASK: Abstract information from a patient record.

CONDITIONS: Use patient record no. 1181 from exercise 8-2, pencil or pen, and abstracting form (form 17).

STANDARDS: Time: _____ minutes
Accuracy: _____
(NOTE: The time element and accuracy criteria may be given by your instructor.)

DIRECTIONS: Complete the Abstracting Form by abstracting information from patient record no. 1181. This will help prepare you for future work, such as abstracting from patient records to complete insurance forms.

NOTE: A Performance Evaluation Checklist for this exercise can be found at the back of the workbook.

EXERCISE 8-6 — PREPARE A HISTORY AND PHYSICAL (H&P)

PERFORMANCE OBJECTIVE

TASK: Prepare a patient record and file folder with label, type a 3" by 5" file card, and make a photocopy of the report.

CONDITIONS: Use an electronic typewriter, word processor, or computer; a photocopy machine; a patient information form of Sun Low Chung (Figure 8-2); one file folder; one label for file folder; one patient record form (form 18); one file card (3" by 5"); two sheets of 8 1/2" by 11" white typing paper.

STANDARDS: Time: _____ minutes
Accuracy: _____
(NOTE: The time element and accuracy criteria may be given by your instructor.)

DIRECTIONS: Using Sun Low Chung's patient information form (Figure 8-2), make up a patient record no. 1182 on form 18 and a file folder. Label the folder and make a 3" by 5" file card. Retype the data in Figure 8-3 into proper history and physical form, using full-block style (see text Figure 8-2A and B). Use the current date as the dictated and transcribed dates. The physician is Gerald Practon, MD. Be careful to use the proper indentations and tab stops. Be alert to topic changes. Make a photocopy of the H&P and store it in the patient's chart.

NOTE: A Performance Evaluation Checklist for this exercise can be found at the back of the workbook.

PATIENT INFORMATION FOR MEDICAL RECORDS *(Please Print)*   DATE: 10 / 25 /--

PATIENT (MR.) MRS. MISS	LAST NAME	FIRST NAME	MIDDLE
	Chung	Sun	Low

PATIENT ADDRESS — STREET: 2375 Laney Street   CITY: Woodland Hills, XY   ZIP: 12345   HOME PHONE: 013/278-6135

SOCIAL SECURITY NUMBER: 738-05-6712   DATE OF BIRTH: 5-20-25   AGE: 56   DRIVER'S LICENSE NO.: 6-0065-178

PATIENT EMPLOYER: Civil Service Maintenance   OCCUPATION: mechanic

EMPLOYER'S ADDRESS — STREET: 742 Redwood Highway   CITY: Port Davis   STATE: XY   ZIP: 12346   BUS PHONE: 013/271-4811

SPOUSE'S NAME: Song Su Chung   MARITAL STATUS: (M)   REFERRED BY: Employer

SPOUSE'S EMPLOYER: Best Market 214 Main Street, Woodland Hills, XY 12345   BUS. PHONE: 013/279-4827

IN CASE OF EMERGENCY CONTACT: Pet Chung (brother) 2851 Laney St Woodland Hills, XY 12345 013/278-7812

MEDICAL INSURANCE INFORMATION

COMPANY: Blue Shield 2751 Courtney St, Woodland Hills, XY 12345   POLICY NUMBER:

COMPANY: POLICY NUMBER: 27894B

COMPANY: POLICY NUMBER:

IF SOMEONE OTHER THAN PATIENT IS RESPONSIBLE FOR PAYMENT PLEASE COMPLETE THIS SECTION

RESPONSIBLE PARTY — MR. MRS. MISS — LAST NAME | FIRST NAME | MIDDLE | RELATION

ADDRESS — STREET | CITY | STATE | ZIP | TELEPHONE

OCCUPATION | EMPLOYED BY

EMPLOYER'S ADDRESS — STREET | CITY | STATE | ZIP | BUS. PHONE

I hereby authorize Dr. Gerald Praxton to furnish to the above insurance company(s) or to a designated attorney, all information which said insurance company(s) or attorney may request. I hereby assign to Dr. Gerald Praxton all money to which I am entitled for medical and/or surgical expense relative to the service rendered by him, but not to exceed my indebtedness to said physician and/or surgeon. It is understood that any money received from the above named insurance company, over and above my indebtedness will be refunded to me when my bill is paid in full. I understand I am financially responsible to said doctor(s) for charges not covered by this assignment. I further agree in the event of non-payment, to bear the cost of collection, and/or Court cost and reasonable legal fees should this be required.

INSURED OR GUARDIAN SIGNATURE

PATIENT'S SIGNATURE: Sun Low Chung

56-8409 © 1976 BIBBERO SYSTEMS, INC., SAN FRANCISCO

Figure 8-2

Sun Low Chung

History. Chief complaint. Palpitations for 1 week. Present illness. This patient has had known hypertension for 4 years. He has been taking Serpasil, two tablets, once a day. About 1 month ago, the medication was changed to Dyazide, one tablet per day. Since that time, the patient has felt more nervous and anxious, with occasional chest tightness. One week ago the patient noted some skipped beats occurring in the evening. There were no other associated symptoms and no history of paroxysmal nocturnal dyspnea, orthopnea, or ankle edema. Palpitation subsided spontaneously but recurred the following night, with a fast throbbing sensation in his right ear. He was seen by Dr. Chan 2 weeks later and had a chest x-ray and cardiac enzymes done. These were normal. An electrocardiogram showed normal sinus rhythm, with nonspecific ST abnormalities. He experiences palpitations in the evening. The patient has been asked to avoid any strenuous exercise and to stay at home until he is seen by the undersigned. Past history. The patient was born in Hankow, China, but has lived in the United States since 1942. He has worked in the Air Force and airplane industry but lately is working for civil service at Port Davis. He has been subjected to some work pressure recently. There was no history of coronary artery disease, heart murmurs, rheumatic fever, or joint problems in childhood. Malaria in his youth in China. Hypothyroidism diagnosed about 10 years ago, and he has been on thyroid 1 grain q.d. Operations none. Allergies none. Medication. Valium 5 milligrams one b.i.d. to t.i.d. p.r.n., Thyroid 1 grain q.d. Social history. The patient smoked one pack of cigarettes per day for 10 years but has discontinued for about 15 years. He does not drink. He consumes about two cups of coffee per day and very little tea. The family history. Most of the family members were separated during the war, and their health conditions are not known. Mother died from an unknown illness at the age of 35. The patient has two children, 36 and 27, both in good health. No known diabetes, hypertension, or heart problems in the family. The review of systems. General. No recent weight gain or weight loss. No unusual fatigue. No recent fevers. The patient has myopia in both eyes. Glasses have not been checked for the past 5 years, and distant vision is not good. EENT. Negative. CR. As in PI. No history of hemoptysis or chronic cough. GI. Negative. GU. Nocturia once a night for many years. NP. No history of headache, syncope, or light-headedness. No history of paralysis. MS. No history of joint problems. Physical examination. General. This patient is an elderly Asian male in no acute distress. Blood pressure is right arm 148 over 80 and left arm 138 over 88. Pulse 80 and regular. Respirations 18. Height 5 feet, 7 inches. Weight 176 1/4 pounds. The patient is afebrile. HEENT. Not pale or cyanotic. Tympanic membranes intact. Fundus normal in the left; right cannot be visualized because of question of early cataract or marked refractive error. Neck. Supple. No jugular venous pulse, thyromegaly, or lymphadenopathy. Carotid upstrokes normal. Chest. Point of maximum, impulse in the fifth intercostal space in the midclavicular line. S1, S2 normal. A soft S4 was heard. No S3. No murmurs. Lungs clear. Abdomen. Soft, nontender. No hepatosplenomegaly. No masses felt. No abdominal bruits. Musculoskeletal. Bilateral hallux valgus. No edema or clubbing. All peripheral pulses normal and equal. Neurological. No gross abnormalities. Diagnosis. 1. Palpitations, probably ventricular premature contractions. Rule out coronary artery disease. Rule out malignant arrhythmias. 2. History of hypertension. 3. History of hypothyroidism. Therapeutic Plan. 1. Review old records. 2. Tumor skin test. 3. EKG with 12-hour Holter monitor. 4. Measure blood pressure at next visit. Decide whether long-term hypertensive medication is necessary. 5. Ophthalmology consult.

Figure 8-3

COMPUTER EXERCISE

Before proceeding, you may want to do more exercises or review the concepts you have learned. Complete the computer exercises on the software for Chapter 8.

CHAPTER 9

Drug and Prescription Records

OBJECTIVES

After completing the exercises, the student will be able to:

1. Write the meanings for chart note abbreviations.
2. Enhance spelling skills by learning new medical words.
3. Record prescription refills in medical records.
4. Translate and write out prescriptions from English to Latin abbreviations and from Latin abbreviations to English.
5. Use the *Physicians' Desk Reference* to identify medication and correctly spell drug names.
6. Interpret a medication log.
7. Record on a medication schedule.
8. Obtain information from the five schedules of controlled substances.

AREAS OF COMPETENCE

Administrative Procedures
■ Perform basic clerical functions

General (Transdisciplinary)

Communication Skills
■ Use medical terminology appropriately

Legal Concepts
■ Prepare and maintain medical records
■ Document accurately
■ Maintain awareness of federal and state health care legislation and regulations

ABBREVIATION AND SPELLING REVIEW LESSON

Read the following patient's chart note and write the meanings for the abbreviations listed below the note. To decode any abbreviations you do not understand or that appear unfamiliar to you, refer to text Tables 8-1 and 9-3. Medical terms in the chart note are italicized; study them for spelling. Use your medical dictionary to look up their definitions. Your instructor may give a test for the spelling and definition of the words and abbreviations.

Lillian M. Chan

February 17, 199X OB case. LMP 12-14-9X. Pt had D & C in 1989 following *spontaneous abortion*. First child delivered by *C-section*. Ordered CBC, Ur, and WR. Pt to ret in 1 mo.

Fran Practon, MD

Fran Practon, MD

OB _____   CBC _____

LMP_____   Ur _____

Pt _____   WR _____

D & C _____   ret _____

C-section _____   mo _____

REVIEW QUESTIONS

Review the objectives, glossary, and chapter information before completing the following review questions.

1. Match the terms in the right column with the definitions in the left column by writing the numbers in the blanks.

   a. Drug that causes general or local loss of sensation to pain and touch   _____   1. generic name

   b. Drug that decreases congestion   _____   2. antiemetic

   c. Drug that exerts a tranquilizing effect   _____   3. stimulant

   d. Drug that increases a secretion of urine   _____   4. diuretic

   e. Nonproprietary name of a drug   _____   5. brand name

   f. Proprietary, or trade, name of a drug   _____   6. sedative

   g. Drug that relieves vomiting   _____   7. hemostatic

   h. Drug that increases activity in the body or any of its organs   _____   8. anesthetic

   i. Drug used to control bleeding   _____   9. antitussive

   j. Drug used to relieve a cough   _____   10. decongestant

2. Name some common side effects associated with medications.

   a. _____   g. _____

   b. _____   h. _____

   c. _____   i. _____

   d. _____   j. _____

   e. _____   k. _____

   f. _____   l. _____

3. If the patient does not have any known allergies, what is the abbreviation listed on the "alert tag" on the front of the patient's chart?

   _____

4. Name several ways the medical assistant can instruct the patient about drug dosages to be sure the patient understands the directions.

   a. _____

   b. _____

   c. _____

   d. _____

   e. _____

5. Name the agency responsible for enforcing all drug legislation, ensuring drug safety, and standarizing drugs in the United States.

   _____

6. Name and define the three types of drug names.

   a. _____

   b. _____

   c. _____

7. Name three important instructions given to patients taking antibiotics.

   a. _____

   b. _____

   c. _____

8. Define a generic drug.

   _____

   _____

   _____

9. In the *Physicians' Desk Reference (PDR)*, which section is used most frequently by the medical assistant?

   _____

10. When must a narcotic license be renewed, and where must the physician register?

    _____

    _____

11. Refer to text Table 9-2, Five Schedules of Controlled Substances, and answer the following questions.

    a. On which schedule may prescriptions be written by the health care worker?

       _____

    b. On which schedule will the medical assistant likely be handling triplicate forms for the doctor? _____

    c. On which schedule do drugs have the most potential for abuse?

       _____

12. Name and define the four components of a prescription.

   a. _____

   b. _____

   c. _____

   d. _____

13. If a pharmacist calls the office and the physician approves a refill on Mr. Hamilton's prescription, what administrative task should the medical assistant then perform? _____

   _____

14. Name two ways a medical assistant can track a patient's drug use habits.

   a. _____

   b. _____

15. Write the abbreviation or symbol for the following pharmaceutical terms.

   a. after meals _____

   b. drops _____

   c. every morning _____

   d. dram _____

   e. ounce _____

   f. every other day _____

16. Mrs. Schwartz telephones and says that the doctor prescribed Hytrin but she cannot remember why. With the physician's permission, you would tell her that the medication is being prescribed for her

   a. headaches   c. nerves

   b. hypertension   d. hypotension

   (Find the answer in the *Physicians' Desk Reference*.)

17. Rewrite the following statements as they would appear on a prescription, using Latin abbreviations.

   a. Proventil Inhaler, one-hundred milligrams per five milliliters, one or two inhalations every four hours whenever necessary.

   _____

   b. Cardizem, thirty milligrams, number one hundred, three times a day before meals, and one before bedtime.

   _____

   c. Lanoxin, zero point one-hundred and twenty-five milligrams, number sixty, one every day.

   _____

   d. Vantin, two-hundred milligrams, number twenty-eight, one by mouth, every twelve hours for fourteen days.

   _____

TRANSLATE PRESCRIPTIONS

PERFORMANCE OBJECTIVE

TASK: Translate ten prescriptions from Latin into common English.

CONDITIONS: Use ten written prescriptions, one sheet of plain paper, and pencil or pen.

STANDARDS: Time: _____ minutes

Accuracy: _____

(NOTE: The time element and accuracy criteria may be given by your instructor.)

DIRECTIONS: Translate the ten prescriptions in Workbook Figure 9-1 into common English by referring to text Table 9-3, Common Prescription Abbreviations and Symbols.

1.
```
Valium          10 mg.
#21
Sig.: ī p.o. t.i.d.
```

2.
```
Deltasone   2.5 mg
#30
Sig.: ī q.i.d.
```

3.
```
Darvocet N-100
Disp Tab #60
Sig.: īī q.4h.
p.r.n. for pain
```

4.
```
Hygroton    100 mg.
#100
Sig.: ī p.o. q.o.d.
```

5.
```
Tenormin      50 mg.
#100
ī q.d. X 7d then
īī q.d.
```

6.
```
Buspar         5 mg.
#100
5 mg. t.i.d. X 3d then
10 mg. t.i.d.
```

7.
```
Isordil
(isosorbide dinitrate)
40 mg. sustained-release
# 30
ī p.o. q.12°
```

8.
```
Comparine
25 mg. suppositories
#14
ī rectally b.i.d.
p.r.n. for vomiting
```

Figure 9-1

```
Vanceril
50 mg./metered spray
#1 bottle
2 inhalations q.i.d.
p.r.n. for asthma
```
9

```
Timoptic Solution
0.25%
1 bottle
Tgt. Ou q.d.
```
10

Figure 9-1 (Continued)

NOTE: A Performance Evaluation Checklist for this exercise can be found at the back of the workbook.

EXERCISE 9-2 **SPELL DRUG NAMES**

PERFORMANCE OBJECTIVE

TASK: Spell ten brand or generic drug names.

CONDITIONS: Use the list of ten drug names, a computer or electronic typewriter, and a drug reference book.

STANDARDS: Time: _____ minutes
Accuracy: _____
(NOTE: The time element and accuracy criteria may be given by your instructor.)

DIRECTIONS: Dr. Gerald Practon has dictated ten drug names, and you have phonetically written the following brand or generic names for the drugs prescribed for several patients. In typing consultation reports, you must complete the list by finding the correct spelling for each drug. Refer to the *Physicians' Desk Reference (PDR)* or other drug reference books (e.g., *Instant Drug Index, Hospital Formulary, Pharmaceutical Terminology*). Be sure to begin all brand names with a capital letter and all generic names with a lowercase letter.

DICTATED DRUG NAMES	
(In Phonetics)	Spelling
1. fy-or-IN-al	_____
2. di-ah-BEN-eze	_____
3. FEE-a-sol	_____
4. NAP-ro-sin	_____
5. HY-gro-ton	_____
6. LAY-six	_____
7. eye-bu-PRO-fen	_____
8. die-AS-a-pam	_____
9. TEN-or-min	_____
10. aug-MEN-tin	_____

NOTE: A Performance Evaluation Checklist for this exercise can be found at the back of the workbook.

<table><tr><td>**EXERCISE 9-3**</td><td>**RECORD PRESCRIPTION REFILLS IN MEDICAL RECORDS**</td></tr></table>

PERFORMANCE OBJECTIVE

TASK: Record four prescription refills on patients' medical records.

CONDITIONS: Use four file folder labels (form 19), pen; medical records of Wayne G. Weather, Sun Low Chung (again see Figures 6-1 and 8-2), and the patient interviewed in workbook exercise 8-2 (i.e., form 15).

STANDARDS: Time: _____ minutes

Accuracy: _____

(NOTE: The time element and accuracy criteria may be given by your instructor.)

DIRECTIONS:

1. The ABC Pharmacy calls about a prescription for Wayne G. Weather. Dr. Practon approves a refill for Darvocet N-100, number twenty, one tablet, every four hours whenever necessary for pain. Record this transaction on a label, initial it, and then paste the label into the patient's medical record as in a real situation. Use pharmaceutical abbreviations and symbols; use a current date.

2. The Dalton Pharmacy calls about the patient you interviewed in Exercise 8-2. The pharmacist asks if a refill on Restoril, fifteen milligram Capsules, number thirty, one by mouth at bedtime, can be approved. Dr. Practon approves. Record this transaction on the label, initial it, and then paste the label into the patient's medical record. Use pharmaceutical abbreviations and symbols. Use a current date.

3. The Georgetown Pharmacy calls regarding Sun Low Chung. He has a urinary tract infection again and would like a refill on his Bactrim double strength, number twenty-eight, one by mouth every twelve hours for fourteen days. Dr. Practon approves. Record this transaction on the label using a current date, initial it, and then paste the label into the patient's medical record. Use pharmaceutical abbreviations and symbols.

4. Two days later, Sun Low Chung calls Dr. Practon reporting an adverse reaction to the Bactrim. Dr. Practon calls the Main Street Pharmacy to order Macrodantin, one-hundred milligram capsules, number forty, one by mouth four times a day, with milk or meals for ten days. He asks that the prescription be sent to the patient. Record this transaction on the label, initial it, and then paste the label into the patient's medical record. Use the pharmaceutical abbreviations and symbols.

NOTE: A Performance Evaluation Checklist for this exercise can be found at the back of the workbook.

EXERCISE 9-4   SPELL DRUG NAMES

PERFORMANCE OBJECTIVE

TASK: Spell ten brand, generic, or over-the-counter drug names.

CONDITIONS: Use a pen or pencil, a drug reference book, and the ten sentences.

STANDARDS: Time: _____ minutes
Accuracy: _____
(NOTE: The time element and accuracy criteria may be given by your instructor.)

DIRECTIONS: Read the following ten sentences and circle the correct spelling from each pair of generic and/or brand medications. You may use a drug reference book (e.g., *Physicians' Desk Reference (PDR), Instant Drug Index, Hospital Formulary,* or *Pharmaceutical Terminology*). For over-the-counter drugs, use your common knowledge, an over-the-counter drug book, or visit a local drug store to locate the medication on the shelf. These sentences contain some frequently misspelled drug names.

1. Dr. Practon's last chart note on Mr. Hoy Cho states "advised the patient to take a) Aspirin, b) aspirin, 1 tab b.i.d."

2. After Ray Nunez suffered a mild heart attack, the physician prescribed a a) nitroglycerin, b) nitroglycerine patch daily.

3. Maria Sanchez telephoned stating she had a cold and wanted to know if it was all right to take a) Contac, b) Contact, an over-the-counter drug.

4. Mrs. Hatakeyama's allergy was easily treated with a) Actafed. b) Actifed.

5. Rosaria LaMacchia suffered a mild respiratory infection, and Dr. Practon gave her a prescription for a) Ceclor. b) Seklor.

6. The patient came in complaining of muscle spasms in the lumbar region, so a prescription for a) Flexeril, b) Flexoril was given.

7. Fayetta Brown's diagnosis was duodenal ulcer, and she was given a prescription for a) Bentil, b) Bentyl.

8. A year ago, Mae James had a urinary tract infection and was prescribed a) Velocef. b) Velosef.

9. Ventricular arrhythmias were diagnosed in Cameron Lesser's case, so a) Quiniglute. b) Quinaglute was given.

10. After the death of her spouse, Danielle La Fleur became depressed, and Dr. Practon prescribed a)Elevil. b) Elavil.

NOTE: A Performance Evaluation Checklist for this exercise can be found at the back of the workbook.

EXERCISE 9-5 — WRITE A PRESCRIPTION

PERFORMANCE OBJECTIVE

TASK: Write prescription.

CONDITIONS: In some regions medical assistants may be allowed to write prescriptions for patients. The physician must sign all originals. This exercise is designed to help understand the different components of a prescription form and the abbreviations used. Use a prescription form (workbook Figure 9-3) and pen.

STANDARDS: Time: _____ minutes
Accuracy: _____
(NOTE: The time element and accuracy criteria may be given by your instructor.)

DIRECTIONS: Write a prescription for the following, using today's date, prescription form (form 20), and text Table 9-3, Common Prescription Abbreviations and Symbols.

Felisha Weiss, 456 Los Angeles Avenue, Woodland Hills, XY 12345. The patient needs treatment for headache prophylaxis, she will be given Calan, eighty-milligrams, number one-hundred and twenty tablets, one by mouth four times a day. She may have two refills.

NOTE: A Performance Evaluation Checklist for this exercise can be found at the back of the workbook.

EXERCISE 9-6 — USE A *PHYSICIANS' DESK REFERENCE (PDR)*

PERFORMANCE OBJECTIVE

TASK: Identify medication in the correct section of the *Physicians' Desk Reference (PDR)*.

CONDITIONS: Use *Physicians' Desk Reference* and pen.

STANDARDS: Time: _____ minutes
Accuracy: _____
(NOTE: The time element and accuracy criteria may be given by your instructor.)

DIRECTIONS: Dr. Practon has just received a prothrombin time report on Mrs. Darcuiel. He asks you to call the patient and verify her present dosage of Coumadin before he makes an adjustment. When you call the patient she states she put all her medications in a medication container and no longer remembers her dosage. She says it is the *only* medication she is taking and it is *yellow*. Look in the P*hysicians' Desk Reference (PDR)* and determine how many milligrams she is taking.

_____

In which section of the *PDR* did you find the information?

_____

NOTE: A Performance Evaluation Checklist for this exercise can be found at the back of the workbook.

EXERCISE 9-7	INTERPRET A MEDICATION LOG

PERFORMANCE OBJECTIVE

TASK: Study the medication log and determine the drug use habits of a patient.

CONDITIONS: Use the medication log, workbook Figure 9-2, and a pen.

STANDARDS: Time: _____ minutes
Accuracy: _____
(NOTE: The time element and accuracy criteria may be given by your instructor.)

DIRECTIONS: Refer to the medication log, Figure 9-2. It is November 17, and Mary Beth Foley calls wanting a refill on her Glucotrol. Look at the medication log in the text and determine:

a) Is she taking the medication? YES/NO

MEDICATION LOG

PATIENT NAME: FOLEY, Mary Beth   **DATE OF BIRTH:** 9-30-52

ALLERGIES: KNA

DATE	MEDICATIONS	DOSE	#	INSTRUCTIONS (SIG)	PRN REG	TEL WRIT	PHARMACY	DR. SIG.
8/5/98	Elavil	100mg.	90	i p.o. h.s.	R	T	ABC Pharm	GMP
10/28/98	Elavil	100mg.	90	i p.o. h.s.	R	T	ABC Pharm	GMP
9/23/98	Glucotrol	10mg.	30	i p.o. a.c./a.m.	R	T	ABC Pharm	GMP
9/23/98	Calan SR	240mg.	30	i p.o. q.a.m.	R	T	ABC Pharm	GMP
10/7/98	Glucotrol	10mg.	90	i p.o. a.c./a.m.	R	W	mail order pharmacy	GMP
10/7/98	Tetracycline	250mg.	30	i p.o. T.I.D. p.r.n. yellow sputum	P	T	ABC Pharm	GMP
10/16/98	Calan SR	240mg.	90	i p.o. q.a.m.	R	W	mail order pharmacy	GMP

Figure 9-2

b) How many days has it been since she got her last refill?

_____DAYS

c) Is it time to refill the medication? YES/NO

d) When may she call for her next refill? _____

NOTE: A Performance Evaluation Checklist for this exercise can be found at the back of the workbook.

EXERCISE 9-8 RECORD ON A MEDICATION SCHEDULE

PERFORMANCE OBJECTIVE

TASK: Record medication name, dosage, and instructions on a medication schedule.

CONDITIONS: Use a medication schedule (form 21) and pen or pencil.

STANDARDS: Time: _____ minutes
Accuracy: _____
(NOTE: The time element and accuracy criteria may be given by your instructor.)

DIRECTIONS: Mr. Delbert Silva has just seen Dr. Fran Practon. She has prescribed Paxil for his depression. He is very confused, and Dr. Practon would like you to record the prescription information in a medication schedule for him. The dosage is 20 milligrams every morning. There is information in his chart indicting he is also taking Sinemet 20/250 mg for his Parkinson's disease. He takes two tablets four times a day. He is also on Lopressor for his hypertension, 100 milligrams twice a day. You have verified that Mr. Silva is still on these medications. Please fill out the medication schedule (form 21) for Mr. Silva.

NOTE: A Performance Evaluation Checklist for this exercise can be found at the back of the workbook.

COMPUTER EXERCISES

Before proceeding, you may want to do more exercises or review the concepts you have learned. Complete the computer exercises on the software for Chapter 9.

CHAPTER 10

Filing Procedures

OBJECTIVES

After completing the exercises, the student will be able to:

1. Write meanings for chart note abbreviations.

2. Enhance spelling skills by learning new medical words.

3. Determine filing units.

4. File patient records using standardized alphabetical rules.

5. Organize a color-coded filing system.

AREAS OF COMPETENCE

Administrative Procedures
■ Perform basic clerical functions

General (Transdisciplinary)

Communication Skills
■ Use medical terminology appropriately

Legal Concepts
■ Prepare and maintain medical records

ABBREVIATION AND SPELLING REVIEW LESSON

Read the following patient's chart note and write the meanings for the abbreviations listed below the note. To decode any abbreviations you do not understand or that appear unfamiliar to you, refer to text Tables 8-1 and 9-3. Medical terms in the chart note are italicized; study them for spelling. Use your medical dictionary to look up their definitions. Your instructor may give a test for the spelling and definition of the words and abbreviations.

DATE	PROGRESS
12-3-9X	Doris A Waxman PC: <u>occipital headaches</u> Px: HEENT NO <u>diplopia</u>, no <u>tinnitus</u>. See PI TPR neg., CV no chest pain, <u>palpitation</u>, <u>orthopnea</u>, <u>dyspnea</u> or <u>exertion</u> or <u>hemoptysis</u>. GI one episode of <u>emesis</u> last night. Some belching & intolerance to fried foods. RUQ abdom pain; no <u>hematemesis</u> or <u>melena</u>. GU no frequency or <u>dysuria</u>. Gyn-no abnormal bleeding. Ordered oral <u>cholecystography</u> Dx rule out GB disease. Fran Practon, MD

PC _____   GI _____

PX _____   RUQ _____

HEENT_____   abdom _____

PI _____   GU _____

TPR _____   Gyn _____

neg. _____   Dx _____

CV _____   GB _____

REVIEW QUESTIONS

Review the objectives, glossary, and chapter information before completing the following review questions.

1. Why is it important for all members of the office staff to master standardized filing rules? _____

    _____

2. A person's first name is also called the _____,
    and the last name is the _____.

3. A married woman may legally write her name three different ways. Give three examples of the way a name can be written.

    a. _____
    b. _____
    c. _____

4. Name two purposes served by file drawer guides.

    a. _____
    b. _____

5. Why is numerical filing considered an indirect method? _____

    _____

    _____

6. What is the purpose of a tickler file? _____

_____

7. What four steps would you take when a patient chart cannot be located?

a. _____

b. _____

c. _____

d. _____

8. What major problem can you anticipate when you prepare to transfer patient files?

_____

_____

9. Give two circumstances that might require cross-referencing of names in alphabetic files.

a. _____

b. _____

10. When determining the choice of a medical filing system, what must be considered?

a. _____

b. _____

c. _____

EXERCISE 10-1 — DETERMINE FILING UNITS

PERFORMANCE OBJECTIVES

TASK: Designate first, second, third, and fourth filing units so that names can be filed alphabetically in the office file.

CONDITIONS: Use pen or pencil.

STANDARDS: Time: _____ minutes
Accuracy: _____
(NOTE: The time element and accuracy criteria may be given by your instructor.)

DIRECTIONS: Underline the first, second, third, and fourth filing units of each name by using pen or pencil to write horizontal lines. Study the example shown in number 1. Refer to filing rules in Chapter 10 of the textbook.

1. A. Marsha Moore
2. Wm. John Taylor Kelly
3. Jamie Trethorn
4. Dan A. DeLeon
5. E. Mary LeVan
6. Amy Kay M'Oeters
7. Shelby C. St. John
8. Robert F. MacGregor
9. S. J. VanderLinder
10. Kelly Saint Thomas
11. Priscilla Ruby DuMont
12. Peter deWinter
13. Sister Mary Beth
14. Mayor Bill A. King
15. Dr. John J. Jackson
16. Mary-Kay deVille
17. Sji Mulzono
18. Mark Philip-DeGeer

19. Pope John Paul
20. Maj. Steve Royal Smith
21. Mrs. Noreen J. Cline
22. Charles T. Lloyd Jr.
23. Charles T. Lloyd II
24. Peter L. Morrison, MD
25. Sarah May Dennis-Brit
26. C. Ngyume
27. Paul Wm. SeValle
28. Foster Memorial Community Hospital
29. Ft. Benning Convalescent Home
30. A-1 Pharmacy
31. American Medical Corp
32. Dr. Spock's Clinic
33. St. Jude's Hospital
34. Russ Wilder Ambulance Service
35. Mt. Blanc Druggist

36. Century 21 Medical Supply
37. College of Ste. Catherine
38. Washington School, St. Paul, MN
39. Mary Cain Pharmacy, Waco, TX
40. Mary Cain Pharmacy, Inc.
41. Riverside County Public Library
42. St. Joseph's Community Hospital, Austin, TX
43. University of California–Los Angeles
44. University of California–Davis
45. St. Louis Publications
46. Father Buechner
47. Sister Sue Ellen
48. C .R. Toll
49. Rebecca Toll (Mrs. John)
50. Mrs. John A. Peterson

NOTE: A Performance Evaluation Checklist for this exercise can be found at the back of the workbook.

EXERCISE 10-2 INDEX AND FILE NAMES ALPHABETICALLY

PERFORMANCE OBJECTIVE

TASK: Demonstrate a knowledge of the standardized alphabetic rules to competently file and find medical records; apply this knowledge as you alphabetize drills for later class discussion.

CONDITIONS: Use pen or pencil.

STANDARDS: Time: _____ minutes
Accuracy: _____
(NOTE: The time element and accuracy criteria may be given by your instructor.)

DIRECTIONS: Underline the first, second, and third units of each name to show proper indexing order, placing one line under the surname, two lines under the given name, and three lines under the third name or initial. After underlining all names, alphabetize each group of three names, writing the corresponding letters in the answer column. Study the example. The first line shows names underlined; the second line shows the names in correct alphabetic arrangement typed as they would appear on file labels.

EXAMPLE:

(a) J. T. Jefferson (b) John Thompson (c) Mrs. T. J. Brown (Marsha)

Jefferson, J. T.; Thompson, John; Brown, Marsha (Mrs. T. J.)   cab

1. (a) Henrietta S. Lamar (b) Greta Lee Mason (c) Mary Lou LaMotte _____

2. (a) Raymond Lorenzana (b) R. Lorenzo (c) Tony Lorenzen _____

3. (a) Roger N. Stephens (b) Garland N. St. John (c) Robert Sprague _____

4. (a) Walter E. Johnston (b) Willard L. Johnson (c) Geo. W.
   Johnstone _____

5. (a) Hugh M. MacAdoo (b) Bruce T. McCall (c) Robert A. Macall _____

6. (a) Lt. Margaret Kim (b) Margaret LaForgeaus (c) Mrs. M.
   LeMaster (Loretta) _____

7. (a) H. King IV (b) H. M. King Jr. (c) Mrs. H. M. King (Alice) _____

8. (a) Mrs. Tina Simmons (Leonard) (b) Richard K. Simmons
   (c) R. K. Simons-Steele _____

9. (a) J. W. Winn, MD, 1404 Rosealea Rd., Cleveland, Ohio
   (b) James W. Winn, 1203 Venetta Drive, Cleveland, Ohio
   (c) J. W. Winn, 18 Maple St., Cleveland, Ohio _____

10. (a) Mary Sue Shelton (b) Martha Lee Shelton-Alston
    (c) Sheila-Lynn Alston (Mrs. Shelton A.) _____

11. (a) Willard Champs, 1072 Main St. (b) Willard Champs,
    290 Main St. (c) Wilfred Champs, 10234 Main St. _____

12. (a) Jas. E. McBean (b) J. L. MacBeen (c) Jason McBean _____

13. (a) W. L. Arthur-Davis (b) Carolyn Archer (Mrs. David)
    (c) Sister Arletta-Marie _____

14. (a) Grace Ayers (b) A. Joseph Almonzaz (c) Mrs. Anthony
    Ayers (Gloria) _____

15. (a) Norman Gilliam (b) N. Gilliam (c) Mrs. N. R. Gilliam (Norma) _____

16. (a) Matthew Kuboushek (b) Toshi Kubota (c) I. M. Kuchenberg _____

17. (a) Dr. Vincent DeLucca (b) Victoria Deems (c) Dr. Carl Deams Jr. _____

18. (a) Mrs. Loretta Maggio (b) Bokker T. Magallon Sr.
    (c) B. L. Magill, Rev. _____

NOTE: A Performance Evaluation Checklist for this exercise can be found at the back of the workbook.

EXERCISE 10-3 — FILE PATIENT NAMES AND BUSINESS NAMES ALPHABETICALLY

PERFORMANCE OBJECTIVE

TASK: Review the rules for alphabetic filing of medical facilities and patient names.

CONDITIONS: Use pen or pencil.

STANDARDS: Time: _____ minutes

Accuracy: _____

(NOTE: The time element and accuracy criteria may be given by your instructor.)

DIRECTIONS: After each group of four names, indicate by letter the order in which the names would be arranged in a file drawer.

1. a. Mrs. Allene Baker
   b. A. Baker
   c. A. Barker, MD
   d. Dr. Barker

   _____

2. a. The Apple Advertising Co.
   b. Apple-Cornwall, Inc.
   c. Appling Health Care
   d. Allan Applesey Corp.

   _____

3. a. Brother Brian Advertising
   b. The Bonita Rehab Facility
   c. B and B Clinic
   d. Bonita Rd. Care

   _____

4. a. Larue-McGuire Canyon Hospital
   b. Los Angeles Community Care
   c. Laruem Medical Clinic
   d. Las Robles Medical Center

   _____

5. a. Fortieth St. Convalescent Center
   b. The Forrest Hospital
   c. The Frew-Forrest Medical Group
   d. Forrest Medical Facility

   _____

6. a. Professor Sam A. Zimmer
   b. Zimmer-Kliev Agency
   c. Prof. A. Zimmer
   d. Z and Z Druggists

   _____

7. a. Robin Persy-Doerr
   b. Philip Persico Retirement Care
   c. Poinsettia Residential Care
   d. Persicona-Philips Mortuary

   _____

8. a. Mcdonald, Calvin
   b. MacDonald, Carl, MD
   c. Macdonald, C. A.
   d. Dr. McDermott

   _____

9. a. Tyler-Hill Medical Ass'n.
   b. Mark Tyler-Hill Mortuary
   c. The Pleasant Hills Pharmacy
   d. Phyllis G. Hills

---

10. a. Kevin St. Mann Jr.
    b. Chauncey A. Southern
    c. Kevin St. Mann
    d. Southwest St. Pharmaceuticals

NOTE: A Performance Evaluation Checklist for this exercise can be found at the back of the workbook.

EXERCISE 10-4 — DETERMINE INDEXING ORDER AND COLOR TO BE USED FOR FOLDER LABELS AND ARRANGE NAMES IN ALPHABETICAL ORDER

PERFORMANCE OBJECTIVE

TASK: Index and key names on file labels uniformly in correct indexing arrangement for alphabetizing.

CONDITIONS: Use forms 22, 23, and 24 and 60 3" x 5" cards or slips of paper.

OPTIONAL: Use highlighter pens in red, orange, green, blue, and violet.

STANDARDS: Time: _____ minutes
Accuracy: _____
(NOTE: The time element and accuracy criteria may be given by your instructor.)

DIRECTIONS: Dr. Practon has asked you to type patient names on cards in proper indexing order and to arrange the cards in alphabetical order. Before beginning to type on the 60 cards, use forms 22, 23, and 24 to write the indexing order for each patient name. Check with the instructor if you have problems in determining units and indexing sequence. If any names need to be cross-referenced, use the blank labels marked "X" at the end of form 24. Then transfer each name with its number to the cards, typing uniformly with even margins. Alphabetize. Make an answer sheet with only the numbers to facilitate checking your work.

OPTIONAL DIRECTIONS: Dr. Practon may ask you to add color to the medical office filing system or he may already use Remington's Variadex color-coding filing system. Highlight the top edge of each label or 3" by 5 card to code the *second* letter of the first unit in the name to a color shown in the following box. When filing the folder, it is first placed in the file drawer according to the alphabetic filing rules. Then the names are filed according to the color code assigned to the *second* letter of the last name. To help you remember the five divisions of the alphabetic system, notice that the first letter of each of the five groups is a vowel except for the last group of letters, which begins with an *r*. Add the appropriate colors before cutting apart the labels.

If the second letter of the patient's surname is:	the tab guide color is:
a, b, c, or d	orange
e, f, g, or h	red
i, j, k, l, m, or n	green
o, p, or q	blue
r, s, t, u, v, w, x, y, or z	violet

NOTE: A Performance Evaluation Checklist for this exercise can be found at the back of the workbook.

COMPUTER EXERCISES

Before proceeding, you may want to do more exercises or review the concepts you have learned. Complete the computer exercises on the software for Chapter 10.

CHAPTER 11

Office Maintenance and Management

OBJECTIVES

After completing the exercises, the student will be able to:

1. Write meanings for chart note abbreviations.

2. Enhance spelling skills by learning new medical words.

3. Compose reference pages for an office procedures manual.

4. Prepare and check invoices and purchase orders.

5. Place an order for office supplies.

6. Perform basic mathematic calculations when ordering supplies.

7. Abstract data from a catalog to place an order.

8. Use touch technique for operation of a calculator.

9. Key an agenda for a staff meeting.

AREAS OF COMPETENCE

Administrative Procedures
■ Perform basic clerical functions

General (Transdisciplinary)

Communication Skills
■ Use medical terminology appropriately

Legal Concepts
■ Maintain and dispose of regulated substances in compliance with government guidelines
■ Comply with established risk management and safety procedures
■ Participate in the development and maintenance of personnel, policy and procedure manuals
■ Maintain supply inventory

ABBREVIATION AND SPELLING REVIEW LESSON

Read the following patient's chart note and write the meanings for the abbreviations listed below the note. To decode any abbreviations you do not understand or that appear unfamiliar to you, refer to text Tables 8-1 and 9-3. Medical terms in the chart note are italicized; study them for spelling. Use your medical dictionary to look up their definitions. Your instructor may give a test for the spelling and definition of the words and abbreviations.

DATE	PROGRESS
12-14-9X	Helen P Craig CC: Back pain originating in the flank + radiating across the abdomen. Pt complains of abdominal distention ; difficulty urinating. Exam reveals increased sensitivity in lumbar ; groin areas. Considerable discomfort c̄ marked urethral stenosis UA: 5-10 RBC occ WBC sp gr 1.012 X: KUB ; IVP revealed small calculus in rt UPJ dilat to 24F c̄ Brev Inc fluid intake, low calcium diet Rx Aluminum hydroxide gel 60 ml q.i.d. Retn 1 wk for FU + decision on whether to operate. G Practon, MD

CC _____ UPJ _____

Pt _____ dilat _____

c̄ _____ 24F _____

UA _____ Brev _____

RBC_____ Inc _____

occ _____ Rx _____

WBC_____ ml _____

sp gr_____ q.i.d. _____

X _____ retn _____

KUB_____ wk. _____

IVP _____ FU _____

rt. _____

REVIEW QUESTIONS

Review the objectives, glossary, and chapter information before completing the following review questions.

1. Why is a service file folder recommended for equipment maintenance?

_____

2. List three security measures that should be taken before the office is closed each day.

    a. _____

    b. _____

    c. _____

3. List three safety habits to aid in preventing physical accidents on the premises of the medical office.

    a. _____

    b. _____

    c. _____

4. What is the purpose of an office procedures manual? _____

    _____

    _____

5. Give four reasons why it might prove unsatisfactory to order supplies in bulk.

    a. _____

    b. _____

    c. _____

    d. _____

6. Why are staff meetings important? _____

    _____

    _____

7. Why should the physician be consulted before expensive items of equipment are ordered? _____

    _____

    _____

8. When an order for merchandise arrives, what steps should be taken after the package is opened? _____

    _____

9. Name two ways the medical assistant can encourage recycling.

    a. _____

    b. _____

10. Name four items that must appear on any type of inventory-control card system.

    a. _____

    b. _____

    c. _____

    d. _____

<table>
<tr><td>EXERCISE
11-1</td><td>**ABSTRACT DATA FROM A CATALOG AND KEY A
PURCHASE ORDER**</td></tr>
</table>

PERFORMANCE OBJECTIVE

TASK: Abstract information from catalog data sheets and type a purchase order form accurately after determining charges.

CONDITIONS: Use order form 25 and pen or pencil.

STANDARDS: Time: _____ minutes
Accuracy: _____
(NOTE: The time element and accuracy criteria may be given by your instructor.)

DIRECTIONS: Dr. Fran and Dr. Gerald Practon want to order some printed letterheads, second sheets, and envelopes from the M & W Printing Company. Study the information on the catalog data sheets (Figures 11-1 and 11-2) so you are able to complete the order form. Refer to one of Dr. Practon's letterheads in this workbook and decide how to attractively arrange additional information to include a second telephone number, 013-487-9003, and a fax number, 013-488-7815. The items to be ordered are

- 2,000 raised-printed 25 percent rag content bond, 8 1/2" by 11"
- 1,000 Hammermill bond stock unprinted second sheets, 8 1/2" by 11"
- 1,000 raised-printed 25 percent rag content bond, 4 1/8" by 9 1/2" (No. 10) envelopes

Type the order form 25 and determine the cost, including the 5 1/2 percent sales tax so you can enclose a check for the items.

NOTE: A Performance Evaluation Checklist for this exercise can be found at the back of the workbook.

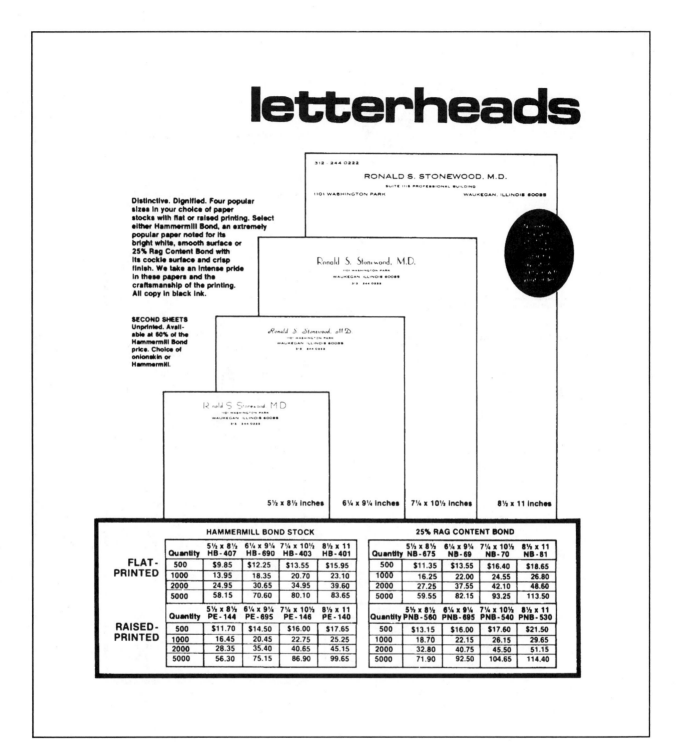

letterheads

312 · 244 0222

RONALD S. STONEWOOD, M.D.

SUITE 1115 PROFESSIONAL BUILDING

1101 WASHINGTON PARK   WAUKEGAN, ILLINOIS 60085

Distinctive. Dignified. Four popular sizes in your choice of paper stocks with flat or raised printing. Select either Hammermill Bond, an extremely popular paper noted for its bright white, smooth surface or 25% Rag Content Bond with its cockle surface and crisp finish. We take an intense pride in these papers and the craftsmanship of the printing. All copy in black ink.

SECOND SHEETS
Unprinted. Available at 60% of the Hammermill Bond price. Choice of onionskin or Hammermill.

5½ x 8½ inches   6¼ x 9¼ inches   7¼ x 10½ inches   8½ x 11 inches

			HAMMERMILL BOND STOCK				25% RAG CONTENT BOND		
	Quantity	5½ x 8½ HB-407	6¼ x 9¼ HB-690	7¼ x 10½ HB-403	8½ x 11 HB-401	Quantity	5½ x 8½ NB-675	6¼ x 9¼ NB-69	7¼ x 10½ NB-70	8½ x 11 NB-81
FLAT-PRINTED	500	$9.85	$12.25	$13.55	$15.95	500	$11.35	$13.55	$16.40	$18.65
	1000	13.95	18.35	20.70	23.10	1000	16.25	22.00	24.55	26.80
	2000	24.95	30.65	34.95	39.60	2000	27.25	37.55	42.10	48.60
	5000	58.15	70.60	80.10	83.65	5000	59.55	82.15	93.25	113.50
	Quantity	5½ x 8½ PE-144	6¼ x 9¼ PE-695	7¼ x 10½ PE-146	8½ x 11 PE-140	Quantity	5½ x 8½ PNB-560	6¼ x 9¼ PNB-695	7¼ x 10½ PNB-540	8½ x 11 PNB-530
RAISED-PRINTED	500	$11.70	$14.50	$16.00	$17.65	500	$13.15	$16.00	$17.60	$21.50
	1000	16.45	20.45	22.75	25.25	1000	18.70	22.15	26.15	29.65
	2000	28.35	35.40	40.65	45.15	2000	32.80	40.75	45.50	51.15
	5000	56.30	75.15	86.90	99.65	5000	71.90	92.50	104.65	114.40

Figure 11-1

envelopes

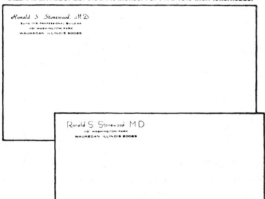

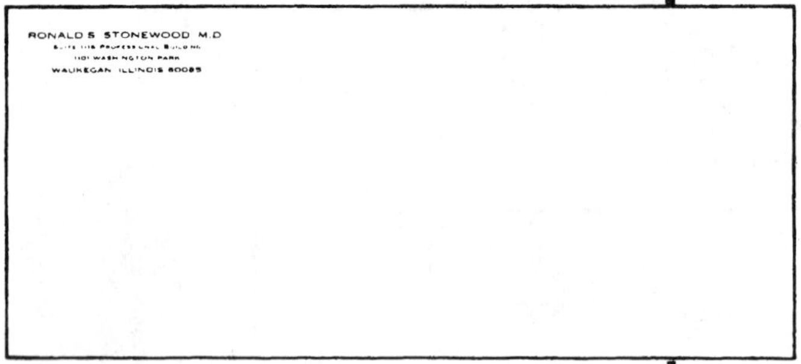

SIZE 10 ENVELOPES: 4⅛ x 9½ inches. For 8½ x 11-inch letterheads.

SIZE 7½ ENVELOPES: 3⅞ x 7½ inches. For 7¼ x 10½-inch letterheads.

SIZE 6¾ ENVELOPES: 3⅝ x 6½ inches. For 6¼ x 9¼-inch letterheads.

Unless specified, we print your copy in the upper left-hand corner on the front of the envelope. Flat-printed envelopes can be imprinted on the back flap as shown.

M&W envelopes are produced on the same fine stocks as our letterheads. Hammermill Bond is a bright white, smooth-surfaced paper. 25% Rag Content Bond is a crisp paper with a cockle finish — a most distinctive stationery. Both available in either flat or raised printing with your copy in 3 or 4 lines in the upper left-hand corner or on the back flap (flat-printed only). All printing in black ink.

HAMMERMILL BOND FLAT-PRINTED

Quantity	Size 6¾ L-500	Size 7½ L-510	Size 10 L-502
500	$13.50	$17.95	$18.50
1000	24.25	28.80	34.55
2000	45.15	50.15	59.30
5000	98.25	110.85	132.75

HAMMERMILL BOND RAISED-PRINTED

Quantity	Size 6¾ PE-220	Size 7½ PE-192	Size 10 PE-190
500	$16.00	$20.50	$21.25
1000	26.30	28.90	34.75
2000	45.40	53.35	59.60
5000	99.00	124.25	133.45

25% RAG CONTENT BOND FLAT-PRINTED

Quantity	Size 6¾ NB-800	Size 7½ NB-600	Size 10 NB-700
500	$18.90	$24.55	$25.20
1000	33.40	34.95	44.60
2000	57.80	67.75	76.95
5000	126.50	149.95	171.90

25% RAG CONTENT BOND RAISED-PRINTED

Quantity	Size 6¾ PNB-520	Size 7½ PNB-510	Size 10 PNB-500
500	$21.60	$27.25	$27.90
1000	33.40	39.55	44.70
2000	58.15	70.95	77.20
5000	127.15	152.55	172.60

Figure 11-2

EXERCISE 11-2 — COMPLETE AN ORDER FORM FOR OFFICE SUPPLIES

PERFORMANCE OBJECTIVE

TASK: Complete an order form, filling in designated spaces and computing total amount ordered by referring to Figure 11-4 in the textbook.

CONDITIONS: Use order form 26 and pen.

STANDARDS: Time: _____ minutes
Accuracy: _____
(NOTE: The time element and accuracy criteria may be given by your instructor.)

DIRECTIONS: Dr. Fran and Dr. Gerald Practon have asked you to order some office supplies. Neatly and accurately complete the order form using a pen. The preferred customer card no. is 667-32-7118-4006. Calculate the extensions, state sales tax at 6 percent, and a $15 two-day shipping and handling charge. There is no shipping and handling charge for orders over $400.

1 carton HCFA-1500 continuous 2-part insurance forms, 8 1/2" by 11", detached, carton pack 1,500, $110/carton (CAT No. RED-25104), page 53

4 boxes 50 poly file folders with fasteners blue, letter size, 1/3" cut tabs, 3/4" expansions, $40.90/box (CAT No. GLW-FF113), page 32

6 daily group practice wirebound appointment books with 15-minute appointments, four columns per page, appointments from 8 A.M. to 7:45 P.M., 11" by 7 7/8", $29.15 each, price break: For each five ordered get one free, (CAT No. GLW-AB402), page 65

5 packages, 9" by 12" clasp envelopes, 28 lb. heavyweight Kraft, 25 to a package, $3.75/package, (CAT No. 42SH-11), page 61

2 packages, double-prong clasp envelopes, reinforced eyelet, gummed flaps, 9" by 12", assorted colors $4.25/package (Cat. No. 387-ACJ), page 62

2 dozen tape flags, style #680-1, 1" by 1.7", 1 dozen red, 1 dozen yellow, $1.49/package (Cat. No. 49WEX-52), page 50

NOTE: A Performance Evaluation Checklist for this exercise can be found at the back of the workbook.

EXERCISE 11-3 — PERFORM BASIC OFFICE MATHEMATICS

PERFORMANCE OBJECTIVE

TASK: Perform basic mathematic calculations on orders for supplies and determine the costs, taking advantage of any special discounts.

CONDITIONS: Use paper and pencil.

STANDARDS: Time: _____ minutes
Accuracy: _____
(NOTE: The time element and accuracy criteria may be given by your instructor.)

DIRECTIONS: The administrative assistant responsible for placing supply orders should be able to figure discounts and sales tax amounts and perform basic office mathematics. If a calculator is available, use it for some problems. To see how wise purchasing and correct math procedures can save the office added expenses, solve the following problems, assuming you pay all bills within the discount period, which is usually ten days. The discounts are subtracted before the sales tax is added.

1. If the laundry bill of $33.80 is paid within ten days, the company allows a 2 1/2 percent discount. Figure the amount of the bill, assuming you pay it within ten days.   _____

2. Mr. Carl McFadden had five office visits at $25 each, three injections at $8.50 each, an x-ray at $26.60, and a home visit of $40.00. He has a $4.60 credit on his account. What will be the amount of his next bill?   _____

3. Mr. Bill Nelson is scheduled to have corrective surgery, which will be $385. He is asked to make a down payment of $50 before the operation, and then he wants to divide his payments into six equal installments. What will be the amount of each installment payment?   _____

4. The following items are on an invoice that arrived today. You are required to check to see that the bill is correct and that the supplies are the ones ordered. The physician will receive a 3 percent discount, and sales tax is 6 percent. The total shown on the invoice is $26.14; if this amount is incorrect, write the correct amount in the space at the right.

> 4 bottles rubbing alcohol @ $2.25 each
> 3 thermometers @ $1.95 each
> 6 boxes cotton @ $.29 each
> 6 bottles mouthwash @ $.89 each
> 11 cartons cotton swabs @ $.39 each
> 3 hypodermic needles @ $.39 each

> Check would be in the amount of: _____

5. Paper towels are sold at the rate of $6.50 a dozen. Figure the cost of ten dozen towels with a 3 1/2 percent discount allowed physicians and a 6 percent sales tax.   _____

6. Dr. Practon needs 500 needles priced at $2.60 a hundred. If she pays within ten days, she receives a 2 percent discount. Sales tax is 5 1/2 percent.   _____

7. Eight thermometers cost $12.42. Dr. Practon wants to order a dozen to take advantage of a 3 percent discount. Sales tax is 5 percent. Determine the amount of the bill for the 12 thermometers.   _____

8. Roberta Mason's account of $98.50 has been delinquent for seven months. According to the office procedures manual, after an account has been delinquent for three months, a 2 percent monthly service charge compounded monthly is added. What will be the amount owed after nine months?   _____

9. Hypodermic needles cost $4.95 per 100.

   a. How much would 300 needles cost? _____

   b. How much would 700 needles cost? _____

10. If the needles are purchased in large lots of 1,000 or more, the manufacturer allows a discount of 15 percent. _____

    a. How much would 3,000 needles cost? _____

    b. How much would 14,000 needles cost? _____

    c. If Dr. Practon uses 200 needles a month, how much would he save in a year by making a single purchase for a year's supply rather than 12 monthly purchases? _____

NOTE: A Performance Evaluation Checklist for this exercise can be found at the back of the workbook.

| EXERCISE 11-4 | USE A CALCULATOR TO FIND TOTAL AMOUNTS |

PERFORMANCE OBJECTIVE

TASK: Determine total amounts by operating a calculator using touch fingering.

CONDITIONS: Use calculator with or without tape, pen or pencil, and Figure 11-3.

STANDARDS: Time: _____ minutes

Accuracy: _____

(NOTE: The time element and accuracy criteria may be given by your instructor.)

DIRECTIONS: Using a calculator, practice touch operation by moving the fingers correctly from the home row to other numbered keys as shown in the diagram. Then determine the total amounts for the problems and write the answer in the space provided. If the calculator prints data on a tape, attach the tape to the worksheet.

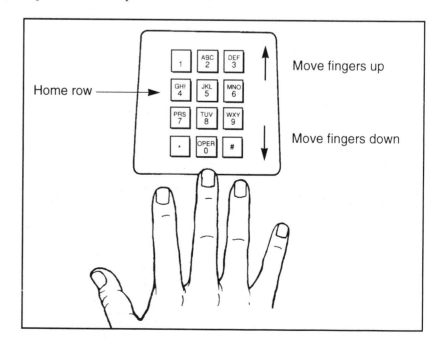

Total the following columns and write your answer in the space provided.

29,837	2,947
106,744	69,301
3,982	881,697
46,671	599
90,567	183,577
288,156	2,106,734

1. _____   2. _____

2,983	40,695
1,067	2,396
398	3,987
466	6,533
71	421
9,056	25,067
173	

3. _____   4. _____

$ 297.81
555.50
63.77
39.88
46.22
1,196.64
782.95
6.07
9,009.31

5. $_____

6. Refer to the checking account transactions slip in Figure 11-3. Assume the previous balance was $8,021.44, determine the amount in the account at the end of March, and write the balance here

_____

7. Refer to textbook Figure 18-4A. Total the amounts of the checks written from June 2 through June 8. Write the total amount disbursed here

_____ (Attach tape if calculator prints data.)

NOTE: A Performance Evaluation Checklist for this exercise can be found at the back of the workbook.

EXERCISE 11-5

PREPARE PURCHASE ORDERS

PERFORMANCE OBJECTIVE

TASK: Type two purchase order forms for medical supplies, using the given information, and determine the total amount owed after taking advantage of the discount. Refer to Figure 11-4 in the textbook. (Note: Photocopies would be made before sending off order.)

CONDITIONS: Use purchase order forms 27 and 28.

```
CHECKING ACCOUNT TRANSACTIONS
CHECKS
```

CHECK NO	DATE	AMOUNT	CHECK NO	DATE	AMOUNT	CHECK NO	DATE	AMOUNT
7246	02-26	30.00	7253*	03-08	5,000.00	7259	03-14	129.48
7247	03-12	500.00	7254	03-07	50.00	7261*	03-19	30.00
7248	03-04	131.45	7255	03-08	33.79	7262	03-20	35.50
7249	03-01	297.41	7256	03-13	29.97	7266*	03-25	400.00
7250	02-26	125.63	7257	03-13	20.00			
7251	02-27	60.84	7258	03-12	163.56			

*Break in check number sequence

ELECTRONIC FUNDS TRANSFERS AND DESCRIPTIVE TRANSACTIONS

DATE	TYPE OF TRANSACTION	WITHDRAWALS	DEPOSITS
03-01	Soc. Sec. US Treasury 2284192B		71.00
03-01	AF Ret Pay AfAfC, Denver, CO 2284192		492.55
03-01	Ret. Benft STRS 2284160 STRS		518.19
03-01	Ret. Benft STRS 2284160A STRS		747.83

Figure 11-3

STANDARDS: Time: _____ minutes

Accuracy: _____

(NOTE: The time element and accuracy criteria may be given by your instructor.)

DIRECTIONS: Using the information given on the following purchase orders no. 235 and no. 236, type two purchase order forms for medical supplies and stationery. Determine the total amount owed, subtract the physician's discount, and then add the sales tax. The supplies are to be shipped to you, and you have authorization from Dr. Practon to sign the form.

PURCHASE ORDER NO. 235

Ordered from Stationers Corporation, 3498 West Olympic Boulevard, Woodland Hills, XY 12345.

Shipped by: United Parcel Service. Discount: 2 percent. Sales tax: 5 1/2 percent.

Quantity	Description	Unit Price
4 reams	8 1/2" by 11" bond paper, 20# weight	$12.95
5 boxes	Lightweight No. 12 carbon paper	3.25
1,500	No. 10 envelopes	5.50M*
6 boxes	Red fine-line ballpoint pens	3.95/box

Amount of check should be _____

PURCHASE ORDER NO. 236

Ordered from: Valley Instrument Corporation, 11335 Almont Boulevard, Denver, CO 80200.

Shipped by: Southwest Delivery Service. Discount: 3 percent. Sales tax: 4 percent.

Quantity	Description	Unit Price
3	Model No. B872C surgeon's handles	$2.95
2 dozen	Scalpel blades, No. F112 (12 to a box)	1.39/box
4	Oval Duplex thermometers,	
	Cage A Rectal, B4	2.95
1 dozen boxes	Sterile cotton balls	1.75/box
3M*	Tongue blades	2.50M
4	Splinter forceps, straight, B112	4.98

Amount of check should be _____

NOTE: A Performance Evaluation Checklist for this exercise can be found at the back of the workbook.

EXERCISE 11-6

PREPARE MATERIAL FOR AN OFFICE PROCEDURE MANUAL

PERFORMANCE OBJECTIVE

TASK: Assemble material on office appointments and type a sample reference sheet for an office procedures manual.

STANDARDS: Time: _____ minutes

CONDITIONS: Use one sheet of white typing paper.
Accuracy: _____
(NOTE: The time element and accuracy criteria may be given by your instructor.)

DIRECTIONS: Dr. Practon wants you to type a reference sheet for the office procedures manual detailing appointment procedures. Refer to office policies in the appendix of this workbook to determine the information Dr. Practon wants outlined for the staff on the subject of appointments. Refer to text Chapter 11, Figure 11-2 to help you plan a well-organized reference sheet.

NOTE: A Performance Evaluation Checklist for this exercise can be found at the back of the workbook.

EXERCISE 11-7

WRITE AN AGENDA FOR AN OFFICE MEETING

PERFORMANCE OBJECTIVE

TASK: Assemble information to type an agenda for an office meeting in outline form.

CONDITIONS: Use one or two sheets of white typing paper and Figure 11-4. Refer to Chapter 11, Figure 11-1.

STANDARDS: Time: _____ minutes
Accuracy: _____
(NOTE: The time element and accuracy criteria may be given by your instructor.)

---

*M is the Roman numeral that means a thousand

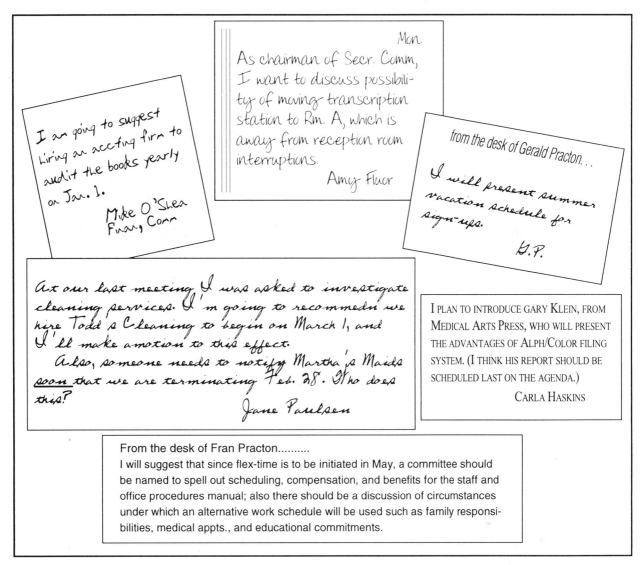

Figure 11-4

DIRECTIONS: Study the following notes in Figure 11-4, gathered from members of the staff, indicating actions they wish to introduce at the February 25 noon lunch meeting. Refer to text Figure 11-1 to learn what occurred at the previous meeting to determine unfinished business. Fran Practon will act as the chairperson for the meeting. The next scheduled meeting will be at 8:30 A.M. on March 20.

NOTE: A Performance Evaluation Checklist for this exercise can be found at the back of the workbook.

COMPUTER EXERCISES

Before proceeding, you may want to do more exercises or review the concepts you have learned. Complete the computer exercises on the software for Chapter 11.

CHAPTER 12

Written Correspondence

OBJECTIVES

After completing the exercises, the student will be able to:

1. Write meanings for chart note abbreviations.

2. Enhance spelling skills by learning new medical words.

3. Edit sentences.

4. Compose and key error-free grammatically correct letters in the proper formats.

5. Key a two-page letter.

6. Abstract information and key properly aligned interoffice memorandums.

(NOTE: Exercises involving the keying of envelopes will be done in chapter 13.)

AREAS OF COMPETENCE

Administrative Procedures
■ Perform basic clerical functions
■ Perform medical transcription

General (Transdisciplinary)

Communication Skills
■ Use effective and correct verbal and written communications
■ Use medical terminology appropriately

ABBREVIATION AND SPELLING REVIEW LESSON

Read the following patient's chart note and write the meanings for the abbreviations listed below the note. To decode any abbreviations you do not understand or that appear unfamiliar to you, refer to text Tables 8-1 and 9-3. Medical terms in the chart note are italicized; study them for spelling. Use your medical dictionary to look up their definitions. Your instructor may give a test for the spelling and definition of the words and abbreviations.

DATE	PROGRESS
1-3-9X	Maria K Morgan CC: Pt complains of back pain, _nausea_, _dysuria_, & _oliguria_ of 1 wk. PH _Congenital_ _stricture_ rt _ureter_ & at _ureterovesical_ junction. UA: Occ WBC occ epith. ph 7, alb 1, sugar 0. Dr. Woodman's summary rev. Dilat to K35 c̄ Brev ordered IVP. _Unilateral_ _nephrectomy_ may be indicated. Dx possible _urinary_ _calculi_ RTO 1 wk for UA & possible Dilat G Practon MD

CC _____   pH _____

Pt _____   alb _____

CVA _____   rev _____

wk. _____   dilat _____

PH _____   K35 _____

rt. _____   c̄ _____

UA _____   Brev _____

Occ _____   IVP _____

WBC_____   Dx _____

epith._____ RTO _____

REVIEW QUESTIONS

Review the objectives, glossary and chapter information before completing the following review questions.

1. List five functions of the electronic memory typewriter.

   a. _____

   b. _____

   c. _____

   d. _____

   e. _____

2. What procedure should be taken when the transcriptionist cannot understand a word or phrase of a physician's dictation?

   _____

   _____

   _____

3. List three flaws, any one of which makes a letter unmailable.

   a. _____

   b. _____

   c. _____

4. A woman's courtesy title is enclosed in parentheses only when used with her

_____

5. What is the best method for correcting an error in typed material being prepared
for photocopying? _____

_____

_____

6. Transcription needs in the physician's office will be based on factors such as the
following:

a. _____
b. _____
c. _____
d. _____

7. List three reasons for using a window envelope.

a. _____
b. _____
c. _____

8. The least personal of the various letter formats is the _____

_____

9. Name three devices you could use to arouse the reader's interest in the first paragraph of a letter you are writing for the physician.

a. _____
b. _____
c. _____

10. List five ways to increase the productivity of photocopy machines.

a. _____
b. _____
c. _____
d. _____
c. _____

EXERCISE 12-1 **SPELL MEDICAL WORDS**

PERFORMANCE OBJECTIVE

TASK: Select the correctly spelled medical word from the choices given.

CONDITIONS: Use pen or pencil.

STANDARDS: Time: _____ minutes
Accuracy: _____
(NOTE: The time element and accuracy criteria may be given by your
instructor.)

DIRECTIONS: Circle the correctly spelled word from the choices given.

1.	conchiousness	consciousness	consceousness
2.	exhaustion	exsaustion	exhausion
3.	theraputic	therapuetic	therapeutic
4.	antidiarretic	antidiarrhetic	antidiarhetic
5.	neurolysis	nuerolysis	neurolosis
6.	medisinal	medicinal	medicenal
7.	roentegenogram	rentegenogram	roentgenogram
8.	kinesiology	kenesiology	kenisiology
9.	pharmasuetical	pharmacuetical	pharmaceutical
10.	humeris	humerus	humerous
11.	esophaglagia	esophagalgia	esopagalgia
12.	critereon	criterion	creiterion
13.	cauterisation	caterization	cauterization
14.	methastasize	metastasize	metasthasize
15.	spontaneous	spontenous	spontaneus
16.	capitation	captation	capitasion
17.	pancretectomy	pancraetectomy	pancreatectomy
18.	indemity	endemnity	indemnity
19.	negoteable	negotiable	negotable
20.	intemperance	intemperence	intemparance
21.	ajudicate	adjudicate	adgudicate
22.	cursor	curser	courser
23.	stethoscope	steathescope	stethescrope
24.	purelent	purulent	peurulent
25.	ausculation	auscultation	auscultasion

NOTE: A Performance Evaluation Checklist for this exercise can be found at the back of the workbook.

EXERCISE 12-2   **KEY A LETTER OF WITHDRAWAL**

PERFORMANCE OBJECTIVE

TASK: Key letter for the physician's signature.

CONDITIONS: Use one sheet of letterhead (form 29) and guide form 29A.

STANDARDS: Time: _____ minutes
Accuracy: _____
(NOTE: The time element and accuracy criteria may be given by your instructor.)

DIRECTIONS: Dr. Gerald Practon has asked you to type a letter of withdrawal on his letterhead to Constance M. Stanfield, 2090 Hope Street, Woodland Hills, XY 12345. Refer to text Chapter 3, Figure 3-5, for format and content. Letter format may be seen in Figure 12-3. Use full-block style with mixed punctuation. Mrs. Stanfield refused to follow the treatment prescribed by Dr. Practon. Watch for proper paragraphing, placement, and punctuation. Be sure to proofread the letter before handing it to your instructor for grading. Grading will be based on neatness, placement, and number of typographical errors. Use the current date on the letter. This letter would be sent certified with return receipt. Do not prepare the envelope at this time.

NOTE: A Performance Evaluation Checklist for this exercise can be found at the back of the workbook.

EXERCISE 12-3   EDIT—REVIEW OF FUNDAMENTALS

PERFORMANCE OBJECTIVE

TASK: Edit sentences to eliminate words, to change the sequence of words, and to eliminate redundant phrases to improve writing.

STANDARDS: Time: _____ minutes
Accuracy: _____
(NOTE: The time element and accuracy criteria may be given by your instructor.)

DIRECTIONS: The following sentences contain unnecessary words that take space and add nothing to content. Strike through the words that are not needed, add a word, or change the sequence of the words to improve the meaning.

1. Mrs. Benson just recovered from an attack of pneumonia.
2. The letter arrived at a time when we were busy.
3. During the year of 19XX the unpaid accounts were numerous.
4. If the population, as in the general case, increases, we'll plan on expanding our practice.
5. The water is for drinking purposes only.
6. The close proximity of the police department scared the thief.
7. It costs the sum of 20 dollars.
8. The young secretary has a beautiful future before her.
9. The wreck occurred at the corner of Fourth and Rampart Streets.
10. The color of the prize rose was dark red.
11. We are now engaged in building a new medical office.
12. Somebody or other must assume the responsibility.
13. The file is made out of steel.
14. There is much construction in the city of Ventura.
15. It happened at the hour of midnight.
16. The package should be there in three weeks' time.
17. We will ship the office supplies at a later date.
18. The character of the road was smooth.
19. The physician spoke at a meeting held in Miami Beach.
20. The patient appeared for her appointment at the hour of 2:30 P.M.

NOTE: A Performance Evaluation Checklist for this exercise can be found at the back of the workbook.

EXERCISE 12-4 — COMPOSE AND KEY A MAILABLE LETTER

PERFORMANCE OBJECTIVE

TASK: Compose and key an original letter dealing with a failed appointment in full-block style with mixed punctuation; assume a file copy will be made of the letter.

CONDITIONS: Use letterhead form 30, guide form 29A, and dictionary.

STANDARDS: Time: _____ minutes
Accuracy: _____
(NOTE: The time element and accuracy criteria may be given by your instructor.)

DIRECTIONS: Mrs. Margaret B. Hanson (Mrs. C. L.) of 2319 Warren Street, Woodland Hills, XY 12345, calls on September 20 to make a 4 P.M. appointment for her son, James P. Hanson, on September 25. The patient does not show (DNS). Write a letter with a reference line to Mrs. Hanson about her son's failure to keep his appointment. Remember that this is a legal document and must be prepared for Dr. Fran Practon's signature. Key this letter in full-block style with mixed punctuation.

NOTE: A Performance Evaluation Checklist for this exercise can be found at the back of the workbook.

EXERCISE 12-5 — COMPOSE AND KEY A MAILABLE LETTER

PERFORMANCE OBJECTIVE

TASK: Compose and key an original letter to a new patient, explaining procedures for the first visit and suggesting insurance information needed; letter is to be keyed in full-block style with mixed punctuation. Assume a file copy will be made of the letter.

CONDITIONS: Use letterhead form 31, guide form 29A and dictionary.

STANDARDS: Time: _____ minutes
Accuracy: _____
(NOTE: The time element and accuracy criteria may be given by your instructor.)

DIRECTIONS: Write a letter over your own signature to Raymond E. Stokes Jr., 4053 Magnolia Boulevard, Woodland Hills, XY 12345, reminding him of his appointment at 2:30 P.M. on Thursday, October 2, and inform him of the fee for a first office visit (intermediate examination). Suggest that he bring all insurance information if he has insurance coverage. (To ascertain the fee for a first visit, look at Dr. Fran Practon's fee schedule in the Appendix, Figure A-1). Use full-block style with mixed punctuation.

NOTE: A Performance Evaluation Checklist for this exercise can be found at the back of the workbook.

EXERCISE 12-6 — COMPOSE AND KEY A MAILABLE LETTER

PERFORMANCE OBJECTIVE

TASK: Compose and key an original letter to a physician, stating that Dr. Fran Practon's patient may need medical attention while on a visit to Mexico; use modified block-style and open punctuation and make a copy to mail to the patient.

CONDITIONS: Use computer letterhead form 32, guide form 29A, and dictionary.

STANDARDS: Time: _____ minutes
Accuracy: _____
(NOTE: The time element and accuracy criteria may be given by your instructor.)

DIRECTIONS: Write a letter to Dr. Manuel Madero-Gonzales, Av. Mexico 131, Parque San Andreas, Mexico 21, D.F., to refer to him Dr. Fran Practon's patient, Mr. Hector Gutierrez, who has been treated for infectious hepatitis. Mention that recent laboratory studies and clinical evaluations were within normal limits. Assume you are enclosing copies of each evaluation. Tell Dr. Madero-Gonzales that you have instructed Mr. Gutierrez to contact him if any medical problems develop during a three-week vacation in Mexico. Use modified-block style with open punctuation and make a copy for the patient. Dr. Practon will sign the letter.

NOTE: A Performance Evaluation Checklist for this exercise can be found at the back of the workbook.

EXERCISE 12-7 — COMPOSE AND KEY A MAILABLE LETTER

PERFORMANCE OBJECTIVE

TASK: Compose and key an original letter over Dr. Gerald Practon's signature, requesting payment on a bill, using modified-block style and open punctuation. Assume a file copy will be made of the letter.

CONDITIONS: Use letterhead form 33, guide form 29A, dictionary, and reference materials.

STANDARDS: Time: _____ minutes
Accuracy: _____
(NOTE: The time element and accuracy criteria may be given by your instructor.)

DIRECTIONS: When checking the financial records, you find that Mrs. Christine LaMairre (Mrs. C. J.), 247 South Lincoln Boulevard, Apartment 5, Topanga, XY 90290, has not paid her bill for three months. Write a firm letter requesting payment (she now owes $52). Enclose a copy of the June statement. Key this letter in modified-block style with open punctuation.

NOTE: A Performance Evaluation Checklist for this exercise can be found at the back of the workbook.

<table>
<tr><td>EXERCISE
12-8</td><td></td></tr>
</table>

EXERCISE 12-8 · KEY MEMORANDA FROM HANDWRITTEN NOTES

PERFORMANCE OBJECTIVE

TASK: Abstract information from a handwritten note and key the message accurately on an interoffice memo form.

CONDITIONS: Use interoffice memo form 34.

STANDARDS: Time: _____ minutes
Accuracy: _____
(NOTE: The time element and accuracy criteria may be given by your instructor.)

DIRECTIONS: Dr. Gerald Practon has written you a note (Figure 12-1), asking you to key a memorandum to Dr. Yong Hall in this clinic. Key an interoffice memo (form 34), aligning the typewritten words with the printed guide words on the memo form. Remember to triple space before you begin the message.

> From the Desk of... *Gerald*
>
> 3-22
>
> Jean:
> Ask Dr. Hall if he saw article "Evaluation of Biofeedback Training + Its Effects Upon Pt's with Tension Headaches" – Jan, 81. <u>AMA Journal</u> by Dr. Hugh James, pgs 21-25 – relevant to Yong's research + very informative!
>
> G.P.
>
> P.S. Ask him if he wants me to send for a reprint.

Figure 12-1

NOTE: A Performance Evaluation Checklist for this exercise can be found at the back of the workbook.

<table>
<tr><td>EXERCISE
12-9</td><td></td></tr>
</table>

EXERCISE 12-9 · KEY MEMORANDA FROM HANDWRITTEN NOTES

PERFORMANCE OBJECTIVE

TASK: Abstract information from a handwritten note and key the message accurately on an interoffice memo form.

CONDITIONS: Use memo form 35.

STANDARDS: Time: _____ minutes
Accuracy: _____
(NOTE: The time element and accuracy criteria may be given by your instructor.)

DIRECTIONS: Dr. Fran Practon has written you a note (Figure 12-2), asking you to key a memorandum to Cathy Crowe, RPT, which Dr. Practon will take to the hospital to place in Cathy's box. Key the appropriate memo, properly aligned and spaced.

From the Desk of... Fran
3-22

J.-
Could you type a memo for me to take to hospital today to Cathy Crowe, RPT, at PT. Lab. Tell her we haven't rec'd copy of muscle strength Evaluation form for pt. Eric Willard. I desperatley need it by 24th before I see Eric.

Thanks!

F.P.

Figure 12-2

NOTE: A Performance Evaluation Checklist for this exercise can be found at the back of the workbook.

EXERCISE 12-10 — ABSTRACT PATIENT INFORMATION FOR A LETTER

PERFORMANCE OBJECTIVE

TASK: Abstract patient information from a chart and then key a mailable letter to a referring physician.

CONDITIONS: Use letterhead form 36.

STANDARDS: Time: _____ minutes
Accuracy: _____
(NOTE: The time element and accuracy criteria may be given by your instructor.)

DIRECTIONS: Dr. Fran Practon has asked you to review the chart notes of Ben Olman (Figure 12-3) and send a letter, dated March 20, 199X, to the referring physician outlining the patient's medical history for the past five weeks and the ensuing surgery. Key the letter for the physician's signature. Use full-block style with mixed punctuation.

NOTE: A Performance Evaluation Checklist for this exercise can be found at the back of the workbook.

PATIENT RECORD

OLMAN,	BEN	ALFRED	03-20-40	M	213/277-8026
LAST NAME	FIRST NAME	MIDDLE NAME	BIRTH DATE	SEX	HOME PHONE

10215 Parthenia Avenue	Woodland Hills	CA	91365
ADDRESS	CITY	STATE	ZIP CODE

Professor, USC	University of Southern California
PATIENT'S OCCUPATION	NAME OF COMPANY

36th St. and University Ave., Los Angeles, CA 90007	213/477-9972
ADDRESS OF EMPLOYER	PHONE

Mary Lou Olman	Housewife
SPOUSE OR PARENT	OCCUPATION

		213/277-8026
EMPLOYER	ADDRESS	PHONE

Pacific Mutual Insurance Co.	USC
NAME OF INSURANCE GROUP	SUBSCRIBER

BLUE SHIELD OR BLUE CROSS CERT. NO.	GROUP NO.	CURRENT COVERAGE NO.	EFFECTIVE DATE
			572-29-4027
MEDICARE NO.	MEDICAID NO.	EFFECTIVE DATE	SOC. SEC. NO.

Ann Coleman, M.D., 4021 Indiana Ave., Suite 2, Pacific Palisades. CA 90272
REFERRED BY:

DATE	PROGRESS
2/3/9X	Pt moved recently to area. States he has a long HX of tonsillitis. Pt seen in ofc complaining of chills, sore throat since January 26. Temp. 102.6°F. CPX shows tonsils that appear enlarged & red. Throat culture taken. Imp: Tonsillitis. R/O strep. Rx penicillin therapy instituted. Adv bed rest. Ret 2 days. *Fran Practon*
	mtf — Fran Practon, MD
2/5/9X	Pt improved. Tonsils appear less swollen. Throat culture neg. for strep. Continue penicillin Rx for 10 days p.o. t.i.d. Call if not improved. *Fran Practon*
	mtf — Fran Practon, MD
2/20/9X	Pt comes in again with severe sore throat. Began 5 days after penicillin was dc. Malaise. Temp. 101.4°F. Tonsil culture taken and await results before prescribing antibiotic. Ret 3 days. *Fran Practon*
	mtf — Fran Practon, MD
2/22/9X	Phone call from Mrs. Olman stating Ben has increased pain in throat, malaise, temp. 102.4°F. Adv retn to ofc in the A.M. *Fran Practon*
	mtf — Fran Practon, MD
2/23/9X	Pt presents with acute sore throat, red & inflamed. Adv tonsillectomy after acute phase subsides. Rx antibiotic, Suprax, 20 mg q.12h. *Fran Practon*
	mtf — Fran Practon, MD
2/23/9X	Letter mailed to Dr. Coleman.
	mtf
3/15/9X	Pt adm to outpatient surgery at College Hospital. T&A with disch. same day. *Fran Practon*
	mtf — Fran Practon, MD
3/21/9X	OC with no complaints. Temp. 98.4°F. To retn p.r.n. *Fran Practon*
	mtf — Fran Practon, MD

Figure 12-3

EXERCISE 12-11 KEY A TWO-PAGE LETTER

PERFORMANCE OBJECTIVE

TASK: Key an accurate two-page letter on letterhead with subject and attention lines, proper paragraphing and capitalization, and an appropriate second-page heading.

CONDITIONS: Use letterhead form 37 and one sheet of white bond paper for second page.

STANDARDS: Time: _____ minutes
Accuracy: _____
(NOTE: The time element and accuracy criteria may be given by your instructor.)

DIRECTIONS: Key the following material in Figure 12-4 written by Dr. Gerald Practon to the education chair of your local county medical society as a two-page letter, using an appropriate second-page heading. Set 1 1/2 inch margins; use open punctuation and full-block format. Determine the paragraphing and make any capitalization corrections required. The subject of the letter is "Work Experience for the Medical Office Student." Use the current date.

In reply to your request for information on work experience, I am enclosing a summary of the material I have found for your group, and I hope it answers some of your questions. Physicians, administrators, educational and medical associations, and officials of school districts have expressed increased interest in the value of on-the-job training and career-related work-study programs for their medical office students. Some colleges have instituted major curriculum changes to provide for internships and hospital work-study assignments. As a result of this interest, employers, including medical agencies, as well as federal agencies, are being asked to support the objectives of this new educational concept by providing new training opportunities for medical office students. Many agencies have inquired as to the role that they may play in making medical facilities available and in providing training to support these work-study medical programs. These inquiries have requested clarification in three general program areas: (1) programs established through legislation; (2) part-time, intermittent, or temporary employment; and (3) the selective exposure of students, in a nonpaid status, to learning projects related to educational objectives. Agencies are now providing and are encouraged to expand work-study opportunities for students and enrollees in programs authorized by legislation. Such legislation includes the higher education, vocational education, economic opportunity, human resources development and training, and Social Security Acts. Under these programs, students receive stipends from financial grants provided by statute. Similar support is urged for part-time, intermittent, and cyclic employment programs for students under appropriate appointment authority. Hospital programs such as cooperative work-study, summer and vacation, and part-time employment during the school year offer agencies an excellent opportunity to make significant contributions through medical-related assignments. These programs are also in keeping with federal long-range recruitment objectives. I hope this summarizes for your group the information you requested. If I can be of any further assistance in setting up the program in your area, please feel free to contact me.

Figure 12-4

NOTE: A Performance Evaluation Checklist for this exercise can be found at the back of the workbook.

COMPUTER EXERCISES

Before proceeding, you may want to do more exercises or review the concepts you have learned. Complete the computer exercises on the software for Chapter 12.

CHAPTER 13

Processing Mail and Telecommunications

OBJECTIVES

After completing the exercises, the student will be able to:

1. Write meanings for chart note abbreviations.
2. Enhance spelling skills by learning new medical words.
3. Process incoming mail and determine the disposition of each communication.
4. Classify outgoing mail.
5. Annotate a letter.
6. Compose letters and prepare envelopes for certified mailing.
7. Complete a mail-order form for postal supplies.
8. Prepare a cover sheet for fax transmission.
9. Address envelopes for optical character reader (OCR) scanning.
10. Key and fold letters, attach enclosures, and insert material into envelopes of different sizes.

AREAS OF COMPETENCE

Administrative Procedures
■ Perform basic clerical functions

General (Transdisciplinary)

Professionalism
■ Prioritize and perform multiple tasks

Communication Skills
■ Receive, organize, prioritize, and transmit information
■ Use medical terminology appropriately

ABBREVIATION AND SPELLING REVIEW LESSON

Read the following patient's chart note and write the meanings for the abbreviations listed below the note. To decode any abbreviations you do not understand or that appear unfamiliar to you, refer to text Tables 8-1 and 9-3. Medical terms in the chart note are italicized; study them for spelling. Use your medical dictionary to look up their definitions. Your instructor may give a test for the spelling and definition of the words and abbreviations.

Stephen L. Boasberg

January 17, 199X OC: Biopsy report pos. for CA of *prostate*. TURP & *bilateral orchiectomy, scrotal*. Adm to hosp in 2 days. Est. TD: 6 wks. Adv dc pain medication in 3 days.

Fran Practon, MD
Fran Practon, MD

OC _____	est. _____
pos. _____	TD _____
CA _____	wks _____
TURP _____	adv _____
adm _____	dc _____
hosp _____	

Terence O. Williams

January 17, 199X Sunday, 4 a.m. pt seen in ER complaining of pain, AD, abt 3 days, PX revealed fluid & pus. Temp. 100°F,

Fran Practon, MD
Fran Practon, MD

a.m. _____	abt _____
pt _____	PX _____
ER _____	temp. _____
AD _____	F _____

REVIEW QUESTIONS

Review the objectives, glossary, and chapter information before completing the following review questions.

1. Describe two situations in which the physician might use facsimile (fax) transmission from the office.

   a. _____

   b. _____

2. List three reasons for using a postage meter.

   a. _____

   b. _____

   c. _____

3. List four legal requirements when faxing confidential medical records.

    a. _____

    b. _____

    c. _____

    d. _____

4. What method of mailing should be used to send a patient chart to a lawyer for use in a malpractice court hearing? _____

5. After the contents are removed from an envelope, what two precautionary steps should be taken.

    a. _____

    b. _____

6. Another physician writes asking for personal information on a new patient referred to him by your employer, who is now on a two-week vacation. How would you handle the situation? _____

    _____

7. Why are envelopes typed for OCR processing? _____

    _____

8. List four items that should be available for opening the mail.

    a. _____

    b. _____

    c. _____

    d. _____

9. Why should all incoming correspondence be dated? _____

    _____

10. Define the word *annotating* as it applies to medical office correspondence.

    _____

    _____

EXERCISE 13-1   PROCESS INCOMING MAIL

PERFORMANCE OBJECTIVE

TASK: Sort and process incoming mail and determine the disbursement for each communication. Circle in red pen the introductory number of any situations you have difficulty processing for class discussion.

CONDITIONS: Use pen or pencil and red pen.

STANDARDS: Time: _____ minutes

Accuracy: _____

(NOTE: The time element and accuracy criteria may be given by your instructor.)

DIRECTIONS: Study the following list of items that arrived in the mail today. Explain what you would do with each piece of mail by writing in the designated space.

1. Letter and check from a patient _____

2. Announcement of a medical society meeting _____

3. Advertisement for an x-ray machine _____

4. Mail-order gardening catalog _____

5. Letter from Mr. C. J. Conway _____

6. Check from Mr. Bill Owen _____

7. Advertisement of a new tranquilizer drug _____

8. *Journal of the American Medical Association* (current issue) _____
_____

9. A reprint of an article written by Dr. Practon is requested _____
_____

10. Letter marked "Personal" to Dr. Fran Practon _____

11. A drug sample _____

12. Letter referring a patient to Dr. Gerald Practon _____

13. A piece of pornographic literature _____

14. Letter announcing a professional meeting in two months _____

15. License tax-due notice _____

16. Charity solicitation letter _____

17. Insurance query about Mrs. Dorothy Ranger _____

18. Medicare payment for Beth Cook _____

19. Lab test results on Mrs. Murdock _____

20. Consultant report on Mr. Bill McKean _____

21. Check from Aetna Insurance Company for service rendered to Samantha Boatman
_____

22. Prudential insurance form on Mr. Tom Patten _____

23. Invoice from V. Mueller Supply Company _____

24. Letter from Mrs. Todd Stark without date or address (these do appear on the envelope) _____

25. Letter from Dr. Lees concerning a research project _____

26. Letter about cancellation of appointment by patient who is on vacation
_____

27. *Time* magazine _____

28. Mutual funds investment letter _____

29. Local medical society agenda for monthly meeting _____

30. Ad for new filing equipment _____

31. Mail-order medical instrument catalog _____

32. Gift parcel from Mrs. Gaspar Whelan (patient) _____

33. Letter notifying Dr. Fran Practon of the death of a colleague _____

34. Telegram from Dr. Perry Cardi congratulating Dr. Gerald Practon on his election as vice president of local medical society _____

35. Personal letter, opened by mistake _____

NOTE: A Performance Evaluation Checklist for this exercise can be found at the back of the workbook.

EXERCISE 13-2 | CLASSIFY OUTGOING MAIL

PERFORMANCE OBJECTIVE

TASK: Identify classes of mail.

CONDITIONS: Use pen or pencil.

STANDARDS: Time: _____ minutes
Accuracy: _____
(NOTE: The time element and accuracy criteria may be given by your instructor.)

DIRECTIONS: You will be mailing various pieces of correspondence for the physicians, and it will be helpful if identification of the following pieces of mail can be determined before going to the post office. After each piece of mail, indicate the appropriate classification you might choose, referring to Chapter 13 in the textbook for help.

Outgoing Mail	Mail Classification
1. Income tax forms	_____
2. Proof that estimated income tax form was mailed by deadline	_____
3. Prescription	_____
4. Postal card	_____
5. Photograph	_____
6. Medical pamphlet	_____
7. Newspaper	_____
8. Bound 28-page manuscript	_____
9. Unsealed circular weighing 12 ounces	_____
10. Green diamond border envelope to enclose an item weighing more than 2 pounds	_____
11. U. S. treasury bond	_____
12. X-rays with letter	_____
13. Cultured pearl necklace	_____
14. Sealed dental catalog	_____
15. Monthly statement	_____

| Outgoing Mail | Mail Classification |

16. Letter with check enclosed _____

17. Laboratory report _____

18. Letter with parcel _____

19. Fastest delivery for a medical tape _____

20. Important item to be delivered within 24 hours; it is Saturday noon _____

21. A third collection letter from medical office _____

22. 30-page book with advertising _____

23. Medical society journal _____

NOTE: A Performance Evaluation Checklist for this exercise can be found at the back of the workbook.

EXERCISE 13-3 ANNOTATE MAIL

PERFORMANCE OBJECTIVE

TASK: Read a letter, annotate significant words or phrases, and make comments in the margins concerning the action to be taken.

CONDITIONS: Use letter in Figure 13-1 for reference and highlighter or colored pen.

STANDARDS: Time: _____ minutes
Accuracy: _____
(NOTE: The time element and accuracy criteria may be given by your instructor.)

DIRECTIONS: Read the letter from Marchall Rents (Figure 13-1) that arrived today. Annotate significant words or phrases by underlining or highlighting and then handwriting in colored pen any action requirements in the right margin.

NOTE: A Performance Evaluation Checklist for this exercise can be found at the back of the workbook.

EXERCISE 13-4 COMPOSE A LETTER AND CERTIFY THE MAIL

PERFORMANCE OBJECTIVE

TASK: Compose and key an important letter in a specified format; address and prepare a large envelope for OCR processing as certified mail.

CONDITIONS: Use one letterhead form 38, a No. 10 envelope (or form 39), form 40 to certify the communication, and pen.

STANDARDS: Time: _____ minutes
Accuracy: _____
(NOTE: The time element and accuracy criteria may be given by your instructor.)

```
                           MARCHALL RENTS
                        23990 WEST VALLEY ROAD
                         SEPULVEDA, XY 93087


      December 2, 199x



      Gerald Practon, MD
      4567 Broad Avenue
      Woodland Hills, XY 12345

      Dear Dr. Practon:

      We have recently opened a rental-sales company in your area
      and are anxious for members of the medical profession to know
      of our specialized home-care equipment.

      Our staff is highly trained to help you determine and meet
      the precise requirements for each patient's comfort and safety.
      We handle only the finest equipment--from oxygen equipment to
      wheelchairs, hospital beds, and patient lifts, and we are on
      24-hour call.

      Because our salesman will be in your area after the first of
      the year about January 13, we are contacting you to see if we
      can set up an appointment for him to show and demonstrate
      pieces of equipment.

      We will follow this communication with a personal telephone
      call to determine a date that is satisfactory.  We hope to meet
      with you soon.

      Sincerely,

      Glenn Marchall
      Mr. Glenn Marchall
      President

      GM:jf
```

Figure 13-1

DIRECTIONS: Mrs. Jane K. Call of 199 Eisenhower Boulevard, Apartment 17-J, Canoga Park, XY 12345-000, telephoned on January 5 stating she wanted no further treatment from Dr. Gerald Practon. Write a letter to confirm this discharge by the patient stating that Dr. Practon feels further treatment is necessary. Date the letter the day you key it, using modified-block style with mixed punctuation. Prepare a No. 10 envelope. Call and ask your local post office to compute the postage necessary, and write the amount where the postage would be placed on the envelope. Key the envelope in OCR format and fill in both sides of the return receipt for certified mail. (See textbook Figure 13-2.) If you are using a No. 10 envelope, fold the letter and insert it correctly.

NOTE: A Performance Evaluation Checklist for this exercise can be found at the back of the workbook.

EXERCISE 13-5 — COMPLETE A MAIL-ORDER FORM FOR POSTAL SUPPLIES

PERFORMANCE OBJECTIVE

TASK: Complete a mail-order form for postal supplies and compute the total amount owed.

CONDITIONS: Use form 41 and pen.

STANDARDS: Time: _____ minutes
Accuracy: _____
(NOTE: The time element and accuracy criteria may be given by your instructor.)

DIRECTIONS: To avoid a special trip to the post office, complete the mail-order form for stamps and other items in ink and determine the total amount owed. A check would ordinarily be written to enclose with the order made out to the U. S. Postmaster. However, since check writing is discussed in Chapter 17, it will not be written for this exercise.

Order:

    5 rolls (100) 32-cent stamps
    250 postal cards
    2 express mail stamps
    300 32-cent stamped No. 10 envelopes
    3 priority mail stamps

NOTE: A Performance Evaluation Checklist for this exercise can be found at the back of the workbook.

EXERCISE 13-6 — PREPARE A COVER SHEET FOR FAX TRANSMISSION

PERFORMANCE OBJECTIVE

TASK: Prepare a transmission slip to accompany a message for fax communication.

CONDITIONS: Use fax transmittal form 42.

STANDARDS: Time: _____ minutes
Accuracy: _____
(NOTE: The time element and accuracy criteria may be given by your instructor.)

DIRECTIONS: Dr. Fran Practon is scheduled to speak at the Massachusetts American Women's Medical Association convention on November 20 in Boston. She asks you to prepare a fax cover sheet to accompany a two-page letter she will write for fax transmission. Dr. Elmo Reardon, 891 So. Revere Way, Boston, MA 02100, will receive the communication. His fax number is 617-326-9923. Complete all pertinent information on the cover slip with date and time indicated as the day you prepare the exercise. Request a prompt confirmation reply by fax.

NOTE: A Performance Evaluation Checklist for this exercise can be found at the back of the workbook.

EXERCISE 13-7	ADDRESS ENVELOPES FOR OCR PROCESSING

PERFORMANCE OBJECTIVE

TASK: Address envelopes for OCR processing using acceptable abbreviations and ZIP codes.

CONDITIONS: Use three No. 6 envelopes or forms 43 and 44.

STANDARDS: Time: _____ minutes
Accuracy: _____
(NOTE: The time element and accuracy criteria may be given by your instructor.)

DIRECTIONS: Dr. Fran Practon has three letters to be placed in No. 6 envelopes (names and addresses listed below) that need the speediest possible mail handling. Use the format recommended for OCR processing and refer to address abbreviations from the National ZIP Code directory in Figure 13-2 for names that cannot be abbreviated to 13 positions by use of standard abbreviations and for ZIP codes. Key the three envelope addresses with standard abbreviations and ZIP codes. Key Dr. Practon's office address in the upper left corner of each envelope. Refer to Figure 13-5 in the textbook.

1. Mr. and Mrs. Arthur L. Duncally
   Post Office Box 286
   West Boothbay Harbor, Maine

2. College Hospital
   8900 West Elvingston Drive
   Brooklyn-Curtis Bay, Maryland
   Attn: Elizabeth Collingswood, MD
   Confidential

3. Mr. Randolph G. Greenworthy Jr.
   49021 67th Avenue North
   Apartment 8
   Washington Grove, Maryland

MAINE

04006-0000	Biddeford Pool	BIDDEFRD POOL
04625-0000	Cranberry Isles	CRANBERRY IS
04021-0000	Cumberland Center	CUMBRLND CTR
04426-0000	Dover-Foxcroft	DOVR FOXCROFT
04940-0000	Farmington Falls	FARMINGTN FLS
04575-0000	West Boothbay Harbor	W BOOTHBY HBR

MARYLAND

21005-0000	Aberdeen Proving Ground	ABRDN PRV GRD
20331-0000	Andrews Air Force Hospital	ANDRS AF HOSP
21225-0000	Brooklyn-Curtis Bay	BKLYN CTS BAY
20622-0000	Charlotte Hall	CHARLOTE HALL
20732-0000	Chesapeake Beach	CHESAPKE BCH
20904-0000	Ednor Cloverly	EDNR CLOVERLY
21713-0000	Fahrney Keedy Memorial Home	FHRN MEM HOME
20755-0000	Fort George G. Meade	FT MEADE
21240-0000	Friendship Airport	FRNDSHP ARPRT
21078-0000	Havre de Grace	HVRE DE GRACE
20014-0000	National Naval Medical Center	NAVAL MED CTR
20390-0000	Naval Air Facility	NAV AIR FACIL
20678-0000	Prince Frederick	PRNC FREDERCK
20788-0000	Prince Georges Plaza	PRNC GEO PLZ
21152-0000	Sparks Glencoe	SPRKS GLENCOE
21784-0000	Springfield State Hospital	SPRINFLD HOSP
20390-0000	U.S. Naval Communications Center	NAV COMMS CTR
20880-0000	Washington Grove	WASHINGTN GRV

Figure 13-2

NOTE: A Performance Evaluation Checklist for this exercise can be found at the back of the workbook.

EXERCISE 13-8

KEY AND FOLD AN ORIGINAL LETTER FOR A SMALL ENVELOPE; ADDRESS AN ENVELOPE FOR OCR PROCESSING; COMPLETE AND ATTACH CERTIFIED MAIL AND RETURN-RECEIPT-REQUESTED FORMS

PERFORMANCE OBJECTIVE

TASK: Key a letter, prepare an envelope for OCR processing, fold and insert the letter into the envelope, and attach special mailing forms.

CONDITIONS: Use letterhead form 45, No. 6 envelope or form 46, certified mail form 47, and pen.

STANDARDS: Time: _____ minutes
Accuracy: _____
(NOTE: The time element and accuracy criteria may be given by your instructor.)

DIRECTIONS: Mr. Henry J. Stone, One April Circle, Pacoima, XY 91331-0000, is negligent about following Dr. Gerald Practon's advice after he has had surgery. Write an appropriate letter to Mr. Stone advising him of Dr. Practon's withdrawal from the case. Dr. Practon will sign the letter. Use full-block style with mixed punctuation and a No. 6 envelope. Fold the letter and insert it into the No. 6 envelope properly. Do not seal the envelope. Complete the information on form 45 and send the letter by certified mail with return receipt requested. (See Figure 13-2 in textbook.)

(NOTE: Refer to text Chapter 12, Figure 12-7 for details on properly inserting the letter into a No. 6 envelope.)

NOTE: A Performance Evaluation Checklist for this exercise can be found at the back of the workbook.

EXERCISE 13-9

KEY AND FOLD AN ORIGINAL LETTER FOR A LARGE ENVELOPE; ADDRESS AN ENVELOPE FOR OCR PROCESSING AND COMPLETE AND ATTACH CERTIFIED MAIL AND RETURN-RECEIPT-REQUESTED FORMS

PERFORMANCE OBJECTIVE

TASK: Key a letter, prepare a large envelope for OCR processing, fold and insert the letter into the envelope, and attach special mailing forms.

CONDITIONS: Use letterhead form 48, No. 10 envelope or form 49, certified mail form 50, and pen.

STANDARDS: Time: _____ minutes
Accuracy: _____
(NOTE: The time element and accuracy criteria may be given by your instructor.)

DIRECTIONS: Miss Henrietta M. Marskovskie of 4311 Eberly Street, Woodland Hills, XY 12345-4700, telephones on September 24. In an angry tone she says she cannot return to work on September 25 and does not want to see Dr. Gerald Practon again because he has failed to solve her medical problem. Write a letter to confirm this discharge by the patient. Suggest she contact the medical society for the names of general practitioners for further care. Key the letter in modified-block style with open punctuation. Use a No. 10 envelope (or form 49) and address it for OCR processing. Dr. Practon will sign the letter. Fold the letter and insert it into the large envelope properly. Do not seal the envelope. Complete the information on form 50 and send the letter by certified mail with return receipt requested.

(NOTE: Refer to text Chapter 12, Figure 12-6, for details on properly inserting the letter into a No. 10 envelope.)

NOTE: A Performance Evaluation Checklist for this exercise can be found at the back of the workbook.

COMPUTER EXERCISES

Before proceeding, you may want to do more exercises or review the concepts you have learned. Complete the computer exercises on the software for Chapter 13.

CHAPTER 14

Professional Reports and Travel Arrangements

OBJECTIVES

After completing the exercises, the student will be able to:

1. Write meanings for chart note abbreviations.

2. Enhance spelling skills by learning new medical words.

3. Key a curriculum vitae for the physician.

4. Key a manuscript for publication.

5. Proofread and key a legal form.

6. Proofread transcription.

7. Prepare a travel expense report.

AREAS OF COMPETENCE

Administrative Procedures
■ Perform basic clerical functions

General (Transdisciplinary)

Communication Skills
■ Use effective and correct verbal and written communications
■ Use medical terminology appropriately

ABBREVIATION AND SPELLING REVIEW LESSON

Read the following patient's chart note and write the meanings for the abbreviations listed below the note. To decode any abbreviations you do not understand or that appear unfamiliar to you, refer to text Tables 8-1 and 9-3. Medical terms in the chart note are italicized; study them for spelling. Use your medical dictionary to look up their definitions. Your instructor may give a test for the spelling and definition of the words and abbreviations.

Mary Ann Stanton

February 5, 199X aet. 18 had Tb. PH: UCHD. T&A aet. 10. Father & mother L&W. HPI: Complaining of back pain on lifting objects & bending over. No injury. PE: SLR, WNL. No joint swelling. AP & Lat *lumbosacral* x-ray films neg. Lab work revealed a sed rate of 32 mm/hr. R/O *arthritis*. Aditional lab work ordered. PT to ret 1 wk.

Gerald Practon, MD
Gerald Practon, MD

aet. _____   AP & Lat _____

Tb _____   neg. _____

PH _____   lab. _____

UCHD _____   sed rate _____

T&A _____   mm/hr _____

L&W _____   R/O _____

HPI _____   Pt _____

PE _____   ret _____

SLR _____   wk. _____

WNL _____

REVIEW QUESTIONS

Review the objectives, glossary, and chapter information before completing the following review questions.

1. Name four specific format changes that have been made in manuscript preparation to accommodate the capabilities of the computer.

   a. _____

   b. _____

   c. _____

   d. _____

2. What is the *Index Medicus*? _____

   _____

3. List three guidelines for typing a speech.

   a. _____

   b. _____

   c. _____

4. When might a physician need an in-office reference file system for research?

   _____

5. A physician's education, experience, and professional activities are outlined in a/an

   _____

   _____

6. How are references treated in manuscript typing?

   a. _____

   b. _____

   c. _____

7. Travel agencies usually do not charge a fee for their services unless

   a. _____

   b. _____

   c. _____

8. Why must the physician personally purchase his or her own traveler's checks?

   _____

   _____

9. List three reasons for carrying credit cards when traveling.

   a. _____

   b. _____

   c. _____

10. Define the word *visa*. _____

    _____

    _____

EXERCISE 14-1

KEY A CURRICULUM VITAE

PERFORMANCE OBJECTIVE

TASK: Key an accurate curriculum vitae in outline form after abstracting information from a memorandum.

CONDITIONS: Use one sheet of white bond paper.

STANDARDS: Time: _____ minutes
Accuracy: _____
(NOTE: The time element and accuracy criteria may be given by your instructor.)

DIRECTIONS: Dr. Fran Practon has been invited to speak before the local medical association next month. The program chair has requested a copy of her curriculum vitae so that an appropriate introduction may be prepared. Refer to text Figure 14-6 to type a similar professional profile using

MEMO.....

Personal Information:	Born Jan. 15 '38, Philadelphia, Pa. married - office address (on letterhead)
Undergraduate Education:	Wash. Univ, St. Louis, Mo. 1959 - B.S. Bacteriology Major (Summa Cum Laude)
Professional Schools:	Univ. of Cincinnati, Oh. - MD, 1965 College of Medicine
Internship:	Rush-Presbyterian, St. Luke's Hosp. Chicago, Ill. '65-'67, Diplomate AAFP
Residency:	LA County/USC Medical Center, F.P., '67
Licensure:	MD, (See appendix for Certif. #)
Honors and Awards:	USC Regents Scholar, '68-'69
Experience:	1968-70, Assoc. Prof. F.P. Medicine USC 1970-to present F.P. physician & Staff member college Hosp.
Professional Activities:	Member AMA, Sec. San Fernando Valley Med. Soc., W. Hills, XX, member of Amer. Medical Woman's Assoc.

Figure 14-1

Dr. Practon's handwritten notes in Figure 14-1. Arrange the information in a balanced format with 1 1/2-inch margins on all sides. A photocopy should be made for the files. Because the curriculum vitae will reflect Dr. Practon's professional stature, key it accurately and proofread it carefully.

NOTE: A Performance Evaluation Checklist for this exercise can be found at the back of the workbook.

EXERCISE 14-2 KEY A MANUSCRIPT FOR PUBLICATION

PERFORMANCE OBJECTIVE

TASK: Key a title page and a manuscript page from a corrected rough draft in acceptable form for publication; prepare manuscript for mailing by writing a cover letter and preparing a large No. 10 envelope for OCR processing.

CONDITIONS: Use several sheets of white bond paper and No. 10 envelope (or Form 51).

STANDARDS: Time: ________________ minutes

Accuracy: ______________

(NOTE: The time element and accuracy criteria may be given by your instructor.)

DIRECTIONS: Dr. Fran Practon has handed you a rough draft (Figure 14-2) of a manuscript she plans to submit to *JAMA* for publication. She asks you to key the manuscript and to prepare a title page to submit with the manuscript. You should also compose and key a letter of transmittal for mailing to: Editor, James L. Reed, MD, 535 No. Dearborn Street, Chicago, IL 60610, and also address a Large No. 10 envelope.

NOTE: A Performance Evaluation Checklist for this exercise can be found at the back of the workbook.

Hypertension →

Hypertension, which is one of the major health problems in the ~~U.S.~~ *United States* is defined as *a*

condition in which the patient has a higher blood pressure than that judged to be

normal ~~healthy~~. Early recognition and treatment could lessen the estimated ~~sixty thousand~~ *60,000*

deaths *a* ~~per~~ year caused by strokes, heart ~~failure~~ *attacks*, and kidney failure in which high

blood pressure and hypertensive heart disease are believed to be a contributing

factor.

Many American s who have high ~~b.p.~~ *blood pressure* are ~~unaware not~~ aware of it. In general

if the systolic pressure is above ~~one hundred fourty millem.~~ *140 mm.* of mercury or the diastolic

above ~~ninety mill.~~ *90 mm.* the person is considered to have ~~elevation b.p.~~ *elevated blood pressure* Since outward symtoms

are negligible, discovery depends all most intirely upon having one's blood pressure

checked by a ~~doctor~~ *physician*. An estimated ~~twenty-three~~ *23* million Americans have high b.p. *blood pressure* only

half ~~½~~ that number are aware of the ~~condition~~ *problem*, and only about ~~1/5~~ *one fifth* are receiving adequate

~~therapies~~ *therapy*.

The AMA is endorsing the development of a National Program by begining a continuing

professional educational program against hypertention. The Federal government, American

heart Assoc*iation*, and another health organizations will be involved.

The AMA's program will concentrate on ~~3~~ *three* approaches:

1. Physicians will be urged to make routine blood pressure ~~checks~~ *readings* of all patients *they see* ~~seen~~.

2. The Public will be ~~asked~~ *urged* to have periodic checks of blood pressure ~~thru~~ *through* an educational *campaign*.

3. A special campaign will be directed at those persons who are aware of having high ~~b.p.~~ *blood pressure* but are not following *proper* therapy.

It is the ~~sincere~~ hope of all those who are interested in ~~the~~ *this* problem *of hypertension* that continuous

publicity and the education of the public will help allevate at least some of the deaths

that occur *each year* as a result of lack of public information and knowledge of ~~the~~ *this* disease.

Figure 14-2

| EXERCISE 14-3 | **PROOFREAD AND KEY A LEGAL FORM** |

PERFORMANCE OBJECTIVE

TASK: Use proofreading marks and symbols to correct a rough draft of a legal form and to key the corrected master for the printer.

CONDITIONS: Use form 52, one sheet of white paper, and pen or pencil.

STANDARDS: Time: _____ minutes
Accuracy: _____
(NOTE: The time element and accuracy criteria may be given by your instructor.)

DIRECTIONS: The Practons have decided to design their own authorization form and their attorney has reviewed it. Proofread the rough draft form 52, marking any additional errors by using appropriate symbols. Also, write the symbols you use in the numbered spaces. Key a double-spaced final copy, centered on a full page, and give both rough draft and final authorization form to your instructor.

NOTE: A Performance Evaluation Checklist for this exercise can be found at the back of the workbook.

| EXERCISE 14-4 | **PROOFREAD TRANSCRIPTION** |

PERFORMANCE OBJECTIVE

TASK: Proofread medical transcription and prepare copy for transfer to patient's chart.

CONDITIONS: Use pen, textbook, glossary, dictionary, Figure 14-1 in the textbook for proofreading marks, and typewriter or computer.

STANDARDS: Time: _____ minutes
Accuracy: _____
(NOTE: The time element and accuracy criteria may be given by your instructor.)

DIRECTIONS: Using a pen, proofread and correct spelling, typographical, and grammatical errors. Use appropriate proofreading marks to indicate errors. After completing the proofreading, key a corrected copy of the four medical reports as they would be transferred to the patient chart. Words in parentheses indicate difficult words to understand.

1. Mrs. Lincoln's x-ray examination showed the plural spaces to be clear and the upper-lungs clear bilateraly. There is some increased density bibasally with the medial portion of the hemidiaphragm obscurred. This most likely represents bibasicular atelektosis (pronounced at-e-LEK-tah-sis); however, a cute infection in the left medial base can not be ruled out. The boney skeletal is unremarkable.

2. The Pathology section of patient, Margaret Spear demonstrates mulitple irreguler fragments of ossious tissue, fibrocallagenous connectile tissue, fibrinus (pronounced FI-bri-nus) debree, anddystrophyic calcfication. A few areas of enkondral (pronounced en-KON-dral) ossification and knew bone formation is also seen. Many of the bone fragment have a necrotic appearance and cavities devoid of osteocytes. A fragment of dense fibrocollaginous scar tissue shows patchey, moderate-to-sever chronic inflammation. There is no evidence of malignancy.

3. Mr. Brown claim that for the past for months he has had problems with laryngitis and nonproductive coughs. Examination of the patients vocal cords showed no evidense of inflammation or disease. Palette and tongue were unremarkable. He was abel to breath normally. Chest was clear to ANP. Heart showed a regular rhythm

without murmers or gallups. Abdominal was soft within normal size. His Extremities were unremarkable.

4. With a presumptive diagnoses of acute appendicitis, rule out performation, Kevin Crenne was started on entervenous anti-biotics in the form of Cefobid and Flagil and taken on an emergent bases to the operating suit. At exploration his appendix was noted to be acutely inflammed and perforated. There was no absesses. There was no fecolith noted. He had a moderate amount of cloudy perineal fluid. Appendectomy was preformed without incidense. The perneal cavity was not drained.

NOTE: A Performance Evaluation Checklist for this exercise can be found at the back of the workbook.

EXERCISE 14-5

PREPARE A TRAVEL EXPENSE REPORT

PERFORMANCE OBJECTIVE

TASK: Complete a travel expense form for the accountant using figures written on a summary form.

CONDITIONS: Use travel expense report form 53, and pen or pencil.

STANDARDS: Time: _____ minutes
Accuracy: _____
(NOTE: The time element and accuracy criteria may be given by your instructor.)

DIRECTIONS: Dr. Gerald Practon presented a paper to a medical convention in Boston and kept a detailed record of all expenses for the week as follows: Parking fees, Monday $5.20; Parkway toll, Monday $4; Tips were $2 on Saturday, $3 on Sunday, $6 on Wednesday, $5.50 on Friday, and $6.25 on Saturday; Hertz car rental was $25 per day; gasoline receipts were $14.20 on Saturday and $10.90 on Monday; Conroy Hotel was $150 per night *for the first four nights*, Commonwealth was $135 per night *for the next two nights*, Shoreham was $165 *for the last night*; phone call on Sunday May 10 to confirm time of report was $1.91. Meal expenses were as follows:

	Breakfast	Lunch	Dinner
Sunday	$8.90	$15.40	$36.20
Monday	5.10	—	26.14
Tuesday	3.40	10.90	31.50
Wednesday	—	13.98	48.14
Thursday	9.15	10.00	20.02
Friday	10.82	22.08	36.33

Transfer the figures to the travel expense report form (form 53). Total the columns vertically and horizontally and explain the purpose of the trip.

NOTE: A Performance Evaluation Checklist for this exercise can be found at the back of the workbook.

COMPUTER EXERCISES

Before proceeding, you may want to do more exercises or review the concepts you have learned. Complete the computer exercises on the software for Chapter 14.

CHAPTER 15

Fees, Credit, and Collection

OBJECTIVES

After completing the exercises, the student will be able to:

1. Write meanings for chart note abbreviations.

2. Enhance spelling skills by learning new medical words.

3. Role-play and discuss how to handle fee collection in various situations.

4. Prepare receipts for cash-paying patients, a credit card authorization form, and a financial agreement.

5. Compose a collection letter and prepare an envelope and ledger card.

6. Use a calculator to compute figures on a ledger card.

7. Document a patient complaint.

AREAS OF COMPETENCE

Administrative Procedures
- Perform basic clerical functions
- Monitor third-party reimbursement
- Understand and adhere to managed care policies and procedures

Practice Finances
- Manage accounts receivable

General (Transdisciplinary)

Communication Skills
- Use medical terminology appropriately

ABBREVIATION AND SPELLING REVIEW LESSON

Read the following patients' chart notes and write the meanings for the abbreviations listed below the notes. To decode any abbreviations you do not understand or that appear unfamiliar to you, refer to text Tables 8-1 and 9-3. Medical terms in the chart notes are italicized; study them for spelling. Use your medical dictionary to look up their definitions. Your instructor may give a test for the spelling and definition of the words and abbreviations.

3-4-98	Robert M Feldman Pt seen for <u>bronchial</u> <u>asthma</u>, ASHD, HBP & <u>sebaceous</u>
	<u>cyst</u>. ECG ordered stat + Lab & x-rays ordered. Comp PX to be done on
	Friday. PTR next wk for I & D of sebaceous cyst of Ⓡ <u>axilla</u>
	Fran Practon, MD

Pt _____   Comp_____

ASHD _____   PX _____

HBP _____   PTR _____

ECG _____   wk. _____

stat _____   I&D _____

Lab. _____   Ⓡ _____

3-15-9X	Marion F. Palmer Pt came in complaining of headaches. Thinks
	she needs stronger lenses PX: c̄c O.D. -1.62 & O.S. -1.50 Gave Rx
	Ret prn.
	G Practon MD

Pt _____   O.S. _____

PX _____   Rx _____

c̄c _____   ret _____

O.D. _____   p.r.n. _____

REVIEW QUESTIONS

Review the objectives, glossary, and chapter information before completing the following review questions.

1. Match the terms in the right column with the definitions in the left column by writing the numbers in the blanks.
   a. Analysis of accounts receivable showing 60, 90, and 120 days' delinquency _____
   b. A legal proceeding in which money (salary) and property are attached so they can be used to pay off a debt _____
   c. A list of the physician's procedures and fees _____
   d. A message to remind a delinquent patient about payment _____
   e. Accounts on the books on which charges are made from time to time _____
   f. To trust in an individual's integrity to meet financial obligations _____
   g. A debtor who moves and does not leave a forwarding address _____

   1. garnishment
   2. credit
   3. open accounts
   4. dun
   5. skip
   6. aging accounts
   7. fee schedule

2. Name four reasons why a patient registration form is valuable for the collection process.

   a. _____

   b. _____

   c. _____

   d. _____

3. How often should a patient information form be updated?

   _____

4. The job of discussing and collecting fees is usually relegated to the _____ . To increase the percentage of patients who pay their bills and for good public relations, how should a person handle himself or herself when approaching a patient?

   a. _____

   b. _____

   c. _____

   d. _____

   e. _____

5. When is a managed care copayment usually collected?

   _____

6. What two things should you obtain from the insurance company before surgical costs are quoted?

   a. _____

   b. _____

7. Name several things to look for in a *deadbeat* patient.

   a. _____   e. _____

   b. _____   f. _____

   c. _____   g. _____

   d. _____   h. _____

8. Name four factors involved in establishing fees for a physician.

   a. _____

   b. _____

   c. _____

   d. _____

9. Explain why an office may have more than one fee schedule.

   _____

   _____

   _____

10. The office policy of giving a discount to a nurse when services are rendered is called _____

11. When is the best time to collect for an office visit and why?

_____

_____

_____

12. What are some names used for a form that serves as a combination bill, insurance form, and routing document?

a. _____   e. _____

b. _____   f. _____

c. _____   g. _____

d. _____   h. _____

13. Explain cycle billing. _____

_____

14. Name four advantages of using a billing service.

a. _____

b. _____

c. _____

d. _____

15. Name three effective bonding methods.

a. _____

b. _____

c. _____

16. If a patient is called about a delinquent bill at 10 P.M., what federal law is being violated? _____

_____

17. If credit is refused to a patient, what federal legislation must be complied with?

_____

18. If, in an obstetrical case, a patient is asked for monthly payments before delivery of the baby, what form must be completed, signed, and given to the patient?

_____

If there are fewer than _____ payment installments, this form is not necessary.

19. If interest is charged on a monthly billing statement, what law requires the disclosure of these costs before the time of service?

_____

20. Which law states the requirements and limitations for the patient and the medical practice when a complaint is registered about a billing statement error?

_____

21. Name the time limit for collection on an open account in your state.

_____

22. Explain aging an account and state why it is necessary.

_____

_____

23. An itemized billing statement is usually sent every _____ days, and when an account becomes delinquent a _____ message is sent to prompt payment.

24. What is the average time frame for turning an account over to a collection agency?
_____

25. If a physician asks you to file a claim in small-claims court, where would you go to get the form and detailed information about the process?
_____

26. Define wage garnishment. _____
_____

27. Name five types of bankruptcy.

    a. _____
    b. _____
    c. _____
    d. _____
    e. _____

28. State where you would file an estate claim and how long you have to file it in your state. _____
_____

29. What do you feel are the most important precautions to take in case a patient becomes a skip and you have to conduct a trace?
_____
_____
_____

EXERCISE 15-1

COLLECTION ROLE-PLAYING

PERFORMANCE OBJECTIVE

TASK: For class discussion, write how you would handle fee collection in the 20 situations of this exercise.

CONDITIONS: Use two sheets of plain bond paper and pencil, pen, or typewriter.

STANDARDS: Time: _____ minutes
Accuracy: _____
(NOTE: The time element and accuracy criteria may be given by your instructor.)

DIRECTIONS: State how you would handle each of the following collection situations, keeping in mind the Practon Medical Group office policies appearing in the Appendix of this workbook.

1. A new patient, Anne Rule, called for an appointment for Monday morning. It is your office policy to ask for the physician's fee at the time of the first visit. Convey this information during your conversation.

2. An established patient, Sylvia Cone, came in on Wednesday for a limited examination. She calls today and says she is not going to pay the bill because she is not satisfied with the treatment. She says, "Go ahead and send my account to a collection agency. I'll call my attorney. I can make trouble for you and Dr. Practon, too." Prepare your response.

3. Mrs. Katrina Frenzel calls to ask you about the bill she just received for her son, Paul, who recently made his first visit to the office. She thinks the bill for $70.92 is "very high" and wonders if there is a mistake because the fee seems out of line. She says she has recently moved into this area. What action would you take? Prepare your response.

4. Today you call Miss Wendy Snow about her account, which is overdue. You have sent her two statements, tried telephoning her, and finally sent her a letter asking her to call the office about the $80 she owes. She has not responded. According to your records, she was seen on November 2, she lives at home with her parents, and she has health insurance. Prepare questions you would ask her.

5. Recently, Dr. Gerald Practon performed a two-hour operation and billed the patient his standard fee, which is what physicians generally charge in your area. But the patient's husband considers the fee exorbitant and has paid only part of it. What action would you take, and how would you collect the outstanding amount?

6. Last week, Dr. Fran Practon made a lengthy long-distance telephone call to check on a patient's previous operation. Should you bill the patient for the phone charges? Explain your answer.

7. Recently, a patient whose account you have turned over to a collection agency meets you in the supermarket and mentions that she will be phoning for an appointment soon. Before making the appointment, you notify Dr. Practon of this circumstance. He insists she pay what she owes, and requires any future bills be paid in cash. Is this ethical? Explain your answer.

8. You routinely bill Dr. Practon's patients the amount that appears on the fee schedule he prepared. In reviewing a ledger, Dr. Practon finds that a certain patient has been charged more than was intended. The patient makes no complaint and pays the bill in full. What action would you take?

9. Dr. Practon gives members of the clergy a professional discount of 20 percent. Sister Mary Benedict Ramer, a new patient, brings you an insurance payment that covers 100 percent of the usual fee. The patient asks for a personal refund, since she feels she is due a 20 percent discount. What action should you take?

10. Dr. Practon's fee for an appendectomy is $586.36. Mr. Jefferson's appendectomy is unusually troublesome. His first symptoms appeared after midnight, and he was admitted to the hospital as an emergency patient. A decision to operate immediately was postponed by Dr. Practon when the patient began to improve. During the following night, however, the patient's condition worsened and the appendectomy was performed, thereby interrupting Dr. Practon's sleep for a second night. After the operation, the patient had a bad case of postanesthesia nausea and while in the hospital was quite demanding. Would Dr. Practon be justified in charging him extra because he was a "lot of trouble"? Explain.

11. You send a bill for $1500 to Mrs. Jamison for major surgery. She tells you that the physician had told her in a presurgery conversation that the charge would be "about $1300." Dr. Practon says he does not remember quoting the figure to her. If his usual charge is $1500 for this procedure, what should you do about the bill? Explain.

12. Mr. French calls in complaining about an overdue refund. He, as well as the insurance company, paid for a procedure, and he is owed a return of his payment. You have been swamped with billing and reply that the statements come first and when you can "get to it" you will mail the refund. What is the proper procedure in this instance? Describe.

ADDITIONAL COLLECTION SCENARIOS

13. "According to our divorce settlement, my husband's insurance should be billed first."
14. "The letter I received from the insurance company said you charged too much."
15. "My wife handles all the bills, you will have to call her."
16. "My insurance should have covered that service."
17. Answering machine—the patient is not home.
18. "My attorney told me not to pay the bill."
19. "I have just declared bankruptcy."
20. The patient is deceased and the spouse answers the phone.

NOTE: A Performance Evaluation Checklist for this exercise can be found at the back of the workbook.

EXERCISE 15-2 — COMPLETE CASH RECEIPTS

PERFORMANCE OBJECTIVE

TASK: Complete four cash receipt forms.

CONDITIONS: Use one sheet of typing paper, one sheet of cash receipt forms (form 54), one sheet of carbon paper or photocopying machine, and pen.

STANDARDS: Time: _____ minutes
Accuracy: _____
(NOTE: The time element and accuracy criteria may be given by your instructor.)

DIRECTIONS: The following patients have paid cash in full for the professional services received today. Complete receipt forms using a carbon and a plain sheet of paper or photocopying machine for Dr. Practon's copy. Refer to the Practon Medical Group fee schedule in the appendix of this workbook (Figure A-1); use 2/16 of current year as date. Give the original receipts to the instructor for grading. (These originals in a real situation would be given to the patient for his or her records.)

- Ms. Beth T. Hobson   Established patient, level I office visit and estrogen injection. No previous account balance.
- Henry P. Morgan   New patient, level IV examination.
- Mrs. Harriet F. Garber   Level II office consultation.
- Miss Carole V. Putnam   Established patient, diptheria, tetanus, pertusis injection; level I office visit; previous account balance $50. Paid for services with check # 4706.

NOTE: A Performance Evaluation Checklist for this exercise can be found at the back of the workbook.

<table>
<tr><td>**EXERCISE 15-3**</td><td>**PREPARE A COLLECTION LETTER, ENVELOPE, AND LEDGER CARD**</td></tr>
</table>

PERFORMANCE OBJECTIVE

TASK: Compose a collection letter, envelope, and ledger card and make a photocopy of the letter.

CONDITIONS: Use one letterhead form (form 55), one No. 10 envelope (form 56), one ledger form (form 57).

STANDARDS: Time: _____ minutes
Accuracy: _____
(NOTE: The time element and accuracy criteria may be given by your instructor.)

DIRECTIONS: In checking your records, you find that Mrs. Mae Van Alystine of 2381 Maple Street, Woodland Hills, XY 12345, has not paid her bill for three months. Compose a letter over your own signature requesting payment. On July 10 she was a new patient and had an intrauterine device inserted as well as a 30-minute office visit (level III). Use a current date and full-block style with open or closed punctuation. Type a No. 10 envelope or use form 56. Complete a ledger card using form 57, and enclose a photocopy with the letter. Mrs. Van Alystine's telephone number is 013-421-8700. Her insurance is with Mutual Insurance Company, policy number J 148. She is employed by TBC Import Company.

NOTE: A Performance Evaluation Checklist for this exercise can be found at the back of the workbook.

<table>
<tr><td>**EXERCISE 15-4**</td><td>**USE A CALCULATOR**</td></tr>
</table>

PERFORMANCE OBJECTIVE

TASK: Compute total charges, payments, and adjustments on a ledger card using a calculator.

CONDITIONS: Use calculator, adding machine, or computer calculator; pencil or pen; and ledger card (form 58).

STANDARDS: Time: _____ minutes
Accuracy: _____
(NOTE: The time element and accuracy criteria may be given by your instructor.)

DIRECTIONS: Use ledger card from workbook with figures already inserted (form 58). Clear the machine (calculator) before you begin. Starting from the top, add the balance forward. Going line by line, add all the charges and subtract all the payments and adjustments, keeping an ongoing balance in the right-hand column. Circle the ending balance as the amount the patient will be billed on his or her next statement. Save the calculator tape to check for errors.

NOTE: A Performance Evaluation Checklist for this exercise can be found at the back of the workbook.

EXERCISE 15-5 — COMPLETE A CREDIT CARD AUTHORIZATION FORM

PERFORMANCE OBJECTIVE

TASK: Fill in authorization to charge credit card with correct information.

CONDITIONS: Use authorization to charge credit card (form 59), and pen or pencil.

STANDARDS: Time: _____ minutes
Accuracy: _____
(NOTE: The time element and accuracy criteria may be given by your instructor.)

DIRECTIONS: Read the case scenario and fill in the authorization to charge credit card (form 59), using pen or pencil. It is May 15 (current year) and you are called to the reception area of Dr. Fran Practon's office because Mr. Stewart Wilson has come in and has a large unpaid balance. It is up to you to discuss the situation with him and come to an agreement on how the account can be paid. After having this discussion, Mr. Wilson agrees to make monthly payments, on the 15th of each month, using his Visa credit card. His account number is 4444 22 8888 7777, and the expiration date is 08/01. His name is listed on the card as Stewart T. Wilson, and his balance is $800. He agrees to have his credit card charged $100 every month until the account is paid in full.

NOTE: A Performance Evaluation Checklist for this exercise can be found at the back of the workbook.

EXERCISE 15-6 — COMPLETE A PATIENT COMPLAINT DOCUMENT

PERFORMANCE OBJECTIVE

TASK: Fill in a patient complaint document.

CONDITIONS: Patient complaint document (form 60) and pen or pencil.

STANDARDS: Time: _____ minutes
Accuracy: _____
(NOTE: The time element and accuracy criteria may be given by your instructor.)

DIRECTIONS: You are working as the receptionist. You answer the phone and a patient starts complaining to you. Read the case scenario and fill in the patient complaint document to hand in to your supervisor. Use the current date. Susan Robels, account number 068941, is on the phone. She is complaining about how she is never able to get through to the doctor when she needs him. The phone lines are always busy, busy, busy! You are speaking to her now, and it is 4:00 P.M. You ask her how many times she has called, and she indicates her phone has been on automatic dialing on and off for two hours. After calming her down, you discuss the times of day she has called. It is discovered that she usually calls around 2:00 P.M. when her children go down for a nap. You apologize, telling her you will document the complaint and give it to your supervisor. Thank her for letting you know there is a problem so it can be corrected.

NOTE: A Performance Evaluation Checklist for this exercise can be found at the back of the workbook.

EXERCISE 15-7	**COMPLETE A FINANCIAL AGREEMENT**

PERFORMANCE OBJECTIVE

TASK: Fill in the financial agreement (form 61) with a schedule of payments.

CONDITIONS: Use financial agreement (form 61), calculator, and pen or pencil.

STANDARDS: Time: _____ minutes
Accuracy: _____
(NOTE: The time element and accuracy criteria may be given by your instructor.)

DIRECTIONS: Read the case scenario. Fill in the information on the financial agreement (form 61), being sure to fill in the schedule of payments. Refer to Figure 15-8 in the textbook. Use the current date. Alan Biederman, 444 Halifax Court, Woodland Hills, XY 12345, telephone number (013) 486-9063, account number 3689, incurred $3,000 for medical services with Dr. Gerald Practon. He has no insurance. He has agreed to pay $600 as a down payment and divide the rest into monthly installments of $200 a month to be paid on the first of every month.

NOTE: A Performance Evaluation Checklist for this exercise can be found at the back of the workbook.

COMPUTER EXERCISES

Before proceeding, you may want to do more exercises and/or review the concepts you have learned. Complete the computer exercises on the software for Chapter 15.

CHAPTER 16

Health Insurance Systems

OBJECTIVES

After completing the exercises, the student will be able to:

1. Write the meanings for chart note abbreviations.

2. Enhance spelling skills by learning new medical words.

3. Select the proper *CPT* codes for given scenarios and examples.

4. Complete a managed care authorization form.

5. Complete a health insurance claim form.

6. Complete a Medicare form.

7. Complete a TRICARE/CHAMPUS claim form.

8. Abstract from patient records to complete the insurance claim forms.

9. Post information to ledger cards after submitting insurance claims.

AREAS OF COMPETENCE

Administrative Procedures

- Perform basic clerical functions
- Understand and apply third-party guidelines
- Obtain reimbursement through accurate claims submission
- Understand and adhere to managed care policies and procedures

Practice Finances

- Perform procedural and diagnostic coding

General (Transdisciplinary)

Communication Skills

- Use medical terminology appropriately

Legal Concepts

- Follow employer's established policies dealing with the health care contract

ABBREVIATION AND SPELLING REVIEW LESSON

Read the following patient's chart note and write the meanings for the abbreviations listed below the note. To decode any abbreviations you do not understand or that appear unfamiliar to you, refer to text Tables 8-1 and 9-3. Medical terms in the chart note are italicized; study them for spelling. Use your medical dictionary to look up their definitions. Your instructor may give a test for the spelling and definition of their words and abbreviations.

Brad Chieu

May 5, 199X Pt came into the hosp c̄ a CC of *dyspnea* & pain in the RUQ. He was adm into the ER. Pt has had *diabetes* since childhood/*hypertension* for 3 years. Smoker. Increasing *malaise, nausea, anorexia* for past 5 days. *Polyuria, polydipsia.* The RN took his FH & vitals & recorded his TPR of 96.5 F & BP of 120/70 on the chart. After exam, the Dr. verified that the pt was suffering from COPD & scheduled him for an IPPB TX b.i.d. AP chest x-rays, a TB test and O2 therapy.

Gerald Practon MD

Gerald Practon, MD

---

c̄ _____   BP _____

CC _____   COPD _____

RUQ _____   IPPB _____

adm _____   TX _____

ER _____   b.i.d. _____

RN _____   AP _____

FH _____   TB _____

TPR _____   O2 _____

F _____

REVIEW QUESTIONS

Review the objectives, glossary, and chapter information before completing the following review questions.

1. Match the terms in the left column with the definition in the right column by writing letters in the blanks.

   copayment _____
   third-party payer _____
   indemnity _____
   deductible _____
   carrier _____
   adjuster _____
   fiscal intermediary _____
   elimination period _____
   assignment _____
   partial disability _____

   a. Claims representative
   b. An agent or contractor that processes payments to providers on behalf of state or federal agencies or insurance companies
   c. An insurance carrier who intervenes to pay hospital or medical expenses on behalf of beneficiaries or recipients
   d. Benefits paid in a predetermined amount in the event of a covered loss
   e. The transfer of one's right to collect an amount payable under an insurance contract
   f. Insurer or underwriter
   g. A form of cost sharing in which the insured pays a specific portion toward the amount of the professional services rendered
   h. Period of time after the beginning of a disability for which no benefits are payable
   i. An illness or injury preventing the insured from performing one or more functions of his or her occupation
   j. The amount the insured must pay in a fiscal year before an insurance company will begin the payment of benefits

2. Name and give a brief definition of three types of private health insurance plans.

   a. _____
   _____
   b. _____
   _____
   c. _____
   _____

3. If the patient is the insured, he or she is also known as a/an _____ or _____ .

4. An elimination period written in an insurance policy may be known as a/an _____ or _____ .

5. An attachment to a policy excluding certain illnesses or disabilities is called a/an
   _____ .

6. Dr. Practon wants to know if Mrs. Snow's managed care plan covers a particular surgical procedure. This process is known as _____ .

7. Dr. Practon completes a form for preauthorization of a diagnostic test to be ordered for Lee Cho. This may also be called a/an _____ or
   _____ .

8. Before scheduling elective surgery on Phyllis Horton, Dr. Practon wants to know the maximum amount the insurance plan will pay. This is a process known as
   _____ .

9. A document from the insurance company that arrives with a check for payment of an insurance claim is called a/an _____ . In the Medicare program, this document is called a/an _____ or
   _____ .

10. A subscriber of a Blue Plan who receives medical care in another state is covered under a program called _____ .

11. Name five popular types of managed care health plans and list their abbreviations.
    a. _____
    b. _____
    c. _____
    d. _____
    e. _____

12. Circle one. Medicare patients   are / are not   permitted to submit claims for reimbursement to the fiscal intermediary.

13. Circle one. A physician who accepts 80 percent of the allowable fee paid by Medicare is considered a/an   participating / nonparticipating   physician.

14. Circle one. A nonparticipating physician   may / may not   bill more than the Medicare limiting charge.

15. There are _____ levels of coding used when billing services rendered to Medicare patients.

16. The time limit for submission of a Medicare claim is _____

    _____ .

17. In submitting a Medicare/Medicaid claim, the physician _____
    accept assignment or payment will go to the patient.

18. A claim processed by Medicare and automatically processed by Medicaid is referred to as a/an _____ claim.

19. The CHAMPUS fiscal year is from _____ to _____ .

20. Define the following terms in relation to disability insurance.

a. Temporary disability: _____

_____

_____

b. Partial disability: _____

_____

_____

c. Total disability: _____

_____

_____

21. After an initial workers' compensation report, insurance carriers want progress reports on the injured worker to be submitted on a _____ basis.

22. The insurance claim form that is accepted by almost all insurance companies, as well as Blue Plans, Medicare, Medicaid, and TRICARE/CHAMPUS programs, is called _____ .

23. If a patient signs an assignment of benefits statement, the insurance payment check is sent to the _____ .

24. The Health Care Financing Administration issues a/an _____ number to physicians who treat and submit claims for Medicare patients.

25. A service that receives insurance claims, edits and sorts them, and then electronically transmits them to insurance companies is called a/an _____ .

26. When completing insurance claim forms, the code numbers required on the claim include

a. _____

b. _____

c. _____

27. For coding purposes, the definition of a *new patient* is _____

_____

_____

28. Explain the difference between a consult and referral of a patient.

    a. Consult is _____

    _____

    b. Referral is _____

    _____

29. Write in the meaning of three symbols that appear in the *Current Procedural Terminology* code book.

    a. ✳ _____

    b. ● _____

    c. ▲ _____

30. Procedure coding is usually _____ -digit number(s) with _____ -digit or _____ - digit modifiers.

31. Diagnostic coding using ICD-9-CM can vary from _____ to _____ digits.

32. The documentation required in a patient's medical record when an injection is given includes

    a. _____
    b. _____
    c. _____

33. The documentation necessary in a patient's medical record for treatment of a laceration includes

    a. _____
    b. _____
    c. _____

34. Mrs. Gary Waxman has brought in a Prudential insurance form for completion. You wish to use the universal health insurance claim form, HCFA 1500. Describe the procedure for submission of the claim.

    _____

    _____

    _____

35. Indicate whether the following statements are true (T) or false (F).

    a. Only an original HCFA-1500 claim form may be optically scanned. _____

    b. It is permissible to type data in lowercase for claims being optically scanned. _____

    c. When entering data on a claim that is to be optically scanned, dates are keyed in using six digits. _____

    d. Staples and paper clips may be used when sending in insurance claims. _____

EXERCISE 16-1 — CODE EVALUATION AND MANAGEMENT

PERFORMANCE OBJECTIVE

TASK: Locate the correct procedure code for each question and/or case scenario.

CONDITIONS: Use pen or pencil and *Current Procedural Terminology*[1] code book.

STANDARDS: Time: _____ minutes
Accuracy: _____
(NOTE: The time element and accuracy criteria may be given by your instructor.)

1. To become acquainted with the sections of the *Current Procedural Terminology (CPT)* code book, match the code number in the left column with the appropriate description in the right column by writing the letters in the blanks. Locate each code number in *Current Procedural Terminology* code book. The problems become more difficult and complex as you progress.

Code		Description
99202	_____	a. X-ray of hip, one view
27500	_____	b. Anesthesia for procedure on esophagus
73500	_____	c. Office visit new patient
00500	_____	d. Poliomyelitis vaccine
80016	_____	e. Closed treatment of femoral shaft fracture
90713	_____	f. Fourteen Clinical chemistry tests

2. Name the section of *CPT* where each of the following codes is located.
   a. 75970 _____
   b. 41872 _____
   c. 86805 _____
   d. 95004 _____
   e. 99261 _____
   f. 01800 _____

3. Evaluation and management (E/M) codes are used by physicians to report a significant portion of their services. Some physicians rank E/M codes on a scale of 1 to 5, with 5 as the highest, most complex level, and 1 as the lowest, least-complex level. This terminology appears on multipurpose billing forms. The levels are broken down as follows:

	Office Visits		Consultations	
	New	Established	Office	Hospital
Level 1	99201	99211	99241	99251
Level 2	99202	99212	99242	99252
Level 3	99203	99213	99243	99253
Level 4	99204	99214	99244	99254
Level 5	99205	99215	99245	99255

[1] *Current Procedural Terminology* codes, descriptions, and two-digit numeric modifiers only are from *CPT* 1997.

Remember, it is the physician's responsibility to assign E/M codes, and the exercises presented are only for familiarization purposes. The problems will acquaint you with terminology for this section of the *CPT* code book. Select the appropriate *new patient* office visit codes using the key components:

a. This is a level 2 case: Expanded problem-focused history   _____
Expanded problem-focused examination
Straightforward medical decision making

b. This is a level 4 case: Comprehensive history   _____
Comprehensive examination
Moderate complexity medical decision making

c. This is a level 1 case: Problem-focused history   _____
Problem-focused examination
Straightforward decision making

4. Select the appropriate *established patient* office visit codes using the key components. Coding these cases illustrates consideration of two out of three components.

a. This is a level 2 case: Problem-focused history   _____
Problem-focused examination
Straightforward medical decision making

b. This is a level 4 case: Detailed history   _____
Detailed examination
Moderate complexity medical decision making

c. This is a level 4 case: Detailed history   _____
Detailed examination
High-complexity decision making

5. Evaluation and management codes 99201 to 99238 are used for services provided in the physician's office, hospital inpatient or outpatient, or other ambulatory facility.

a. Office visit for a four-year-old male, established patient,   _____
with an expanded problem-focused history for earache
and dyshidrosis of feet and low-complexity medical
decision making.

b. Office visit for a 35-year-old male, established patient,   _____
with a detailed history and examination for a new onset RLQ
pain. Medical decision making was of moderate complexity.

c. Initial hospital visit for a 15-year-old male with a detailed   _____
comprehensive history and examination for infectious
mononucleosis and dehydration. Medical decision making
was of low complexity.

d. Subsequent hospital visit for a nine-year-old female admitted   _____
for lobar pneumonia with vomiting and dehydration. A
problem-focused interval history was made because she is
becoming afebrile but tolerates oral fluids. An expanded
problem-focused examination was done, with straightforward
decision making.

e. Office visit for a nine-year-old male, established patient, who   _____
has been taking swimming lessons and now presents with a

two-day history of left ear pain with purulent drainage. This visit required a problem-focused history and examination, with straightforward decision making.

6. Evaluation and management codes 99241 to 99275 are used for consultations provided in the physician's office, hospital inpatient or outpatient, or other ambulatory facility. Read the brief statement and then locate the code number in the *Current Procedural Terminology*[1] code book.

   a. Office consultation for a 67-year-old male with chronic low back pain radiating to the left leg requiring a detailed history and examination and low-complexity decision making. _____

   b. Initial office consultation for a 21-year-old female with acute upper respiratory tract symptoms that required an expanded problem-focused history and examination with straightforward decision making. _____

   c. Office consult for 30-year-old female with chronic pelvic inflammatory disease who now has left lower quadrant pain with a palpable pelvic mass. This visit required a comprehensive history and examination and moderate-complexity decision making. _____

   d. Initial office consultation for a 60-year-old carpenter with olecranon bursitis requiring a problem-focused history and examination. Medical decision making was straightforward. _____

   e. Follow-up consultation for a highly functional 70-year-old male to complete review of previously unavailable studies. A problem-focused interval history was taken, and a comprehensive examination was performed. Medical decision making was of low complexity. _____

7. Evaluation and management codes 99281 to 99499 are used for emergency department, critical care, nursing facility, rest home, custodial care, home, prolonged, physician standby, and preventive medicine services. Read the brief statement and then locate the code number in the *Current Procedural Terminology*[1] code book.

   a. First hour of critical care of a 16-year-old male with acute respiratory failure from asthma. _____

   b. A child is seen in the emergency department with rash on both legs after exposure to poison ivy. This visit required an expanded problem-focused history and examination but low-complexity medical decision making. _____

   c. Initial nursing facility visit to evaluate a 70-year-old male found confused and wandering, admitted by Adult Protective Services without a qualifying stay or inpatient diagnostic work-up. Patient lives alone and has no relatives in the area. A comprehensive history and examination was performed. Medical decision making was of moderate complexity. _____

---

[1] *Current Procedural Terminology* codes, descriptions, and two-digit numeric modifiers only are from *CPT* 1997. © 1996 American Medical Association. All rights reserved.

d. Subsequent visit in a skilled nursing facility to a female   _____
with controlled dementia, hypertension, and diabetes.
During the visit, she seems to exhibit flu symptoms. An
expanded problem-focused interval history and examination
was performed. Medical decision making was of low complexity.

e. Emergency department visit for a female who received an   _____
abrasion and needs a tetanus toxoid immunization. A problem-
focused history and examination was performed, and medical
decision making was straightforward.

NOTE: A Performance Evaluation Checklist for this exercise can be found at the back
of the workbook.

EXERCISE 16-2   CODE SURGICAL PROCEDURES AND SERVICES

PERFORMANCE OBJECTIVE

TASK: Locate the correct procedure code for each question and/or case scenario.

CONDITIONS: Use *Current Procedural Terminology*[1] code book and pen or pencil.

STANDARDS: Time: _____ minutes
Accuracy: _____
(NOTE: The time element and accuracy criteria may be given by your instructor.)

DIRECTIONS: Surgery codes 10040 to 69979 are used for each anatomic part of the body. Read each case carefully. Use the *Current Procedural Terminology*[1] code book to obtain the correct code number for each descriptor given. Full descriptors for services rendered have been omitted in some instances to give you practice in abstracting the correct two-digit modifier if necessary. The skill of critical thinking enters this section of the exercises, because you may have to use your judgment to code since the cases do not contain full details. Definitions for abbreviations may be found in the workbook's appendix. You will notice that Blocks 21 through 24E of the HCFA-1500 claim form are shown partially completed. This will introduce you to a portion of the form before you tackle completing the entire claim.

Integumentary system 10040-19499

1. Excision, benign lesion, face, 0.5 cm   _____
2. Repair layer closure of lt leg 2.7 cm laceration   _____

Musculoskeletal System 20000-29909

3. Closed reduction of rt humerus fracture, no manipulation   _____
4. Subsequent application of long leg cast with a walker   _____

Respiratory System 30000-32999

5. Extract fried potato from left nostril of child   _____
6. Excise small nasal polyp   _____

Cardiovascular System 33010-37799

7. Introduction of catheter into superior vena cava   _____

8. Coronary artery bypass using arterial graft   _____

Hemic/lymphatic/diaphragm 38100-39599

9. Biopsy of cervical lymph nodes   _____

10. Excision of total spleen   _____

Digestive System 40490-49999

11. Liver biopsy   _____

12. Excision of gallbladder (cholecystectomy)   _____

Urinary System/Male and Female Genitals 50010-55980

13. Drainage of deep periurethral abscess   _____

14. Aspiration of bladder by needle   _____

Laparoscopy/peritoneoscopy/hysteroscopy/female genitals/maternity 56300-59899

15. Removal of IUD   _____

16. Cesarean delivery including obstetric/antepartum/postpartum care   _____

NOTE: A Performance Evaluation Checklist for this exercise can be found at the back of the workbook.

EXERCISE 16-3   CODE RADIOLOGY AND PATHOLOGY PROCEDURES AND SERVICES

PERFORMANCE OBJECTIVE

TASK: Locate the correct procedure code for each question and case scenario.

CONDITIONS: Use *Current Procedural Terminology*[1] code book and pen or pencil.

STANDARDS: Time: _____ minutes
Accuracy: _____
(NOTE: The time element and accuracy criteria may be given by your instructor.)

RADIOLOGY 70010-79999 AND PATHOLOGY 80002-89399

1. X-rays of hand, four views   _____

2. Bilateral renal angiography   _____

3. Fifteen laboratory multichannel chemistry tests, automated   _____

4. Bacterial culture of specimen from leg, anaerobic (isolation)   _____

NOTE: A Performance Evaluation Checklist for this exercise can be found at the back of the workbook.

---

[1] *Current Procedural Terminology* codes, descriptions, and two-digit numeric modifiers only are from *CPT* 1997.

| EXERCISE 16-4 | CODE PROCEDURES AND SERVICES |

PERFORMANCE OBJECTIVE

TASK: Locate the correct procedure code for each case scenario.

CONDITIONS: Use *Current Procedural Terminology*[1] code book and pen or pencil.

STANDARDS: Time: _____ minutes
Accuracy: _____
(NOTE: The time element and accuracy criteria may be given by your instructor.)

MODIFIERS AND MEDICINE SECTION 90700-99199

DIRECTIONS: This exercise will familiarize you with Blocks 21 through 24F of the HCFA-1500 insurance claim form. It will reinforce what you have already learned about procedural coding, since code numbers for the problems presented are located in all sections of the *CPT* code book. To further enhance your coding skill, insert two-digit modifiers if necessary and search for codes in the medicine section. Look up fees using a mock fee schedule and insert them for each descriptor.

1. On February 3, a Blue Shield (new) patient is seen in the office with effusion or fluid (hydrathrosis) of the right knee. The physician does an arthrocentesis, aspirates, and sends a specimen to the laboratory for evaluation. Applied dressing and patient is to return in one week. Insert diagnosis code 719.06 in Block 21, on line 1.

19. RESERVED FOR LOCAL USE						20. OUTSIDE LAB? ☐ YES ☐ NO	$ CHARGES					
21. DIAGNOSIS OR NATURE OF ILLNESS OR INJURY. (RELATE ITEMS 1,2,3 OR 4 TO ITEM 24E BY LINE)						22. MEDICAID RESUBMISSION CODE	ORIGINAL REF. NO.					
1. L___.__			3. L___.__			23. PRIOR AUTHORIZATION NUMBER						
2. L___.__			4. L___.__									

24. A DATE(S) OF SERVICE From MM DD YY To MM DD YY	B Place of Service	C Type of Service	D PROCEDURES, SERVICES, OR SUPPLIES (Explain Unusual Circumstances) CPT/HCPCS | MODIFIER	E DIAGNOSIS CODE	F $ CHARGES	G DAYS OR UNITS	H EPSDT Family Plan	I EMG	J COB	K RESERVED FOR LOCAL USE
	11			1						
	11			1						

2. On May 6, a patient is seen in the office of an otologist after referral by a family physician to evaluate and treat diminished hearing in right ear. The physician performed an expanded problem-focused history and examination. A comprehensive audiometry threshold evaluation and speech recognition was performed, revealing a conductive right ear low-frequency loss of hearing. Patient was referred to an audiologist for hearing aid examination and selection. Decision making was straightforward. Patient asked to return in one month. Insert diagnosis code 389.8 in Block 21.

[1]*Current Procedural Terminology* codes, descriptions, and two-digit numeric modifiers only are from *CPT* 1997.

19. RESERVED FOR LOCAL USE							20. OUTSIDE LAB?		$ CHARGES		

19. RESERVED FOR LOCAL USE

20. OUTSIDE LAB? ☐ YES ☐ NO $ CHARGES

21. DIAGNOSIS OR NATURE OF ILLNESS OR INJURY. (RELATE ITEMS 1,2,3 OR 4 TO ITEM 24E BY LINE)

22. MEDICAID RESUBMISSION CODE   ORIGINAL REF. NO.

1. |___ . __| 3. |___ . __|

23. PRIOR AUTHORIZATION NUMBER

2. |___ . __| 4. |___ . __|

24. A						B	C	D		E	F	G	H	I	J	K
DATE(S) OF SERVICE						Place of Service	Type of Service	PROCEDURES, SERVICES, OR SUPPLIES (Explain Unusual Circumstances)		DIAGNOSIS CODE	$ CHARGES	DAYS OR UNITS	EPSDT Family Plan	EMG	COB	RESERVED FOR LOCAL USE
From			To					CPT/HCPCS	MODIFIER							
MM	DD	YY	MM	DD	YY											
						11				1						
						11				1						

NOTE: A Performance Evaluation Checklist for this exercise can be found at the back of the workbook.

EXERCISE 16-5 CODE CLINICAL EXAMPLES

PERFORMANCE OBJECTIVE

TASK: Locate the correct procedure code for each question and case scenario.

CONDITIONS: Use *Current Procedural Terminology* code book and pen or pencil.

STANDARDS: Time: _____ minutes
Accuracy: _____
(NOTE: The time element and accuracy criteria may be given by your instructor.)

DIRECTIONS: The clinically oriented format of the E/M codes mandates that the physician analyze his or her services to be able to choose the appropriate level of service. Codes for these levels should be either printed on the multipurpose billing form or the physician should use a checklist. The physician should circle or check the appropriate level of service after each patient is seen. Code these cases. Begin by selecting the appropriate E/M category. Refer to your *CPT* book or use text Table 16-6 or 16-7 to assess the key components. To assist you, scenario examples are presented in the *CPT* book within the E/M section and in Appendix D, Clinical Examples Supplement.

PROBLEM 1

4/15/9X Maria Gomez

S: A 35-year-old female established patient is seen for left lower quadrant pain of 1 wk. duration. Symptoms: mild fevers, decreased appetite, and mild constipation of 1 wk. Pt denies abdominal injury, change in urination or menstruation. LMP: 3/12/9X.

O: Temp: 100.2°F; BP 130/80, HR 80; RR 18.

Lungs: Clear.

Abdomen: Both sides mildly hyperactive, flat, mild guarding LLQ, rebound neg; fullness LLQ; no discrete masses; no HSM.

Rectal: Normal tone; no masses; guaiac positive.

Pelvic: Cervix closed, uterus and ovaries normal, fullness lt lat adnexa c̄ tenderness.

CBC, elevated. WBC c̄ mild lt shift; UA, normal; HCG, negative.

A/P: Probable diverticulitis of sigmoid colon based on clinical picture; will obtain barium enema to R/O diverticulitis. Will begin antibiotics and dietary restriction during acute phase and follow up in three days.

_____
Gerald Practon, MD

mtf

CPT E/M Code _____

PROBLEM 2

A physician does a history and examination for five minutes, performs acne surgery (code 10040) on an established patient for ten minutes, and counsels the patient on skin care and diet for ten minutes.

CPT E/M Code _____

PROBLEM 3

DIRECTIONS: Code these items and/or procedures using the Medicare HCPCS codes that appear in the mock fee schedule of this workbook (See appendix).

1. Ace bandage   _____
2. Chiropractic manipulation of spine   _____
3. 2 cc gamma globulin inj IM   _____
4. Pap smear   _____

NOTE: A Performance Evaluation Checklist for this exercise can be found at the back of the workbook.

EXERCISE 16-6 — COMPLETE A MANAGED CARE AUTHORIZATION FORM

PERFORMANCE OBJECTIVE

TASK: Complete a managed care authorization form.

CONDITIONS: Use one managed care authorization form (form 62), and typewriter or computer.

STANDARDS: Time: _____ minutes
Accuracy: _____
(NOTE: The time element and accuracy criteria may be given by your instructor.)

DIRECTIONS: Complete the managed care authorization (form 62) referring to the case scenario. Date it August 3 of current year and submit it to the managed care plan. Refer to textbook Figure 16-1 for visual guidance. Antoyan Gagonian comes into Dr. Gerald Practon's office complaining of low back pain of two weeks duration. Dr. Practon is the primary care physician for the managed care program, Healthnet, of which Mr. Gagonian is a member. Mr. Gagonian lives at 2345 West Bath Street, Woodland Hills, XY 12340-0324, telephone number 013-765-0720. His plan identification number is GAG56921, and he was born October 10, 1963.

After taking a history and completing physical and neurological examinations, Dr. Practon orders x-rays of the lower back. A diagnosis was made of lumbago due to displacement of lumbar intervertebral disc, ICD-9-CM diagnosis code 722.10. He gives him a prescription for pain medication and muscle relaxant for muscle spasm. He says it is necessary to order a magnetic resonance imaging (MRI) scan of the lumbar spine to investigate any other lumbar problems. This scan is to be done as an outpatient at College Hospital. An authorization must be obtained for this study. The procedure number for an MRI is 72158.

NOTE: A Performance Evaluation Checklist for this exercise can be found at the back of the workbook.

EXERCISE 16-7 — COMPLETE A HEALTH INSURANCE CLAIM FORM

PERFORMANCE OBJECTIVE

TASK: Complete a health insurance claim form and post the information to the patient's ledger card.

CONDITIONS: Use Cathy B. Maywood's patient record, Cathy B. Maywood's ledger card, E/M code checklist (Figure 16-3, page 148), one health insurance claim form (form 63), and typewriter, computer, or pen.

STANDARDS: Time: _____ minutes
Accuracy: _____
(NOTE: The time element and accuracy criteria may be given by your instructor.)

DIRECTIONS: Complete the health insurance claim form for Colonial Health Insurance Company on Mrs. Cathy B. Maywood by referring to her patient record (Figure 16-1) and ledger card (Figure 16-2). Date the claim June 30. Refer to Tables 16-4 and 16-5 in the text to locate the correct *CPT* E/M code and enter it at the bottom of the E/M code checklist (Figure 16-3, page 148). Then refer to the Practon Medical Group's mock fee schedule in the appendix of this workbook (Figure A-1) to find the correct five-digit procedure code number for each professional service rendered. Remember to include modifiers if necessary. Record the proper information on the patient's ledger card when you have submitted the claim to the insurance company.

PATIENT RECORD

Maywood,	Cathy	B.	11-24-62	F	013/592-1841
LAST NAME	FIRST NAME	MIDDLE NAME	BIRTH DATE	SEX	HOME PHONE

384 Gary Street,	Woodland Hills,	XY	12345
ADDRESS	CITY	STATE	ZIP CODE

public relations secretary	St. Joseph's Hospital
PATIENT'S OCCUPATION	NAME OF COMPANY

4501 Main Street, Woodland Hills, XY 12345	013/581-2600
ADDRESS OF EMPLOYER	PHONE

Robert M. Maywood	supervisor
SPOUSE OR PARENT	OCCUPATION

United Parcel	261 Jeffers St., Woodland Hills, XY 12345	
EMPLOYER	ADDRESS	PHONE 013/521-8011

Colonial Health Insurance Company	Cathy B. Maywood
NAME OF INSURANCE GROUP	SUBSCRIBER

11 Royal Street, Woodland Hills, XY 12345			1-1-80
BLUE SHIELD OR BLUE CROSS CERT. NO.	GROUP NO.	CURRENT COVERAGE NO.	EFFECTIVE DATE

Policy No. 265012B			458-11-2601
MEDICARE NO.	MEDICAID NO.	EFFECTIVE DATE	SOC. SEC. NO.

REFERRED BY: ID#000 654 111
Bert B. Evans, MD, 100 S. Maple St., Woodland Hills. XY 12345   013/490-1100

DATE	PROGRESS
6/2/9X	This new pt was referred for consultation & came in complaining of irregular vaginal bleeding. Pt asked for evaluaton for possible infertility. Pelvic exam showed cervicitis and cervical erosion. Retn in 3 days for cauterization. Pap smear & cervical mucosa smear taken and sent to outside lab. Cauterization of cervix performed. *Fran Practon, MD*
6/25/9X	Pt reports to outpatient surgery at College Hospital for diag. tests. Endometrial biopsy done & inj proc for hysterosalpingography perf. Dx: cervicitis c̄ erosion (ICD-9-CM diag. code # 616.0) & infertility assoc c̄ congenital cervical anomaly (ICD-9-CM diag. code # 628.4). Pt discharged to retn for OV in 3 days. *Fran Practon, MD*

Figure 16-1

STATEMENT

Practon Medical Group, Inc.
4567 Broad Avenue
Woodland Hills, XY 12345
Tel. 013-486-9002

Name ____ Cathy B. Maywood _____

Address ____ 384 Gary Street _____ Phone No. ____ 013/592-1841 ____

____ Woodland Hills, XY 12345 ____ Policy No. ____ 265012B ____

Insurance Co. ____ Colonial Health Ins. Co. 11 Royal St., Woodland Hills, XY 12345 ____

DATE	Service Description	CPT Code	CHARGE	CREDITS		CURRENT BALANCE
				Payments	Adjustments	
6-2-9x	Consult, comp. exam					
6-5-9x	Cauterization of cervix					
6-25-9x	Endometrial biopsy					
6-25-9x	Hysterosalpingography with inj procedure					

Due and payable within 10 days.   **Pay last amount in balance column** ↑

Figure 16-2

NOTE: A Performance Evaluation Checklist for this exercise can be found at the back of the workbook.

EXERCISE 16-8   **COMPLETE A MEDICARE CLAIM FORM**

PERFORMANCE OBJECTIVE

TASK: Complete a Medicare HCFA 1500 claim form and post information to the ledger card.

CONDITIONS: Use Michael T. Donlevy's patient record, Michael T. Donlevy's ledger card, one health insurance claim form (form 64), typewriter or pen.

STANDARDS: Time: _____ minutes
Accuracy: _____
(NOTE: The time element and accuracy criteria may be given by your instructor.)

DIRECTIONS: Complete the Medicare claim form, directing it to your local fiscal intermediary (you may have to obtain this information from your

Physician Checklist Simplifies
E/M Code Selection for Staff

Physician offices may want to adopt a checklist like the one below, which physicians can complete in full or in part. This tool is an efficient way of gathering the information needed to select the correct E/M codes.

Patient name: _Cathy Maywood_   Account number: _____   Date of service: _6-2-9x_

Providing physician: _Fran Procton_   Requesting physician's name and UPIN: _Bert B Evans MD_
_000 662 988_

Diagnoses:
1. _616.0_   3. _____
2. _628.4_   4. _____

Type of Patient: **Type of Visit:**   **Place of Service (POS Code):**
☑ New   ☑ Initial   ☑ Office (11)   ☐ ER (23)
☐ Established   ☐ Subsequent   ☐ Inpatient hospital (21)   ☐ Nursing home (31)
                              ☐ Outpatient hospital (22)   ☐ Other:_____

Type of History (check one only):
☐ **Problem-focused** (chief complaint, brief history of present problem)
☐ **Expanded problem-focused** (chief complaint, brief history and system review pertinent to problem)
☐ **Detailed** (chief complaint, extended history, extended system review and pertinent past, family and/or social history)
☑ **Comprehensive** (chief complaint, extended history, complete system review and complete past, family and social history)

Type of Examination (check one only):
☐ **Problem-focused** (affected body area or organ system)
☐ **Expanded problem-focused** (affected body area or system and other related systems)
☐ **Detailed** (extended exam of affected body area or system and extended exam of related systems)
☑ **Comprehensive** (complete single system specialty exam or complete multisystem exam)

Level of Medical Decision Making:	Straight-forward	Low Complexity	Moderate Complexity	High Complexity
Number of diagnoses or management options	☐ Minimal	☐ Limited	☑ Multiple	☐ Extensive
Amount/complexity of data to be reviewed	☐ Minimal	☐ Limited	☑ Moderate	☐ Extensive
Risk of complications and/or morbidity or mortality	☐ Minimal	☐ Low	☑ Moderate	☐ High

Select highest level for which two or more criteria are met or exceeded:
☐ High complexity   ☑ Moderate complexity   ☐ Low complexity   ☐ Straightforward

Time:
Total face-to-face time spent with patient: _60 min_ (required only if more than 50 percent of the face-to-face time was spent in counseling or coordination of care—documentation of the extent of counseling and coordination of care is required)

CPT Code: _____

St. Anthony's Coding for Physician Reimbursement, March 1992—Special Supplement

Figure 16-3

instructor). Refer to Michael T. Donlevy's patient record and ledger card (Figures 16-4 and 16-5) for information. Date the claim June 30. Dr. Practon is accepting assignment in this particular case and will bill as a participating physician using the limiting charge. Mr. Donlevy has already met his deductible for the year, owing to previous medical

PATIENT RECORD

Donlevy,	Michael	T.	3-10-17	M	013/421-0015
LAST NAME	FIRST NAME	MIDDLE NAME	BIRTH DATE	SEX	HOME PHONE

2821 Georgia Street,	Woodland Hills,	XY	12345
ADDRESS	CITY	STATE	ZIP CODE

retired truck driver
PATIENT'S OCCUPATION   NAME OF COMPANY

ADDRESS OF EMPLOYER   PHONE

Patricia M. Donlevy	retired	
SPOUSE OR PARENT	OCCUPATION	

EMPLOYER   ADDRESS   PHONE

Medicare
NAME OF INSURANCE GROUP   SUBSCRIBER

BLUE SHIELD OR BLUE CROSS CERT. NO.	GROUP NO.	CURRENT COVERAGE NO.	EFFECTIVE DATE
451-82-9003A			451-82-9003
MEDICARE NO.	MEDICAID NO.	EFFECTIVE DATE	SOC. SEC. NO.

REFERRED BY:
Harry Donlevy (brother)

DATE	PROGRESS
6/3/9X	Called to ER at 7 p.m. on request of pt who fell at home and cut head.
	Sutured intermed laceration of scalp 3.5 cm (ICD-9-CM diag. code
	# 873.0). Pt to come to the office in 4 days for dressing change.
	Gerald Practon, MD
6/7/9X	Dressing change by Mary Atkins, RN *M. Atkins, RN*

Figure 16-4

STATEMENT

Practon Medical Group, Inc.
4567 Broad Avenue
Woodland Hills, XY 12345
Tel. 013-486-9002

Name _____ Michael T. Donlevy _____

Address _____ 2821 Georgia Street _____   Phone No. _____ 013/421-0015

_____ Woodland Hills, XY 12345 _____   Policy No. _____ 451-82-9003A

Insurance Co. ___ Medicare _____

DATE	Service Description	CPT Code	CHARGE	CREDITS Payments	Adjustments	CURRENT BALANCE
6-3-9x	ER visit, low complexity est pt					
6-3-9x	3.5 cm intermed lacer. repair					
6-7-9x	Dressing change by R.N. (minimal service) (5 min)					

Due and payable within 10 days.   Pay last amount in balance column   ↑

Figure 16-5

expenses with another physician. Refer to the fee schedule to find the correct five-digit procedure code number for each professional service rendered. Remember to include the modifiers if necessary. Low-complexity emergency room care was rendered to Mr. Donlevy. Record the proper information on the patient's ledger card when you have submitted the claim to Medicare.

After completing the claim form, refer to the mock fee schedule (Figure A-1) and answer these questions for class discussion.

1. If Dr. Practon is **participating**, how much will he receive for the **hospital visit**? $ _____

2. If Dr. Practon is **not participating**, how much will he receive for the **repair**? $ _____

3. If Dr. Practon is a **nonparticipating** physician in the Medicare program, what is the **maximum** limiting charge he can bill on the **office visit**? $ _____

NOTE: A Performance Evaluation Checklist for this exercise can be found at the back of the workbook.

EXERCISE 16-9 | COMPLETE A TRICARE/CHAMPUS CLAIM FORM

PERFORMANCE OBJECTIVE

TASK: Complete a TRICARE/CHAMPUS claim form HCFA 1500, and post information to the patient's ledger card.

CONDITIONS: Use Frances O. Davidson's patient record, Frances O. Davidson's ledger card, Insur-a-bill (superbill form Figure 16-8), one health insurance claim form 65, and typewriter or pen.

STANDARDS: Time: _____ minutes
Accuracy: _____
(NOTE: The time element and accuracy criteria may be given by your instructor.)

DIRECTIONS: Complete the TRICARE/CHAMPUS claim form, directing it to your local CHAMPUS fiscal intermediary (obtain this information from your instructor). Refer to Mrs. Frances O. Davidson's patient record (Figure 16-6), ledger card (Figure 16-7), and Insur-a-bill (Figure 16-8) for information. Date the claim June 30. Dr. Practon is accepting assignment. This patient met her deductible last November when seen by a previous physician. Refer to the mock fee schedule to find the correct five-digit procedure code number for each professional service rendered and use the mock fee column. Remember to include modifiers if necessary. Record the proper information on the patient's ledger card when you have submitted the claim to TRICARE/CHAMPUS.

NOTE: A Performance Evaluation Checklist for this exercise can be found at the back of the workbook.

COMPUTER EXERCISES

Before proceeding, you may want to do more exercises and/or review the concepts you have learned. Complete the computer exercises on the software for Chapter 16.

PATIENT RECORD

Davidson,	Frances	O.	4-10-50	F	013/217-8105
LAST NAME	FIRST NAME	MIDDLE NAME	BIRTH DATE	SEX	HOME PHONE

128 Watson Street	Woodland Hills,	XY	12345
ADDRESS	CITY	STATE	ZIP CODE

tailor	Sampson Department Store
PATIENT'S OCCUPATION	NAME OF COMPANY

7841 Broadway, Woodland Hills, XY 12345	013/289-7811
ADDRESS OF EMPLOYER	PHONE

William C. Davidson	U.S. Navy Lieutenant (L/C) Active Status
SPOUSE OR PARENT	OCCUPATION

Service #821-78-2601	Soc.Sec.No. 821-78-2601	Grade 12
EMPLOYER	ADDRESS	PHONE

P.O. Box 1978, APO New York, NY 09194
NAME OF INSURANCE GROUP   SUBSCRIBER

BLUE SHIELD OR BLUE CROSS CERT. NO.	GROUP NO.	CURRENT COVERAGE NO.	EFFECTIVE DATE
TRICARE/CHAMPUS ID Card # 57521		1/1/--	283-07-1651
MEDICARE NO.	MEDICAID NO.	EFFECTIVE DATE	Pt.'s SOC. SEC. NO.
Issue Date 12/15/--		Expir. Date 1/1/--	

REFERRED BY:
Martha B. Emory (friend)

DATE	PROGRESS
6/4/9X	New pt comes in with CC of chest pain (moderate to severe), weakness, fatigue, & dizziness. EKG and spirometry, total and timed capacity. Took spec. for 16 panel tests, CBC, T-3 uptake sent to outside lab. UA in ofc neg. PE: BP 140/110. Edema throughout lower extremities Dx: Possible congestive heart failure (ICD-9-CM diag. code # 428.0) Adv hospitalization as soon as possible. *Gerald Practon MD*

Figure 16-6

STATEMENT

Practon Medical Group, Inc.
4567 Broad Avenue
Woodland Hills, XY 12345
Tel. 013-486-9002

Name _____Frances O. Davidson_____

Address _____128 Watson Street_____   Phone No. _____013/217-8105_____

_____Woodland Hills, XY 12345_____   Policy No. _____CHAMPUS ID #57521_____

Insurance Co. ___CHAMPUS_____

DATE	Service Description	CPT Code	CHARGE	Payments	Adjustments	CURRENT BALANCE
				CREDITS		
6-4-9x	Comp. Exam					
6-4-9x	EKG					
6-4-9x	Spirometry					
6-4-9x	UA					

Due and payable within 10 days.   Pay last amount in balance column   ↑

Figure 16-7

General Practice
CAL. LIC. #

TAX ID #

157631

✓ CHAMPUS

☐ PRIVATE   ☐ BLUE CROSS/SHIELD   ☐ CCHP   ☐ IND.   ☐ MEDI-CAL   ☐ MEDICARE   ☐ S.S.   ☐ BRIDGEWAY

PATIENT INFORMATION							
PATIENT'S LAST NAME	FIRST	INITIAL		BIRTHDATE	SEX		TODAY'S DATE
Davidson,	Frances	O.		/ /	☐ MALE ☐ FEMALE		/ /
ADDRESS	CITY	STATE	ZIP	RELATION TO SUBSCRIBER		REFERRING PHYSICIAN	
SUBSCRIBER OR POLICYHOLDER				INSURANCE CARRIER			
ADDRESS	CITY	STATE	ZIP	INS. ID	COVERAGE CODE		GROUP

OTHER HEALTH COVERAGE? ☐ NO ☐ YES — IDENTIFY   DISABILITY RELATED TO: ☐ IND. ☐ ACCIDENT ☐ PREGNANCY ☐ OTHER   DATE SYMPTOMS APPEARED, INCEPTION OF PREGNANCY, OR ACCIDENT OCCURRED: / /

ASSIGNMENT & RELEASE: I hereby assign my insurance benefits to be paid directly to the undersigned physician. I am financially responsible for non-covered services. I also authorize the physician to release any information required to process this claim.
SIGNED (Patient, or Parent, if Minor)   DATE: / /

✓ DESCRIPTION	CODE/MD	FEE	✓ DESCRIPTION	CODE/MD	FEE	✓ DESCRIPTION	CODE/MD	FEE
1. OFFICE VISIT			2. PROCEDURES			4. INJECTIONS		
NEW PATIENT			Joint Aspiration	20610		Benadryl	00107	
Focused	99201		Ear Irrigation	69210		Kenalog 90782	11230	
Expanded	99202		TB Skin Test	86585		Lincocin 90788	01003	
Detailed	99203		Unna Boot	29580		Vitamin B12	14730	
✓ Comprehensive	99204					Flu Vaccine 90724	12823	
			Supplies & Material	99070		Immun:		
ESTABLISHED PATIENT								
Minimal	99211		3. LABORATORY					
Focused	99212		Urinalysis	81005				
Expanded	99213		UA Complete	81000		6. MISCELLANEOUS		
Detailed	99214		Blood - Stick Test	82948				
Comprehensive	99215		VDRL	86592				
			Premarital - Male	1001				
			- Female	1002				

DIAGNOSIS:	ICD-9				
☐ Abscess	682.9	☐ Cephalgia 784.0	☐ Hemorrhoids 455	☐ Obesity 278.0
☐ Abdominal Pain	789.0	☐ CVA 431	☐ Hernia 550	☐ Pancreatitis 577.1
☐ Acne	706.1	☐ Chest Pain 786.5	☐ Hepatitis AC / CH	☐ Pharyngitis 462
☐ Acute Stress Reaction	308	☐ Cholecystitis AC / CH	☐ Herpes Simplex 054.9	☐ Parkinsonism 332.0
☐ Allergic Dermatitis	692.9	☐ Cirrhosis 571	☐ Herpes Zoster 053.9	☐ Pleurisy 511.0
☐ Allergic Rhinitis	477	☒ Congestive Heart Failure .. 428.0	☐ Hyperthyroidism 242.9	☐ Pneumonia 485
☐ Anemia	280	☐ Conjunctivitis 372.00	☐ Hypertension Essential .. 401	☐ Prostatism 600
☐ Anxiety Reaction	300.00	☐ Constipation 564.0	☐ Indigestion 536.9	☐ Sinusitis: AC / CH 473
☐ Angina Pectoris	413.9	☐ Dermatophytosis 110.9	☐ Infectious Dermatitis ... 686.9	☐ Tachycardia 785.0
☐ ASCVD	429.2	☐ Diabetes Mellitus 250.0	☐ Influenza 487	☐ TBC 011
☐ Asthma	493.9	☐ Emphysema 492	☐ Insomnia 307.41	☐ Tonsillitis: AC / CH 463
☐ Arthritis, AC / CH	716.9	☐ Epicondylitis 726.32	☐ Kidney Stone 592.0	☐ Ulcer of:
☐ Arrhythmia	427.9	☐ Fibrositis, Acute 729.0	☐ Lower Back Pain 724.2	☐ Uremia AC / CH 585
☐ Bronchitis	466.0	☐ Fracture of:	☐ Lumbosacral Strain .. 846.0	☐ UTI 599.0
☐ Burn	949.0	☐ Gallstones 574.0	☐ Laryngitis 464.0	☐ URI 487.1
☐ Bursitis, Knee	726.60	☐ Gastritis 535	☐ Measles 055.9	☐ Urticaria 708.9
☐ Bursitis, Shoulder	726.10	☐ Gastroenteritis 558.9	☐ Myocardial Inf. AC / CH ... 410	☐ Vertigo 780.4
☐ CA of:		☐ Gastro Intest. Bleeding .. 578.9	☐ Neuritis 729.2	☐ Varicose Veins 454
☐ Cellulitis	682.9	☐ Gingivitis, Acute 523.0	☐ Nodule, Thyroid 241.0	☐ Verrucae 078.1
		☐ Gouty Arthritis 274.0	☐ NSU 099.4	☐ Viral Infect., Unspecified .. 079.9

DIAGNOSIS: (IF NOT CHECKED ABOVE)

PLACE OF SERVICE: ☐ OFFICE	RETURN APPT. INFO.: DAYS: WEEKS: MONTHS:	NEXT APPOINTMENT: M — T — W — TH — F — S DATE: / / TIME: AM PM	DOCTOR'S SIGNATURE / DATE *Gerald Practon, MD*

INSTRUCTIONS TO PATIENT FOR FILING INSURANCE CLAIMS: ACCEPT ASSIGNMENT? ☑ YES ☐ NO

Complete upper portion of this form. — Sign & Date. — Attach all miscellaneous bills pertaining to this claim such as: X-Ray Bills, Lab Bills, Hospital Bills, Prescriptions, etc. — If you have a deductible policy hold your claim forms until you have met your deductible. Mail this form and all attachments directly to your insurance company. You may attach your own insurance company's form if you wish.
PLEASE remember that payment is your obligation, regardless of insurance or other third party involvement.

TOTAL TODAY'S FEE
PAYMENT
REC'D. BY: ☐ CASH   ☐ CHECK   ☐

Figure 16-8

CHAPTER 17

Banking

OBJECTIVES

After completing the exercises, the student will be able to:

1. Write meanings for chart note abbreviations.

2. Enhance spelling skills by learning new medical words.

3. Pay invoices by writing checks.

4. Endorse a check that has been received.

5. Post entries to ledger cards.

6. Reconcile a monthly bank statement.

7. Scan a check.

AREAS OF COMPETENCE

Administrative Procedures

■ Perform basic clerical functions

Practice Finances

■ Document and maintain accounting and banking records

General (Transdisciplinary)

Communication Skills

■ Use medical terminology appropriately

ABBREVIATION AND SPELLING REVIEW LESSON

Read the following patient's chart note and write the meanings for the abbreviations listed below the note. To decode any abbreviations you do not understand or that appear unfamiliar to you, refer to text Tables 8-1 and 9-3. Medical terms in the chart note are italicized; study them for spelling. Use your medical dictionary to look up their definitions. Your instructor may give a test for the spelling and definition of the words and abbreviations.

Etta Chan

June 22, 199X Pt was born with *cystic hydromas* and has had *epileptic seizures* without *vomiting* or *dyspnea*. Pt is on *Dilantin*. Pt is to be started on *phenobarbital* 100 mg t.i.d. i.e., 2 mg/kg per day. Ordered CT scan.

Gerald Practon MD
Gerald Practon, MD

Pt _____   kg _____

mg _____   i.e. _____

t.i.d. _____   CT _____

mg _____

NOTE: i.e. is a Latin abbreviation and may be found in an English dictionary.

REVIEW QUESTIONS

Review the objectives, glossary, and chapter information before completing the following review questions.

1. Match the terms in the left column with the definitions in the right column by writing the letters in the blanks.

    debit _____   a. A check stub
    payee _____   b. Deposit or addition to a bank account
    voucher _____   c. The person signing a check to pay out
    ABA number _____   funds from a checking account
    payer _____   d. Withdrawal from or charge to a bank
    credit _____   account
                           e. A fee assessed by a bank for processing
                              transactions
                           f. The person named on a check as the
                              recipient of the amount shown
                           g. Bank, or transit, number

2. Name the three general types of checking accounts.
    a. _____
    b. _____
    c. _____

3. Give the meaning of the following abbreviations.
    a. NSF _____
    b. EFTS _____
    c. POS _____
    d. MICR _____
    e. ATM _____

4. The following check endorsements are either blank, restrictive, or full. Note next to each statement the type of endorsement.

a. For deposit only
Jane Garner   _____

b. Ronald P. Yeager   _____

c. Pay to the order of
Stationer's Corporation
Betty T. White
Harold M. Jeffers   _____

5. Explain what procedures follow if an error is made in typing a check.

_____

_____

6. In reconciling the monthly bank statement, indicate whether to add or subtract the following from the balance appearing on the bank statement or the balance in the checkbook.

a. outstanding checks   _____

b. bank service charges   _____

c. deposits not shown on the bank statement _____

7. In adjusting the checkbook balance to obtain a reconciliation with the bank statement, what other debits might you list and subtract from the checkbook balance?

a. _____

b. _____

c. _____

8. Divide the amount of the error by what number to find out if a transposition error has been made on the check stub register. _____

_____

EXERCISE 17-1   WRITE CHECKS

PERFORMANCE OBJECTIVE

TASK: Handwrite or type two checks.

CONDITIONS: Use two blank checks and two invoices (form 66), and pen.

STANDARDS: Time: _____ minutes
Accuracy: _____
(NOTE: The time element and accuracy criteria may be given by your instructor.)

DIRECTIONS: This exercise will prepare you for the disbursement bookkeeping exercises in the next chapter. You have received two invoices (form 66) for the Practon Medical Group. Handwrite or type two checks (form 66) for Dr. Practon's signature to pay these bills. Date one check May 27 and the other check May 28. Enter the information on the check stub. Write in the beginning checkbook balance as $9,825.55. Record date paid, check number, and amount of check on the invoices.

NOTE: A Performance Evaluation Checklist for this exercise can be found at the back of the workbook.

EXERCISE 17-2

ENDORSE A CHECK

PERFORMANCE OBJECTIVE

TASK: Handwrite a restrictive endorsement on a check in the proper location.

CONDITIONS: Use a check from a patient (Figure 17-1), and pen.

STANDARDS: Time: _____ minutes

Accuracy: _____

(NOTE: The time element and accuracy criteria may be given by your instructor.)

DIRECTIONS: Handwrite a restrictive endorsement on a check received from patient Jeffrey Brown.

NOTE: A Performance Evaluation Checklist for this exercise can be found at the back of the workbook.

EXERCISE 17-3

POST TO A LEDGER CARD

PERFORMANCE OBJECTIVE

TASK: Post a check to a patient's ledger card.

CONDITIONS: Use check in Workbook Exercise 17-2 (again see Figure 17-1), ledger card, (Figure 17-2), and pen.

STANDARDS: Time: _____ minutes

Accuracy: _____

(NOTE: The time element and accuracy criteria may be given by your instructor.)

DIRECTIONS: Refer to the check used in Exercise 17-2, and post in ink the delinquent payment received on the ledger card shown in Figure 17-2.

```
Jeffrey Brown                                    90-7177
7827 Minnow Street                               ------- 750              164
Woodland Hills, XY 12345                          3222
Phone: 013-482-1976                              7504003778

                                                 Date Dec. 15, 199x

Pay to the
order of    Practon Medical Group, Inc.                    $ 199.03

One hundred ninety-nine and 03/100 ——————————— Dollars

College National Bank
741 Main Street
Woodland Hills, XY  12345

Memo _____        Jeffrey Brown                    NP

⑆3222717791⑆0164 ⑈750 4003778⑈
```

Figure 17-1

Figure 17-1 Continued

STATEMENT

PRACTON MEDICAL GROUP, INC.
4567 Broad Avenue
Woodland Hills, XY 12345-4700
Tel. 013/486-9002
Fax No. 013/488-7815

Mr. Jeffrey Brown
230 Main Street
Woodland Hills, XY 12345-0001

DATE	REFERENCE	DESCRIPTION	CHARGES	CREDITS PYMNTS.	ADJ.	BALANCE	
1-9-9X		BALANCE FORWARD →				20	00
1-9-9X	99213	Level III OV	36.80			56	80
1-10-9X	(1-9-9X)	Medicare billed				56	80
3-5-9X	(1-9-9X)	Medicare pmt		29 44		27	36
4-3-9X	47600		937.74			965	10
4-5-9X	(4-3-9X)	Medicare billed				965	10
6-2-9X	(4-3-9X)	Medicare pmt		686 68		278	42
6-2-9X	(4-3-9X)	Medicare adj.			79 39	199	03

MEDICARE HAS PAID THEIR PORTION OF THIS CLAIM. THE
BALANCE IS YOUR RESPONSIBILITY. PLEASE REMIT.

RB40BC-2-96   PLEASE PAY LAST AMOUNT IN BALANCE COLUMN →

THIS IS A COPY OF YOUR ACCOUNT AS IT APPEARS ON OUR RECORDS

Figure 17-2

NOTE: A Performance Evaluation Checklist for this exercise can be found at the back of the workbook.

POST TO LEDGER CARDS

PERFORMANCE EVALUATION

TASK: Post entries to patients' ledger cards.

CONDITIONS: Use pen and five ledger cards (Figures 17-3 through 17-7).

STANDARDS: Time: _____ minutes
Accuracy: _____
(NOTE: The time element and accuracy criteria may be given by your instructor.)

DIRECTIONS: Complete the following ledger card entries.

1. Elizabeth Hooper has a balance due, but Dr. Practon said he wishes to accept the insurance check as payment in full. Post the correct entry for closing the account and complete the balance column.

2. Maria Sanchez has made several payments. Post to the balance column for each entry showing the final balance due.

3. Brett Walker paid on his account and his insurance paid, resulting in an overpayment. The patient is to receive a refund. Make the appropriate entries.

4. Edna Holgrove issued a check on her last office visit, but it was returned today by the bank marked insufficient funds (NSF). Record this, as well as the $10 bank charge on the ledger card.

5. Beth Jones is expecting her first child. Dr. Practon expects 15 percent of the obstetrical care and delivery fee paid today so that by the time the baby is delivered, the entire fee is paid. She also had a urinalysis nonautomated without microscopy done today. Use the current date. Post the correct entries in all columns for today's transactions by referring to the mock fee schedule in the appendix.

NOTE: A Performance Evaluation Checklist for this exercise can be found at the back of the workbook.

Elizabeth Hooper						
		CPT		\u200bCREDITS		CURRENT
DATE	Service Description	Code	CHARGE	Payments	Adjustments	BALANCE
6-1-9x	OV	99203	70.92			
	Penicillin inj	90782	4.77			
	Pap smear (coll)	99000	5.00			
8-15-9x	Insurance check			69.00		

Figure 17-3

Maria Sanchez

DATE	Service Description	CPT Code	CHARGE	CREDITS		CURRENT BALANCE
				Payments	Adjustments	
7-6-9x	Consultation, comp	99244	145.05			
7-20-9x	Personal ck 432			25.00		
8-15-9x	Personal ck 451			50.00		
9-18-9x	Personal ck 463			25.00		

Figure 17-4

Brett Walker

DATE	Service Description	CPT Code	CHARGE	CREDITS		CURRENT BALANCE
				Payments	Adjustments	
7-1-9x	OV	99203	70.92			
7-15-9x	Proctosigmoidoscopy with biopsy	45308	135.34			
7-20-9x	Personal ck 2005			50.00		
9-1-9x	Blue Cross payment			165.01		

Figure 17-5

Edna Holgrove

DATE	Service Description	CPT Code	CHARGE	CREDITS		CURRENT BALANCE
				Payments	Adjustments	
8-1-9x	OV intermed	99213	40.20			
	IUD insertion	58300	100.00			
8-14-9x	Personal ck 101			100.00		
current date	NSF bank retn'd ck					

Figure 17-6

Beth Jones

DATE	Service Description	CPT Code	CHARGE	CREDITS		CURRENT BALANCE
				Payments	Adjustments	

Figure 17-7

EXERCISE 17-5	**RECONCILE A BANK STATEMENT**

PERFORMANCE OBJECTIVE

TASK: Reconcile a bank statement.

CONDITIONS: Use a bank statement, pencil or pen, and bank reconciliation form (form 67).

STANDARDS: Time: _____ minutes

Accuracy: _____

(NOTE: The time element and accuracy criteria may be given by your instructor.)

DIRECTIONS: Refer to Figure 17-8, showing a bank statement. Assume you have made deposits of $3,500 and $1,800, which do not show on the state-

---

College National Bank
700 West Main Street
Woodland Hills, XY 12345

(800) 540-5060

COLLEGE NATIONAL BANK
ACCOUNT ACTIVITY

STATEMENT PERIOD: May 17, THROUGH
June 16, 199X

PRACTON MEDICAL GROUP, INC 140
4567 BROAD AVENUE
WOODLAND HILLS XY   12345

ACCOUNT
12345-6789
ACCESS# 0082

PAGE   1

ITEM COUNT   30

CHECKING	ACCOUNT 12345-6789

SUMMARY

BEGINNING STATEMENT BALANCE ON 5-12-9X .... $ 633.87

TOTAL OF   4 DEPOSITS/OTHER CREDITS 1414.75

TOTAL OF   25 CHECKS PAID.......................................   271.53
                5 WITHDRAWALS/OTHER CHARGES.................................   73.00

ENDING STATEMENT BALANCE ON   6-16-9X 1704.09

CHECKS/ WITHDRAWALS/ OTHER CHARGES

CHECKS:

NUMBER	DATE	AMOUNT		NUMBER	DATE	AMOUNT
0317	06-08	17.40		0328	06-10	29.90
1319	05-25	30.00		0329	05-26	32.05
0320	05-30	7.59		0330	06-02	2.75
0321	05-27	9.00		0331	06-02	30.79
0322	05-24	1.00		0332	06-02	11.47
0323	06-03	6.13				
0324	05-30	1.78				
0325	06-02	67.50				
0326	05-25	21.92				
0327	06-03	2.25				

TOTAL OF   25   CHECKS PAID $271.53–

WITHDRAWALS/OTHER CHARGES:

DATE	TRANSACTION DESCRIPTION	AMOUNT
06-10	SURGICAL SUPPLY PAYMENT AT ELECTRONIC BANKING	34.30
06-07	STAR FREE PRESS PAYMENT AT ELECTRONIC BANKING	2.00
06-07	MARINER'S MAIL PAYMENT AT ELECTRONIC BANKING	1.00
06-07	CELLULAR ONE PAYMENT AT ELECTRONIC BANKING	16.00
06-03	CLINT PHARMACY PAYMENT AT ELECTRONIC BANKING	19.70

DEPOSITS/ OTHER CREDITS

DEPOSITS:

DATE	TRANSACTION DESCRIPTION	AMOUNT
06-07	BRANCH DEPOSIT	250.24
06-09	BRANCH DEPOSIT	1000.00
06-15	BRANCH DEPOSIT	156.69
06-16	CHECK DEPOSIT AT BANK BY MAIL	7.82

DAILY BALANCES

DATE	BALANCE	DATE	BALANCE	DATE	BALANCE
05-24	632.87	06-02	418.02	06-09	1605.78
05-25	580.95	06-03	389.94	06-10	1573.88
05-26	548.90	06-07	623.18	06-15	1730.57
05-27	539.90	06-08	605.78	06-16	1704.09
05-30	530.53				

Figure 17-8

ment. The outstanding checks are #318 for $25, #337 for $60, #338 for $78, #340 for $15, and #341 for $18.20. The checkbook balance is $6,807.89. Using form 67, reconcile the bank statement given this additional information.

NOTE: A Performance Evaluation Checklist for this exercise can be found at the back of the workbook.

EXERCISE 17-6   SCAN A CHECK

PERFORMANCE OBJECTIVE

TASK: Scan a check and answer questions.

CONDITIONS: Use information given for the case and questions, pen or pencil, and illustration of a handwritten check (Figure 17-9).

STANDARDS: Time: _____ minutes
Accuracy: _____
(NOTE: The time element and accuracy criteria may be given by your instructor.)

DIRECTIONS: As learned after reading Chapter 17 in the textbook, a handwritten check has certain requirements that must be met to be valid. An established patient, Rita Stevens, wrote a check before leaving the office on May 21, 199X for a level III office visit, $40.20. Scan the check shown in Figure 17-9 and answer the questions.

1. What two personal identification items should be obtained from the patient before accepting a check?

    a. _____

    b. _____

2. Does the check list the complete name, address, and phone number of the patient? If not, what is missing? _____

3. Is the check dated correctly? _____

```
RITA STEVENS                                    90-7177  750          164
126 Sunset Lane                                 3222
Woodland Hills, XY   12345                      7504003778

                                                Date May 25, 199x

Pay to the
order of   Dr. Gerald Practon                              $

           Forty and 20/100                                   Dollars

College National Bank
741 Main Street
Woodland Hills, XY  12345

Memo  Level III OV              Rita Stevens                    MP

⑆322271779⑆0164 ⑈750 4003778⑈
```

Figure 17-9

4. Is the check postdated? _____

5. Is the check made out to the correct payee? _____

6. Did Mrs. Stevens make the check out for the correct amount? _____

7. Do the numerical and written amounts agree? _____

8. If not, what is the amount Dr. Practon will receive? $ _____

9. Is the check signed? _____

NOTE: A Performance Evaluation Checklist for this exercise can be found at the back of the workbook.

COMPUTER EXERCISES

Before proceeding, you may want to do more exercises and/or review the concepts you have learned. Complete the computer exercises on the software for Chapter 17.

CHAPTER 18

Bookkeeping

OBJECTIVES

After completing the exercises, the student will be able to:

1. Write meanings for chart note abbreviations.

2. Enhance spelling skills by learning new medical words.

3. Complete and post ledger cards.

4. Prepare a deposit slip and checks.

5. Prepare a daily journal.

6. Complete cash receipts.

7. Set up and replenish petty cash transactions.

8. Write checks to pay bills.

9. Complete the check register or disbursement record and enter deposits.

10. Reconcile a bank statement.

AREAS OF COMPETENCE

Administrative Procedures
- Perform basic clerical functions

Practice Finances
- Apply bookkeeping principles
- Manage accounts receivable
- Manage accounts payable

General (Transdisciplinary)

Communication Skills
- Use medical terminology appropriately

ABBREVIATION AND SPELLING REVIEW LESSON

Read the following patient's chart note and write the meanings for the abbreviations listed below the note. To decode any abbreviations you do not understand or that appear unfamiliar to you, refer to text Tables 8-1 and 9-3. Medical terms in the chart note are italicized; study them for spelling. Use your medical dictionary to look up their definitions. Your instructor may give a test for the spelling and definition of the words and abbreviations.

> Kevin T. Dusseau
>
> June 30, 199X Pt has off and on problems with eye. Dx: Acute *bacterial conjunctivitis* O.S. Treat O.D. at first sign of *symptoms*. Cold compresses O.S. ad lib. for comfort. Retn p.r.n.
>
> *Fran Practon, MD*
> Fran Practon, MD

Dx _____   ad lib. _____

O.S. _____   retn _____

O.D. _____   p.r.n. _____

REVIEW QUESTIONS

Review the objectives, glossary, and chapter information before completing the following review questions.

1. Match the terms in the left column with the definitions in the right column by writing the letters in the blanks.

debit	_____	a. A bookkeeping entry that decreases an asset and increases a liability
post	_____	
accounts receivable	_____	b. Amounts due to a creditor for supplies, equipment, or services rendered
asset	_____	
liability	_____	c. The owner's net worth
collateral	_____	d. To transfer financial entries, debit or credit, to an account
credit	_____	
proprietorship	_____	e. Real or personal property pledged by a borrower to guarantee a loan
accounts payable	_____	
trial balance	_____	f. That which is owned, tangible, or intangible

g. A record of all open debit and credit items of individual accounts. The ledgers are in balance with the journal

h. A legal obligation to pay a definite amount at a certain time in return for goods or services

i. The total sum of money owed to the physician by patients for professional services rendered

j. A bookkeeping entry that records increases in assets and expenses and decreases in liabilities

2. On the daily record sheet, the total of what patients have paid by cash and check must equal the total _____ for that day.

3. Mrs. Landry's account shows a delinquent balance of $3, and Dr. Practon wants the account to be closed, showing an adjusted entry. How would you show this figure on the patient's ledger card and in which column?

   _____

4. Explain how to determine the new accounts receivable figure at the end of the month.

   _____
   _____
   _____
   _____
   _____

5. An amount divisible by _____ may indicate a transposed figure, and an amount divisible by _____ may indicate posting to the wrong column.

6. Name three items written on an invoice after payment has been made by check. (Refer back to Chapter 8, if you do not remember the answer.)

   a. _____
   b. _____
   c. _____

7. At the end of the month, on the disbursement (accounts payable) record, the total of the _____must agree with the _____ .

8. The _____ and _____ on hand must total the amount of the petty cash fund at all times.

PEGBOARD BOOKKEEPING EXERCISES

To gain experience in step-by-step bookkeeping procedures, Exercises 18-1 through 18-5 incorporate the same forms used in *Delmar's Medical Pegboard Procedures,* 3rd Edition (ISBN 0-8273-7548-4). Complete Chapter 18 exercises for a basic introduction of medical pegboard activities kit. If more extensive knowledge of the pegboard is desired, you may also wish to use the Medical Pegboard Procedures Kit. This kit will allow for an even better understanding of this complex aspect of financial practices.

EXERCISE
18-1
COMPLETE LEDGER CARDS

PERFORMANCE OBJECTIVE

TASK: Complete 28 ledger cards.

CONDITIONS: Use 14 sheets of ledger cards (forms 68 through 82) (total of 28 ledger cards), and typewriter or pen.

STANDARDS: Time: _____ minutes
Accuracy: _____
(NOTE: The time element and accuracy criteria may be given by your instructor.)

DIRECTIONS: Type the following information for each patient on the ledger cards (forms 68-82). Cut the cards apart and put them in alphabetical sequence. Your instructor may want you to complete Exercises 18-1 through 18-5 before handing in any part of the bookkeeping practice set. Staple the ledger cards in order before you hand them in. Each member of a family has a separate ledger card for this exercise. The last ledger card may be typed with a heading "Miscellaneous Other Income" for keeping records when receiving checks for lectures, published articles, and so forth. When payments are posted for miscellaneous items, the charges are usually posted at the same time the check is received.

Name	Address and Phone Number	Previous Balance
Miss Mary Lou Chaney	4902 Saviers Road Woodland Hills, XY 12345-0000 Tel: 013-490-8755 DOB: 7/30/30 Ins.: Medicare ID # 459-08-7655	new pt
Russell P. Smith	2336 East Manly Street Woodland Hills, XY 12345-0000 Tel: 013-786-0123 DOB: 5/6/56 Ins.: Blue Cross/Blue Shield Group # T8471811A Cert. # 58557AT	0
Miss Jody F. Swinney	4300 Saunders Road Woodland Hills, XY 12345-0000 Tel: 013-908-6605 DOB: 1/16/64 Ins: Aetna Casualty Company Policy # 7821-11	$25.00
Miss Adrienne Cane	6502 North J Street Woodland Hills, XY 12345-0000 Tel: 013-498-2110 DOB: 7/29/46 Ins: R. L. Kautz & Company Policy # 7821-1KBM	$85.00

Name	Address and Phone Number	Previous Balance
Mark B. Hanson	2560 South M Street Woodland Hills, XY 12345-0000 Tel: 013-980-2210 DOB: 6/22/49 Ins: Prudential Insurance Co. Policy # 4579	0
Robert T. Jenner	1300 Hampshire Road Woodland Hills, XY 12345-0000 Tel: 013-986-6790 DOB: 2/28/68 Ins: Guarantee Insurance Company Policy # 67021	0
Harold B. Mason	6107 Harcourt Street Woodland Hills, XY 12345-0000 Tel: 013-615-0123 DOB: 8/20/46 Ins: Allstate Insurance Company Policy # 7632111 BA	0
J. B. Haupman	15761 Dickens Street Woodland Hills, XY 12345-0000 Tel: 013-457-0561 DOB: 7/23/28 Ins: Medicare Medicare ID # 987-43-0988A	$1,466.56
Mrs. Betty K. Lawson	6400 Best Way Woodland Hills, XY 12345-0000 Tel: 013-450-9533 DOB: 1/27/69 Ins: CHAMPUS ID # 5430982	0
Miss Carol M. Wolf	2765 Honey Lane Street Woodland Hills, XY 12345-0000 Tel: 013-892-0651 DOB: 8/25/76 Ins: Blue Cross/Blue Shield Group # T8461320A Cert. # 76502 AT	0
Margaret Jenkins, RN	5692 Rose Avenue Woodland Hills, XY 12345-0000 Tel: 013-760-3211 DOB: 6/29/70 Ins: Blue Cross/ Blue Shield Group # T7693209A Cert. # 65923AT	new pt

Name	Address and Phone Number	Previous Balance
Roger T. Simpson	792 Baker Street Woodland Hills, XY 12345-0000 Tel: 013-549-0879 DOB: 11/2/52 Ins: Farmers Insurance Group Policy # 56892	$45.00
Joan Gomez	4391 Wooden Street Woodland Hills, XY 12345-000 Tel: 013-459-2399 DOB: 3/15/37 Ins. Fremont Indemnity Company Policy # 56702111	$60.00
Maria Bargioni	4892 Simpson Street Woodland Hills, XY 12345-0000 Tel: 013-549-2344 DOB: 4/5/76 Ins: Fireman's Fund Insurance Companies Policy # 568 MB 2111	$25.00
Jack J. Johnson	5490 Olive Mill Road Woodland Hills, XY 12345-0000 Tel: 013-857-9920 DOB: 5/27/59 Ins: Medicaid ID # 458962016	0
Lois A. Conrad	8920 Canton Street Woodland Hills, XY 12345-000 Tel: 013-569-2201 DOB: 5/8/55 Ins: Gates, McDonald & Company Policy # 4591 XT	$31.50
Miss Marylou Conrad c/o Lois Conrad	8920 Canton Street Woodland Hills, XY 12345-0000 Tel: 013-569-2201 DOB: 4/22/95 Ins: Gates, McDonald & Company Policy # 4591 XT	0
Hannah F. Riley	459 Fifth Avenue Woodland Hills, XY 12345-0000 Tel: 013-789-2201 DOB: 10/8/62 Ins: Hartford Insurance Group Policy # 5601221	0
Stephen B. Riley, Jr.	459 Fifth Avenue Woodland Hills, XY 12345-0000 Tel: 013-789-2201 DOB: 6/29/62 Ins: Hartford Insurance Group Policy # 5601221	new pt

Name	Address and Phone Number	Previous Balance
Rosa K. Okida	7900 Shatto Place Woodland Hills, XY 12345-0000 Tel: 013-420-1121 DOB: 11/2/58 Ins: Home Insurance Company Policy # 789-1191-21K	$201.00
Howard S. Chan	3200 Shaw Avenue Woodland Hills, XY 12345-0000 Tel: 013-660-3211 DOB: 8/3/58 Ins: Imperial Insurance Company Policy # 21019KBM	0
Rachel T. O'Brien	5598 East 17 Street Woodland Hills, XY 12345-0000 Tel: 013-566-2199 DOB: 3/19/68 Ins: North America Health Net Policy # 54901	$50.00
Martin P. Owens	430 Herndon Place Woodland Hills, XY 12345-0000 Tel: 013-542-2232 DOB: 12/3/73 Ins: John Deere Insurance Company Policy # 67401 J	$25.00
Joseph C. Smith	P.O. Box 4301 Woodland Hills, XY 12345-0000 Tel: 013-549-1124 DOB: 6/20/73 Ins: Home Insurance Company Policy # 589102K	new pt
Kathryn L. Hope	6680 Bascom Road Woodland Hills, XY 12345-0000 Tel: 013-210-9980 DOB: 8/14/60 Ins: Met Life (managed care plan) Policy # 8921	$75.00
Russell O. Smith	459 University Avenue Woodland Hills, XY 12345-0000 Tel: 013-129-1980 DOB: 2/15/65 Ins: International Insurance Company Policy # 8901	new pt
Charlotte J. Brown	769 Sky Park Circle Woodland Hills, XY 12345-0000 Tel: 013-780-2341 DOB: 9/5/66 Ins: Kemper Insurance Company Policy # 5769	$35.00

NOTE: A Performance Evaluation Checklist for this exercise can be found at the back of the workbook.

Complete the Day Sheet (General Ledger)

Columns of the day sheet may be completed as follows:

1. Date: Enter date of posting in the first column.

2. Reference: When doing pegboard bookkeeping, enter the transaction slip number for audit control. When doing bookkeeping manually, use this column for check numbers. It may be used for other items depending on the needs of the office.

3. Description: When doing bookkeeping manually, enter the procedure code numbers for professional services rendered or enter "Miscellaneous other income" for checks received from other sources.

4. Charge: List total charge for professional services rendered.

5. Credits: List payment and adjustment amounts.

6. Balance: Add previous balance to charges and subtract credit to post balance.

7. Previous balance: Obtain amount extended from patient's ledger.

8. Name: Enter last name, first name, and middle initial.

9. Numbered lines: Line numbers for posting.

10. Receipt number: Enter cash receipt and/or check number.

11. Record of deposit: Enter Bank ABA number in column 1; cash amount in column 2; check amount in column 3.

12. Business analysis summaries: Enter copayment amount in column 1; other columns may be used for various entries depending on the needs of the office.

13. Total all columns on the day sheet.

14. Balance the day sheet by posting the totals as directed on the proof of posting accounts receivable control and accounts receivable proof.

15. Verify total bank deposit against individual checks and cash received; then total the deposit section.

16. Cash control: Balance cash on hand using cash control guidelines.

EXERCISE 18-2   BOOKKEEPING—PARTS 1, 2, AND 3

PERFORMANCE OBJECTIVE FOR PART 1

TASK: Post ledger cards, prepare deposit slip and checks, prepare daily journal, and complete cash receipts.

CONDITIONS: Use ledger cards from Exercise 18-1, Practon Medical Group fee schedule (Appendix and Tables 16-6 and 16-7 in the textbook), five checks received (forms 83 and 84), one daily journal (form 85), two cash receipts (form 88), pocket call record cards (form 89), and pen.

STANDARDS: Time: _____ minutes
Accuracy: _____
(NOTE: The time element and accuracy criteria may be given by your instructor.)

DIRECTIONS:

1. Read the entire exercise before beginning.

2. Refer to Dr. Fran and Dr. Gerald Practon's fee schedule in the appendix of the workbook (Figure A-1) and, if coding E/M procedures, see Table 16-6 and 16-7 in the text. For bookkeeping exercises, Dr. Fran Practon and Dr. Gerald Practon are nonparticipating physicians in the Medicare program and elect to use a limiting charge for professional services rendered. For all other insurance types, use the mock fees.

3. Pull your ledger cards for each patient seen today, and type in the information given in the exercise.

4. It is June 28. The Practons ask you to deposit all money collected daily. Prepare a deposit slip by making a photocopy of the section of the day sheet showing the record of deposits. At the top of the photocopied deposit slip, insert the name of the bank, The First National Bank, and the checking account number 8765432. Practon Medical Group's checking account number is 12345-6789. Cut out the checks for patients who pay on their accounts, add the proper endorsement, and put them with the bank deposit.

5. Prepare a journal of daily charges, payments, and deposits. The figures needed to complete the bottom of the day sheet are:
   Totals from previous page for

Column A	Column B-1	Column B-2	Column C	Column D
$14,336.60	$8,592.41	$450.00	$1,387.56	$980.00

   Accounts receivable balance forward from June 27 *($30,526.32)* and first of month figure *($25,232.13)* should be placed under the accounts receivable proof. The cash on hand at the beginning of the day is $50. This is used to make change if necessary when patients pay in cash on their accounts and is not considered petty cash.

6. The following is the appointment schedule for June 28. Unless otherwise noted, the patients are established patients.

   JUNE 28 APPOINTMENT SCHEDULE

Mark B. Hanson	level II OV (pt pd cash today for visit)
Russell O. Smith	new pt consult, level III
Betty K. Lawson	OV level I, vit B12 inj. (pt pd $15 on account today)
Jody F. Swinney	level II OV (pt was previously new pt who belongs to a fee-for-service managed care plan. It requires a copayment of $15 per visit)
Mary Lou Chaney	new pt first visit, level IV comp hx & ex with moderate complex decision making & moderate problem), UA (in office), basic audiometric and medication ($9) (pt pd cash) from non-automated with microscopy.
Carol M. Wolf	OV Level I est pt DPT inj only
Harold B. Mason	OV Levil II est pt ECG & medication ($2.50)

7. Robert T. Jenner was seen at the College Hospital this A.M. for hospital admission H & P (comprehensive history and physical exam), low-complexity decision making & low problem, 30 min.

8. Mr. J. B. Haupman had surgery on May 1 (prostatectomy) and called today for an exam. You scheduled the patient to be seen on June 30.

9. In today's mail, Drs. Practon received a check from *Family Health* magazine for an article that was submitted and accepted for publication. Drs. Practon received a check from Colony Boys School for a lecture delivered recently. Miss Adrienne Cane sent in a payment on her account.

10. Write receipts for the patients who paid cash.

NOTE: A Performance Evaluation Checklist for this exercise can be found at the back of the workbook.

PERFORMANCE OBJECTIVE FOR PART 2

TASK: Post ledger cards, prepare deposit slips and checks, prepare daily journal, complete cash receipts, and complete petty cash transactions.

CONDITIONS: Use ledger cards from Exercise 18-1, Practon Medical Group fee schedule (Figure A-1), three checks received (form 86), one daily journal (form 87), one cash receipt (form 88), one receipt for expenditures (form 95), one office fund voucher envelope (form 96), and pen.

STANDARDS: Time: _____ minutes
Accuracy: _____
(NOTE: The time element and accuracy criteria may be given by your instructor.)

DIRECTIONS:

1. Read the entire exercise before beginning.
2. Refer to the fee schedule (Figure A-1).
3. Pull the appropriate patient ledger cards and add the information below that belongs on each of them.
4. It is June 29. Prepare your daily deposit slip and the checks to accompany it as done on the previous day.
5. Prepare your daily journal by posting all entries below. Obtain the accounts receivable figure from the June 28 day sheet.
6. The following is the appointment schedule for June 29. Unless otherwise stated, the patients are established.

JUNE 29 APPOINTMENT SCHEDULE

Margaret Jenkins	comprehen. hx & ex consultation, mod. complexity, mod. problem (level IV)
Roger T. Simpson	level IV follow-up detailed hx and exam mod. prob. & decision making (pt pd by ck on his acct)
Joan Gomez	ECG only; after reading the ECG, Dr. Practon had Joan Gomez admitted to the College Hospital. Initial hosp care 50 min
Harold B. Mason	post-op visit level II (10 min exam)
Maria Bargioni	OV (bad headaches) expanded prob hx & exam, low complexity & low problem, level III
Jack J. Johnson	OV level I (min problem) inj for tetanus (pt pd $15 Medicaid copayment)

Lois A. Conrad	Pap smear (coll) & level III 15 min exam medication ($7)
Marylou Conrad	polio vaccine & 10 min exam (level II)
Hannah F. Riley	level IV, detailed hx & exam & med complex decision making & mod prob. & insert IUD
Stephen B. Riley, Jr.	level IV comprehen. hx & ex consult mod complex decision making & mod prob. (pt pd $25 cash)
Rosa K. Okida	OV level I min problem allergy inj by RN
Howard S. Chan	OV level IV detailed hx & ex, mod complex decision making & mod problem

7. Robert T. Jenner was seen at the hospital

8. The morning mail contained a check from Prudential Insurance Company for a life insurance claim.

9. Petty cash is $100. At lunch time, you purchase one roll of one hundred 32-cent stamps. Number the petty cash voucher (receipt for expenditures) 101 and enter it on the office fund voucher envelope.

10. Write receipts for the patients who paid cash.

NOTE: A Performance Evaluation Checklist for this exercise can be found at the back of the workbook.

PERFORMANCE OBJECTIVE FOR PART 3

TASK: Post ledger cards, prepare deposit slip and checks, prepare daily journal, complete cash receipts, and complete petty cash transactions.

CONDITIONS: Use ledger cards from Exercise 18-1, Practon Medical Group fee schedule (Figure A-1), two checks received (form 91), one daily journal (form 92), one cash receipt (form 88), one receipt for expenditures (form 95), office fund voucher envelope (form 96), and pen.

STANDARDS: Time: _____ minutes
Accuracy: _____
(NOTE: The time element and accuracy criteria may be given by your instructor.)

DIRECTIONS:

1. Read the entire exercise before beginning.

2. Refer to the fee schedule (Figure A-1).

3. Pull the pertinent patient ledger cards and add the information below that should appear on them.

4. It is June 30, the last day of the month. Prepare your deposit slip and the checks to accompany it.

5. Prepare your daily journal by posting all entries below. Obtain the accounts receivable figure from the June 29 day sheet.

6. The following is the appointment schedule for June 30. Unless otherwise stated, the patients are established.

JUNE 30 APPOINTMENT SCHEDULE

J. B. Haupman	level II, 10 min OV
Rachel T. O'Brien	level II, 10 min OV (pt pd managed care plan copayment by ck)
Martin P. Owens	level II, 10 min OV diathermy
Joseph C. Smith	new pt level III, detailed hx and exam (premarital) low complex decision making & moderate prob. & esophageal intubation (pt pd by ck on account)
Kathryn L. Hope	level II, 10 min OV (pt pd managed care plan copayment of $10 cash)
Russell P. Smith	dressing change OV level II, 10 min
Stephen B. Riley, Jr.	CBC only (pt was a no show—Dr. Practon said since this was not for an office visit, but only for a blood draw that no charge should be rendered)
Charlotte J. Brown	OV expanded hx & exam, low complex decision making & low prob (level III)

7. Mr. Howard S. Chan telephoned and said he was unable to pay his bill. After the patient talked with the physician, Dr. Practon told you to cancel the bill. Show this transaction on the patient's ledger card.

8. At lunch time, you purchased a soft soap refill for the treatment room from Thrifty Drug Store. (Total cost $2.45 + .17 tax.) Number the petty cash voucher receipt for expenditures 102 and enter it on the cover of the office fund voucher envelope.

9. Dr. Practon made hospital rounds this morning and saw Joan Gomez for 15 min.

10. Robert T. Jenner was discharged

11. Write receipts for the patients who paid cash.

NOTE: A Performance Evaluation Checklist for this exercise can be found at the back of the workbook.

EXERCISE 18-3   DISBURSEMENTS

PERFORMANCE OBJECTIVE

TASK: Write checks for disbursement, enter transactions on the check register, and post deposits.

CONDITIONS: Use check register (forms 93 and 94), three sheets of checks (forms 98 through 103), office fund voucher envelope (form 96), blue or black pen, and red pen for recording deposits.

STANDARDS: Time: _____ minutes
Accuracy: _____
(NOTE: The time element and accuracy criteria may be given by your instructor.)

DIRECTIONS:

1. Read the entire exercise before beginning.
2. Prepare a check register showing the following disbursements made during the month of June. Post each check in the gross amount and the amount of check columns. Then post the check amount to the appropriate disbursement column(s). Handwrite or type a check for each disbursement. The checkbook beginning balance is $9,745.45.

6/1	Security Pacific Company 2091 Mission Street Woodland Hills, XY 12345	$1900.00	(rent)
6/3	Central Laboratories 351 Robin Avenue Woodland Hills, XY 12345	74.50	(medical supplies)
	Broadway Garage 4560 Broad Avenue Woodland Hills, XY 12345	300.00	(parking fee)
6/4	Union Oil Company P.O. Box 232 Woodland Hills, XY 12345	87.75	(diesel fuel)
6/15	Woodland Hills Tax Commission 2200 James Street Woodland Hills, XY 12345	162.00	(quarterly city tax)
	Eli Lilly and Company Lilly Corporate Center Indianapolis, IN 46285	226.00	(medications)
6/20	Woodland Hills Gas Company 50 South M Street Woodland Hills, XY 12345	87.80	(utility)
	Sargents Pharmacy 711 Wheeler Road Woodland Hills, XY 12345	38.75	(drugs)
	United Fund P.O. Box 400 New York, NY 10015	200.00	(donation)
6/25	Woodland Hills Telephone company 505 Peppermint Street Woodland Hills, XY 12345	79.60	(utility)
	Woodland Hills Electric Company 320 Banyon Avenue Woodland Hills, XY 12345	85.78	(utility)
	Rite-Way Laundry 2500 Torrance Way Woodland Hills, XY 12345	45.00	(office linens)

3. Include the following deposits on the appropriate dates, and use a red ball-point pen to enter the transactions on the checks. Deposits: 6/1 $130; 6/3 $95; 6/4 $195; 6/15 $80; 6/20 $160; and 6/25 $105.
4. Enter the deposits you prepared for June 28 and 29.
5. Bank balance column: obtain running balance by subtracting amount of check and adding any deposit on each line of the check register.

NOTE: A Performance Evaluation Checklist for this exercise can be found at the back of the workbook.

PAY BILLS AND REPLENISH PETTY CASH

PERFORMANCE OBJECTIVE

TASK: Write checks for invoices received, complete the check register, enter deposit, and replenish petty cash.

CONDITIONS: Use four invoices, check register (forms 93 and 94), five checks (forms 102 and 103), office fund voucher envelope (form 96), blue or black pen, and red pen for recording deposit.

STANDARDS: Time: _____ minutes
Accuracy: _____
(NOTE: The time element and accuracy criteria may be given by your instructor.)

DIRECTIONS:

1. Read the entire exercise before beginning.
2. Today is June 30. Enter the deposit you prepared for June 30 before beginning to pay the invoices in Figure 18-1. (Cut these invoices apart, since they would arrive separately.)

```
Central Medical Supply Company
     859 East Santa Clara Drive
    Woodland Hills, XY 12345-0012

            STATEMENT

199X
6-15   Ophthalmoscope       $350.00
                 tax          24.50
       Shipping & handling   10.00
       BALANCE DUE          $384.50
```

```
          Thrifty Drug Store
          540 West Main Street
       Woodland Hills, XY 12345-6785

              STATEMENT

199X

6-20  1 roll bandages        $6.50
      2 boxes tissues          3.00
      1 box cotton swabs       4.50
                   tax          .98
               TOTAL        $14.98
```

```
      Prudential Life Insurance
        2603 Underpass Street
     Woodland Hills, XY 12345-9822

              INVOICE

199X

6-30  Gerald Practon
      Life Insurance
      6 months premium

      PLEASE PAY  $1969.42
```

```
             ABC MOTORS
            610 Main Street
      Woodland Hills, XY 12345-2389

                INVOICE
199X

6-15   Lube and oil
       1998 Toyota          $65.00
       5 qts oil             10.00
       filter                 5.00
       TOTAL BALANCE DUE    $80.00
```

Figure 18-1

3. Write checks to pay invoices.

4. Petty cash must be balanced and replenished at the end of the month. The beginning petty cash balance was $100. The following expenses are represented by voucher, and should be entered on the office fund voucher envelope, as should the petty cash transactions performed on June 29 and June 30.

Voucher Number	Vendor	Item	Amount
103	Crown Stationers	stationery supplies	$5.70
104	U.S. Postal Service	postage due	.95
105	Thrifty Drug Store	medical supplies	10.32
106	TG & Y Store	miscellaneous (office plant)	3.40

Prepare a check for the amount necessary to replenish petty cash, and enter this transaction on the check register, disbursed under the proper columns.

5. Total all columns of the check register. Balance the check register by using proof formulas shown at the bottom of the register.

NOTE: A Performance Evaluation Checklist for this exercise can be found at the back of the workbook.

EXERCISE 18-5 — BANK RECONCILIATION

PERFORMANCE OBJECTIVE

TASK: Reconcile a bank statement.

CONDITIONS: Use one bank account reconciliation form (Form 104), checkbook stubs completed in Exercises 18-3 and 18-4, bank statement (Figure 18-2), and pencil or pen.

STANDARDS: Time: _____ minutes

Accuracy: _____

(NOTE: The time element and accuracy criteria may be given by your instructor.)

DIRECTIONS: Reconcile the bank statement using your checkbook stubs for June, the bank statement (Figure 18-2), and the bank reconciliation form 104. The checks that have not been returned by the bank are 488, 489, and 490. Notice also that the checks written on June 30 as well as the deposits made on June 28, 29, and 30, are not recorded on the bank statement.

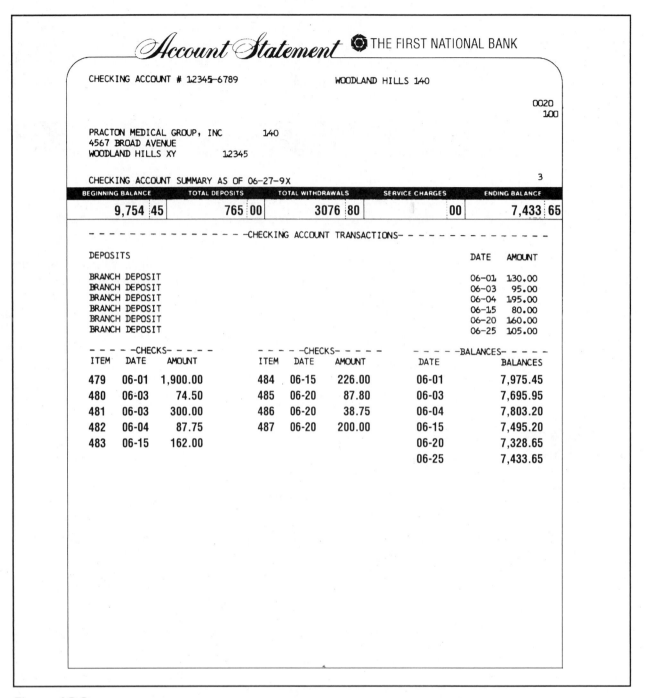

Figure 18-2

NOTE: A Performance Evaluation Checklist for this exercise can be found at the back of the workbook.

COMPUTER EXERCISES

Before proceeding, you may want to do more exercises or review the concepts you have learned. Complete the computer exercises on the software for Chapter 18.

CHAPTER 19

Payroll Procedures

OBJECTIVES

After completing the exercises, the student will be able to:

1. Write meanings for chart note abbreviations.

2. Enhance spelling skills by learning new medical words.

3. Prepare payroll figures.

4. Complete payroll register.

5. Prepare an employee earnings record.

6. Document correct information on an employee's withholding allowance certificate.

7. Abstract information to complete an employee benefit form.

AREAS OF COMPETENCE

Administrative Procedures
- Perform basic clerical functions

Practice Finances
- Process payroll

General (Transdisiplinary)

Communication Skills
- Use medical terminology appropriately

ABBREVIATION AND SPELLING REVIEW LESSON

Read the following patients' chart notes and write the meanings for the abbreviations listed below the notes. To decode any abbreviations you do not understand or that appear unfamiliar to you, refer to text Tables 8-1 and 9-3. Medical terms in the chart notes are italicized; study them for spelling. Use your medical dictionary to look up their definitions. Your instructor may give a test for the spelling and definition of the words and abbreviations.

Bernice Saxon

April 10, 199X Pt had closed reduction of *telescoping* nasal *ethmoidal fracture* with sutures and application of an *external nasal* splint. When pt ret'nd from surg, she was given 100 mg of *Demerol* q.3h. IM. Her vital signs were taken q.i.d. for the first 2 days & then b.i.d. p that. Sleeping medication was given h.s. She will be seen in the office in 4 days for follow-up.

Gerald Practon MD
Gerald Practon, MD

Pt _____   IM _____

ret'nd_____   q.i.d. _____

surg _____   b.i.d. _____

mg _____   p _____

q.3h._____   h.s. _____

Lucy Corsentino

July 7, 199X Pt, a 3-year-old, has had temp 100.1 for 2 days. Exam reveals strep throat. DX: Acute *streptococcal pharyngitis.* Plan: *Penicillin* V *potassium* 250 mg/tsp to be taken in a dose of 1 tsp q.i.d. X 10 days, *Tylenol* up to 1 gm q.4h. for pain & fever. Mother advised not to give ASA.

Fran Practon, MD
Fran Practon, MD

DX _____   1 gm _____

250 mg/tsp _____   q.4h. _____

tsp _____   ASA _____

q.i.d. X 10 days _____

REVIEW QUESTIONS

Review the objectives, glossary, and chapter information before completing the following review questions.

1. Name some responsibilities of the medical assistant when he or she is in complete charge of the payroll.

    a. _____

    b. _____

    c. _____

    d. _____

2. Explain how to obtain a tax identification number (EIN) for a physician/employer.

   _____

   _____

3. Explain how an employee obtains a tax identification number.

   _____

   _____

4. Why do you have an employee complete an employee's withholding allowance certificate, form W-4? _____

   _____

5. Under FICA, both _____ and _____ contribute at a rate specified by law.

6. Name three programs financed under Social Security (FICA), from one payroll tax, and list what they provide.
   a. 1st Program: _____
      Provides: _____
   b. 2nd Program: _____
      Provides: _____
   c. 3rd Program: _____
      Provides: _____

7. List three names used for state disability insurance deductions.
   a. _____
   b. _____
   c. _____

8. List several optional payroll deductions; also called _____.
   a. _____   d. _____
   b. _____   e. _____
   c. _____   f. _____

9. How often are federal unemployment tax deposits made and reported on form 508? _____ How often must employers report payments by using form 940? _____

10. In what publication does the Department of the Treasury, Internal Revenue Service, publish submission guidelines and requirements for quarterly reports, federal tax deposits, and unemployment tax payments?

    _____

11. The employer's quarterly federal tax return must be filed by an employer on or before _____ , _____ , and _____ on form _____ .

12. Agnes Baker terminated her employment with Dr. Jeffries on August 31. What document must be given to her by the employer and what is the time limit?

    _____

13. State the deductions from a payroll check required in your state.

    a. _____

    b. _____

    c. _____

    d. _____

14. Spell out the following payroll abbreviations.

    FICA _____

    FUTA _____

    UCD _____

15. You may have difficulty remembering whether *biweekly* means "twice a week" or "every 2 weeks," it can mean both. However, *semiweekly* is usually used for "twice a week" and in accounting *biweekly* is used for "every 2 weeks." In the following list, check the correct definitions.

    biyearly   _____ a. twice a year

                      _____ b. once a year

                      _____ c. every two years

    biweekly   _____ a. twice a week

                      _____ b. every two weeks

                      _____ c. semiweekly

    quarterly   _____ a. twice a year

                      _____ b. every four weeks

                      _____ c. four times a year

    semiannually   _____ a. every six months

                      _____ b. every two years

                      _____ c. once a year

    semimonthly   _____ a. every other month

                      _____ b. twice a month

                      _____ c. monthly

    weekly   _____ a. every weekday

                      _____ b. once a week

                      _____ c. every other week

| EXERCISE 19-1 | **PREPARE PAYROLL** |

PERFORMANCE OBJECTIVE

TASK: Prepare payroll figures.

CONDITIONS: Use payroll information for seven employees, income tax tables (Figures 19-1 through 19-8), pencil or pen, and calculator.

STANDARDS: Time: _____ minutes
Accuracy: _____
(NOTE: The time element and accuracy criteria may be given by your instructor.)

DIRECTIONS: It is May 28 and time to prepare the payroll and to record the information in the payroll register. Hourly employees are paid only once each month, on the first; full-time and part-time, salaried employees are paid semimonthly. A few full-time employees have elected to pay 2 percent of their gross pay into the College Hospital Insurance Plan. If you reside in California, Hawaii, New Jersey, New York, Puerto Rico, or Rhode Island, assume state disability insurance (SDI) is 1 percent of gross pay; in all other states, disregard this deduction. Refer to the tax tables that follow this exercise to determine the deductions (unless told to do otherwise by your instructor). Figure FICA deductions at 6.2 percent and Medicare deductions at 1.45 percent of gross earnings. Divorced persons are considered single on federal tax table and head of household on state tax tables that appear in this exercise.

Single persons with a dependent parent are considered "Unmarried Head of Household" with the state.

1. Hillary Sheehan is the physician's part-time bookkeeper. She is married and claims herself as an exemption. She earns $225 per week.

Gross Pay	FICA	Fed. Inc. Tax	State Inc. Tax	SDI	Medicare	Other	Total Deduc.	Net pay

2. Roger Young works part-time as a custodian on weekends. He is single and claims himself and a dependent mother. He is paid $6.50 per hour. He worked 18 hours this month.

Gross Pay	FICA	Fed. Inc. Tax	State Inc. Tax	SDI	Medicare	Other	Total Deduc.	Net pay

3. Kelley Jones is the office receptionist. She is single and claims herself only. She is paid $1650 per month, and she elected not to enroll in the hospital insurance plan.

Gross Pay	FICA	Fed. Inc. Tax	State Inc. Tax	SDI	Medicare	Other	Total Deduc.	Net pay

4. Maryjane Moran works part-time doing insurance. She is paid hourly and earns $12.50 per hour. She is married and claims no dependents because her husband claims her. She worked 80 hours this month.

Gross Pay	FICA	Fed. Inc. Tax	State Inc. Tax	SDI	Medicare	Other	Total Deduc.	Net pay

5. Carla O'Hare is the administrative medical assistant. She is divorced and has three children. She claims herself and her children. She is paid $1,675 a month, and she is a member of the hospital plan.

Gross Pay	FICA	Fed. Inc. Tax	State Inc. Tax	SDI	Medicare	Other	Total Deduc.	Net pay

6. Amy Seaforth is a part-time laboratory technician. She is married; her husband does not claim her, and she does not wish to claim herself either. She joined the hospital plan. She earns $145 per week plus car expense figured at $0.34 per mile. She drove 36 miles this month. Amy is a new employee hired on May 1, 199X, so it is necessary to complete an employee earning record card for her. Her address is: 29926 West Ridgeway Avenue, Woodland Hills, XY 12345; telephone 013-692-4408; Social Security number 043-19-1945; birth date 8-4-50.

Gross Pay	FICA	Fed. Inc. Tax	State Inc. Tax	SDI	Medicare	Other	Total Deduc.	Net pay

7. Lisa Adams is the clinical medical assistant. She is married and has one child, whom she claims as a deduction. She is paid $1,750 per month, and she joined the hospital plan.

Gross Pay	FICA	Fed. Inc. Tax	State Inc. Tax	SDI	Medicare	Other	Total Deduc.	Net pay

NOTE: A Performance Evaluation Checklist for this exercise can be found at the back of the workbook.

SINGLE Persons—SEMIMONTHLY Payroll Period
(For Wages Paid in 1997)

If the wages are—		And the number of withholding allowances claimed is—										
At least	But less than	0	1	2	3	4	5	6	7	8	9	10
		The amount of income tax to be withheld is—										
$0	$115	0	0	0	0	0	0	0	0	0	0	0
115	120	1	0	0	0	0	0	0	0	0	0	0
120	125	2	0	0	0	0	0	0	0	0	0	0
125	130	3	0	0	0	0	0	0	0	0	0	0
130	135	3	0	0	0	0	0	0	0	0	0	0
135	140	4	0	0	0	0	0	0	0	0	0	0
140	145	5	0	0	0	0	0	0	0	0	0	0
145	150	6	0	0	0	0	0	0	0	0	0	0
150	155	6	0	0	0	0	0	0	0	0	0	0
155	160	7	0	0	0	0	0	0	0	0	0	0
160	165	8	0	0	0	0	0	0	0	0	0	0
165	170	9	0	0	0	0	0	0	0	0	0	0
170	175	9	0	0	0	0	0	0	0	0	0	0
175	180	10	0	0	0	0	0	0	0	0	0	0
180	185	11	0	0	0	0	0	0	0	0	0	0
185	190	12	0	0	0	0	0	0	0	0	0	0
190	195	12	0	0	0	0	0	0	0	0	0	0
195	200	13	0	0	0	0	0	0	0	0	0	0
200	205	14	0	0	0	0	0	0	0	0	0	0
205	210	15	0	0	0	0	0	0	0	0	0	0
210	215	15	0	0	0	0	0	0	0	0	0	0
215	220	16	0	0	0	0	0	0	0	0	0	0
220	225	17	0	0	0	0	0	0	0	0	0	0
225	230	18	1	0	0	0	0	0	0	0	0	0
230	235	18	2	0	0	0	0	0	0	0	0	0
235	240	19	3	0	0	0	0	0	0	0	0	0
240	245	20	3	0	0	0	0	0	0	0	0	0
245	250	21	4	0	0	0	0	0	0	0	0	0
250	260	22	5	0	0	0	0	0	0	0	0	0
260	270	23	7	0	0	0	0	0	0	0	0	0
270	280	25	8	0	0	0	0	0	0	0	0	0
280	290	26	10	0	0	0	0	0	0	0	0	0
290	300	28	11	0	0	0	0	0	0	0	0	0
300	310	29	13	0	0	0	0	0	0	0	0	0
310	320	31	14	0	0	0	0	0	0	0	0	0
320	330	32	16	0	0	0	0	0	0	0	0	0
330	340	34	17	1	0	0	0	0	0	0	0	0
340	350	35	19	2	0	0	0	0	0	0	0	0
350	360	37	20	4	0	0	0	0	0	0	0	0
360	370	38	22	5	0	0	0	0	0	0	0	0
370	380	40	23	7	0	0	0	0	0	0	0	0
380	390	41	25	8	0	0	0	0	0	0	0	0
390	400	43	26	10	0	0	0	0	0	0	0	0
400	410	44	28	11	0	0	0	0	0	0	0	0
410	420	46	29	13	0	0	0	0	0	0	0	0
420	430	47	31	14	0	0	0	0	0	0	0	0
430	440	49	32	16	0	0	0	0	0	0	0	0
440	450	50	34	17	1	0	0	0	0	0	0	0
450	460	52	35	19	2	0	0	0	0	0	0	0
460	470	53	37	20	4	0	0	0	0	0	0	0
470	480	55	38	22	5	0	0	0	0	0	0	0
480	490	56	40	23	7	0	0	0	0	0	0	0
490	500	58	41	25	8	0	0	0	0	0	0	0
500	520	60	43	27	10	0	0	0	0	0	0	0
520	540	63	46	30	13	0	0	0	0	0	0	0
540	560	66	49	33	16	0	0	0	0	0	0	0
560	580	69	52	36	19	3	0	0	0	0	0	0
580	600	72	55	39	22	6	0	0	0	0	0	0
600	620	75	58	42	25	9	0	0	0	0	0	0
620	640	78	61	45	28	12	0	0	0	0	0	0
640	660	81	64	48	31	15	0	0	0	0	0	0
660	680	84	67	51	34	18	1	0	0	0	0	0
680	700	87	70	54	37	21	4	0	0	0	0	0
700	720	90	73	57	40	24	7	0	0	0	0	0
720	740	93	76	60	43	27	10	0	0	0	0	0
740	760	96	79	63	46	30	13	0	0	0	0	0
760	780	99	82	66	49	33	16	0	0	0	0	0
780	800	102	85	69	52	36	19	3	0	0	0	0
800	820	105	88	72	55	39	22	6	0	0	0	0
820	840	108	91	75	58	42	25	9	0	0	0	0

Figure 19-1

MARRIED Persons—SEMIMONTHLY Payroll Period

(For Wages Paid in 1997)

If the wages are—		And the number of withholding allowances claimed is—										
At least	But less than	0	1	2	3	4	5	6	7	8	9	10
		The amount of income tax to be withheld is—										
$0	$270	0	0	0	0	0	0	0	0	0	0	0
270	280	1	0	0	0	0	0	0	0	0	0	0
280	290	2	0	0	0	0	0	0	0	0	0	0
290	300	4	0	0	0	0	0	0	0	0	0	0
300	310	5	0	0	0	0	0	0	0	0	0	0
310	320	7	0	0	0	0	0	0	0	0	0	0
320	330	8	0	0	0	0	0	0	0	0	0	0
330	340	10	0	0	0	0	0	0	0	0	0	0
340	350	11	0	0	0	0	0	0	0	0	0	0
350	360	13	0	0	0	0	0	0	0	0	0	0
360	370	14	0	0	0	0	0	0	0	0	0	0
370	380	16	0	0	0	0	0	0	0	0	0	0
380	390	17	1	0	0	0	0	0	0	0	0	0
390	400	19	2	0	0	0	0	0	0	0	0	0
400	410	20	4	0	0	0	0	0	0	0	0	0
410	420	22	5	0	0	0	0	0	0	0	0	0
420	430	23	7	0	0	0	0	0	0	0	0	0
430	440	25	8	0	0	0	0	0	0	0	0	0
440	450	26	10	0	0	0	0	0	0	0	0	0
450	460	28	11	0	0	0	0	0	0	0	0	0
460	470	29	13	0	0	0	0	0	0	0	0	0
470	480	31	14	0	0	0	0	0	0	0	0	0
480	490	32	16	0	0	0	0	0	0	0	0	0
490	500	34	17	1	0	0	0	0	0	0	0	0
500	520	36	20	3	0	0	0	0	0	0	0	0
520	540	39	23	6	0	0	0	0	0	0	0	0
540	560	42	26	9	0	0	0	0	0	0	0	0
560	580	45	29	12	0	0	0	0	0	0	0	0
580	600	48	32	15	0	0	0	0	0	0	0	0
600	620	51	35	18	2	0	0	0	0	0	0	0
620	640	54	38	21	5	0	0	0	0	0	0	0
640	660	57	41	24	8	0	0	0	0	0	0	0
660	680	60	44	27	11	0	0	0	0	0	0	0
680	700	63	47	30	14	0	0	0	0	0	0	0
700	720	66	50	33	17	0	0	0	0	0	0	0
720	740	69	53	36	20	3	0	0	0	0	0	0
740	760	72	56	39	23	6	0	0	0	0	0	0
760	780	75	59	42	26	9	0	0	0	0	0	0
780	800	78	62	45	29	12	0	0	0	0	0	0
800	820	81	65	48	32	15	0	0	0	0	0	0
820	840	84	68	51	35	18	1	0	0	0	0	0
840	860	87	71	54	38	21	4	0	0	0	0	0
860	880	90	74	57	41	24	7	0	0	0	0	0
880	900	93	77	60	44	27	10	0	0	0	0	0
900	920	96	80	63	47	30	13	0	0	0	0	0
920	940	99	83	66	50	33	16	0	0	0	0	0
940	960	102	86	69	53	36	19	3	0	0	0	0
960	980	105	89	72	56	39	22	6	0	0	0	0
980	1,000	108	92	75	59	42	25	9	0	0	0	0
1,000	1,020	111	95	78	62	45	28	12	0	0	0	0
1,020	1,040	114	98	81	65	48	31	15	0	0	0	0
1,040	1,060	117	101	84	68	51	34	18	1	0	0	0
1,060	1,080	120	104	87	71	54	37	21	4	0	0	0
1,080	1,100	123	107	90	74	57	40	24	7	0	0	0
1,100	1,120	126	110	93	77	60	43	27	10	0	0	0
1,120	1,140	129	113	96	80	63	46	30	13	0	0	0
1,140	1,160	132	116	99	83	66	49	33	16	0	0	0
1,160	1,180	135	119	102	86	69	52	36	19	3	0	0
1,180	1,200	138	122	105	89	72	55	39	22	6	0	0
1,200	1,220	141	125	108	92	75	58	42	25	9	0	0
1,220	1,240	144	128	111	95	78	61	45	28	12	0	0
1,240	1,260	147	131	114	98	81	64	48	31	15	0	0
1,260	1,280	150	134	117	101	84	67	51	34	18	1	0
1,280	1,300	153	137	120	104	87	70	54	37	21	4	0
1,300	1,320	156	140	123	107	90	73	57	40	24	7	0
1,320	1,340	159	143	126	110	93	76	60	43	27	10	0
1,340	1,360	162	146	129	113	96	79	63	46	30	13	0
1,360	1,380	165	149	132	116	99	82	66	49	33	16	0
1,380	1,400	168	152	135	119	102	85	69	52	36	19	3
1,400	1,420	171	155	138	122	105	88	72	55	39	22	6

Figure 19-2

SINGLE Persons—MONTHLY Payroll Period

(For Wages Paid in 1997)

If the wages are—		And the number of withholding allowances claimed is—										
At least	But less than	0	1	2	3	4	5	6	7	8	9	10
		The amount of income tax to be withheld is—										
$0	$220	0	0	0	0	0	0	0	0	0	0	0
220	230	1	0	0	0	0	0	0	0	0	0	0
230	240	2	0	0	0	0	0	0	0	0	0	0
240	250	4	0	0	0	0	0	0	0	0	0	0
250	260	5	0	0	0	0	0	0	0	0	0	0
260	270	7	0	0	0	0	0	0	0	0	0	0
270	280	8	0	0	0	0	0	0	0	0	0	0
280	290	10	0	0	0	0	0	0	0	0	0	0
290	300	11	0	0	0	0	0	0	0	0	0	0
300	320	13	0	0	0	0	0	0	0	0	0	0
320	340	16	0	0	0	0	0	0	0	0	0	0
340	360	19	0	0	0	0	0	0	0	0	0	0
360	380	22	0	0	0	0	0	0	0	0	0	0
380	400	25	0	0	0	0	0	0	0	0	0	0
400	420	28	0	0	0	0	0	0	0	0	0	0
420	440	31	0	0	0	0	0	0	0	0	0	0
440	460	34	1	0	0	0	0	0	0	0	0	0
460	480	37	4	0	0	0	0	0	0	0	0	0
480	500	40	7	0	0	0	0	0	0	0	0	0
500	520	43	10	0	0	0	0	0	0	0	0	0
520	540	46	13	0	0	0	0	0	0	0	0	0
540	560	49	16	0	0	0	0	0	0	0	0	0
560	580	52	19	0	0	0	0	0	0	0	0	0
580	600	55	22	0	0	0	0	0	0	0	0	0
600	640	60	27	0	0	0	0	0	0	0	0	0
640	680	66	33	0	0	0	0	0	0	0	0	0
680	720	72	39	6	0	0	0	0	0	0	0	0
720	760	78	45	12	0	0	0	0	0	0	0	0
760	800	84	51	18	0	0	0	0	0	0	0	0
800	840	90	57	24	0	0	0	0	0	0	0	0
840	880	96	63	30	0	0	0	0	0	0	0	0
880	920	102	69	36	3	0	0	0	0	0	0	0
920	960	108	75	42	9	0	0	0	0	0	0	0
960	1,000	114	81	48	15	0	0	0	0	0	0	0
1,000	1,040	120	87	54	21	0	0	0	0	0	0	0
1,040	1,080	126	93	60	27	0	0	0	0	0	0	0
1,080	1,120	132	99	66	33	0	0	0	0	0	0	0
1,120	1,160	138	105	72	39	5	0	0	0	0	0	0
1,160	1,200	144	111	78	45	11	0	0	0	0	0	0
1,200	1,240	150	117	84	51	17	0	0	0	0	0	0
1,240	1,280	156	123	90	57	23	0	0	0	0	0	0
1,280	1,320	162	129	96	63	29	0	0	0	0	0	0
1,320	1,360	168	135	102	69	35	2	0	0	0	0	0
1,360	1,400	174	141	108	75	41	8	0	0	0	0	0
1,400	1,440	180	147	114	81	47	14	0	0	0	0	0
1,440	1,480	186	153	120	87	53	20	0	0	0	0	0
1,480	1,520	192	159	126	93	59	26	0	0	0	0	0
1,520	1,560	198	165	132	99	65	32	0	0	0	0	0
1,560	1,600	204	171	138	105	71	38	5	0	0	0	0
1,600	1,640	210	177	144	111	77	44	11	0	0	0	0
1,640	1,680	216	183	150	117	83	50	17	0	0	0	0
1,680	1,720	222	189	156	123	89	56	23	0	0	0	0
1,720	1,760	228	195	162	129	95	62	29	0	0	0	0
1,760	1,800	234	201	168	135	101	68	35	2	0	0	0
1,800	1,840	240	207	174	141	107	74	41	8	0	0	0
1,840	1,880	246	213	180	147	113	80	47	14	0	0	0
1,880	1,920	252	219	186	153	119	86	53	20	0	0	0
1,920	1,960	258	225	192	159	125	92	59	26	0	0	0
1,960	2,000	264	231	198	165	131	98	65	32	0	0	0
2,000	2,040	270	237	204	171	137	104	71	38	5	0	0
2,040	2,080	276	243	210	177	143	110	77	44	11	0	0
2,080	2,120	282	249	216	183	149	116	83	50	17	0	0
2,120	2,160	288	255	222	189	155	122	89	56	23	0	0
2,160	2,200	294	261	228	195	161	128	95	62	29	0	0
2,200	2,240	305	267	234	201	167	134	101	68	35	2	0
2,240	2,280	316	273	240	207	173	140	107	74	41	8	0
2,280	2,320	328	279	246	213	179	146	113	80	47	14	0
2,320	2,360	339	285	252	219	185	152	119	86	53	20	0

Figure 19-3

MARRIED Persons—MONTHLY Payroll Period

(For Wages Paid in 1997)

If the wages are—		And the number of withholding allowances claimed is—										
At least	But less than	0	1	2	3	4	5	6	7	8	9	10
		The amount of income tax to be withheld is—										
$0	$540	0	0	0	0	0	0	0	0	0	0	0
540	560	2	0	0	0	0	0	0	0	0	0	0
560	580	5	0	0	0	0	0	0	0	0	0	0
580	600	8	0	0	0	0	0	0	0	0	0	0
600	640	12	0	0	0	0	0	0	0	0	0	0
640	680	18	0	0	0	0	0	0	0	0	0	0
680	720	24	0	0	0	0	0	0	0	0	0	0
720	760	30	0	0	0	0	0	0	0	0	0	0
760	800	36	3	0	0	0	0	0	0	0	0	0
800	840	42	9	0	0	0	0	0	0	0	0	0
840	880	48	15	0	0	0	0	0	0	0	0	0
880	920	54	21	0	0	0	0	0	0	0	0	0
920	960	60	27	0	0	0	0	0	0	0	0	0
960	1,000	66	33	0	0	0	0	0	0	0	0	0
1,000	1,040	72	39	6	0	0	0	0	0	0	0	0
1,040	1,080	78	45	12	0	0	0	0	0	0	0	0
1,080	1,120	84	51	18	0	0	0	0	0	0	0	0
1,120	1,160	90	57	24	0	0	0	0	0	0	0	0
1,160	1,200	96	63	30	0	0	0	0	0	0	0	0
1,200	1,240	102	69	36	3	0	0	0	0	0	0	0
1,240	1,280	108	75	42	9	0	0	0	0	0	0	0
1,280	1,320	114	81	48	15	0	0	0	0	0	0	0
1,320	1,360	120	87	54	21	0	0	0	0	0	0	0
1,360	1,400	126	93	60	27	0	0	0	0	0	0	0
1,400	1,440	132	99	66	33	0	0	0	0	0	0	0
1,440	1,480	138	105	72	39	6	0	0	0	0	0	0
1,480	1,520	144	111	78	45	12	0	0	0	0	0	0
1,520	1,560	150	117	84	51	18	0	0	0	0	0	0
1,560	1,600	156	123	90	57	24	0	0	0	0	0	0
1,600	1,640	162	129	96	63	30	0	0	0	0	0	0
1,640	1,680	168	135	102	69	36	3	0	0	0	0	0
1,680	1,720	174	141	108	75	42	9	0	0	0	0	0
1,720	1,760	180	147	114	81	48	15	0	0	0	0	0
1,760	1,800	186	153	120	87	54	21	0	0	0	0	0
1,800	1,840	192	159	126	93	60	27	0	0	0	0	0
1,840	1,880	198	165	132	99	66	33	0	0	0	0	0
1,880	1,920	204	171	138	105	72	39	6	0	0	0	0
1,920	1,960	210	177	144	111	78	45	12	0	0	0	0
1,960	2,000	216	183	150	117	84	51	18	0	0	0	0
2,000	2,040	222	189	156	123	90	57	24	0	0	0	0
2,040	2,080	228	195	162	129	96	63	30	0	0	0	0
2,080	2,120	234	201	168	135	102	69	36	3	0	0	0
2,120	2,160	240	207	174	141	108	75	42	9	0	0	0
2,160	2,200	246	213	180	147	114	81	48	15	0	0	0
2,200	2,240	252	219	186	153	120	87	54	21	0	0	0
2,240	2,280	258	225	192	159	126	93	60	27	0	0	0
2,280	2,320	264	231	198	165	132	99	66	33	0	0	0
2,320	2,360	270	237	204	171	138	105	72	39	5	0	0
2,360	2,400	276	243	210	177	144	111	78	45	11	0	0
2,400	2,440	282	249	216	183	150	117	84	51	17	0	0
2,440	2,480	288	255	222	189	156	123	90	57	23	0	0
2,480	2,520	294	261	228	195	162	129	96	63	29	0	0
2,520	2,560	300	267	234	201	168	135	102	69	35	2	0
2,560	2,600	306	273	240	207	174	141	108	75	41	8	0
2,600	2,640	312	279	246	213	180	147	114	81	47	14	0
2,640	2,680	318	285	252	219	186	153	120	87	53	20	0
2,680	2,720	324	291	258	225	192	159	126	93	59	26	0
2,720	2,760	330	297	264	231	198	165	132	99	65	32	0
2,760	2,800	336	303	270	237	204	171	138	105	71	38	5
2,800	2,840	342	309	276	243	210	177	144	111	77	44	11
2,840	2,880	348	315	282	249	216	183	150	117	83	50	17
2,880	2,920	354	321	288	255	222	189	156	123	89	56	23
2,920	2,960	360	327	294	261	228	195	162	129	95	62	29
2,960	3,000	366	333	300	267	234	201	168	135	101	68	35
3,000	3,040	372	339	306	273	240	207	174	141	107	74	41
3,040	3,080	378	345	312	279	246	213	180	147	113	80	47

Figure 19-4

STATE

SINGLE PERSONS, DUAL INCOME MARRIED
OR MARRIED WITH MULTIPLE EMPLOYERS----SEMI-MONTHLY PAYROLL PERIOD

(FOR WAGES PAID IN 1997)

IF WAGES ARE...   AND THE NUMBER OF WITHHOLDING ALLOWANCES CLAIMED IS...

AT LEAST	BUT LESS THAN	0	1	2	3	4	5	6	7	8	9	10 OR MORE
		...THE AMOUNT OF INCOME TAX TO BE WITHHELD SHALL BE...										
$1	$300	0.00										
300	320	2.05										
320	340	2.44										
340	360	2.84	0.05									
360	380	3.24	0.45									
380	400	3.64	0.85									
400	420	4.04	1.25									
420	440	4.44	1.65									
440	460	4.84	2.05									
460	480	5.24	2.45									
480	500	5.64	2.85	0.06									
500	540	6.24	3.45	0.66									
540	580	7.04	4.25	1.46									
580	620	8.04	5.25	2.46									
620	660	9.64	6.85	4.06	1.26								
660	700	11.24	8.45	5.66	2.86	0.07							
700	740	12.84	10.05	7.26	4.46	1.67							
740	780	14.44	11.65	8.86	6.06	3.27	0.48						
780	820	16.04	13.25	10.46	7.66	4.87	2.08						
820	860	17.64	14.85	12.06	9.26	6.47	3.68	0.89					
860	900	19.44	16.65	13.86	11.07	8.28	5.48	2.69					
900	940	21.84	19.05	16.26	13.47	10.68	7.88	5.09	2.30				
940	980	24.24	21.45	18.66	15.87	13.08	10.28	7.49	4.70	1.91			
980	1020	26.64	23.85	21.06	18.27	15.48	12.68	9.89	7.10	4.31	1.52		
1020	1060	29.04	26.25	23.46	20.67	17.88	15.08	12.29	9.50	6.71	3.92	1.13
1060	1100	31.44	28.65	25.86	23.07	20.28	17.48	14.69	11.90	9.11	6.32	3.53
1100	1140	33.84	31.05	28.26	25.47	22.68	19.88	17.09	14.30	11.51	8.72	5.93
1140	1180	36.24	33.45	30.66	27.87	25.08	22.28	19.49	16.70	13.91	11.12	8.33
1180	1220	39.30	36.51	33.71	30.92	28.13	25.34	22.55	19.76	16.96	14.17	11.38
1220	1260	42.50	39.71	36.91	34.12	31.33	28.54	25.75	22.96	20.16	17.37	14.58
1260	1300	45.70	42.91	40.11	37.32	34.53	31.74	28.95	26.16	23.36	20.57	17.78
1300	1340	48.90	46.11	43.31	40.52	37.73	34.94	32.15	29.36	26.56	23.77	20.98
1340	1380	52.10	49.31	46.51	43.72	40.93	38.14	35.35	32.56	29.76	26.97	24.18
1380	1420	55.30	52.51	49.71	46.92	44.13	41.34	38.55	35.76	32.96	30.17	27.38
1420	1460	58.50	55.71	52.91	50.12	47.33	44.54	41.75	38.96	36.16	33.37	30.58
1460	1500	62.13	59.34	56.55	53.76	50.97	48.17	45.38	42.59	39.80	37.01	34.22
1500	1540	65.85	63.06	60.27	57.48	54.69	51.89	49.10	46.31	43.52	40.73	37.94
1540	1580	69.57	66.78	63.99	61.20	58.41	55.61	52.82	50.03	47.24	44.45	41.66
1580	1620	73.29	70.50	67.71	64.92	62.13	59.33	56.54	53.75	50.96	48.17	45.38
1620	1660	77.01	74.22	71.43	68.64	65.85	63.05	60.26	57.47	54.68	51.89	49.10
1660	1700	80.73	77.94	75.15	72.36	69.57	66.77	63.98	61.19	58.40	55.61	52.82
1700	1750	84.92	82.13	79.33	76.54	73.75	70.96	68.17	65.38	62.58	59.79	57.00
1750	1800	89.57	86.78	83.98	81.19	78.40	75.61	72.82	70.03	67.23	64.44	61.65
1800	1850	94.22	91.43	88.63	85.84	83.05	80.26	77.47	74.68	71.88	69.09	66.30
1850	1900	98.87	96.08	93.28	90.49	87.70	84.91	82.12	79.33	76.53	73.74	70.95
1900	1950	103.52	100.73	97.93	95.14	92.35	89.56	86.77	83.98	81.18	78.39	75.60
1950	2000	108.17	105.38	102.58	99.79	97.00	94.21	91.42	88.63	85.83	83.04	80.25
2000	2100	115.14	112.35	109.56	106.77	103.98	101.18	98.39	95.60	92.81	90.02	87.23
2100	2200	124.44	121.65	118.86	116.07	113.28	110.48	107.69	104.90	102.11	99.32	96.53
2200	2300	133.74	130.95	128.16	125.37	122.58	119.78	116.99	114.20	111.41	108.62	105.83
2300	2400	143.04	140.25	137.46	134.67	131.88	129.08	126.29	123.50	120.71	117.92	115.13

2400 and over   (Table Amount PLUS 9.3 Percent of the Amount Over 2400)

Figure 19-5

STATE

MARRIED PERSONS----SEMI-MONTHLY PAYROLL PERIOD

(FOR WAGES PAID IN 1997)

IF WAGES ARE... AND THE NUMBER OF WITHHOLDING ALLOWANCES CLAIMED IS...

AT LEAST	BUT LESS THAN	0	1	2	3	4	5	6	7	8	9	10 OR MORE
					...THE AMOUNT OF INCOME TAX TO BE WITHHELD SHALL BE...							
$1	$300	0.00										
300	320	2.05										
320	340	2.25										
340	360	2.45										
360	380	2.65										
380	400	2.85	0.06									
400	420	3.05	0.26									
420	440	3.25	0.46									
440	460	3.45	0.66									
460	480	3.65	0.86									
480	500	3.85	1.06									
500	520	4.05	1.26									
520	540	4.41	1.62									
540	560	4.81	2.02									
560	580	5.21	2.42									
580	600	5.61	2.82									
600	620	6.01	3.22									
620	640	6.41	3.62									
640	660	6.81	4.02									
660	680	7.21	4.42									
680	700	7.61	4.82									
700	720	8.01	5.22	0.33								
720	740	8.41	5.62	0.73								
740	760	8.81	6.02	1.13								
760	780	9.21	6.42	1.53								
780	800	9.61	6.82	1.93								
800	820	10.01	7.22	2.33								
820	840	10.41	7.62	2.73								
840	860	10.81	8.02	3.13	0.33							
860	880	11.21	8.42	3.53	0.73							
880	900	11.61	8.82	3.93	1.13							
900	920	12.01	9.22	4.33	1.53							
920	940	12.41	9.62	4.73	1.93							
940	960	12.81	10.02	5.13	2.33							
960	980	13.21	10.42	5.53	2.73							
980	1000	13.61	10.82	5.93	3.13	0.34						
1000	1040	14.21	11.42	6.53	3.73	0.94						
1040	1090	15.01	12.22	7.33	4.53	1.74						
1080	1120	16.33	13.54	8.13	5.33	2.54						
1120	1160	17.93	15.14	8.93	6.13	3.34	0.55					
1160	1200	19.53	16.74	9.73	6.94	4.15	1.36					
1200	1240	21.13	18.34	11.33	8.54	5.75	2.96	0.17				
1240	1280	22.73	19.94	12.93	10.14	7.35	4.56	1.77				
1280	1320	24.33	21.54	14.53	11.74	8.95	6.16	3.37	0.57			
1320	1360	25.93	23.14	16.13	13.34	10.55	7.76	4.97	2.18			
1360	1400	27.53	24.74	17.73	14.94	12.15	9.36	6.57	3.78	0.98		
1400	1440	29.13	26.34	19.33	16.54	13.75	10.96	8.17	5.38	2.58		
1440	1480	30.73	27.94	20.93	18.14	15.35	12.56	9.77	6.98	4.18	1.39	
1480	1520	32.33	29.54	22.53	19.74	16.95	14.16	11.37	8.58	5.78	2.99	0.20
1520	1560	33.93	31.14	24.13	21.34	18.55	15.76	12.97	10.18	7.38	4.59	1.80
1560	1600	35.53	32.74	25.73	22.94	20.15	17.36	14.57	11.78	8.98	6.19	3.40

--- CONTINUED NEXT PAGE ---

Figure 19-6

STATE

SINGLE PERSONS, DUAL INCOME MARRIED
OR MARRIED WITH MULTIPLE EMPLOYERS----MONTHLY PAYROLL PERIOD

(FOR WAGES PAID IN 1997)

IF WAGES ARE... AND THE NUMBER OF WITHHOLDING ALLOWANCES CLAIMED IS...

AT LEAST	BUT LESS THAN	0	1	2	3	4	5	6	7	8	9	10 OR MORE
		...THE AMOUNT OF INCOME TAX TO BE WITHHELD SHALL BE...										
$1	$600	0.00										
600	640	4.10										
640	680	4.90										
680	720	5.70	0.11									
720	760	6.50	0.92									
760	800	7.30	1.72									
800	840	8.10	2.52									
840	880	8.90	3.32									
880	920	9.70	4.12									
920	960	10.50	4.92									
960	1000	11.30	5.72	0.13								
1000	1050	12.20	6.62	1.03								
1050	1100	13.20	7.62	2.03								
1100	1150	14.20	8.62	3.03								
1150	1200	15.20	9.62	4.03								
1200	1250	17.11	11.52	5.94	0.36							
1250	1300	19.11	13.52	7.94	2.36							
1300	1350	21.11	15.52	9.94	4.36							
1350	1400	23.11	17.52	11.94	6.36	0.77						
1400	1450	25.11	19.52	13.94	8.36	2.77						
1450	1500	27.11	21.52	15.94	10.36	4.77						
1500	1600	30.11	24.52	18.94	13.36	7.77	2.19					
1600	1700	34.11	28.52	22.94	17.36	11.77	6.19	0.61				
1700	1800	38.30	32.71	27.13	21.55	15.96	10.38	4.80				
1800	1900	44.30	38.71	33.13	27.55	21.96	16.38	10.80	5.21			
1900	2000	50.30	44.71	39.13	33.55	27.96	22.38	16.80	11.21	5.63	0.05	
2000	2100	56.30	50.71	45.13	39.55	33.96	28.38	22.80	17.21	11.63	6.05	0.46
2100	2200	62.30	56.71	51.13	45.55	39.96	34.38	28.80	23.21	17.63	12.05	6.46
2200	2300	68.30	62.71	57.13	51.55	45.96	40.38	34.80	29.21	23.63	18.05	12.46
2300	2400	74.60	69.02	63.44	57.85	52.27	46.69	41.10	35.52	29.94	24.35	18.77
2400	2500	82.60	77.02	71.44	65.85	60.27	54.69	49.10	43.52	37.94	32.35	26.77
2500	2600	90.60	85.02	79.44	73.85	68.27	62.69	57.10	51.52	45.94	40.35	34.77
2600	2700	98.60	93.02	87.44	81.85	76.27	70.69	65.10	59.52	53.94	48.35	42.77
2700	2800	106.60	101.02	95.44	89.85	84.27	78.69	73.10	67.52	61.94	56.35	50.77
2800	2900	114.60	109.02	103.44	97.85	92.27	86.69	81.10	75.52	69.94	64.35	58.77
2900	3000	123.32	117.74	112.16	106.57	100.99	95.41	89.82	84.24	78.66	73.07	67.49
3000	3100	132.62	127.04	121.46	115.87	110.29	104.71	99.12	93.54	87.96	82.37	76.79
3100	3200	141.92	136.34	130.76	125.17	119.59	114.01	108.42	102.84	97.26	91.67	86.09
3200	3300	151.22	145.64	140.06	134.47	128.89	123.31	117.72	112.14	106.56	100.97	95.39
3300	3400	160.52	154.94	149.36	143.77	138.19	132.61	127.02	121.44	115.86	110.27	104.69
3400	3500	169.82	164.24	158.66	153.07	147.49	141.91	136.32	130.74	125.16	119.57	113.99
3500	3600	179.12	173.54	167.96	162.37	156.79	151.21	145.62	140.04	134.46	128.87	123.29
3600	3700	188.42	182.84	177.26	171.67	166.09	160.51	154.92	149.34	143.76	138.17	132.59
3700	3800	197.72	192.14	186.56	180.97	175.39	169.81	164.22	158.64	153.06	147.47	141.89
3800	3900	207.02	201.44	195.86	190.27	184.69	179.11	173.52	167.94	162.36	156.77	151.19
3900	4000	216.32	210.74	205.16	199.57	193.99	188.41	182.82	177.24	171.66	166.07	160.49
4000	4200	230.27	224.69	219.11	213.52	207.94	202.36	196.77	191.19	185.61	180.02	174.44
4200	4400	248.87	243.29	237.71	232.12	226.54	220.96	215.37	209.79	204.21	198.62	193.04
4400	4600	267.47	261.89	256.31	250.72	245.14	239.56	233.97	228.39	222.81	217.22	211.64
4600	4800	286.07	280.49	274.91	269.32	263.74	258.16	252.57	246.99	241.41	235.82	230.24
4800	5000	304.67	299.09	293.51	287.92	282.34	276.76	271.17	265.59	260.01	254.42	248.84

5000 and over (Table Amount PLUS 9.3 Percent of the Amount Over 5000)

Figure 19-7

STATE

UNMARRIED HEAD OF HOUSEHOLD----MONTHLY PAYROLL PERIOD

(FOR WAGES PAID IN 1997)

IF WAGES ARE...   AND THE NUMBER OF WITHHOLDING ALLOWANCES CLAIMED IS...

AT LEAST	BUT LESS THAN	0	1	2	3	4	5	6	7	8	9	10 OR MORE
					...THE AMOUNT OF INCOME TAX TO BE WITHHELD SHALL BE...							
$1	1200	0.00										
1200	1220	7.89	2.31									
1220	1240	8.09	2.51									
1240	1260	8.40	2.81									
1260	1280	8.80	3.21									
1280	1300	9.20	3.61									
1300	1320	9.60	4.01									
1320	1340	10.00	4.41									
1340	1360	10.40	4.81									
1360	1380	10.80	5.21									
1380	1400	11.20	5.61	0.03								
1400	1420	11.60	6.01	0.43								
1420	1440	12.00	6.41	0.83								
1440	1460	12.40	6.81	1.23								
1460	1480	12.80	7.21	1.63								
1480	1520	13.40	7.81	2.23								
1520	1560	14.20	8.61	3.03								
1560	1600	15.00	9.41	3.83								
1600	1640	15.80	10.21	4.63								
1640	1680	16.60	11.01	5.43								
1680	1720	17.40	11.81	6.23	0.65							
1720	1760	18.20	12.61	7.03	1.45							
1760	1800	19.00	13.41	7.83	2.25							
1800	1840	19.80	14.21	8.63	3.05							
1840	1880	20.60	15.01	9.43	3.85							
1880	1920	21.40	15.81	10.23	4.65							
1920	1960	22.20	16.61	11.03	5.45							
1960	2000	23.00	17.41	11.83	6.25	0.66						
2000	2050	23.90	18.31	12.73	7.15	1.56						
2050	2100	24.90	19.31	13.73	8.15	2.56						
2100	2150	25.90	20.31	14.73	9.15	3.56						
2150	2200	26.90	21.31	15.73	10.15	4.56						
2200	2250	27.90	22.31	16.73	11.15	5.56						
2250	2300	28.90	23.31	17.73	12.15	6.56	0.98					
2300	2350	29.90	24.31	18.73	13.15	7.56	1.98					
2350	2400	31.18	25.60	20.02	14.43	8.85	3.27					
2400	2450	33.18	27.60	22.02	16.43	10.85	5.27					
2450	2500	35.18	29.60	24.02	18.43	12.85	7.27	1.68				
2500	2600	38.18	32.60	27.02	21.43	15.85	10.27	4.68				
2600	2700	42.18	36.60	31.02	25.43	19.85	14.27	8.68	3.10			
2700	2800	46.18	40.60	35.02	29.43	23.85	18.27	12.68	7.10	1.52		
2800	2900	50.18	44.60	39.02	33.43	27.85	22.27	16.68	11.10	5.52		
2900	3000	54.80	49.22	43.63	38.05	32.47	26.88	21.30	15.72	10.13	4.55	
3000	3100	60.80	55.22	49.63	44.05	38.47	32.88	27.30	21.72	16.13	10.55	4.97
3100	3200	66.80	61.22	55.63	50.05	44.47	38.88	33.30	27.72	22.13	16.55	10.97
3200	3300	72.80	67.22	61.63	56.05	50.47	44.88	39.30	33.72	28.13	22.55	16.97
3300	3400	78.80	73.22	67.63	62.05	56.47	50.88	45.30	39.72	34.13	28.55	22.97
3400	3600	87.80	82.22	76.63	71.05	65.47	59.88	54.30	48.72	43.13	37.55	31.97
3600	3800	103.51	97.92	92.34	86.76	81.17	75.59	70.01	64.42	58.84	53 26	47.67
3800	4000	119.51	113.92	108.34	102.76	97.17	91.59	86.01	80.42	74.84	69.26	63.67
4000	4200	135.87	130.29	124.71	119.12	113.54	107.96	102.37	96.79	91.21	85.62	80.04

4200 and over   (Table Amount PLUS 9.3 Percent of the Amount Over 4200)

Figure 19-8

| EXERCISE 19-2 | **COMPLETE A PAYROLL REGISTER** |

PERFORMANCE OBJECTIVE

TASK: Complete a payroll register.

CONDITIONS: Use the payroll information obtained for seven employees from Exercise 19-1 and one payroll register (form 105); and typewriter, pen, or pencil.

STANDARDS: Time: _____ hours _____ minutes
Accuracy: _____
(NOTE: The time element and accuracy criteria may be given by your instructor.)

DIRECTIONS: After you have determined the net pay for each employee in Exercise 19-1, alphabetize the names and record the information in the payroll register (form 105).

NOTE: A Performance Evaluation Checklist for this exercise can be found at the back of the workbook.

| EXERCISE 19-3 | **COMPLETE AN EMPLOYEE EARNING RECORD** |

PERFORMANCE OBJECTIVE

TASK: Complete an employee earning record card.

CONDITIONS: Use the information from Exercise 19-1 and one employee earnings record (form 106); and typewriter, pen, or pencil.

STANDARDS: Time: _____ hours _____ minutes
Accuracy: _____
(NOTE: The time element and accuracy criteria may be given by your instructor.)

DIRECTIONS: Complete an employee earning record card (form 106) for Amy Seaforth, a new employee.

NOTE: A Performance Evaluation Checklist for this exercise can be found at the back of the workbook.

| EXERCISE 19-4 | **COMPLETE AN EMPLOYEE'S WITHHOLDING ALLOWANCE CERTIFICATE** |

PERFORMANCE OBJECTIVE

TASK: Complete an employee's withholding allowance certificate.

CONDITIONS: Use the employee's withholding allowance certificate (form 107), and typewriter, pen or pencil.

STANDARDS: Time: _____ hours _____ minutes
Accuracy: _____
(NOTE: The time element and accuracy criteria may be given by your instructor.)

DIRECTIONS: Complete an employee's withholding allowance certificate for yourself as if you were being hired by Drs. Gerald and Fran Practon. Use form 107, and a typewriter, pen or pencil.

NOTE: A Performance Evaluation Checklist for this exercise can be found at the back of the workbook.

EXERCISE 19-5 — COMPLETE AN EMPLOYEE BENEFIT FORM

PERFORMANCE OBJECTIVE

TASK: Complete an employee benefit form.

CONDITIONS: Use the information in the case scenario to complete an employee benefit form. Use a computer, typewriter, pen or pencil, calculator, and employee benefit form (form 108).

STANDARDS: Time: _____ hours _____ minutes
Accuracy: _____
(NOTE: The time element and accuracy criteria may be given by your instructor.)

DIRECTIONS: You have just been hired by Drs. Gerald and Fran Practon. Read the information pertaining to your salary and benefit package in the case scenario. Extract the information to fill in the employee benefit form. Determine your actual compensation by adding the dollar amount from the benefit package and the amount you actually pay for the entire year.

CASE SCENARIO: Dr. Practon has hired you as a full-time administrative medical assistant and has agreed to pay you $1,760 per month, which amounts to approximately $10 per hour. You receive six paid holidays per year and one week paid vacation after the first year. You have ten sick days per year and $150 for a uniform allowance per year. There are no retirement benefits; occasionally there may be an incentive bonus. The practice pays for your medical insurance which costs $60 per month, and you elect to get life insurance at your own expense, at $12 per month for $100,000 coverage. You also elect to get accident insurance at an additional $4.60 per month for $200,000 coverage. Dr. Practon pays $15.35 per month for your workers' compensation insurance and an additional $17.60 per month for your disability insurance. He pays for your dues to the American Association of Medical Assistants, which are $90 per year.

NOTE: A Performance Evaluation Checklist for this exercise can be found at the back of the workbook.

COMPUTER EXERCISES

Before proceeding, you may want to do more exercises or review the concepts you have learned. Complete the computer exercises on the software for Chapter 19.

CHAPTER 20

Seeking a Position as an Administrative Medical Assistant

OBJECTIVES

After completing the exercises, the student will be able to:

1. Write meanings for chart note abbreviations.

2. Enhance spelling skills by learning new medical words.

3. Prepare an outline for a resumé following specific guidelines.

4. Key an error-free resumé.

5. Compose a cover letter.

6. Compose and key a follow-up thank-you letter.

AREAS OF COMPETENCE

Administrative Procedures
■ Perform basic clerical functions

General (Transdisciplinary)

Communication Skills
■ Use medical terminology appropriately

Legal Concepts
■ Participate in the development and maintenance of personnel, policy and procedures manuals.

ABBREVIATION AND SPELLING REVIEW LESSON

Read the following patient's chart note and write the meanings for the abbreviations listed below the note. To decode any abbreviations you do not understand or that appear unfamiliar to you, refer to text Tables 8-1 and 9-3. Medical terms in the chart note are italicized; study them for spelling. Use your medical dictionary to look up their definitions. Your instructor may give a test for the spelling and definition of the words and abbreviations.

Mary Lee Brau

August 24, 199X Pt comes in complaining of *postmenopausal* bleeding with known *cystic endometrial hyperplasia* associated with *fibroid* uterus and *uterine prolapse*. PH: I&D L breast, *abscess*. Pelvic done two months ago revealed Pap smr Class II. *Menstrual:* The pt is a Para 3, 2-0-1-2, Rh-, unsensitized. Scheduled for *hysterectomy* in two weeks. Pt to have preop HX and PX day before surg.

Gerald Practon, MD
Gerald Practon, MD

Pt _____   Rh- _____

PH _____   preop _____

I&D _____   HX _____

L _____   PX _____

Pap smr _____ Surg. _____

Para 3 _____

NOTE: Translation for 2-0-1-2 = 2 term infants, 0 premature, 1 abortion, 2 live births. What would be the translation for 3-1-0-3? _____

_____

REVIEW QUESTIONS

Review the objectives, glossary, and chapter information before completing the following review questions.

1. What are the four primary reasons employers reject job applicants?

    a. _____
    b. _____
    c. _____
    d. _____

2. Name three steps you would take to find medical job openings.

    a. _____
    b. _____
    c. _____

3. Define *resumé*. _____

_____

4. Why should you read the fine print of any contract an employment agency asks you to sign? _____

_____

5. A customized letter accompanying a resumé is called a _____

    _____ , or _____ letter.

6. A resumé style that stresses work experience dates is the _____
   format; the _____ format highlights job skills.

7. List five items that might be included in a medical assistant's personnel file.

    a. _____

    b. _____

    c. _____

    d. _____

    e. _____

8. Name three personal items that legally do not have to be included on a resumé or
   discussed at a job interview.

    a. _____

    b. _____

    c. _____

9. If three days have elapsed since your interview and you have had no word from the
   office, what two follow-up steps could you initiate?

    a. _____

    b. _____

10. One way to demonstrate interest in a job interview is to:

    _____

    _____

EXERCISE 20-1 — OUTLINE A RESUMÉ

PERFORMANCE OBJECTIVE

TASK: Research information and complete worksheets in preparation for
keying a resumé.

CONDITIONS: Use worksheet forms 109 and 110, and pen or pencil.

STANDARDS: Time: _____ minutes
Accuracy: _____
(NOTE: The time element and accuracy criteria may be given by your
instructor.)

DIRECTIONS: In preparation for keying your resumé, complete the spaces on the
information worksheet. Note that some items on the worksheet should
not appear on the resumé, such as references, but you should have
them available if you are asked to provide them.

NOTE: A Performance Evaluation Checklist for this exercise can be found at the back
of the workbook.

| EXERCISE 20-2 | **KEY A RESUMÉ** |

PERFORMANCE OBJECTIVE

TASK: Key an accurate resumé in an attractive format.

CONDITIONS: Use two sheets of white paper.

STANDARDS: Time: _____ minutes
Accuracy: _____
(NOTE: The time element and accuracy criteria may be given by your instructor.)

DIRECTIONS: The advertisements shown in Figure 20-1 appeared in your local newspaper. You decide to follow up on one of them. Abstract the data you think is relevant from your resumé information worksheet and key a resumé in rough draft. Ask you instructor for suggestions to improve the resumé. Refer to text Chapter 20, Figures 20-2, 20-3, and 20-4 to help organize your resumé into an attractive format before keying the final copy.

NOTE: A Performance Evaluation Checklist for this exercise can be found at the back of the workbook.

ADMINISTRATIVE MEDICAL ASSISTANT—Challenging, full-time opportunity for take-charge person with mature personality to use skills at a multiphysician practice in a suburban and pleasant working environment. Typing of 60 wpm, knowledge of grammar, spelling, and medical terminology essential. We offer top salary with excellent fringe benefits; outstanding potential for right person. Send resumé and salary history with your application letter telling us why you think you are the best candidate for the position. Reply to: Office Manager, Butler Medical Group, Salisbury, MD 21801.

RECEPTIONIST FOR A MEDICAL OFFICE—A rural, pediatric clinic is looking for a person who has PR skills with children to make appointments, to assist and direct patients, and to become involved in general health care. Some filing and typing are required. High school education, business math courses, minimum typing speed of 50 wpm, and previous medical office experience would be helpful but right person without all qualifications will be considered. Salary based on experience. Excellent benefits with opportunity for swift advancement. Pleasant working environment for candidate interested in joining our team. Reply with handwritten letter and attach a resumé. Give salary history and references. All information is confidential. Reply to: Personnel Office, Lasalle Pediatric Clinic, 145 Hobart Ave., Dade City, FL 33425.

Figure 20-1

MEDICAL SECRETARY—A busy midtown general family practice physician is accepting applications from persons with outgoing, empathetic personality who wish to work in stimulating environment. Basic MD terminology and secretarial skills with typing at 80 wpm and some health insurance background are essential. Top salary, excellent fringe benefits, flexible hours, and pleasant working conditions. Outstanding potential for right person. Send resumé and salary history with your letter telling us why you think you are qualified for this position. K. Cain, CMA, 44901 Valley View Blvd., 2215 West University Dr., Suite F1088, Rochester, MN 55904.

Figure 20-1 Continued

EXERCISE 20-3 COMPOSE A COVER LETTER OF INTRODUCTION

PERFORMANCE OBJECTIVE

TASK: Compose and key a letter of introduction to accompany the resumé and place in a prepared envelope.

CONDITIONS: Use two sheets of white paper rough and final drafts, and No. 10 envelope (or form 111).

STANDARDS: Time: _____ minutes
Accuracy: _____
(NOTE: The time element and accuracy criteria may be given by your instructor.)

DIRECTIONS: Compose a cover letter of introduction in rough draft to accompany your resumé from Workbook Exercise 20-2. Show it to your instructor for suggestions. Key the cover letter on white paper in perfect mailable form. Refer to the sample letter in text Figure 20-1 as a guide to help organize your thoughts. Prepare a No. 10 envelope and insert the letter with the resumé.

NOTE: A Performance Evaluation Checklist for this exercise can be found at the back of the workbook.

EXERCISE 20-4 PREPARE A FOLLOW-UP THANK-YOU LETTER

PERFORMANCE OBJECTIVE

TASK: Compose and key a follow-up thank-you letter and address a No. 6 envelope.

CONDITIONS: Use one sheet of white paper, and one No. 6 envelope (or form 112).

STANDARDS: Time: _____ minutes
Accuracy: _____
(NOTE: The time element and accuracy criteria may be given by your instructor.)

DIRECTIONS: It has been two days since you had an interview for one of the two positions advertised in the local newspaper. You have decided to send a follow-up thank-you letter to the person who interviewed you. Key a letter and address a No. 6 envelope. Refer to text Figure 20-6 to help organize your thoughts.

NOTE: A Performance Evaluation Checklist for this exercise can be found at the back of the workbook.

COMPUTER EXERCISES

Before proceeding, you may want to do more exercises or review the concepts you have learned. Complete the computer exercises on the software for Chapter 20.

Part II

Blank Forms

Insurance cards copied ❑
Date: _____

Patient Registration
Information
Please PRINT AND complete ALL sections below!

Account # : _____
Insurance # : _____
Co-Payment: $ _____

Is your condition a result of a work injury? YES NO   An auto accident? YES NO   Date of injury: _____

PATIENT'S PERSONAL INFORMATION Marital Status: ❑ Single ❑ Married ❑ Divorced ❑ Widowed Sex: ❑ Male ❑ Female

Name:_____
            last name   first name   initial

Street address: _____ (Apt # _____) City: _____ State: _____ Zip: _____

Home phone: (___) _____ Work phone: (___) _____ Social Security # _____ - _____ - _____

Date of Birth: _____ / _____ / _____ Driver's License: (State & Number) _____
                    month   day   year

Employer / Name of School _____ ❑ Full Time ❑ Part Time

Spouse's Name: _____ _____ _____ Spouse's Work phone: (___) _____
                           last name   first name   initial

How do you wish to be addressed? _____ Social Security # _____ - _____ - _____

PATIENT'S / RESPONSIBLE PARTY INFORMATION

Responsible party: _____ Date of Birth: _____

Relationship to Patient: ❑ Self ❑ Spouse ❑ Other _____ Social Security # _____ - _____ - _____

Responsible party's home phone: (_____) _____ Work phone: (_____) _____

    Address: _____ (Apt # _____) City: _____ State: _____ Zip: _____

Employer's name: _____ Phone number: (_____) _____

    Address: _____ City: _____ State: _____ Zip: _____

    Your occupation: _____

Spouse's Employer's name: _____ Spouse's Work phone: (___) _____

    Address: _____ City: _____ State: _____ Zip: _____

PATIENT'S INSURANCE INFORMATION Please present insurance cards to receptionist.

PRIMARY insurance company's name: _____

Insurance address: _____ City: _____ State: _____ Zip: _____

Name of insured: _____ Date of Birth: _____ Relationship to insured: ❑ Self ❑ Spouse ❑ Other ❑ Child

Insurance ID number: _____ Group number: _____

SECONDARY insurance company's name: _____

Insurance address: _____ City: _____ State: _____ Zip: _____

Name of insured: _____ Date of Birth: _____ Relationship to insured: ❑ Self ❑ Spouse ❑ Other ❑ Child

Insurance ID number: _____ Group number: _____

Check if appropriate: ❑ Medigap policy ❑ Retiree coverage

PATIENT'S REFERRAL INFORMATION   (please circle one)

Referred by: _____ If referred by a friend, may we thank her or him? YES NO

Name(s) of other physician(s) who care for you: _____
_____

EMERGENCY CONTACT

Name of person not living with you: _____ Relationship: _____

Address: _____ City: _____ State: _____ Zip: _____

Phone number (home): (_____) _____ Phone number (work): (_____) _____

Assignment of Benefits • Financial Agreement

I hereby give lifetime authorization for payment of insurance benefits to be made directly to _____ , and any assisting physicians, for services rendered. I understand that I am financially responsible for all charges whether or not they are covered by insurance. In the event of default, I agree to pay all costs of collection, and reasonable attorney's fees. I hereby authorize this healthcare provider to release all information necessary to secure the payment of benefits.

I further agree that a photocopy of this agreement shall be as valid as the original.

Date: _____ Your Signature: _____

Method of Payment: ❑ Cash ❑ Check ❑ Credit Card

FORM # 58-8424 • BIBBERO SYSTEMS, INC. • PETALUMA, CA. • TO ORDER CALL TOLL FREE : 800-BIBBERO (800-242-2376) • FAX (800) 242-9330 © 7/94

PATIENT REGISTRATION

Form 1

DMV
A Public Service Agency

APPLICATION/STATEMENT OF FACTS FOR
DISABLED PERSON PARKING PLACARD OR PLATES

MAIL TO:
DMV PLACARD
P. O. Box 942869
Sacramento, CA 94269-0001
— DO NOT MAIL CASH —

☐ **License Plates** .... **No Fee** — Applicant completes Sections A, B, C, D, and E
☐ **Parking Placard** .... **$6.00** — Applicant completes Sections A, C, and E
☐ **Temporary Parking Placard** ...... **$6.00** — Applicant completes Sections A, and E
☐ **Travel Parking Placard** .... **$6.00** — Applicant completes Sections A, C, and E
NOTE: Applicant's doctor must complete Sections F or G, and H

A. TRUE FULL NAME AS SHOWN ON DRIVER LICENSE OR ID CARD *(PRINT LAST, FIRST, MIDDLE)*

DATE OF BIRTH
MO. __ __ — DA. __ __ — YR. __ __

ADDRESS

DRIVER LICENSE/ID NUMBER *(If any)*

CITY   STATE   ZIP CODE

TELEPHONE NUMBER
(   )

B. VEHICLE LICENSE NUMBER   VEHICLE IDENTIFICATION NUMBER

VEHICLE MAKE

C. 1. Are you a resident of California? .... ☐ Yes ☐ No
2. If you currently have California disabled person or disabled veteran license plates or a California disabled person permanent disability parking placard, please provide the number, and doctor's certification will not be required.   NUMBER:_____

D.   **COMMERCIAL VEHICLE EXEMPTION (Applications for license plates only)**
☐ This is the only commercial vehicle for which I will request exemption from weight fees.

E.   **APPLICANT'S CERTIFICATION**
I certify under penalty of perjury under the laws of the State of California that I am ☐ permanently ☐ temporarily
disabled due to _____ *and the information entered by me on this document is true and correct.*

DATE   APPLICANT'S SIGNATURE
                   X

F.   **DOCTOR'S CERTIFICATION FOR TEMPORARY DISABILITY**

The applicant is/will be temporarily disabled due to _____

_____

until (month) _____ (day) _____ (year) _____

NOTE: See reverse side for placard time periods.

G.   **DOCTOR'S CERTIFICATION OF PERMANENT DISABILITY**
The applicant suffers from the following disability.

1. ☐ Lung disease to such an extent that forced (respiratory) expiratory volume for one second when measured by spirometry is less than one liter, or arterial oxygen tension (PO_2) is less than 60 mm/HG on room air at rest.
2. ☐ Cardiovascular disease impairment limitations classified in severity as Class III or Class IV according to standards accepted by the American Heart Association.
3. ☐ A significant limitation in the use of the lower extremities which substantially impairs or interferes with mobility, or requires the aid of an assistant device for mobility (e.g., cane, walker, crutches, etc.).
4. ☐ A diagnosed disease or disorder which substantially impairs or interferes with mobility, or requires the aid of an assistant device for mobility (e.g., cane, walker, crutches, etc.).
5. ☐ Loss, or loss of the use of, one or both lower extremities.
6. ☐ Loss, or loss of use of, both hands
7. ☐ Central visual acuity not exceeding 20/200 in the better eye, with corrective lenses, as measured by the Snellen test, or visual acuity greater than 20/200 with a limitation in the field of vision such that the widest diameter of the visual field subtends an angle not greater than 20 degrees.

Any licensed physician may certify 1-7.
A licensed chiropractor may certify to 3, 4, and 5 and 6.
Only a licensed ophthalmologist or optometrist may certify to 7.
You may self-certify to the loss of one or both lower extremities or both hands if you present this form in person.

H. *I certify that as a*
☐ Physician ☐ Chiropractor ☐ Ophthalmologist ☐ Optometrist ☐ Other _____
under penalty of perjury under the laws of the State of California that the information entered by me on this document is true and correct.

DATE   SIGNATURE
                   X

PRINTED NAME

MEDICAL LICENSE NUMBER

ADDRESS

DAYTIME TELEPHONE NUMBER
(   )

REG 195 (REV. 9/95)

Form 2

72623

PRIORITY ☐

PATIENT Michael JACKson   AGE

CALLER same

TELEPHONE (410) Michael 776-1111

REFERRED TO

CHART #

CHART ATTACHED ☐ YES ☐ NO

DATE 10 / /   TIME   REC'D BY SW

TELEPHONE RECORD ☎

MESSAGE nose still hurts can you call in something stronger

TEMP   ALLERGIES NKDA

RESPONSE

PHY/RN INITIALS | DATE / / | TIME | HANDLED BY

PRIORITY ☐

PATIENT Bob Denver   AGE 4

CALLER John Denver

TELEPHONE 410 222-1333

REFERRED TO

CHART #

CHART ATTACHED ☐ YES ☐ NO

DATE / /   TIME   REC'D BY

TELEPHONE RECORD ☎

MESSAGE cough, runny nose x 2 days No appts avail.

TEMP 101 4   ALLERGIES

RESPONSE

PHY/RN INITIALS | DATE / / | TIME | HANDLED BY

PRIORITY ☐

PATIENT Brad Pitt   AGE

CALLER

TELEPHONE 410 2225554

REFERRED TO

CHART #

CHART ATTACHED ☐ YES ☐ NO

DATE / /   TIME   REC'D BY

TELEPHONE RECORD ☎

MESSAGE in last wk, diarrhea still has no appts avail

TEMP NONE   ALLERGIES

RESPONSE

PHY/RN INITIALS | DATE / / | TIME | HANDLED BY

PRIORITY ☐

PATIENT Joe Millionaire   AGE

CALLER

TELEPHONE 410 215 4110

REFERRED TO

CHART #

CHART ATTACHED ☐ YES ☐ NO

DATE / /   TIME   REC'D BY

TELEPHONE RECORD ☎

MESSAGE fell, thinks he sprained his ankle, what to do NA

TEMP   ALLERGIES

RESPONSE

PHY/RN INITIALS | DATE / / | TIME | HANDLED BY

Form 3

72623

Card 1

	PRIORITY ☐
PATIENT	Monica Lewinsky
CALLER	
TELEPHONE	215 221 4444
REFERRED TO	
CHART #	
CHART ATTACHED ☐ YES ☐ NO	
DATE / /	TIME	REC'D BY

Copyright © 1978 Bibbero Systems, Inc. Printed in the U.S.A.

TELEPHONE RECORD ☎

MESSAGE: Okay to give referral to ENT, chronic sinusitis

TEMP	ALLERGIES

RESPONSE

| PHY/RN INITIALS | DATE / / | TIME | HANDLED BY |

Card 2

	PRIORITY ☐
PATIENT	AGE
CALLER	Jamie Curtis
TELEPHONE	610 215 6621
REFERRED TO	
CHART #	
CHART ATTACHED ☐ YES ☐ NO	
DATE / /	TIME	REC'D BY

Copyright © 1978 Bibbero Systems, Inc. Printed in the U.S.A.

TELEPHONE RECORD ☎

MESSAGE: electric turned off wants Doctors note stating electric med. nece.

TEMP	ALLERGIES

RESPONSE

| PHY/RN INITIALS | DATE / / | TIME | HANDLED BY |

Card 3

	PRIORITY ☐
PATIENT	Bill Clinton AGE
CALLER	
TELEPHONE	610 211 4554
REFERRED TO	
CHART #	
CHART ATTACHED ☐ YES ☐ NO	
DATE / /	TIME	REC'D BY

Copyright © 1978 Bibbero Systems, Inc. Printed in the U.S.A.

TELEPHONE RECORD ☎

MESSAGE: called for Jury Duty wants Doctors note to not have to serve

TEMP	ALLERGIES

RESPONSE

| PHY/RN INITIALS | DATE / / | TIME | HANDLED BY |

Card 4

	PRIORITY ☐
PATIENT	Jesse James AGE
CALLER	
TELEPHONE	215 913 3445
REFERRED TO	
CHART #	
CHART ATTACHED ☐ YES ☐ NO	
DATE / /	TIME	REC'D BY

Copyright © 1978 Bibbero Systems, Inc. Printed in the U.S.A.

TELEPHONE RECORD ☎

MESSAGE: needs refill. HA med blue pill white little imitrex

TEMP	ALLERGIES NKDA

RESPONSE

| PHY/RN INITIALS | DATE / / | TIME | HANDLED BY |

Form 4a

72623

PRIORITY ☐

TELEPHONE RECORD ☎

PATIENT	AGE

MESSAGE

CALLER

TELEPHONE

TEMP	ALLERGIES

REFERRED TO

CHART #

RESPONSE

CHART ATTACHED ☐ YES ☐ NO

DATE / /	TIME	REC'D BY

Copyright © 1978 Bibbero Systems, Inc.
Printed in the U.S.A.

PHY/RN INITIALS	DATE / /	TIME	HANDLED BY

PRIORITY ☐

TELEPHONE RECORD ☎

PATIENT	AGE

MESSAGE

CALLER

TELEPHONE

TEMP	ALLERGIES

REFERRED TO

CHART #

RESPONSE

CHART ATTACHED ☐ YES ☐ NO

DATE / /	TIME	REC'D BY

Copyright © 1978 Bibbero Systems, Inc.
Printed in the U.S.A.

PHY/RN INITIALS	DATE / /	TIME	HANDLED BY

PRIORITY ☐

TELEPHONE RECORD ☎

PATIENT	AGE

MESSAGE

CALLER

TELEPHONE

TEMP	ALLERGIES

REFERRED TO

CHART #

RESPONSE

CHART ATTACHED ☐ YES ☐ NO

DATE / /	TIME	REC'D BY

Copyright © 1978 Bibbero Systems, Inc.
Printed in the U.S.A.

PHY/RN INITIALS	DATE / /	TIME	HANDLED BY

PRIORITY ☐

TELEPHONE RECORD ☎

PATIENT	AGE

MESSAGE

CALLER

TELEPHONE

TEMP	ALLERGIES

REFERRED TO

CHART #

RESPONSE

CHART ATTACHED ☐ YES ☐ NO

DATE / /	TIME	REC'D BY

Copyright © 1978 Bibbero Systems, Inc.
Printed in the U.S.A.

PHY/RN INITIALS	DATE / /	TIME	HANDLED BY

Form 4b

72623

PRIORITY ☐ / TELEPHONE RECORD ☎

PATIENT   AGE

CALLER

TELEPHONE

REFERRED TO

CHART #

CHART ATTACHED ☐ YES ☐ NO

DATE   /   /   **TIME**   **REC'D BY**

Copyright © 1978 Bibbero Systems, Inc.
Printed in the U.S.A.

MESSAGE

TEMP   **ALLERGIES**

RESPONSE

PHY/RN INITIALS   **DATE**   /   /   **TIME**   **HANDLED BY**

PRIORITY ☐ / TELEPHONE RECORD ☎

PATIENT   AGE

CALLER

TELEPHONE

REFERRED TO

CHART #

CHART ATTACHED ☐ YES ☐ NO

DATE   /   /   **TIME**   **REC'D BY**

Copyright © 1978 Bibbero Systems, Inc.
Printed in the U.S.A.

MESSAGE

TEMP   **ALLERGIES**

RESPONSE

PHY/RN INITIALS   **DATE**   /   /   **TIME**   **HANDLED BY**

PRIORITY ☐ / TELEPHONE RECORD ☎

PATIENT   AGE

CALLER

TELEPHONE

REFERRED TO

CHART #

CHART ATTACHED ☐ YES ☐ NO

DATE   /   /   **TIME**   **REC'D BY**

Copyright © 1978 Bibbero Systems, Inc.
Printed in the U.S.A.

MESSAGE

TEMP   **ALLERGIES**

RESPONSE

PHY/RN INITIALS   **DATE**   /   /   **TIME**   **HANDLED BY**

PRIORITY ☐ / TELEPHONE RECORD ☎

PATIENT   AGE

CALLER

TELEPHONE

REFERRED TO

CHART #

CHART ATTACHED ☐ YES ☐ NO

DATE   /   /   **TIME**   **REC'D BY**

Copyright © 1978 Bibbero Systems, Inc.
Printed in the U.S.A.

MESSAGE

TEMP   **ALLERGIES**

RESPONSE

PHY/RN INITIALS   **DATE**   /   /   **TIME**   **HANDLED BY**

Form 5

APPOINTMENT RECORD

		DOCTOR		
		DATE		
		DAY		

		AM	00		
		8	15		
			30		
			45		
		9	00		
			15		
			30		
			45		
		10	00		
			15		
			30		
			45		
		11	00		
			15		
			30		
			45		
		12	00		
			15		
			30		
			45		
		PM	00		
		1	15		
			30		
			45		
		2	00		
			15		
			30		
			45		
		3	00		
			15		
			30		
			45		
		4	00		
			15		
			30		
			45		
		5	00		
			15		
			30		
			45		

REMARKS & NOTES

FORM # 56-8315 ©1965 BIBBERO SYSTEMS, INC., PETALUMA, CA.   TO ORDER CALL TOLL FREE: 800-BIBBERO (CA) OR 800/358-8240 (U.S.)

Form 6

APPOINTMENT RECORD

		DOCTOR			
		DATE			
		DAY			
		AM	00		
		8	15		
			30		
			45		
		9	00		
			15		
			30		
			45		
		10	00		
			15		
			30		
			45		
		11	00		
			15		
			30		
			45		
		12	00		
			15		
			30		
			45		
		PM 1	00		
			15		
			30		
			45		
		2	00		
			15		
			30		
			45		
		3	00		
			15		
			30		
			45		
		4	00		
			15		
			30		
			45		
		5	00		
			15		
			30		
			45		

REMARKS & NOTES

FORM # 56-8315 ©1965 BIBBERO SYSTEMS, INC., PETALUMA, CA.   TO ORDER CALL TOLL FREE: 800-BIBBERO (CA) OR 800/358-8240 (U.S.)

Form 7

APPOINTMENT RECORD

		DOCTOR		
		DATE		
		DAY		

		AM		
		8	00	
			15	
			30	
			45	
		9	00	
			15	
			30	
			45	
		10	00	
			15	
			30	
			45	
		11	00	
			15	
			30	
			45	
		12	00	
			15	
			30	
			45	
		1 PM	00	
			15	
			30	
			45	
		2	00	
			15	
			30	
			45	
		3	00	
			15	
			30	
			45	
		4	00	
			15	
			30	
			45	
		5	00	
			15	
			30	
			45	

REMARKS & NOTES

FORM # 56-8315 ©1965 BIBBERO SYSTEMS, INC., PETALUMA, CA.   TO ORDER CALL TOLL FREE: 800-BIBBERO (CA) OR 800/358-8240 (U.S.)

Form 8

M_____

has an appointment with

PRACTON MEDICAL GROUP, INC.
4567 Broad Avenue
Woodland Hills, XY 12345
Tel. 013/486-9002

for

Mon. _____at_____

Tues. _____at_____

Wed. _____at_____

Thurs._____at_____

Fri. _____at_____

Sat. _____at_____

If unable to keep this appointment
kindly give 24 hours notice.

M_____

has an appointment with

PRACTON MEDICAL GROUP, INC.
4567 Broad Avenue
Woodland Hills, XY 12345
Tel. 013/486-9002

for

Mon. _____at_____

Tues. _____at_____

Wed. _____at_____

Thurs._____at_____

Fri. _____at_____

Sat. _____at_____

If unable to keep this appointment
kindly give 24 hours notice.

M_____

has an appointment with

PRACTON MEDICAL GROUP, INC.
4567 Broad Avenue
Woodland Hills, XY 12345
Tel. 013/486-9002

for

Mon. _____at_____

Tues. _____at_____

Wed. _____at_____

Thurs._____at_____

Fri. _____at_____

Sat. _____at_____

If unable to keep this appointment
kindly give 24 hours notice.

M_____

has an appointment with

PRACTON MEDICAL GROUP, INC.
4567 Broad Avenue
Woodland Hills, XY 12345
Tel. 013/486-9002

for

Mon. _____at_____

Tues. _____at_____

Wed. _____at_____

Thurs._____at_____

Fri. _____at_____

Sat. _____at_____

If unable to keep this appointment
kindly give 24 hours notice.

Form 9

HOSPITAL/SURGERY SCHEDULING FORM

Section 1   **Completed by physician**

1. _____   Patient's name_____
2. _____   Procedure_____
3. _____   Emergency: Urgent_____   Elective_____
4. _____   Diagnoses 1. _____
                         2. _____
5. _____   Hospital/Facility name_____
6. _____   Inpatient_____   Outpatient_____   Day Surgery_____
7. _____   Surgical assistant required?   Yes_____   No_____
                Who preferred?_____
8. _____   Anesthesia required?   Yes_____   No_____   General_____   Local_____
                Who preferred?_____
9. _____   Referring physician_____

Section 2   **Completed by patient**

10. _____   Age of patient_____   Date of birth _____   Smoker_____Nonsmoker_____
11. _____   Room accommodations: Private_____   Semi-private_____   Ward_____
12. _____   Telephone numbers: Home (_____)_____   Work (_____)_____
13. _____   Insurance Company_____Policy number_____
                Secondary insurance_____Policy number_____
14. _____   Second surgical opinion needed for insurance?   Yes_____   No_____
15. _____   Name of nearest relative_____
                Address_____Phone number_____
16. _____   Admitted to this facility previous?   Yes_____   No_____
                Date_____ Type of procedure_____
17. _____   Patient has had preadmission testing of CBC_____, EKG_____, Chest x-ray_____within
                _____ weeks.
18. _____   Admission and procedures reported to patient on   Date:_____
19. _____   Preadmission and operation instructions given to me?   Yes_____   No_____
20. _____   Insurance and financial arrangements discussed with me? Yes_____   No_____

Section 3   **Completed by medical assistant**

21. _____   Operation room reserved for surgery on this date_____and time_____
                Name of hospital employee that scheduled surgery_____
22. _____   Name of surgical assistant scheduled and called_____
23. _____   Name of anesthesiologist scheduled and called_____
24. _____   Reported to referring physician's office and talked to_____
25. _____   Hospital/Facility admission confirmed/preadmission test scheduled
26. _____   Prior authorizations/second opinions obtained
                Authorization/precertification #_____Date provided_____
                Who provided number?_____
27. _____   Admitting date and surgical procedure entered in appointment book
28. _____   Arrangements confirmed with patient
29. _____   History and physical report ready
                Name of office employee that scheduled surgery_____Date_____

Form 10

FRAN T. PRACTON, MD
Family Practice

GERALD M. PRACTON, MD
General Practice

PRACTON MEDICAL GROUP, INC.
4567 Broad Avenue
Woodland Hills, XY 12345-4700
Tel. 013/486-9002
Fax No. 013/488-7815

_____
_____
_____

The following arrangements have been made for your hospitalization under the care of

_____. You are to enter _____ on _____,_____

at _____

Your procedure, _____, is scheduled for _____, _____ at

_____ (subject to change in time). A _____ room has been reserved for you as requested.

You should take pajamas or night gown, robe, slippers and ordinary toilet articles with

you. Please leave valuables at home. If it should become necessary for you to cancel these

arrangements, please notify me immediately.

Sincerely,

_____, Secretary

Surgeon: _____   Assistant: _____

Anesthetist: _____

SPECIAL NOTE to patients covered by Medicare. Medicare will only pay for a semi-private room;

therefore, patients requesting private rooms will be required to pay the difference in cost.

Form 11

I.D.#	PATIENT LAST NAME		FIRST	M.I.	REFERRING PHYSICIAN

REFERRED BY	SS #:	BILL: ☐ PHYSICIAN ☐ MEDI-CAL ☐ HMO ☐ CHDP ☐ MEDICARE ☐ INSURANCE ☐ PATIENT PLEASE COMPLETE BILLING INFORMATION AT BOTTOM	D.O.B.	AGE	SEX
		ADDRESS PHONE NUMBER ( )	DATE COLLECTED	TIME COLLECTED	
		CITY STATE ZIP CODE	FASTING YES | NO	STAT	CALL RESULT
		MEDICARE # MEDICAL #	INFO. BELOW WILL APPEAR ON REPORT		

CUSTOM PROFILES & ADDITIONAL TESTS

```
173    [ ] CHEMISTRY PANEL, COMPLETE BLOOD COUNT (ZPP), LIPID PROFILE, T4
05050  [ ] CHOL, TRIG, HDL CHOL, VLDL CHOL, LDL CHOL, RISK FACTOR
```

PROFILES

Code	Test		Code	Test			
00011	☐ SPECIAL COMPREHENSIVE	2 SS,L	03536	☐ HYPERTHYROID PROFILE			SS
00001	☐ COMPREHENSIVE HEALTH SURVEY	SS,L	05037	☐ HYPOTHYROID PROFILE			SS
00002	☐ GENERAL SURVEY	SS,L	05051	☐ LIPID PROFILE			SS
00003	☐ CHEMISTRY PANEL	SS	05021	☐ LIVER PROFILE			SS
CH7	☐ CHEM 7 PANEL	SS	03350	☐ LUPUS PROFILE			SS
03280	☐ ANEMIA PROFILE	SS	03959	☐ MENOPAUSAL PROFILE	SS / 03960	☐ POST MENOPAUSAL	SS
05016	☐ ARTHRITIS PROFILE	SS,L	02280	☐ OVARIAN FUNCTION PROFILE	SS / 02281	☐ TESTICULAR FUNC. PROF.	SS
05726	☐ COMPREHENSIVE THYROID SURVEY	SS	02808	☐ PRENATAL PROFILE			L,R
02691	☐ EPSTEIN BARR PROFILE	SS	05006	☐ THYROID PROFILE			SS
05010	☐ ELECTROLYTES	SS	03191	☐ TORCH PANEL			SS
06826	☐ HEPATITIS PROFILE	SS	5756	☐ URINE DRUG SCREEN	U /	☐ VENIPUNCTURE	

TESTS

Code	Test		Code	Test		Code	Test		Code	Test	
0361	☐ ABO & Rh TYPE	R, L	0141	☐ C-REACTIVE PROTEIN	SS	0673	☐ HEPATITIS B SURFACE ANTIGEN	SS	0237	☐ PTT	B
0302	☐ ALKALINE PHOSPHATASE	SS	1341	☐ DHEA-S	SS	0245	☐ HEPATITIS C ANTIBODY	SS	0317	☐ RA FACTOR	SS
0109	☐ AMYLASE	SS	0119	☐ DIGOXIN	SS	0257	☐ IRON	SS	0321	☐ RUBELLA	SS
0613	☐ ANA	SS	0224	☐ DILANTIN	SS	LDL-A	☐ LDL CHOLESTEROL	SS	0381	☐ RPR	SS
0366	☐ ANTIBODY SCREEN	R	0835	☐ ESTRADIOL	SS	0283	☐ LEAD BLOOD	RB	0335	☐ SEMEN ANALYSIS	SEMEN
0110	☐ ASO (STREPTOZYME)	SS	0833	☐ FERRITIN	SS	0281	☐ LIPASE	SS	0328	☐ SEDIMENTATION RATE (ESR)	L
0126	☐ BILIRUBIN TOTAL	SS	0003	☐ FOLIC ACID & VITAMIN B12	SS	8225	☐ LH	SS	0349	☐ SGOT (AST)	SS
0132	☐ BUN	SS	0651	☐ FSH	SS	0247	☐ MONONUCLEOSIS	SS	0348	☐ SGPT (ALT)	SS
8728	☐ CA125	SS	0140	☐ FTA-ABS	SS	0778	☐ PHENOBARBITAL	SS	0330	☐ SICKLE CELL SCREEN	L
0142	☐ CALCIUM	SS	0210	☐ GGTP	SS	0307	☐ POTASSIUM	SS	0354	☐ T4 (THYROXINE)	SS
0130	☐ CBC	L	0536	☐ GLUCOSE, FASTING	GY	0557	☐ PREGNANCY (SERUM)	SS	1358	☐ T4 FREE	SS
0388	☐ CEA-ROCHE	SS		☐ GLUCOSE, ____ HR PP	GY	0308	☐ PREGNANCY (URINE)	U	8456	☐ TESTOSTERONE	SS
0152	☐ CHOLESTEROL	SS	0771	☐ GLYCOHEMOGLOBIN	L	0859	☐ PROGESTERONE	SS	0624	☐ THEOPHYLLINE	SS
0786	☐ CORTISOL	SS	0534	☐ H. PYLORI	SS	8041	☐ PROLACTIN	SS	0360	☐ TRIGLYCERIDE	SS
0162	☐ CPK	SS	0823	☐ HCG QUANTITATIVE	SS	0103	☐ PROTEIN, TOTAL	SS	0672	☐ TSH	SS
0445	☐ CKMB ISOENZYME	SS	1856	☐ HIV (ANTIBODY)	SS	2000	☐ PROSTATE SPECIFIC ANTIGEN (PSA)	SS	0373	☐ URIC ACID	SS
0161	☐ CREATININE	SS	0558	☐ HDL CHOLESTEROL	SS	0310	☐ PT (PROTHROMBIN TIME)	B	0219	☐ URINALYSIS	U

CYTOPATHOLOGY

☐ PREGNANT   ☐ ABORTION   ☐ POST-PARTUM   ☐ POST-MENOPAUSE
HISTORY

PREV. ABNORMAL CYTOL FINDINGS   DATE
☐ CONTRACEPTIVES   ☐ HORMONES   ☐ IUD
☐ HYSTERECTOMY   ☐ TOTAL   ☐ SUPRA CX
☐ OOPHORECTOMY   DATE
☐ RADIATION Rx   ☐ HORMONES Rx   ☐ CHEMO Rx
☐ OTHER

LMP: DATE COLLECTED:
SOURCE ☐ CERVIX   ☐ ENDOCERVIX   ☐ VAGINA
       ☐ CYTOBRUSH   ☐ OTHERSITE

LAB USE ONLY (DO NOT WRITE BELOW THIS SPACE)

DATE RECEIVED   DATE REPORTED

STATEMENT OF SPECIMEN ADEQUACY

GENERAL CATEGORIZATION

DESCRIPTIVE DIAGNOSIS

HORMONAL EVALUATION   MI

ADDITIONAL COMMENT

CYTOTECHNOLOGIST   PATHOLOGIST

MICROBIOLOGY

THCUL ☐ THROAT	URTHC ☐ URETHRAL	9391 ☐ CHLAMYDIA DNA
EACUL ☐ EAR	VACUL ☐ VAGINAL	9390 ☐ GONORRHEA DNA
EYCUL ☐ EYE	WOCUL ☐ WOUND	9391 ☐ OCCULT BLOOD
GOCUL ☐ GC	ROCUL ☐ CULTURE (Routine)	0293 ☐ OVA & PARASITE
SPCUL ☐ SPUTUM	URCUL ☐ URINE	WTM ☐ WET MOUNT
STCUL ☐ STOOL	GSP ☐ GRAM STAIN	

SOURCE_____ OTHER_____

DIAGNOSIS OR COMMENTS

BILLING INFORMATION

PRIMARY INSURED	INSURANCE COMPANY
ADDRESS	
POLICY NO. & I.D. NO.	ICD9 CODE

LEGEND

SS Serum Separator	GY Grey	B Blue	U Urine
R Red	L Lavender	RB Royal Blue	G Green

Form 12

DATE ORDERED _____ AGE _____ **X-RAY REQUEST** DATE PERFORMED _____

PATIENT _____

CHART # ☐☐☐☐☐☐ DOB _____

X-RAY # _____

13 188

REFERRING
PHYSICIAN: _____

BILL TO: _____

STREET _____

CALL
REPORT EXT: _____

CITY _____

☐ TYPE

✔ NEW ADDRESS ☐

☐ ASAP   ☐ TODAY

Examination _____

Chief Complaint _____

Clinical Findings _____

✔	SC	Description	CPT	Mod	Fee	✔	SC	Description	CPT	Mod	Fee	✔	SC	Description	CPT	Mod	Fee
		CHEST						**UPPER EXTREMITY**						**HEAD**			
	5085	P.A. & Lat Chest	71020				5158	Shoulder Complete	73030				5042	Facial Bones	70150		
	5083	P.A. Chest	71010				5155	Clavicle	73000				5043	Nose	70160		
	5088	Chest Fluoro	71023				5156	Scapula	73010				5048	Sinuses	70220		
	5098	Ribs Unilateral	71101				5160	A-C Joints	73050				5047	Sinuses, Ltd.	70210		
	5100	Ribs Bilateral	71111				5102	S-C Joints	71130				5051	Skull, Complete	70260		
	5101	Sternum	71120				5161	Humerus	73060				5050	Skull, Ltd.	70250		
	5352	Mammo, Diag	76091				5163	Elbow, Complete	73080				5039	Mastoids	70130		
	5351	Mammo, Unilat	76090				5162	Elbow, 2 views	73070				5046	Orbits	70200		
	5353	Mammo, Screen	76092				5165	Forearm	73090				5037	Mandible	70110		
							5168	Wrist Complete	73110				5056	T.M. Joints	70330		
		ABDOMEN					5167	Wrist, 2 views	73100								
	5204	A.P.	74000				5171	Hand, Complete	73130					**SPINE-PELVIS**			
	5207	Acute Series	74022				5170	Hand, 2 views	73120				5110	C-Spine, Comp	72050		
							5172	Finger(s)	73140				5108	C-Spine, Ltd.	72020		
		GASTROINTESTINAL					5341	Bone Age	76020				5113	T-Spine	72070		
	5212	Swallowing - Eso	74210										5119	L-Spine, Comp	72110		
	5213	Esophagram	74220					**LOWER EXTREMITY**					5118	L-Spine, Ltd.	72100		
	5217	UGI Series	74241				5179	Hip	73510				5140	Pelvis	72170		
	5218	UGI & Sm Bowel	74245				5180	Bilateral Hips	73520				5147	Sacro-Iliac Joints	72202		
	5224	BA Enema	74270				5183	Infant Hips	73540				5148	Sacrum/Coccyx	72220		
	5225	BA Air Contrast	74280				5184	Femur (Thigh)	73550				5112	Scoliosis Study	72069		
	5227	GB Oral	74290				5187	Knee, Complete	73564								
	5228	GB Repeat	74291				5185	Knee, 2 views	73560					**MISCELLANEOUS**			
	5222	Small Bowel	74250				5186	Patella	73562				5337	Fluoroscopy	76000		
	5231	T-Tube Cholangio	74305				5190	Leg (Tibia)	73590				5344	Bone Survey	76062		
	5348	Sinogram	76080				5193	Ankle, Complete	73610				5362	Outside Films	76140		
	5061	Soft Tissue Neck	70360				5192	Ankle, 2 views	73600				5354	Needle Loc	76096		
							5196	Foot, Complete	73630				5356	Specimen Film	76098		
		GENITOURINARY					5195	Foot, 2 views	73620				5159	Shoulder Arthro	73040		
	5242	I.VP.	74400				5197	Os Calcis	73650								
	5258	Salpingogram	74740				5198	Toe(s)	73660					**SUPPLIES**			
	5248	Cystogram	74430				5342	Bone Length Scan	76040								

5-10

Form 13

PATIENT RECORD

| LAST NAME | FIRST NAME | MIDDLE NAME | BIRTH DATE | SEX | HOME PHONE |

| ADDRESS | CITY | STATE | ZIP CODE |

PATIENT'S OCCUPATION   NAME OF COMPANY

ADDRESS OF EMPLOYER   PHONE

SPOUSE OR PARENT   OCCUPATION

EMPLOYER   ADDRESS   PHONE

NAME OF INSURANCE GROUP   SUBSCRIBER

BLUE SHIELD OR BLUE CROSS CERT. NO.   GROUP NO.   CURRENT COVERAGE NO.   EFFECTIVE DATE

MEDICARE NO.   MEDICAID NO.   EFFECTIVE DATE   SOC. SEC. NO.

REFERRED BY:

DATE	PROGRESS

Form 14

PATIENT RECORD

LAST NAME	FIRST NAME	MIDDLE NAME	BIRTH DATE	SEX	HOME PHONE

ADDRESS	CITY	STATE	ZIP CODE

PATIENT'S OCCUPATION   NAME OF COMPANY

ADDRESS OF EMPLOYER   PHONE

SPOUSE OR PARENT   OCCUPATION

EMPLOYER   ADDRESS   PHONE

NAME OF INSURANCE GROUP   SUBSCRIBER

BLUE SHIELD OR BLUE CROSS CERT. NO.   GROUP NO.   CURRENT COVERAGE NO.   EFFECTIVE DATE

MEDICARE NO.   MEDICAID NO.   EFFECTIVE DATE   SOC. SEC. NO.

REFERRED BY:

DATE	PROGRESS

Form 15

MESSAGE FROM

For Dr.	Name of Caller	Rel. to Pt.	Patient	Pt. Age	Pt. Temp.	Message Date	Message Time AM PM	Urgent ☐ Yes ☐ No

Message: | Allergies

Respond to Phone #	Best Time to Call AM PM	Pharmacy Name / #	Patient's Chart Attached ☐ Yes ☐ No	Patient's Chart #	Initials

DOCTOR - STAFF RESPONSE

Doctor's / Staff Orders / Follow-Up Action

Call Back ☐ Yes ☐ No	Chart Mess. ☐ Yes ☐ No	Follow-Up Date / /	Follow-Up Completed-Date/Time / / AM PM	Response by

Product #78-9156 Pkg., #78-9157 Pads, Bibbero Systems, Inc., Petaluma, CA. To order, call toll free 800-Bibbero (800-242-2376) or Fax 800-242-9330.

MESSAGE FROM

For Dr.	Name of Caller	Rel. to Pt.	Patient	Pt. Age	Pt. Temp.	Message Date	Message Time AM PM	Urgent ☐ Yes ☐ No

Message: | Allergies

Respond to Phone #	Best Time to Call AM PM	Pharmacy Name / #	Patient's Chart Attached ☐ Yes ☐ No	Patient's Chart #	Initials

DOCTOR - STAFF RESPONSE

Doctor's / Staff Orders / Follow-Up Action

Call Back ☐ Yes ☐ No	Chart Mess. ☐ Yes ☐ No	Follow-Up Date / /	Follow-Up Completed-Date/Time / / AM PM	Response by

Product #78-9156 Pkg., #78-9157 Pads, Bibbero Systems, Inc., Petaluma, CA. To order, call toll free 800-Bibbero (800-242-2376) or Fax 800-242-9330.

MESSAGE FROM

For Dr.	Name of Caller	Rel. to Pt.	Patient	Pt. Age	Pt. Temp.	Message Date	Message Time AM PM	Urgent ☐ Yes ☐ No

Message: | Allergies

Respond to Phone #	Best Time to Call AM PM	Pharmacy Name / #	Patient's Chart Attached ☐ Yes ☐ No	Patient's Chart #	Initials

DOCTOR - STAFF RESPONSE

Doctor's / Staff Orders / Follow-Up Action

Call Back ☐ Yes ☐ No	Chart Mess. ☐ Yes ☐ No	Follow-Up Date / /	Follow-Up Completed-Date/Time / / AM PM	Response by

Product #78-9156 Pkg., #78-9157 Pads, Bibbero Systems, Inc., Petaluma, CA. To order, call toll free 800-Bibbero (800-242-2376) or Fax 800-242-9330.

MESSAGE FROM

For Dr.	Name of Caller	Rel. to Pt.	Patient	Pt. Age	Pt. Temp.	Message Date	Message Time AM PM	Urgent ☐ Yes ☐ No

Message: | Allergies

Respond to Phone #	Best Time to Call AM PM	Pharmacy Name / #	Patient's Chart Attached ☐ Yes ☐ No	Patient's Chart #	Initials

DOCTOR - STAFF RESPONSE

Doctor's / Staff Orders / Follow-Up Action

Call Back ☐ Yes ☐ No	Chart Mess. ☐ Yes ☐ No	Follow-Up Date / /	Follow-Up Completed-Date/Time / / AM PM	Response by

Product #78-9156 Pkg., #78-9157 Pads, Bibbero Systems, Inc., Petaluma, CA. To order, call toll free 800-Bibbero (800-242-2376) or Fax 800-242-9330.

Form 16

ABSTRACTING FROM MEDICAL RECORDS   _____

Patient's Name:_____

Did this patient have surgery?_____

If so, what was done?_____

What is the patient's chief complaint?_____
_____

What is the diagnosis?_____

Was any medication prescribed?_____

If so, what is the name of the medication and the dosage?_____
_____

Does the patient's past history show anything of consequence?_____
If so, what is it?_____

Does this patient have any drug or food allergies?_____
If so, what are they?_____

What is the etiology of this disease, injury or illness?_____
_____

What is the prognosis in this case?_____

Was any laboratory work performed?_____
If so, was there anything of consequence shown?_____
_____

List the abbreviations from the patient record and give their definitions:

_____   _____

_____   _____

_____   _____

_____   _____

_____   _____

_____   _____

_____   _____

_____   _____

_____   _____

What reports or material helped you ascertain the above answers?

_____   _____

_____   _____

Form 17

PATIENT RECORD

LAST NAME	FIRST NAME	MIDDLE NAME	BIRTH DATE	SEX	HOME PHONE

ADDRESS	CITY	STATE	ZIP CODE

PATIENT'S OCCUPATION   NAME OF COMPANY

ADDRESS OF EMPLOYER   PHONE

SPOUSE OR PARENT   OCCUPATION

EMPLOYER   ADDRESS   PHONE

NAME OF INSURANCE GROUP   SUBSCRIBER

BLUE SHIELD OR BLUE CROSS CERT. NO.	GROUP NO.	CURRENT COVERAGE NO.	EFFECTIVE DATE

MEDICARE NO.	MEDICAID NO.	EFFECTIVE DATE	SOC. SEC. NO.

REFERRED BY:

DATE	PROGRESS

Form 18

Form 19

PRACTON MEDICAL GROUP, INC.
4567 Broad Avenue
Woodland Hills, XY 12345-4700

Phone: 013/486-6789   FAX: 013/488-7815

NAME_____DATE_____
ADDRESS_____CITY_____STATE_____

Rx

N.E. REP.____
REP.____TIMES

_____ MD

BNDD NO. AJ8706723

Gerald M. Practon, MD C 14021
Fran T. Practon, MD   C 15038

Form 20

PRACTON MEDICAL GROUP, INC.
4567 Broad Avenue
Woodland Hills, XY 12345-4700
Tel. 013/486-9002

Patient's name:

_____

Please bring this card with you
for each appointment.

Your primary physician is:

_____

With so many potent medicines available today, the possibility of undesirable effects of single drugs, or adverse interactions of multiple drugs, is always present. If there is any question of side effects of drugs, or their potential toxicity, feel free to call and discuss this with your physician.

It is vital that you, and all health care professionals involved in your care, know exactly the names and dosages of ALL medicines you are currently taking. Please keep this card with you and show it to your doctor or dentist, during office visits, and to your pharmacist when prescriptions and/or over-the-counter preparations are purchased.

MEDICATION SCHEDULE

Name of Medication	Strength	Times to be Taken					

If you have any questions or problems with medications, please call 486-9002

Form 21

1. Walter Louis McDougall

2. Marilyn Marvel

3. Ms. Margaret McKinney

4. Roberta Nelson
   6428 Lorraine Rd. Sherman Oaks, XY

5. Rev. Jack Rowe
   462 Twelve Oaks Dr. Encino, XY

6. Renee T. Moore (Mrs. C. H.)

7. Marilyn P. Marvel (Mrs. Paul P.)

8. Roger C. Camp

9. Mrs. John M. White (Jane B.)

10. Anna F. Rolf

11. Mrs. Roger G. Camp (Jane)

12. Raymond E. Stokes, Jr.

13. Nancy Jeffers

14. Mrs. Alfred Hall (Martha)

15. Ms. Carla St. John

16. Wm. L. MacPherson

17. Benjamin Thomas

18. L. William McPherson

19. A. Buckley

20. Vincent DeLuca

Form 22

21. John Lee-Barry

22. Alice Buckley

23. Tufo Skroff

24. Mrs. Andrew Hall (Mary Jones)

25. Mrs. Winifred LaSalle (Robert L.)

26. Alice-Ruth Buckely

27. Dr. Jack Rowe
    409 - 23 St., Encino, XY

28. Robert Nelson
    321 April Ave., Woodland Hills, XY

29. Professor Carl Starr

30. Margo Hawkins, RN

31. Paul P. Marvel

32. Carl Saintelley

33. Professor Carl Procter

34. Frank Albert

35. Mr. C. H. Moore

36. Larry J. Riley

37. Karen Ruth-Ann Klein

38. Robert Nelson, III
    421 April Ave., Woodland Hills, XY

39. Mr. C. Howard Moore

40. Mary Faye Jeffers

Form 23

41. Edward R. Mackey

51. Edward S. Mackey

42. M. Robert DeAriolla

52. Raymond E. Stokes

43. Marvin N. Riley

53. Walter L. McDougall

44. Hannah R. Sentry (Mrs. Randolph E.)

54. Mary MacKay

45. Rock C. Stetson

55. Donald Morris, Mr., II
    26 Avocado Place, Logan, XY

46. Senator Griffith

56. Chas. R. Bennett

47. Mr. Donald Morris, III
    771 So. Main St., Long Beach, XY

57. C. Richard Bennett

48. Dr. John S. Richards

58. Donald Morris
    14 Meridian St., Logan, XY

49. Robert LaVelle

59. X

50. John C. Richards, M D

60. X

Form 24

ORDER FORM

Ship to _____

Your name _____

Address _____

City _____ State _____

Zip _____ Telephone _____

☐ Check enclosed. M&W pays delivery charges in continental U.S. ☐ Bill me. M&W adds delivery.

M&W PRINTING COMPANY

**1101 WASHINGTON PARK
WAUKEGAN, ILL. 60085**

OFFICE USE	5 Category	Shop code	300 Effort key	Premium	Type

QUANTITY	ITEM NO.	DESCRIPTION	TYPE STYLE	PRICE

Reg. number for prescription forms _____

Starting number for receipt books _____

Color choice (where applicable) _____

Codes: ☐ Standard ☐ Special ☐ No codes

SALES TAX (Ill. residents only)	
DELIVERY (where applicable)	
TOTAL	

OFFICE USE

Quantity _____

Item no. _____

Description _____

Type style _____

Starting no. _____

Reg. no. _____

Codes _____

☐ Standard _____

☐ Special _____

☐ No codes _____

Hand print or typewrite your copy here. If possible send us a printed sample. We print your copy only as indicated

Form 25

ORDER FORM

photocopy this form for ordering convenience

24 HOUR FAX LINE: 916.638.0116

TOLL FREE DIRECT ORDER LINE

1.800.800.4930

MSI, Incorporated
20 Main Street, Third Floor
Irvine, California 92714

PLEASE FILL IN YOUR CUSTOMER NUMBER IF YOU HAVE PURCHASED FROM US BEFORE:

NAME _____
ADDRESS _____
CITY/STATE/ZIP _____
SPECIALTY _____
TELEPHONE _____
SHIP TO: (IF DIFFERENT FROM ABOVE _____

If you are a new customer, or have recently moved, help us expedite your order by providing us with your state registration number.

State License # _____
Expiration Date: _____

PRODUCT PART NUMBER	PAGE #	PRODUCT DESCRIPTION	PKG SIZE	UNITS	QTY	EXTN

IF YOU WISH TO PAY FOR YOUR ORDER BY CREDIT CARD, PLEASE COMPLETE THE FOLLOWING INFORMATION:

□ VISA □ MASTERCARD □ DISCOVER □ PREFERRED CUSTOMER CARD

YOUR CARD # : ☐☐☐☐☐☐☐☐☐☐☐☐☐☐☐☐☐☐

SIGNATURE _____ CARD EXP. DATE _____

STATE TAX (CA, IN, KY, OH, WA, WV)	
SHIPPING & HANDLING	
TOTAL	

THANK YOU FOR YOUR ORDER!

Form 26

PURCHASE ORDER

TO.

PURCHASE
ORDER NO.

DATE

SHIP TO ATTENTION OF:

TERMS	F.O.B.	SHIP VIA	DATE NEEDED

QUANTITY	DESCRIPTION	UNIT PRICE	AMOUNT

TOTAL VALUE

DELIVER NO GOODS WITHOUT A WRITTEN ORDER ON THIS FORM

By _____

PURCHASING AGENT

PLEASE FORWARD
ACKNOWLEDGEMENT AT ONCE

Form 27

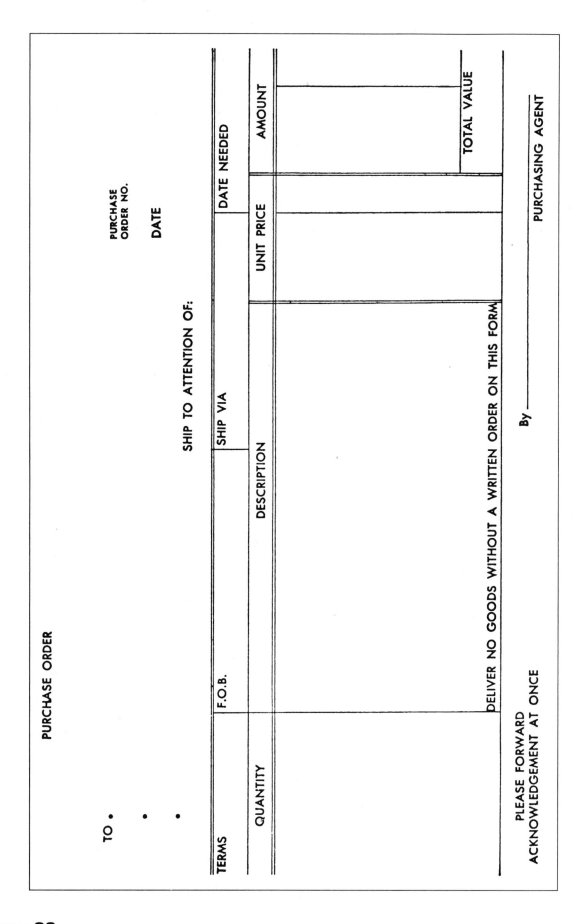

Form 28

FRAN T. PRACTON, MD
Family Practice

GERALD M. PRACTON, MD
General Practice

PRACTON MEDICAL GROUP, INC.
4567 Broad Avenue
Woodland Hills, XY 12345-4700
Tel. 013/486-9002
Fax No. 013/488-7815

Form 29

Date line   line 13—15

Inside address   line 18—24

1—100 words   Short letter   4 inches (40P/50E)

100—200 words Medium length letter 5 inches (50P/60E)

200 + words   Long letter 6 inches (60P/70E)

Form 29A

FRAN T. PRACTON, MD
Family Practice

GERALD M. PRACTON, MD
General Practice

PRACTON MEDICAL GROUP, INC.
4567 Broad Avenue
Woodland Hills, XY 12345-4700
Tel. 013/486-9002
Fax No. 013/488-7815

Form 30

FRAN T. PRACTON, MD
Family Practice

GERALD M. PRACTON, MD
General Practice

PRACTON MEDICAL GROUP, INC.
4567 Broad Avenue
Woodland Hills, XY 12345-4700
Tel. 013/486-9002
Fax No. 013/488-7815

Form 31

FRAN T. PRACTON, MD
Family Practice

GERALD M. PRACTON, MD
General Practice

PRACTON MEDICAL GROUP, INC.
4567 Broad Avenue
Woodland Hills, XY 12345-4700
Tel. 013/486-9002
Fax No. 013/488-7815

Form 32

FRAN T. PRACTON, MD
Family Practice

GERALD M. PRACTON, MD
General Practice

PRACTON MEDICAL GROUP, INC.
4567 Broad Avenue
Woodland Hills, XY 12345-4700
Tel. 013/486-9002
Fax No. 013/488-7815

Form 33

INTER-OFFICE MEMO   Date_____

TO:

FROM:

SUBJECT:

Form 34

MEMO

TO:

FROM:

DATE:

SUBJECT:

Form 35

FRAN T. PRACTON, MD
Family Practice

GERALD M. PRACTON, MD
General Practice

PRACTON MEDICAL GROUP, INC.
4567 Broad Avenue
Woodland Hills, XY 12345-4700
Tel. 013/486-9002
Fax No. 013/488-7815

Form 36

FRAN T. PRACTON, MD
Family Practice

GERALD M. PRACTON, MD
General Practice

PRACTON MEDICAL GROUP, INC.
4567 Broad Avenue
Woodland Hills, XY 12345-4700
Tel. 013/486-9002
Fax No. 013/488-7815

Form 37

FRAN T. PRACTON, MD
Family Practice

GERALD M. PRACTON, MD
General Practice

PRACTON MEDICAL GROUP, INC.
4567 Broad Avenue
Woodland Hills, XY 12345-4700
Tel. 013/486-9002
Fax No. 013/488-7815

Form 38

PRACTON MEDICAL GROUP, INC.
4567 Broad Avenue
Woodland Hills, XY 12345-4700

Forwarding and Service Requested

Form 39

UNITED STATES POSTAL SERVICE

First-Class Mail
Postage & Fees Paid
USPS
Permit No. G-10

● Print your name, address, and ZIP Code in this box ●

SENDER:
- Complete items 1 and/or 2 for additional services.
- Complete items 3, 4a, and 4b.
- Print your name and address on the reverse of this form so that we can return this card to you.
- Attach this form to the front of the mailpiece, or on the back if space does not permit.
- Write *"Return Receipt Requested"* on the mailpiece below the article number.
- The Return Receipt will show to whom the article was delivered and the date delivered.

I also wish to receive the following services (for an extra fee):

1. ☐ Addressee's Address
2. ☐ Restricted Delivery

Consult postmaster for fee.

Is your RETURN ADDRESS completed on the reverse side?

Thank you for using Return Receipt Service.

3. Article Addressed to:

4a. Article Number

4b. Service Type
☐ Registered   ☐ Certified
☐ Express Mail   ☐ Insured
☐ Return Receipt for Merchandise ☐ COD

7. Date of Delivery

5. Received By: *(Print Name)*

8. Addressee's Address *(Only if requested and fee is paid)*

6. Signature: *(Addressee or Agent)*
X

PS Form **3811,** December 1994   Domestic Return Receipt

P 300 578 329

US Postal Service
Receipt for Certified Mail
No Insurance Coverage Provided.
Do not use for International Mail (*See reverse*)

Sent to

Street & Number

Post Office, State, & ZIP Code

Postage | $

Certified Fee

Special Delivery Fee

Restricted Delivery Fee

Return Receipt Showing to Whom & Date Delivered

Return Receipt Showing to Whom, Date, & Addressee's Address

TOTAL Postage & Fees | $

Postmark or Date

PS Form **3800,** April 1995

Fold at line over top of envelope to the right of the return address

CERTIFIED

P 300 578 329

MAIL

Form 40

UNITED STATES POSTAL SERVICE™

Stamps By Mail Order Form

555   0495

Area Code   **Daytime Phone Number**

☐☐☐   ☐☐☐ - ☐☐☐☐

Last Name   First Initial   Middle Initial

Company Name (if applicable)

Mailing Address/PO Box   Apt./Suite

City   State   ZIP+4 Code

ITEM	DESCRIPTION	PRICE	QTY.	COST
1	(100) 32¢ Stamps - 1 Roll First-Class rate	$32.00		
2	(50) 32¢ Stamps - 1 Sheet First-Class rate	16.00		
3	(20) 32¢ Stamps - 1 Booklet First-Class rate	6.40		
4	(500) 32¢ Stamps - 1 Roll First-Class rate	160.00		
5	(100) 32¢ Stamps - 1 Sheet First-Class rate	32.00		
6	(100) 23¢ Stamps - 1 Roll First-Class rate, 2nd ounce	23.00		
7	(50) 32¢ Love Stamps - 1 Sheet First-Class rate	16.00		
8	(100) 20¢ Stamps - 1 Sheet First-Class postcard rate	20.00		
9	(50) 20¢ Stamped Postal Cards First-Class, pre-stamped	10.00		
10	(100) 32¢ Stamped Envelopes - #10 First-Class, pre-stamped	38.00		
11	Express Mail Stamp (Up to 8 ozs.)	10.75		
12	Priority Mail Stamp (Up to 2 lbs.)	3.00		
13	(20) 32¢ Stamps - Self Adhesive First-Class rate	6.40		
14				

TOTAL COST OF ORDER _____

Thank you

PLEASE DO NOT SEND CASH. REQUESTS FOR ITEMS NOT LISTED WILL BE HONORED IF ITEM IS AVAILABLE. Orders of $200.00 or more will be sent by Certified Mail and must be signed for upon delivery. Information you provide will be protected and only disclosed in accordance with the Privacy Act of 1974. USPS eagle symbol and logotype are trademarks of the United States Postal Service. All rights reserved.

PS Form **3227-G** April 1995   ♲ *printed on recycled paper*

Form 41

FAX TRANSMITTAL SHEET

To: _____   Date _____

Fax Number: _____   Time _____

Number of Pages (including this one): _____

From: _____   Phone _____

Note: This transmittal is intended only for the use of the individual or entity to which it
is addressed, and may contain information that is privileged, confidential, and exempt from
disclosure under applicable law. If you are not the intended recipient, any dissemination,
distribution, or photocopying of this communication is strictly prohibited. If you have
received this communication in error, please notify this office immediately by telephone and
return the original FAX to us at the address below by U. S. Postal Service. Thank you.

Remarks:_____

_____

_____

If you cannot read this FAX or if pages are missing, please contact:

PRACTON MEDICAL GROUP, INC.
4567 Broad Avenue
Woodland Hills, XY 12345-4700
Tel. 013/486-9002
Fax No. 013/488-7815

Form 42

PRACTON MEDICAL GROUP, INC.
4567 Broad Avenue
Woodland Hills, XY 12345-4700

Forwarding Service Requested

PRACTON MEDICAL GROUP, INC.
4567 Broad Avenue
Woodland Hills, XY 12345-4700

Forwarding Service Requested

Form 43

PRACTON MEDICAL GROUP, INC.
4567 Broad Avenue
Woodland Hills, XY 12345-4700

Forwarding Service Requested

Form 44

FRAN T. PRACTON, MD
Family Practice

GERALD M. PRACTON, MD
General Practice

PRACTON MEDICAL GROUP, INC.
4567 Broad Avenue
Woodland Hills, XY 12345-4700
Tel. 013/486-9002
Fax No. 013/488-7815

Form 45

PRACTON MEDICAL GROUP, INC.
4567 Broad Avenue
Woodland Hills, XY 12345-4700

Forwarding Service Requested

Form 46

UNITED STATES POSTAL SERVICE

||||||||

First-Class Mail
Postage & Fees Paid
USPS
Permit No. G-10

● Print your name, address, and ZIP Code in this box ●

SENDER:
- Complete items 1 and/or 2 for additional services.
- Complete items 3, 4a, and 4b.
- Print your name and address on the reverse of this form so that we can return this card to you.
- Attach this form to the front of the mailpiece, or on the back if space does not permit.
- Write *"Return Receipt Requested"* on the mailpiece below the article number.
- The Return Receipt will show to whom the article was delivered and the date delivered.

I also wish to receive the following services (for an extra fee):
1. ☐ Addressee's Address
2. ☐ Restricted Delivery
Consult postmaster for fee.

3. Article Addressed to:

4a. Article Number

4b. Service Type
☐ Registered　☐ Certified
☐ Express Mail　☐ Insured
☐ Return Receipt for Merchandise　☐ COD

7. Date of Delivery

5. Received By: *(Print Name)*

8. Addressee's Address *(Only if requested and fee is paid)*

6. Signature: *(Addressee or Agent)*
X

Is your **RETURN ADDRESS** completed on the reverse side?

Thank you for using Return Receipt Service.

PS Form **3811,** December 1994

Domestic Return Receipt

P 300 578 329

US Postal Service
Receipt for Certified Mail
No Insurance Coverage Provided.
Do not use for International Mail *(See reverse)*

Sent to

Street & Number

Post Office, State, & ZIP Code

Postage $

Certified Fee

Special Delivery Fee

Restricted Delivery Fee

Return Receipt Showing to Whom & Date Delivered

Return Receipt Showing to Whom, Date, & Addressee's Address

TOTAL Postage & Fees $

Postmark or Date

PS Form **3800,** April 1995

Fold at line over top of envelope to the right of the return address

CERTIFIED

P 300 578 329

MAIL

Form 47

FRAN T. PRACTON, MD
Family Practice

GERALD M. PRACTON, MD
General Practice

PRACTON MEDICAL GROUP, INC.
4567 Broad Avenue
Woodland Hills, XY 12345-4700
Tel. 013/486-9002
Fax No. 013/488-7815

Form 48

PRACTON MEDICAL GROUP, INC.
4567 Broad Avenue
Woodland Hills, XY 12345-4700

Forwarding and Service Requested

Form 49

UNITED STATES POSTAL SERVICE

First-Class Mail
Postage & Fees Paid
USPS
Permit No. G-10

• Print your name, address, and ZIP Code in this box •

Is your **RETURN ADDRESS** completed on the reverse side?

SENDER:
- Complete items 1 and/or 2 for additional services.
- Complete items 3, 4a, and 4b.
- Print your name and address on the reverse of this form so that we can return this card to you.
- Attach this form to the front of the mailpiece, or on the back if space does not permit.
- Write *"Return Receipt Requested"* on the mailpiece below the article number.
- The Return Receipt will show to whom the article was delivered and the date delivered.

I also wish to receive the following services (for an extra fee):

1. ☐ Addressee's Address

2. ☐ Restricted Delivery

Consult postmaster for fee.

3. Article Addressed to:

4a. Article Number

4b. Service Type
☐ Registered   ☐ Certified
☐ Express Mail   ☐ Insured
☐ Return Receipt for Merchandise   ☐ COD

7. Date of Delivery

5. Received By: *(Print Name)*

8. Addressee's Address *(Only if requested and fee is paid)*

6. Signature: *(Addressee or Agent)*
X

Thank you for using Return Receipt Service.

PS Form **3811,** December 1994   Domestic Return Receipt

P 300 578 329

US Postal Service
Receipt for Certified Mail
No Insurance Coverage Provided.
Do not use for International Mail *(See reverse)*

Sent to

Street & Number

Post Office, State, & ZIP Code

Postage $

Certified Fee

Special Delivery Fee

Restricted Delivery Fee

Return Receipt Showing to Whom & Date Delivered

Return Receipt Showing to Whom, Date, & Addressee's Address

TOTAL Postage & Fees $

Postmark or Date

PS Form **3800,** April 1995

Fold at line over top of envelope to the right of the return address

CERTIFIED

P 300 578 329

MAIL

Form 50

PRACTON MEDICAL GROUP, INC.
4567 Broad Avenue
Woodland Hills, XY 12345-4700

Forwarding and Service Requested

Form 51

Authorization for medical and/or surgical treatment →center all caps   Symbols

I, the under signed, a patinet of Dr._____, in   1._____

_____hospital, do herebuy authorise Dr._____   2._____

_____and the following designated assistant's:_____,   3._____

_____,_____ to perfrom the following opera-   4._____

tion_____at_____hospital.   5._____

I further authorise addedprocedures or surgery as are considered ther-   6._____

apuetically necessary on the basis of any findings during the coarse   7._____

of the operation, and I consent to the administration of such anes-   8._____

thesia as are deemed necessary with the exception of_____   9._____

Any tissues or parts removedd by surgery maybe disposed of by the   10._____

Hospital in accordance with accustomed practice.   11._____

I herebuy acknowlege that I have read and that I fully understand the above   12._____

authorization for Medical and/or Surgical treatment, the reasons why for   13._____

the above-names surgery is necessary; its advantages and possbile   14._____

complications as well as possibly optional modes of treatment which   15._____

were explained by Doctor_____. I also certify   16._____

that no assurance or guaranty has been made as to the results that   17._____

maybe the direct result of the this surgery.   18._____

DATE_____   Singed_____   19._____

                                    Patient →center

WITNESS_____   oR _____   20._____

                                    Nearest Relative →

                                            21._____

Form 52

TRAVEL EXPENSE REPORT

TRIP BEGINNING_____   TRIP ENDING_____

DATE	SAT		SUN		MON		TUES		WED		THURS		FRI		SAT		TOTALS
LODGING																	
BREAKFAST																	
LUNCH																	
DINNER																	
LOCAL FARES																	
AUTO EXPENSES																	
PARKING FEES																	
PHONE/TELEGRAM																	
ENTERTAINMENT																	
TIPS																	
TOLLS																	
MISCELLANEOUS																	
OTHER																	
TOTALS																	

Description of Business Purpose/Locations

Form 53

DATE	REFERENCE	DESCRIPTION	CHARGES	PYMNTS.	ADJ.	BALANCE	PREVIOUS BALANCE	N A M E
				CREDITS				

This is your RECEIPT for this amount
This is a STATEMENT of your account to date _____

Please present this slip to receptionist
before leaving office.

PRACTON MEDICAL GROUP, INC.
4567 Broad Avenue
Woodland Hills, XY 12345-4700
Tel. 013-488-7815
Fax. No. 013-488-7815

Thank You!

ROA – Received on Account

OT – Other _____

_____

RB40BC-3-96

NEXT APPOINTMENT _____ **143**

DATE	REFERENCE	DESCRIPTION	CHARGES	PYMNTS.	ADJ.	BALANCE	PREVIOUS BALANCE	N A M E
				CREDITS				

This is your RECEIPT for this amount
This is a STATEMENT of your account to date _____

Please present this slip to receptionist
before leaving office.

PRACTON MEDICAL GROUP, INC.
4567 Broad Avenue
Woodland Hills, XY 12345-4700
Tel. 013-488-7815
Fax. No. 013-488-7815

Thank You!

ROA – Received on Account

OT – Other _____

_____

RB40BC-3-96

NEXT APPOINTMENT _____ **144**

DATE	REFERENCE	DESCRIPTION	CHARGES	PYMNTS.	ADJ.	BALANCE	PREVIOUS BALANCE	N A M E
				CREDITS				

This is your RECEIPT for this amount
This is a STATEMENT of your account to date _____

Please present this slip to receptionist
before leaving office.

PRACTON MEDICAL GROUP, INC.
4567 Broad Avenue
Woodland Hills, XY 12345-4700
Tel. 013-488-7815
Fax. No. 013-488-7815

Thank You!

ROA – Received on Account

OT – Other _____

_____

RB40BC-3-96

NEXT APPOINTMENT _____ **145**

DATE	REFERENCE	DESCRIPTION	CHARGES	PYMNTS.	ADJ.	BALANCE	PREVIOUS BALANCE	N A M E
				CREDITS				

This is your RECEIPT for this amount
This is a STATEMENT of your account to date _____

Please present this slip to receptionist
before leaving office.

PRACTON MEDICAL GROUP, INC.
4567 Broad Avenue
Woodland Hills, XY 12345-4700
Tel. 013-488-7815
Fax. No. 013-488-7815

Thank You!

ROA – Received on Account

OT – Other _____

_____

RB40BC-3-96

NEXT APPOINTMENT _____ **146**

Form 54

FRAN T. PRACTON, MD
Family Practice

GERALD M. PRACTON, MD
General Practice

PRACTON MEDICAL GROUP, INC.
4567 Broad Avenue
Woodland Hills, XY 12345-4700
Tel. 013/486-9002
Fax No. 013/488-7815

Form 55

PRACTON MEDICAL GROUP, INC.
4567 Broad Avenue
Woodland Hills, XY 12345-4700

Forwarding and Service Requested

Form 56

STATEMENT
PRACTON MEDICAL GROUP, INC.
4567 Broad Avenue
Woodland Hills, XY 12345-4700
Tel. 013-486-9002
Fax No. 013-488-7815

Phone No.(H)_____ (W)_____ Birthdate_____
Insurance Co._____Policy No._____

DATE	REFERENCE	DESCRIPTION	CHARGES	CREDITS		BALANCE
				PYMNTS.	ADJ.	
		BALANCE FORWARD ⟶				

RB40BC-2-96 PLEASE PAY LAST AMOUNT IN BALANCE COLUMN ⟶

THIS IS A COPY OF YOUR ACCOUNT AS IT APPEARS ON OUR RECORDS

Form 57

STATEMENT
PRACTON MEDICAL GROUP, INC.
4567 Broad Avenue
Woodland Hills, XY 12345-4700
Tel. 013-486-9002
Fax No. 013-488-7815

Phone No.(H)_____(W)_____ Birthdate_____

Insurance Co._____Policy No._____

DATE	REFERENCE	DESCRIPTION	CHARGES		CREDITS PYMNTS.		ADJ.		BALANCE	
			BALANCE FORWARD →						25	00
1/25/XX		OV level III	40	20						
1/25/XX		ECG	34	26						
1/25/XX		Spirometry	38	57						
1/25/XX		Handling Spec	5	00						
1/25/XX		Ua	8	00						
1/26/XX		Billed Aetna Ins. (1/25/XX)								
2/12/XX		OV level II	28	55						
2/12/XX		ECG	34	26						
2/12/XX		ROA pt ck. #1692			25	00				
3/2/XX		ROA Aetna ck. # 5093			90	74				
3/2/XX		Aetna Adj					12	60		
3/2/XX		Billed Aetna (2/12/XX)								
3/17/XX		ROA pt ck.# 1701			22	69				
4/11/XX		ROA Aetna ck. #7948			45	22				
4/11/XX		Aetna adj.					6	28		

RB40BC-2-96

PLEASE PAY LAST AMOUNT IN BALANCE COLUMN ⬏

THIS IS A COPY OF YOUR ACCOUNT AS IT APPEARS ON OUR RECORDS

Form 58

FRAN T. PRACTON, MD
Family Practice

GERALD M. PRACTON, MD
General Practice

PRACTON MEDICAL GROUP, INC.
4567 Broad Avenue
Woodland Hills, XY 12345-4700
Tel. 013/486-9002
Fax No. 013/488-7815

AUTHORIZATION TO CHARGE CREDIT CARD

Patient Name _____

Cardholder Name _____

Credit Card Company_____

Card Number_____ Expiration Date_____

I authorize _____ to charge my credit card $_____ on the _____ of each month until my balance of $_____ is paid in full. I understand that if the charge is not accepted by my credit card company, I will immediately make the monthly payment to the practice.

I understand that I may cancel this authorization at any time, but by doing so I acknowledge that the balance owing will be due and payable in full.

_____   _____
                Signature   Date

Form 59

FRAN T. PRACTON, MD
Family Practice

GERALD M. PRACTON, MD
General Practice

PRACTON MEDICAL GROUP, INC.
4567 Broad Avenue
Woodland Hills, XY 12345-4700
Tel. 013/486-9002
Fax No. 013/488-7815

PATIENT COMPLAINT DOCUMENT

Date of complaint _____ Account number _____

Patient name _____ Account balance _____

Complaint_____

_____

_____

_____

Action taken to resolve complaint_____

_____

_____

_____

_____   _____
           Employee signature   Date

Form 60

FINANCIAL AGREEMENT

For PROFESSIONAL SERVICES rendered or to be rendered to :

Daytime
Phone _____

Patient _____

Parent if patient is a minor _____

1. Cash price for services .... $ _____
2. Cash down payment .... $ _____
3. Charges covered by insurance service plan ...... $ _____
4. Unpaid balance of cash price .... $ _____
5. Amount financed (the amount of credit provided to you) .... $ _____
6. **FINANCE CHARGE** (the dollar amount the credit will cost you) ... $ _____
7. **ANNUAL PERCENTAGE RATE** (the cost of credit as a year-ly rate) _____ %
8. Total of payments (5 + 6 above- The amount you will have paid when you have made all scheduled payments) $ _____
9. Total sales price (1 + 6 above-Sum of cash price, financing charge and any other amounts financed by the creditor, not part of the finance charge) .... $ _____

You have the right at anytime to pay the unpaid balance due under this agreement without penalty.
You have the right at this time to receive an itemization of the amount financed.
☐ I want an itemization   ☐ I do not want an itemization

Total of payments (# 8 above) is payable to Dr. _____
in _____ monthly installments of $ _____ each and
installments of $ _____ each. The first installment being payable on
_____ 19 _____ and subsequent installments on the same day of each
consecutive month until paid in full.

NOTICE TO PATIENT

Do not sign this agreement if it contains any blank spaces. You are entitled to an exact copy of any agreement you sign. You have the right at any time to pay the unpaid balance due under this agreement.

The patient (parent or guardian) agrees to be and is fully responsible for total payment of services performed in this office including any amounts not covered by any health insurance or prepayment program the responsible party may have. See your contract documents for any additional information about nonpayment, default, any required prepayment in full before the scheduled date and prepayment refunds and penalties.

Signature of patient or one parent if patient is a minor:

X _____

Doctor's Signature _____

Form 1826 • 1982

SCHEDULE OF PAYMENT

No.	Date Due	Amount of Installment	Date Paid	Amount Paid	Balance Owed
D.P.		Total Amount			
1					
2					
3					
4					
5					
6					
7					
8					
9					
10					
11					
12					
13					
14					
15					
16					
17					
18					
19					
20					
21					
22					
23					

Form 61

MANAGED CARE PLAN
TREATMENT AUTHORIZATION REQUEST

**TO BE COMPLETED BY PRIMARY CARE PHYSICIAN
OR OUTSIDE PROVIDER**

Health Net	☐	Met Life	☐
Pacificare	☐	Travelers	☐
Secure Horizons	☐	Pru Care	☐

Patient Name:_____Date:_____

M_____ F_____ Birthdate_____ Home telephone number_____

Address_____

Primary Care Physician_____Member ID#_____

Referring Physician_____Member ID#_____

Referred to_____ Address_____

_____ Office telephone no._____

Diagnosis Code_____ Diagnosis_____

Diagnosis Code_____ Diagnosis_____

Treatment Plan:_____

Authorization requested for procedures/tests/visits:

Procedure Code_____ Description_____

Procedure Code_____ Description_____

Facility to be used:_____Estimated length of stay_____

Office ☐   Outpatient ☐   Inpatient ☐   Other ☐

List of potential consultants (i.e., anesthetists, assistants, or medical/surgical):

_____

Physician's signature_____

TO BE COMPLETED BY PRIMARY CARE PHYSICIAN

PCP Recommendations:_____PCP Initials_____

Eligibility checked_____Effective date_____

TO BE COMPLETED BY UTILIZATION MANAGEMENT

Authorized_____ Not authorized_____

Deferred_____ Modified_____

Authorization Request #_____

Comments:_____

Form 62

PLEASE
DO NOT
STAPLE
IN THIS
AREA

APPROVED OMB-0938-0008

↑
CARRIER
↓

| | PICA | | | | **HEALTH INSURANCE CLAIM FORM** | PICA | | |

1. MEDICARE MEDICAID CHAMPUS CHAMPVA GROUP HEALTH PLAN FECA BLK LUNG OTHER
☐ (Medicare #) ☐ (Medicaid #) ☐ (Sponsor's SSN) ☐ (VA File #) ☐ (SSN or ID) ☐ (SSN) ☐ (ID)

1a. INSURED'S I.D. NUMBER   (FOR PROGRAM IN ITEM 1)

2. PATIENT'S NAME (Last Name, First Name, Middle Initial)

3. PATIENT'S BIRTH DATE MM DD YY SEX M ☐ F ☐

4. INSURED'S NAME (Last Name, First Name, Middle Initial)

5. PATIENT'S ADDRESS (No., Street)

6. PATIENT RELATIONSHIP TO INSURED
Self ☐ Spouse ☐ Child ☐ Other ☐

7. INSURED'S ADDRESS (No., Street)

CITY   STATE

8. PATIENT STATUS
Single ☐ Married ☐ Other ☐
Employed ☐ Full-Time Student ☐ Part-Time Student ☐

CITY   STATE

ZIP CODE   TELEPHONE (Include Area Code) ( )

ZIP CODE   TELEPHONE (INCLUDE AREA CODE) ( )

9. OTHER INSURED'S NAME (Last Name, First Name, Middle Initial)

10. IS PATIENT'S CONDITION RELATED TO:

11. INSURED'S POLICY GROUP OR FECA NUMBER

a. OTHER INSURED'S POLICY OR GROUP NUMBER

a. EMPLOYMENT? (CURRENT OR PREVIOUS)
☐ YES ☐ NO

a. INSURED'S DATE OF BIRTH MM DD YY SEX M ☐ F ☐

b. OTHER INSURED'S DATE OF BIRTH MM DD YY SEX M ☐ F ☐

b. AUTO ACCIDENT?   PLACE (State)
☐ YES ☐ NO

b. EMPLOYER'S NAME OR SCHOOL NAME

c. EMPLOYER'S NAME OR SCHOOL NAME

c. OTHER ACCIDENT?
☐ YES ☐ NO

c. INSURANCE PLAN NAME OR PROGRAM NAME

d. INSURANCE PLAN NAME OR PROGRAM NAME

10d. RESERVED FOR LOCAL USE

d. IS THERE ANOTHER HEALTH BENEFIT PLAN?
☐ YES ☐ NO *If yes,* return to and complete item 9 a-d.

READ BACK OF FORM BEFORE COMPLETING & SIGNING THIS FORM.

12. PATIENT'S OR AUTHORIZED PERSON'S SIGNATURE I authorize the release of any medical or other information necessary to process this claim. I also request payment of government benefits either to myself or to the party who accepts assignment below.

SIGNED   DATE

13. INSURED S OR AUTHORIZED PERSON'S SIGNATURE I authorize payment of medical benefits to the undersigned physician or supplier for services described below.

SIGNED

↑
PATIENT AND INSURED INFORMATION
↓

14. DATE OF CURRENT: MM DD YY ◄ ILLNESS (First symptom) OR INJURY (Accident) OR PREGNANCY(LMP)

15. IF PATIENT HAS HAD SAME OR SIMILAR ILLNESS. GIVE FIRST DATE MM DD YY

16. DATES PATIENT UNABLE TO WORK IN CURRENT OCCUPATION
FROM MM DD YY TO MM DD YY

17. NAME OF REFERRING PHYSICIAN OR OTHER SOURCE

17a. I.D. NUMBER OF REFERRING PHYSICIAN

18. HOSPITALIZATION DATES RELATED TO CURRENT SERVICES
FROM MM DD YY TO MM DD YY

19. RESERVED FOR LOCAL USE

20. OUTSIDE LAB? $ CHARGES
☐ YES ☐ NO

21. DIAGNOSIS OR NATURE OF ILLNESS OR INJURY. (RELATE ITEMS 1,2,3 OR 4 TO ITEM 24E BY LINE)

1. |___.___| 3. |___.___|
2. |___.___| 4. |___.___|

22. MEDICAID RESUBMISSION CODE   ORIGINAL REF. NO.

23. PRIOR AUTHORIZATION NUMBER

24. A DATE(S) OF SERVICE			B Place of Service	C Type of Service	D PROCEDURES, SERVICES, OR SUPPLIES (Explain Unusual Circumstances)		E DIAGNOSIS CODE	F $ CHARGES	G DAYS OR UNITS	H EPSDT Family Plan	I EMG	J COB	K RESERVED FOR LOCAL USE
From MM DD YY	To MM DD YY				CPT/HCPCS	MODIFIER							
1													
2													
3													
4													
5													
6													

25. FEDERAL TAX I.D. NUMBER   SSN EIN ☐ ☐

26. PATIENT'S ACCOUNT NO.

27. ACCEPT ASSIGNMENT? (For govt. claims, see back) ☐ YES ☐ NO

28. TOTAL CHARGE $

29. AMOUNT PAID $

30. BALANCE DUE $

31. SIGNATURE OF PHYSICIAN OR SUPPLIER INCLUDING DEGREES OR CREDENTIALS (I certify that the statements on the reverse apply to this bill and are made a part thereof.)

SIGNED   DATE

32. NAME AND ADDRESS OF FACILITY WHERE SERVICES WERE RENDERED (If other than home or office)

33. PHYSICIAN'S, SUPPLIER'S BILLING NAME, ADDRESS, ZIP CODE & PHONE #

PIN#   GRP#

↑
PHYSICIAN OR SUPPLIER INFORMATION
↓

(APPROVED BY AMA COUNCIL ON MEDICAL SERVICE 8/88)

PLEASE PRINT OR TYPE

FORM HCFA-1500 (U2) (12-90)
FORM OWCP-1500   FORM RRB-1500

Form 63

APPROVED OMB-0938-0008

HEALTH INSURANCE CLAIM FORM

PLEASE
DO NOT
STAPLE
IN THIS
AREA

CARRIER

PICA | | | PICA | |

1. MEDICARE MEDICAID CHAMPUS CHAMPVA GROUP HEALTH PLAN FECA BLK LUNG OTHER
(Medicare #) (Medicaid #) (Sponsor's SSN) (VA File #) (SSN or ID) (SSN) (ID)

1a. INSURED'S I.D. NUMBER (FOR PROGRAM IN ITEM 1)

2. PATIENT'S NAME (Last Name, First Name, Middle Initial)

3. PATIENT'S BIRTH DATE MM DD YY SEX M F

4. INSURED'S NAME (Last Name, First Name, Middle Initial)

5. PATIENT'S ADDRESS (No., Street)

6. PATIENT RELATIONSHIP TO INSURED
Self Spouse Child Other

7. INSURED'S ADDRESS (No., Street)

CITY STATE

8. PATIENT STATUS
Single Married Other
Employed Full-Time Student Part-Time Student

CITY STATE

ZIP CODE TELEPHONE (Include Area Code) ( )

ZIP CODE TELEPHONE (INCLUDE AREA CODE) ( )

9. OTHER INSURED'S NAME (Last Name, First Name, Middle Initial)

10. IS PATIENT'S CONDITION RELATED TO:

11. INSURED'S POLICY GROUP OR FECA NUMBER

a. OTHER INSURED'S POLICY OR GROUP NUMBER

a. EMPLOYMENT? (CURRENT OR PREVIOUS) YES NO

a. INSURED'S DATE OF BIRTH MM DD YY SEX M F

b. OTHER INSURED'S DATE OF BIRTH MM DD YY SEX M F

b. AUTO ACCIDENT? PLACE (State) YES NO

b. EMPLOYER'S NAME OR SCHOOL NAME

c. EMPLOYER'S NAME OR SCHOOL NAME

c. OTHER ACCIDENT? YES NO

c. INSURANCE PLAN NAME OR PROGRAM NAME

d. INSURANCE PLAN NAME OR PROGRAM NAME

10d. RESERVED FOR LOCAL USE

d. IS THERE ANOTHER HEALTH BENEFIT PLAN? YES NO *If yes,* return to and complete item 9 a-d.

READ BACK OF FORM BEFORE COMPLETING & SIGNING THIS FORM.
12. PATIENT'S OR AUTHORIZED PERSON'S SIGNATURE I authorize the release of any medical or other information necessary to process this claim. I also request payment of government benefits either to myself or to the party who accepts assignment below.
SIGNED DATE

13. INSURED'S OR AUTHORIZED PERSON'S SIGNATURE I authorize payment of medical benefits to the undersigned physician or supplier for services described below.
SIGNED

14. DATE OF CURRENT: MM DD YY ILLNESS (First symptom) OR INJURY (Accident) OR PREGNANCY(LMP)

15. IF PATIENT HAS HAD SAME OR SIMILAR ILLNESS. GIVE FIRST DATE MM DD YY

16. DATES PATIENT UNABLE TO WORK IN CURRENT OCCUPATION FROM MM DD YY TO MM DD YY

17. NAME OF REFERRING PHYSICIAN OR OTHER SOURCE

17a. I.D. NUMBER OF REFERRING PHYSICIAN

18. HOSPITALIZATION DATES RELATED TO CURRENT SERVICES FROM MM DD YY TO MM DD YY

19. RESERVED FOR LOCAL USE

20. OUTSIDE LAB? YES NO $ CHARGES

21. DIAGNOSIS OR NATURE OF ILLNESS OR INJURY. (RELATE ITEMS 1,2,3 OR 4 TO ITEM 24E BY LINE)
1. 3.
2. 4.

22. MEDICAID RESUBMISSION CODE ORIGINAL REF. NO.

23. PRIOR AUTHORIZATION NUMBER

24. A DATE(S) OF SERVICE		B Place of Service	C Type of Service	D PROCEDURES, SERVICES, OR SUPPLIES (Explain Unusual Circumstances) CPT/HCPCS MODIFIER	E DIAGNOSIS CODE	F $ CHARGES	G DAYS OR UNITS	H EPSDT Family Plan	I EMG	J COB	K RESERVED FOR LOCAL USE
From MM DD YY	To MM DD YY										
1											
2											
3											
4											
5											
6											

25. FEDERAL TAX I.D. NUMBER SSN EIN

26. PATIENT'S ACCOUNT NO.

27. ACCEPT ASSIGNMENT? (For govt. claims, see back) YES NO

28. TOTAL CHARGE $

29. AMOUNT PAID $

30. BALANCE DUE $

31. SIGNATURE OF PHYSICIAN OR SUPPLIER INCLUDING DEGREES OR CREDENTIALS (I certify that the statements on the reverse apply to this bill and are made a part thereof.)
SIGNED DATE

32. NAME AND ADDRESS OF FACILITY WHERE SERVICES WERE RENDERED (If other than home or office)

33. PHYSICIAN'S, SUPPLIER'S BILLING NAME, ADDRESS, ZIP CODE & PHONE #
PIN# GRP#

PATIENT AND INSURED INFORMATION / PHYSICIAN OR SUPPLIER INFORMATION

(APPROVED BY AMA COUNCIL ON MEDICAL SERVICE 8/88) **PLEASE PRINT OR TYPE**

FORM HCFA-1500 (U2) (12-90) FORM OWCP-1500 FORM RRB-1500

Form 64

PLEASE
DO NOT
STAPLE
IN THIS
AREA

APPROVED OMB-0938-0008

CARRIER

| | PICA | | | **HEALTH INSURANCE CLAIM FORM** | PICA | |

1. MEDICARE (Medicare #) **MEDICAID** (Medicaid #) **CHAMPUS** (Sponsor's SSN) **CHAMPVA** (VA File #) **GROUP HEALTH PLAN** (SSN or ID) **FECA BLK LUNG** (SSN) **OTHER** (ID)

1a. INSURED'S I.D. NUMBER (FOR PROGRAM IN ITEM 1)

2. PATIENT'S NAME (Last Name, First Name, Middle Initial)

3. PATIENT'S BIRTH DATE MM DD YY **SEX** M F

4. INSURED'S NAME (Last Name, First Name, Middle Initial)

5. PATIENT'S ADDRESS (No., Street)

6. PATIENT RELATIONSHIP TO INSURED Self Spouse Child Other

7. INSURED'S ADDRESS (No., Street)

CITY STATE

8. PATIENT STATUS Single Married Other

Employed Full-Time Student Part-Time Student

CITY STATE

ZIP CODE TELEPHONE (Include Area Code) ( )

ZIP CODE TELEPHONE (INCLUDE AREA CODE) ( )

9. OTHER INSURED'S NAME (Last Name, First Name, Middle Initial)

10. IS PATIENT'S CONDITION RELATED TO:

11. INSURED'S POLICY GROUP OR FECA NUMBER

a. OTHER INSURED'S POLICY OR GROUP NUMBER

a. EMPLOYMENT? (CURRENT OR PREVIOUS) YES NO

a. INSURED'S DATE OF BIRTH MM DD YY **SEX** M F

b. OTHER INSURED'S DATE OF BIRTH MM DD YY **SEX** M F

b. AUTO ACCIDENT? PLACE (State) YES NO

b. EMPLOYER'S NAME OR SCHOOL NAME

c. EMPLOYER'S NAME OR SCHOOL NAME

c. OTHER ACCIDENT? YES NO

c. INSURANCE PLAN NAME OR PROGRAM NAME

d. INSURANCE PLAN NAME OR PROGRAM NAME

10d. RESERVED FOR LOCAL USE

d. IS THERE ANOTHER HEALTH BENEFIT PLAN? YES NO *If yes*, return to and complete item 9 a-d.

READ BACK OF FORM BEFORE COMPLETING & SIGNING THIS FORM.

12. PATIENT'S OR AUTHORIZED PERSON'S SIGNATURE I authorize the release of any medical or other information necessary to process this claim. I also request payment of government benefits either to myself or to the party who accepts assignment below.

SIGNED _____ DATE _____

13. INSURED'S OR AUTHORIZED PERSON'S SIGNATURE I authorize payment of medical benefits to the undersigned physician or supplier for services described below.

SIGNED _____

14. DATE OF CURRENT: ILLNESS (First symptom) OR INJURY (Accident) OR PREGNANCY(LMP) MM DD YY

15. IF PATIENT HAS HAD SAME OR SIMILAR ILLNESS. GIVE FIRST DATE MM DD YY

16. DATES PATIENT UNABLE TO WORK IN CURRENT OCCUPATION FROM MM DD YY TO MM DD YY

17. NAME OF REFERRING PHYSICIAN OR OTHER SOURCE

17a. I.D. NUMBER OF REFERRING PHYSICIAN

18. HOSPITALIZATION DATES RELATED TO CURRENT SERVICES FROM MM DD YY TO MM DD YY

19. RESERVED FOR LOCAL USE

20. OUTSIDE LAB? YES NO $ CHARGES

21. DIAGNOSIS OR NATURE OF ILLNESS OR INJURY. (RELATE ITEMS 1,2,3 OR 4 TO ITEM 24E BY LINE)

1. ____ . ____   3. ____ . ____

2. ____ . ____   4. ____ . ____

22. MEDICAID RESUBMISSION CODE ORIGINAL REF. NO.

23. PRIOR AUTHORIZATION NUMBER

24. A DATE(S) OF SERVICE		B Place of Service	C Type of Service	D PROCEDURES, SERVICES, OR SUPPLIES (Explain Unusual Circumstances)		E DIAGNOSIS CODE	F $ CHARGES	G DAYS OR UNITS	H EPSDT Family Plan	I EMG	J COB	K RESERVED FOR LOCAL USE
From MM DD YY	To MM DD YY			CPT/HCPCS	MODIFIER							
1												
2												
3												
4												
5												
6												

25. FEDERAL TAX I.D. NUMBER SSN EIN

26. PATIENT'S ACCOUNT NO.

27. ACCEPT ASSIGNMENT? (For govt. claims, see back) YES NO

28. TOTAL CHARGE $

29. AMOUNT PAID $

30. BALANCE DUE $

31. SIGNATURE OF PHYSICIAN OR SUPPLIER INCLUDING DEGREES OR CREDENTIALS (I certify that the statements on the reverse apply to this bill and are made a part thereof.)

SIGNED _____ DATE _____

32. NAME AND ADDRESS OF FACILITY WHERE SERVICES WERE RENDERED (If other than home or office)

33. PHYSICIAN'S, SUPPLIER'S BILLING NAME, ADDRESS, ZIP CODE & PHONE #

PIN# GRP#

PATIENT AND INSURED INFORMATION

PHYSICIAN OR SUPPLIER INFORMATION

(APPROVED BY AMA COUNCIL ON MEDICAL SERVICE 8/88)

PLEASE PRINT OR TYPE

FORM HCFA-1500 (U2) (12-90)
FORM OWCP-1500   FORM RRB-1500

Form 65

DATE	ITEM	AMOUNT

PRACTON MEDICAL GROUP, INC.
4567 Broad Avenue
Woodland Hills, XY 12345-4700

FOR INSTRUCTIONAL USE ONLY

485

3-2
310

PAY _____ **DOLLARS**

PAY TO THE ORDER OF	DATE	GROSS	DISC.

CHECK AMOUNT

$ _____

NOT VALID

THE FIRST NATIONAL BANK – Princeton, NJ, 08540-2222
RB40BC-4-96

⑂"000000"⑂ ⑂:123456789⑂: "876 543 2"

DATE	ITEM	AMOUNT

PRACTON MEDICAL GROUP, INC.
4567 Broad Avenue
Woodland Hills, XY 12345-4700

FOR INSTRUCTIONAL USE ONLY

486

3-2
310

PAY _____ **DOLLARS**

PAY TO THE ORDER OF	DATE	GROSS	DISC.

CHECK AMOUNT

$ _____

NOT VALID

THE FIRST NATIONAL BANK – Princeton, NJ, 08540-2222
RB40BC-4-96

⑂"000000"⑂ ⑂:123456789⑂: "876 543 2"

Stationer's Corporation
340 West Main Street
Woodland Hills, XY 12345

STATEMENT

199x
5-11 1 pkg pens $10.00
      1 box 3 x 5 cards   5.50
      1 sm file box   8.00

      6% tax   1.50

TOTAL BALANCE DUE $25.00

Randolph Electrical Supply
458 State Street
Woodland Hills, XY 12345

STATEMENT

199x
5-15 Small vacuum $51.80

      6% tax   3.30

TOTAL BALANCE DUE $55.10

Form 66

FOUR EASY STEPS TO HELP YOU BALANCE YOUR CHECKBOOK

1. UPDATE YOUR CHECKBOOK
   - Compare and check-off each transaction recorded in your check register with those listed on this statement. These include checks, direct deposits, direct debits, deposits, ATM transactions, etc.
   - Add interest and subtract service charges

2. DETERMINE OUTSTANDING ITEMS
   - Use the charts below to list transactions shown in your check register but not included on this statement.
   - Include any from previous months.

OUTSTANDING CHECKS OR OTHER WITHDRAWALS				DEPOSITS NOT CREDITED	
CHECK NO.	AMOUNT	CHECK NO.	AMOUNT	DATE	AMOUNT
	$		$		$
		TOTAL	$	TOTAL	$

3. BALANCE YOUR ACCOUNT
   - Enter Ending Statement Balance shown on this statement. $ _____
   - Add deposits listed in your register and not shown on this statement. + _____
   - Subtract outstanding checks/withdrawals. - _____
   - **ADJUSTED TOTAL** (should agree with your checkbook balance). $ _____

4. IF THE BALANCE IN YOUR CHECKBOOK DOES NOT AGREE WITH THE ADJUSTED TOTAL, THEN
   - Check all addition and subtraction.
   - Make sure all outstanding checks, withdrawals and deposits have been listed in the appropriate chart above.
   - Compare the amount of each check, withdrawal and deposit in your checkbook with the amounts on this statement.
   - Review the figures on last month's statement.

IN CASE OF ERRORS OR QUESTIONS ABOUT YOUR ELECTRONIC TRANSFERS, telephone us at the telephone number shown on this statement, or write us at: P.O. Box 30987, City of Industry, CA 91896-7987 as soon as you can if you think your statement or receipt is wrong or if you need more information about a transfer on the statement or receipt. We must hear from you no later than 60 days after we sent you the FIRST statement on which the error or problem appeared. Tell us your name and account number, and describe the error or the transfer you are unsure about. Please explain as clearly as you can why you believe there is an error or why you need more information. You must also tell us the exact dollar amount of the suspected error. If you tell us orally, we require that you send us your complaint or question in writing within 10 business days. If you do not put your complaint or questions in writing or we do not receive it within 10 business days, we may not recredit your account. If we decide that there was no error, we will send you a written explanation within 3 business days after we finish our investigation. You may ask for copies of the documents that we used in our investigation. For purposes of error resolution, our business days are Monday through Friday, 8:30 a.m. to 5:00 p.m., Pacific Time. We are closed Saturdays, Sundays and federal holidays.

All Non-POS, MasterMoney™ or Foreign Transactions
We will tell you the results of our investigation within 10 business days after we receive your written complaint and will correct any error promptly. If we need more time, however, we may take up to 45 days to investigate your complaint or questions. If we decide we need additional time, we will recredit your account within 10 business days for the amount you think is in error, so that you will have the use of the money during the time it takes us to complete our investigation.

POS, MasterMoney™ and Foreign Transactions
If the transfer results from a point-of-sale transaction, MasterMoney™ transaction or a transfer initiated outside the United States, we will still correct any error promptly. However, we may take up to 20 business days after we receive your written complaint to tell you the results of our investigation. If we need more time, we may use an additional 90 days. Should we take this additional time, we will recredit your account within 20 business days for the amount you think is in error. This will allow you to have the use of this money while we complete our investigation.

CF 5299F (5/96)

Form 67

STATEMENT
PRACTON MEDICAL GROUP, INC.
4567 Broad Avenue
Woodland Hills, XY 12345-4700
Tel. 013-486-9002
Fax No. 013-488-7815

Phone No.(H)_____ (W)_____ Birthdate_____
Insurance Co._____ Policy No._____

DATE	REFERENCE	DESCRIPTION	CHARGES	CREDITS		BALANCE
				Pymnts	Adj	
		BALANCE FORWARD				

STATEMENT
PRACTON MEDICAL GROUP, INC.
4567 Broad Avenue
Woodland Hills, XY 12345-4700
Tel. 013-486-9002
Fax No. 013-488-7815

Phone No.(H)_____ (W)_____ Birthdate_____
Insurance Co._____ Policy No._____

DATE	REFERENCE	DESCRIPTION	CHARGES	CREDITS		BALANCE
				Pymnts	Adj	
		BALANCE FORWARD				

Form 68

STATEMENT
PRACTON MEDICAL GROUP, INC.
4567 Broad Avenue
Woodland Hills, XY 12345-4700
Tel. 013-486-9002
Fax No. 013-488-7815

Phone No.(H)_____(W)_____ Birthdate_____
Insurance Co._____ Policy No._____

DATE	REFERENCE	DESCRIPTION	CHARGES	CREDITS		BALANCE	
				Pymnts	Adj		
		BALANCE FORWARD					

STATEMENT
PRACTON MEDICAL GROUP, INC.
4567 Broad Avenue
Woodland Hills, XY 12345-4700
Tel. 013-486-9002
Fax No. 013-488-7815

Phone No.(H)_____(W)_____ Birthdate_____
Insurance Co._____ Policy No._____

DATE	REFERENCE	DESCRIPTION	CHARGES	CREDITS		BALANCE	
				Pymnts	Adj		
		BALANCE FORWARD					

Form 69

STATEMENT
PRACTON MEDICAL GROUP, INC.
4567 Broad Avenue
Woodland Hills, XY 12345-4700
Tel. 013-486-9002
Fax No. 013-488-7815

Phone No.(H)_____(W)_____ Birthdate_____
Insurance Co._____Policy No._____

DATE	REFERENCE	DESCRIPTION	CHARGES	CREDITS		BALANCE
				Pymnts	Adj	
		BALANCE FORWARD				

STATEMENT
PRACTON MEDICAL GROUP, INC.
4567 Broad Avenue
Woodland Hills, XY 12345-4700
Tel. 013-486-9002
Fax No. 013-488-7815

Phone No.(H)_____(W)_____ Birthdate_____
Insurance Co._____Policy No._____

DATE	REFERENCE	DESCRIPTION	CHARGES	CREDITS		BALANCE
				Pymnts	Adj	
		BALANCE FORWARD				

Form 70

STATEMENT
PRACTON MEDICAL GROUP, INC.
4567 Broad Avenue
Woodland Hills, XY 12345-4700
Tel. 013-486-9002
Fax No. 013-488-7815

Phone No.(H)_____ (W)_____ Birthdate_____
Insurance Co._____ Policy No._____

DATE	REFERENCE	DESCRIPTION	CHARGES	CREDITS		BALANCE
				Pymnts	Adj	
		BALANCE FORWARD				

STATEMENT
PRACTON MEDICAL GROUP, INC.
4567 Broad Avenue
Woodland Hills, XY 12345-4700
Tel. 013-486-9002
Fax No. 013-488-7815

Phone No.(H)_____ (W)_____ Birthdate_____
Insurance Co._____ Policy No._____

DATE	REFERENCE	DESCRIPTION	CHARGES	CREDITS		BALANCE
				Pymnts	Adj	
		BALANCE FORWARD				

Form 71

STATEMENT
PRACTON MEDICAL GROUP, INC.
4567 Broad Avenue
Woodland Hills, XY 12345-4700
Tel. 013-486-9002
Fax No. 013-488-7815

Phone No.(H)_____ (W)_____ Birthdate_____
Insurance Co._____ Policy No._____

DATE	REFERENCE	DESCRIPTION	CHARGES	CREDITS		BALANCE
				Pymnts	Adj	
		BALANCE FORWARD				

STATEMENT
PRACTON MEDICAL GROUP, INC.
4567 Broad Avenue
Woodland Hills, XY 12345-4700
Tel. 013-486-9002
Fax No. 013-488-7815

Phone No.(H)_____ (W)_____ Birthdate_____
Insurance Co._____ Policy No._____

DATE	REFERENCE	DESCRIPTION	CHARGES	CREDITS		BALANCE
				Pymnts	Adj	
		BALANCE FORWARD				

Form 72

STATEMENT
PRACTON MEDICAL GROUP, INC.
4567 Broad Avenue
Woodland Hills, XY 12345-4700
Tel. 013-486-9002
Fax No. 013-488-7815

Phone No.(H)_____(W)_____ Birthdate_____
Insurance Co._____Policy No._____

DATE	REFERENCE	DESCRIPTION	CHARGES	CREDITS		BALANCE
				Pymnts	Adj	
		BALANCE FORWARD				

STATEMENT
PRACTON MEDICAL GROUP, INC.
4567 Broad Avenue
Woodland Hills, XY 12345-4700
Tel. 013-486-9002
Fax No. 013-488-7815

Phone No.(H)_____(W)_____ Birthdate_____
Insurance Co._____Policy No._____

DATE	REFERENCE	DESCRIPTION	CHARGES	CREDITS		BALANCE
				Pymnts	Adj	
		BALANCE FORWARD				

Form 73

STATEMENT
PRACTON MEDICAL GROUP, INC.
4567 Broad Avenue
Woodland Hills, XY 12345-4700
Tel. 013-486-9002
Fax No. 013-488-7815

Phone No.(H)_____(W)_____ Birthdate_____
Insurance Co._____Policy No._____

DATE	REFERENCE	DESCRIPTION	CHARGES	CREDITS		BALANCE
				Pymnts	Adj	
		BALANCE FORWARD				

STATEMENT
PRACTON MEDICAL GROUP, INC.
4567 Broad Avenue
Woodland Hills, XY 12345-4700
Tel. 013-486-9002
Fax No. 013-488-7815

Phone No.(H)_____(W)_____ Birthdate_____
Insurance Co._____Policy No._____

DATE	REFERENCE	DESCRIPTION	CHARGES	CREDITS		BALANCE
				Pymnts	Adj	
		BALANCE FORWARD				

Form 74

STATEMENT
PRACTON MEDICAL GROUP, INC.
4567 Broad Avenue
Woodland Hills, XY 12345-4700
Tel. 013-486-9002
Fax No. 013-488-7815

Phone No.(H)_____(W)_____ Birthdate_____
Insurance Co._____Policy No._____

DATE	REFERENCE	DESCRIPTION	CHARGES	CREDITS		BALANCE
				Pymnts	Adj	
		BALANCE FORWARD				

STATEMENT
PRACTON MEDICAL GROUP, INC.
4567 Broad Avenue
Woodland Hills, XY 12345-4700
Tel. 013-486-9002
Fax No. 013-488-7815

Phone No.(H)_____(W)_____ Birthdate_____
Insurance Co._____Policy No._____

DATE	REFERENCE	DESCRIPTION	CHARGES	CREDITS		BALANCE
				Pymnts	Adj	
		BALANCE FORWARD				

Form 75

STATEMENT
PRACTON MEDICAL GROUP, INC.
4567 Broad Avenue
Woodland Hills, XY 12345-4700
Tel. 013-486-9002
Fax No. 013-488-7815

Phone No.(H)_____(W)_____ Birthdate_____
Insurance Co._____Policy No._____

DATE	REFERENCE	DESCRIPTION	CHARGES	CREDITS		BALANCE
				Pymnts	Adj	
		BALANCE FORWARD				

STATEMENT
PRACTON MEDICAL GROUP, INC.
4567 Broad Avenue
Woodland Hills, XY 12345-4700
Tel. 013-486-9002
Fax No. 013-488-7815

Phone No.(H)_____(W)_____ Birthdate_____
Insurance Co._____Policy No._____

DATE	REFERENCE	DESCRIPTION	CHARGES	CREDITS		BALANCE
				Pymnts	Adj	
		BALANCE FORWARD				

Form 76

STATEMENT
PRACTON MEDICAL GROUP, INC.
4567 Broad Avenue
Woodland Hills, XY 12345-4700
Tel. 013-486-9002
Fax No. 013-488-7815

Phone No.(H)_____ (W)_____ Birthdate_____
Insurance Co._____Policy No._____

DATE	REFERENCE	DESCRIPTION	CHARGES	CREDITS		BALANCE	
				Pymnts	Adj		
		BALANCE FORWARD					

STATEMENT
PRACTON MEDICAL GROUP, INC.
4567 Broad Avenue
Woodland Hills, XY 12345-4700
Tel. 013-486-9002
Fax No. 013-488-7815

Phone No.(H)_____ (W)_____ Birthdate_____
Insurance Co._____Policy No._____

DATE	REFERENCE	DESCRIPTION	CHARGES	CREDITS		BALANCE	
				Pymnts	Adj		
		BALANCE FORWARD					

Form 77

STATEMENT
PRACTON MEDICAL GROUP, INC.
4567 Broad Avenue
Woodland Hills, XY 12345-4700
Tel. 013-486-9002
Fax No. 013-488-7815

Phone No.(H)_____(W)_____ Birthdate_____
Insurance Co._____Policy No._____

DATE	REFERENCE	DESCRIPTION	CHARGES	CREDITS		BALANCE
				Pymnts	Adj	
		BALANCE FORWARD				

STATEMENT
PRACTON MEDICAL GROUP, INC.
4567 Broad Avenue
Woodland Hills, XY 12345-4700
Tel. 013-486-9002
Fax No. 013-488-7815

Phone No.(H)_____(W)_____ Birthdate_____
Insurance Co._____Policy No._____

DATE	REFERENCE	DESCRIPTION	CHARGES	CREDITS		BALANCE
				Pymnts	Adj	
		BALANCE FORWARD				

Form 78

STATEMENT
PRACTON MEDICAL GROUP, INC.
4567 Broad Avenue
Woodland Hills, XY 12345-4700
Tel. 013-486-9002
Fax No. 013-488-7815

Phone No.(H)_____(W)_____ Birthdate_____
Insurance Co._____Policy No._____

DATE	REFERENCE	DESCRIPTION	CHARGES	CREDITS		BALANCE
				Pymnts	Adj	
		BALANCE FORWARD				

STATEMENT
PRACTON MEDICAL GROUP, INC.
4567 Broad Avenue
Woodland Hills, XY 12345-4700
Tel. 013-486-9002
Fax No. 013-488-7815

Phone No.(H)_____(W)_____ Birthdate_____
Insurance Co._____Policy No._____

DATE	REFERENCE	DESCRIPTION	CHARGES	CREDITS		BALANCE
				Pymnts	Adj	
		BALANCE FORWARD				

Form 79

STATEMENT
PRACTON MEDICAL GROUP, INC.
4567 Broad Avenue
Woodland Hills, XY 12345-4700
Tel. 013-486-9002
Fax No. 013-488-7815

Phone No.(H)_____(W)_____ Birthdate_____
Insurance Co._____Policy No._____

DATE	REFERENCE	DESCRIPTION	CHARGES	CREDITS		BALANCE
				Pymnts	Adj	
		BALANCE FORWARD				

STATEMENT
PRACTON MEDICAL GROUP, INC.
4567 Broad Avenue
Woodland Hills, XY 12345-4700
Tel. 013-486-9002
Fax No. 013-488-7815

Phone No.(H)_____(W)_____ Birthdate_____
Insurance Co._____Policy No._____

DATE	REFERENCE	DESCRIPTION	CHARGES	CREDITS		BALANCE
				Pymnts	Adj	
		BALANCE FORWARD				

Form 80

STATEMENT
PRACTON MEDICAL GROUP, INC.
4567 Broad Avenue
Woodland Hills, XY 12345-4700
Tel. 013-486-9002
Fax No. 013-488-7815

Phone No.(H)_____(W)_____ Birthdate_____
Insurance Co._____Policy No._____

DATE	REFERENCE	DESCRIPTION	CHARGES	CREDITS			BALANCE	
				Pymnts		Adj		
		BALANCE FORWARD						

STATEMENT
PRACTON MEDICAL GROUP, INC.
4567 Broad Avenue
Woodland Hills, XY 12345-4700
Tel. 013-486-9002
Fax No. 013-488-7815

Phone No.(H)_____(W)_____ Birthdate_____
Insurance Co._____Policy No._____

DATE	REFERENCE	DESCRIPTION	CHARGES	CREDITS			BALANCE	
				Pymnts		Adj		
		BALANCE FORWARD						

Form 81

STATEMENT
PRACTON MEDICAL GROUP, INC.
4567 Broad Avenue
Woodland Hills, XY 12345-4700
Tel. 013-486-9002
Fax No. 013-488-7815

Phone No.(H)_____(W)_____ Birthdate_____
Insurance Co._____Policy No._____

DATE	REFERENCE	DESCRIPTION	CHARGES	CREDITS		BALANCE
				Pymnts	Adj	
		BALANCE FORWARD				

STATEMENT
PRACTON MEDICAL GROUP, INC.
4567 Broad Avenue
Woodland Hills, XY 12345-4700
Tel. 013-486-9002
Fax No. 013-488-7815

Phone No.(H)_____(W)_____ Birthdate_____
Insurance Co._____Policy No._____

DATE	REFERENCE	DESCRIPTION	CHARGES	CREDITS		BALANCE
				Pymnts	Adj	
		BALANCE FORWARD				

Form 82

FAMILY HEALTH MAGAZINE
3490 Broadway Street
New York, NY 10010

0136

June 26, 19--

16-66/1220

PAY TO THE ORDER OF Gerald Practon, M.D. $50.00

Fifty and NO/100 —————————————— DOLLARS

VOID

BANK OF AMERICA NT&SA

⑈122000661⑈0136⑈ 10386⑈60402⑈

COLONY BOYS SCHOOL
659 Manchester Avenue
Woodland Hills, XY 12345

785

June 26, 19-- 16-36/208
1220

Pay to the Order of Fran Practon, M. D. ————— $ 75.00

Seventy-five and no/100------- ——————————— Dollars

VOID

BARCLAYS BANK

memo lecture

⑈122000360⑈0785 208913379⑈

Adrienne Cane
6502 North J Street
Woodland Hills, XY 12345
Tel. 013/498-2110

0425

June 26, 19--

16-4
1220

PAY TO THE ORDER OF Practon Medical Group, Inc. $50.00

Fifty and no/100 —————————— DOLLARS

VOID

SECURITY PACIFIC NATIONAL BANK

Adrienne Cane

⑈122000043⑈0425⑈ 229⑈048596⑈

Form 83

Betty K. Lawson
6400 Best Way
Woodland Hills, XY 12345
Tel: 013/450-9533

192

June 28, 19-- $\frac{90-1692}{1222}$

PAY TO THE
ORDER OF *Practon Medical Group, Inc.* $15.00

Fifteen and $\frac{no}{100}$ ——— VOID ——— DOLLARS

UCB · UNITED BANK

MEMO *flu inj*

Betty K. Lawson

⊕ ⑈1222⑈1692⑈: 2044 1361 1⑈ 0192 ⑈

DELUXE CHECK PRINTERS - LH

Jody F. Swinney
4300 Saunders Road
Woodland Hills, XY 12345
Tel: 013/908-6605

No. 150

June 28, 19-- 16-8/1220

Pay to the order of *Practon Medical Group, Inc.* $15.00

Fifteen and $\frac{No}{100}$ ——— VOID ——— DOLLARS

◆ **CROCKER NATIONAL BANK**

Memo *on acct*

Jody. F. Swinney

⑈122000085⑈: 0150 1400 5060 1⑈ 3333

Form 84

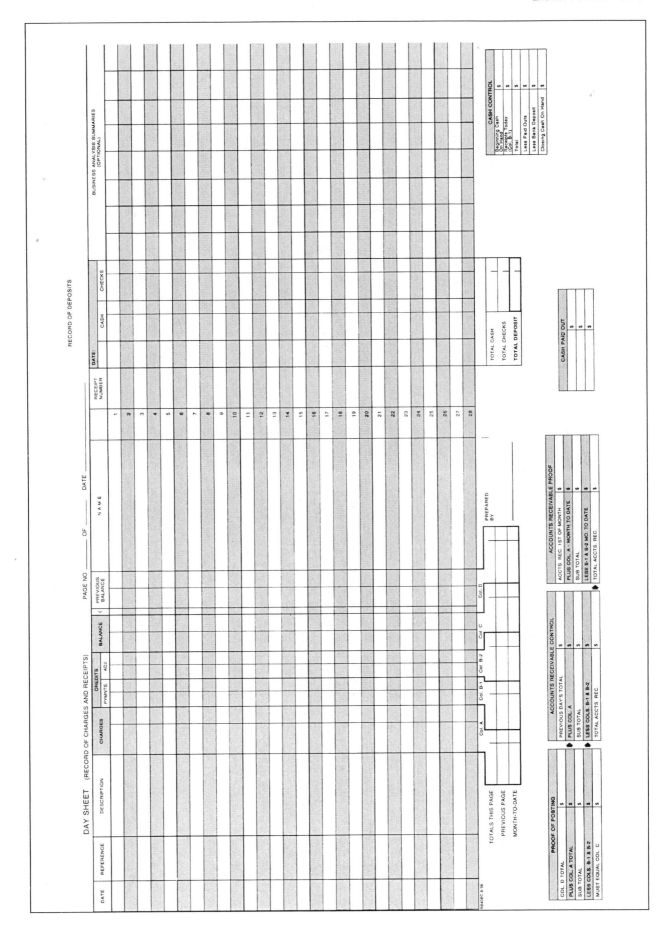

Form 85

Roger T. Simpson
792 Baker Street
Woodland Hills, XY 12345
Tel: 013/549-0879

3000

16-1493/343
1220

June 29, 19--

PAY TO THE
ORDER OF Practon Medical Group Inc. $15.00

Fifteen and No/100 ——————————————— DOLLARS

VOID

Channel Islands Office
UNION BANK

MEMO on acct.

Roger T. Simpson

⑈:1220149321:95178000171⑈ 000

DELUXE CHECK PRINTERS-LH

Bank of A. Levy

№ 553

June 29, 19--

90-372/1222

Pay to the Order of Practon Medical Group, Inc. $15.00

Fifteen and no/100 ——————— VOID ——————— Dollars

Jack J. Johnson
5490 Olive Mill Road
Woodland Hills, XY 12345
Tel: 013/857-9920

Memo fees inj.

Signed Jack J. Johnson

⑈:122203727: 2145⑈878⑈

Prudential Insurance Company
4680 Cowper Street
Woodland Hills, XY 12345

189

90-3219
1222

June 27, 19--

PAY TO THE
ORDER OF Practon Medical Group, Inc.----- --------- $15.00

Fifteen and No/100-------------- ——————— VOID ——————— DOLLARS

OJAI VALLEY STATE BANK

FOR completion life ins form

:122232196:0189⑈ 260⑈ 100742⑈

Form 86

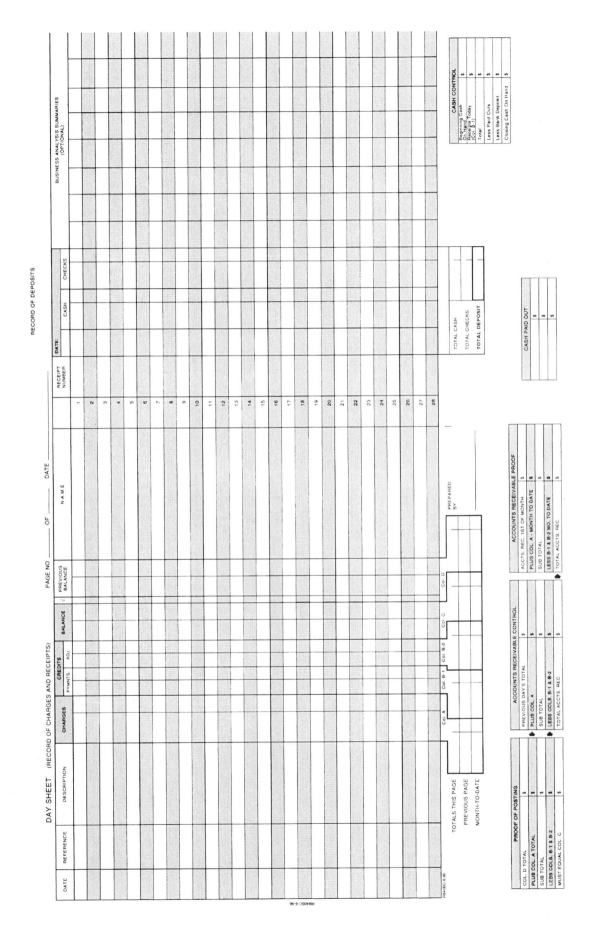

Form 87

DATE	REFERENCE	DESCRIPTION	CHARGES	PYMNTS.	ADJ.	BALANCE	PREVIOUS BALANCE	N A M E
				CREDITS				

This is your RECEIPT for this amount
This is a STATEMENT of your account to date

Please present this slip to receptionist before leaving office.

PRACTON MEDICAL GROUP, INC.
4567 Broad Avenue
Woodland Hills, XY 12345-4700
Tel. 013-488-7815
Fax. No. 013-488-7815

Thank You!

ROA – Received on Account

OT – Other _____

NEXT APPOINTMENT _____

147

RB40BC-3-96

DATE	REFERENCE	DESCRIPTION	CHARGES	PYMNTS.	ADJ.	BALANCE	PREVIOUS BALANCE	N A M E
				CREDITS				

This is your RECEIPT for this amount
This is a STATEMENT of your account to date

Please present this slip to receptionist before leaving office.

PRACTON MEDICAL GROUP, INC.
4567 Broad Avenue
Woodland Hills, XY 12345-4700
Tel. 013-488-7815
Fax. No. 013-488-7815

Thank You!

ROA – Received on Account

OT – Other _____

NEXT APPOINTMENT _____

148

RB40BC-3-96

DATE	REFERENCE	DESCRIPTION	CHARGES	PYMNTS.	ADJ.	BALANCE	PREVIOUS BALANCE	N A M E
				CREDITS				

This is your RECEIPT for this amount
This is a STATEMENT of your account to date

Please present this slip to receptionist before leaving office.

PRACTON MEDICAL GROUP, INC.
4567 Broad Avenue
Woodland Hills, XY 12345-4700
Tel. 013-488-7815
Fax. No. 013-488-7815

Thank You!

ROA – Received on Account

OT – Other _____

NEXT APPOINTMENT _____

149

RB40BC-3-96

DATE	REFERENCE	DESCRIPTION	CHARGES	PYMNTS.	ADJ.	BALANCE	PREVIOUS BALANCE	N A M E
				CREDITS				

This is your RECEIPT for this amount
This is a STATEMENT of your account to date

Please present this slip to receptionist before leaving office.

PRACTON MEDICAL GROUP, INC.
4567 Broad Avenue
Woodland Hills, XY 12345-4700
Tel. 013-488-7815
Fax. No. 013-488-7815

Thank You!

ROA – Received on Account

OT – Other _____

NEXT APPOINTMENT _____

150

RB40BC-3-96

Form 88

Diagnosis _Congestive heart_
failure _____ 428.0

Month _June_ _____ Year _199X_

1 2 3 4 5 6 7 8 9 10 11 12 13 14 15 16 17 18 19 20 21 22 23 24 25 26 27 28 29 30 31

Patient Name _Joan Gomez_

Birthdate _____

Admission Date _6-29-9X_

Discharge Date _____

Hospital _College Hospital_

	INITIAL HOSPITAL VISIT		
X	99221	(99222)	99223
	SUBSEQUENT HOSPITAL VISIT		
X	(99231)	99232	99233
	HOSPITAL CONSULT		
	99251	99252	99253
	99254	99255	
	FOLLOW-UP CONSULT		
	99261	99262	99263
	EMERGENCY		
	99281	99282	99283
	99284	99285	
	CRITICAL CARE 99291		99292
	HOSPITAL DISCHARGE		99238

Consultation Referred By:
Practon Medical Group, Inc.

Dr. _Gerald Practon_

Provider # _C14021_

#10829 — Medical Arts Press   1-800-328-2179

Diagnosis _Phlebitis, deep_
femoral vein _____ 451.11

Month _June_ _____ Year _199X_

1 2 3 4 5 6 7 8 9 10 11 12 13 14 15 16 17 18 19 20 21 22 23 24 25 26 27 28 29 30 31

Patient Name _Robert T. Jenner_

Birthdate _6-10-9X_

Admission Date _6-28-9X_

Discharge Date _____

Hospital _College Hospital_

	INITIAL HOSPITAL VISIT		
X	(99221)	99222	99223
	SUBSEQUENT HOSPITAL VISIT		
X	(99231)	99232	99233
	HOSPITAL CONSULT		
	99251	99252	99253
	99254	99255	
	FOLLOW-UP CONSULT		
	99261	99262	99263
	EMERGENCY		
	99281	99282	99283
	99284	99285	
	CRITICAL CARE 99291		99292
X	HOSPITAL DISCHARGE		(99238)

Consultation Referred By:
Practon Medical Group, Inc.

Dr. _Fran Practon_

Provider # _C15038_

#10829 — Medical Arts Press   1-800-328-2179

Form 89

RECEIPT FOR EXPENDITURES

No _____

PAY TO _____

_____ Date _____

DESCRIPTION OF ITEMS	ACCOUNT NUMBER	AMOUNT	

APPROVED	ENTERED	RECEIVED PAYMENT

WILMER "SERVICE" LINE   FORM 11-45

RECEIPT FOR EXPENDITURES

No _____

PAY TO _____

_____ Date _____

DESCRIPTION OF ITEMS	ACCOUNT NUMBER	AMOUNT	

APPROVED	ENTERED	RECEIVED PAYMENT

WILMER "SERVICE" LINE   FORM 11-45

Form 90

Joseph C. Smith
P.O. Box 4301
Woodland Hills, XY 12345
Tel: 013/549-1124

217

90-2055 / 1222

June 30, 19--

PAY TO THE ORDER OF *Practon Medical Group, Inc.* $ 75.00

Seventy five and no/100 VOID DOLLARS

SAMPLE VOID

SECURITY PACIFIC NATIONAL BANK

For PE + lab test

Joseph C. Smith

⑈000217⑈ ⑈1222⑈2055⑈437⑈23456⑈

UCB UNITED BANK

16-21/204 / 1220

4800

June 30, 19--

pay to the order of *Practon Medical Group, Inc.* $ 10.00

Ten and NO/100 VOID dollars

Rachel T. O'Brien
5598 East 17 Street
Woodland Hills, XY 12345
Tel: 013/566-2119

Rachel T. O'Brien

⑈122000218⑈20450 2843⑈ 4800 11

Recycled and Recyclable

Form 91

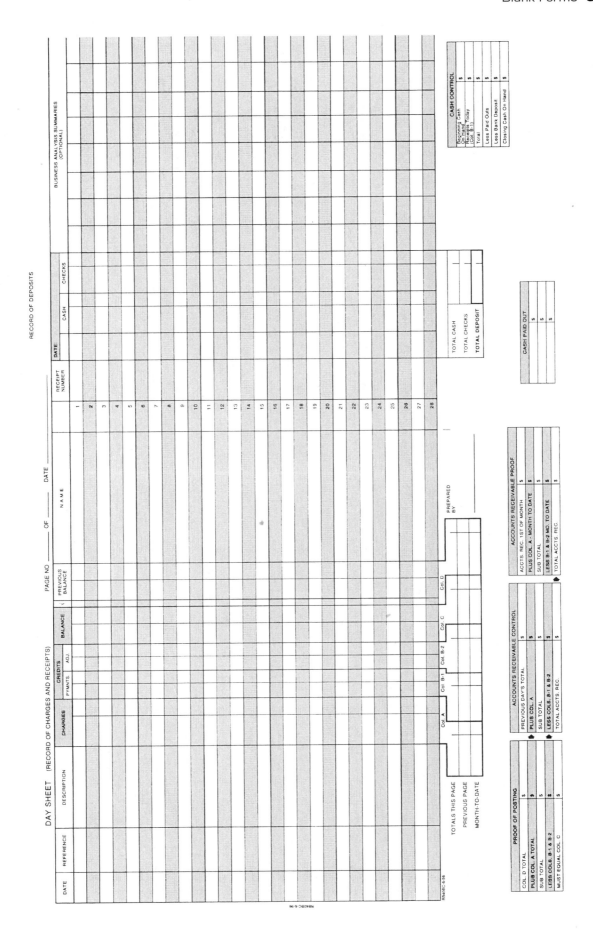

Form 92

CHECK REGISTER

RECORD OF CHECKS DRAWN ON _____

MONTH OF _____ 19 _____ PAGE NO. _____

BALANCE FORWARD ⟶

Ⓐ Ⓑ Ⓒ

PROOF FORMULAS:
DISBURSEMENTS – COL'S. Ⓑ + Ⓒ = Ⓐ

COL. Ⓐ TOTAL = TOTAL OF COLUMNS USED FOR EXPENSE DISTRIBUTION.

Form 93

LINE NO.		DATE	AMOUNT	1	2	3	4	5	6	7	8	9	10	11	
1															
2															
3															
4															
5															
6															
7															
8															
9															
10															
11															
12															
13															
14															
15															
16															
17															
18															
19															
20															
21															
22															
23															
24															
25															
26															
27															
28															
29															
30															

PREPARED BY _____

Form 94

RECEIPT FOR EXPENDITURES

No_____

PAY TO_____

_____ DATE_____

DESCRIPTION OF ITEMS	ACCOUNT NUMBER	AMOUNT	

APPROVED	ENTERED	RECEIVED PAYMENT

WILMER "SERVICE" LINE   FORM 11-45

RECEIPT FOR EXPENDITURES

No_____

PAY TO_____

_____ DATE_____

DESCRIPTION OF ITEMS	ACCOUNT NUMBER	AMOUNT	

APPROVED	ENTERED	RECEIVED PAYMENT

WILMER "SERVICE" LINE   FORM 11-45

Form 95

OFFICE FUND VOUCHER ENVELOPE

Voucher No. _____

From _____ 19 ___ To _____ 19 ___ Paid by Check No. _____

ENTERED	AUDITED	APPROVED	PAID

DATE	NO.	TO WHOM PAID	FOR WHAT	ACCT.	AMOUNT

OFFICE FUND AMOUNT	$_____		VOUCHERS PAID	$_____
TOTAL VOUCHERS AND CASH	$_____		CASH ON HAND	$_____
(OVER OR SHORT)	$_____		TOTAL	$_____

DISTRIBUTION OF VOUCHERS

										SUNDRY ITEMS
									TOTALS

WILMER ★ 'Service' line   FORM 11-71

Form 96

PRACTON MEDICAL GROUP, INC.
4567 Broad Avenue
Woodland Hills, XY 12345-4700

FOR INSTRUCTIONAL USE ONLY

DATE	ITEM	AMOUNT

479

3-2
310

PAY _____ **DOLLARS**

PAY TO THE ORDER OF	DATE	GROSS	DISC.	CHECK AMOUNT
				$

NOT VALID

THE FIRST NATIONAL BANK – Princeton, NJ, 08540-2222
RB40BC-4-96

⑈000000⑈ ⑆123456789⑆ ⑈8765432⑈

PRACTON MEDICAL GROUP, INC.
4567 Broad Avenue
Woodland Hills, XY 12345-4700

FOR INSTRUCTIONAL USE ONLY

DATE	ITEM	AMOUNT

480

3-2
310

PAY _____ **DOLLARS**

PAY TO THE ORDER OF	DATE	GROSS	DISC.	CHECK AMOUNT
				$

NOT VALID

THE FIRST NATIONAL BANK – Princeton, NJ, 08540-2222
RB40BC-4-96

⑈000000⑈ ⑆123456789⑆ ⑈8765432⑈

PRACTON MEDICAL GROUP, INC.
4567 Broad Avenue
Woodland Hills, XY 12345-4700

FOR INSTRUCTIONAL USE ONLY

DATE	ITEM	AMOUNT

481

3-2
310

PAY _____ **DOLLARS**

PAY TO THE ORDER OF	DATE	GROSS	DISC.	CHECK AMOUNT
				$

NOT VALID

THE FIRST NATIONAL BANK – Princeton, NJ, 08540-2222
RB40BC-4-96

⑈000000⑈ ⑆123456789⑆ ⑈8765432⑈

Form 97

PRACTON MEDICAL GROUP, INC.
4567 Broad Avenue
Woodland Hills, XY 12345-4700

FOR INSTRUCTIONAL USE ONLY

DATE	ITEM	AMOUNT

482

3-2
310

PAY _____ **DOLLARS**

PAY TO THE ORDER OF	DATE	GROSS	DISC.		CHECK AMOUNT
					$

NOT VALID

THE FIRST NATIONAL BANK – Princeton, NJ, 08540-2222
RB40BC-4-96

⑈000000⑈ ⑆123456789⑆ ⑈8765432⑈

PRACTON MEDICAL GROUP, INC.
4567 Broad Avenue
Woodland Hills, XY 12345-4700

FOR INSTRUCTIONAL USE ONLY

DATE	ITEM	AMOUNT

483

3-2
310

PAY _____ **DOLLARS**

PAY TO THE ORDER OF	DATE	GROSS	DISC.		CHECK AMOUNT
					$

NOT VALID

THE FIRST NATIONAL BANK – Princeton, NJ, 08540-2222
RB40BC-4-96

⑈000000⑈ ⑆123456789⑆ ⑈8765432⑈

PRACTON MEDICAL GROUP, INC.
4567 Broad Avenue
Woodland Hills, XY 12345-4700

FOR INSTRUCTIONAL USE ONLY

DATE	ITEM	AMOUNT

484

3-2
310

PAY _____ **DOLLARS**

PAY TO THE ORDER OF	DATE	GROSS	DISC.		CHECK AMOUNT
					$

NOT VALID

THE FIRST NATIONAL BANK – Princeton, NJ, 08540-2222
RB40BC-4-96

⑈000000⑈ ⑆123456789⑆ ⑈8765432⑈

Form 98

PRACTON MEDICAL GROUP, INC.
4567 Broad Avenue
Woodland Hills, XY 12345-4700

FOR INSTRUCTIONAL USE ONLY

DATE	ITEM	AMOUNT

485

3-2
310

PAY _____ DOLLARS

PAY TO THE ORDER OF	DATE	GROSS	DISC.

CHECK AMOUNT

$ _____

NOT VALID

THE FIRST NATIONAL BANK – Princeton, NJ, 08540-2222
RB40BC-4-96

⑈000000⑈ ⑉123456789⑉ ⑊876543 2⑊

PRACTON MEDICAL GROUP, INC.
4567 Broad Avenue
Woodland Hills, XY 12345-4700

FOR INSTRUCTIONAL USE ONLY

DATE	ITEM	AMOUNT

486

3-2
310

PAY _____ DOLLARS

PAY TO THE ORDER OF	DATE	GROSS	DISC.

CHECK AMOUNT

$ _____

NOT VALID

THE FIRST NATIONAL BANK – Princeton, NJ, 08540-2222
RB40BC-4-96

⑈000000⑈ ⑉123456789⑉ ⑊876543 2⑊

PRACTON MEDICAL GROUP, INC.
4567 Broad Avenue
Woodland Hills, XY 12345-4700

FOR INSTRUCTIONAL USE ONLY

DATE	ITEM	AMOUNT

487

3-2
310

PAY _____ DOLLARS

PAY TO THE ORDER OF	DATE	GROSS	DISC.

CHECK AMOUNT

$ _____

NOT VALID

THE FIRST NATIONAL BANK – Princeton, NJ, 08540-2222
RB40BC-4-96

⑈000000⑈ ⑉123456789⑉ ⑊876543 2⑊

Form 99

PRACTON MEDICAL GROUP, INC.
4567 Broad Avenue
Woodland Hills, XY 12345-4700

FOR INSTRUCTIONAL USE ONLY

DATE	ITEM	AMOUNT

488

3-2
310

PAY _____ **DOLLARS**

PAY TO THE ORDER OF	DATE	GROSS	DISC.	CHECK AMOUNT
				$

NOT VALID

THE FIRST NATIONAL BANK – Princeton, NJ, 08540-2222
RB40BC-4-96

⑈000000⑈ ⑈123456789⑈ ⑈876543 2⑈

PRACTON MEDICAL GROUP, INC.
4567 Broad Avenue
Woodland Hills, XY 12345-4700

FOR INSTRUCTIONAL USE ONLY

DATE	ITEM	AMOUNT

489

3-2
310

PAY _____ **DOLLARS**

PAY TO THE ORDER OF	DATE	GROSS	DISC.	CHECK AMOUNT
				$

NOT VALID

THE FIRST NATIONAL BANK – Princeton, NJ, 08540-2222
RB40BC-4-96

⑈000000⑈ ⑈123456789⑈ ⑈876543 2⑈

PRACTON MEDICAL GROUP, INC.
4567 Broad Avenue
Woodland Hills, XY 12345-4700

FOR INSTRUCTIONAL USE ONLY

DATE	ITEM	AMOUNT

490

3-2
310

PAY _____ **DOLLARS**

PAY TO THE ORDER OF	DATE	GROSS	DISC.	CHECK AMOUNT
				$

NOT VALID

THE FIRST NATIONAL BANK – Princeton, NJ, 08540-2222
RB40BC-4-96

⑈000000⑈ ⑈123456789⑈ ⑈876543 2⑈

Form 100

DATE	ITEM	AMOUNT

PRACTON MEDICAL GROUP, INC.
4567 Broad Avenue
Woodland Hills, XY 12345-4700

FOR INSTRUCTIONAL USE ONLY

491   3-2 / 310

PAY _____ **DOLLARS**

PAY TO THE ORDER OF	DATE	GROSS	DISC.	CHECK AMOUNT
				$

NOT VALID

THE FIRST NATIONAL BANK – Princeton, NJ, 08540-2222
RB40BC-4-96

⑆000000⑆ ⑆123456789⑆ ⑆8765432⑆

DATE	ITEM	AMOUNT

PRACTON MEDICAL GROUP, INC.
4567 Broad Avenue
Woodland Hills, XY 12345-4700

FOR INSTRUCTIONAL USE ONLY

492   3-2 / 310

PAY _____ **DOLLARS**

PAY TO THE ORDER OF	DATE	GROSS	DISC.	CHECK AMOUNT
				$

NOT VALID

THE FIRST NATIONAL BANK – Princeton, NJ, 08540-2222
RB40BC-4-96

⑆000000⑆ ⑆123456789⑆ ⑆8765432⑆

DATE	ITEM	AMOUNT

PRACTON MEDICAL GROUP, INC.
4567 Broad Avenue
Woodland Hills, XY 12345-4700

FOR INSTRUCTIONAL USE ONLY

493   3-2 / 310

PAY _____ **DOLLARS**

PAY TO THE ORDER OF	DATE	GROSS	DISC.	CHECK AMOUNT
				$

NOT VALID

THE FIRST NATIONAL BANK – Princeton, NJ, 08540-2222
RB40BC-4-96

⑆000000⑆ ⑆123456789⑆ ⑆8765432⑆

Form 101

PRACTON MEDICAL GROUP, INC.
4567 Broad Avenue
Woodland Hills, XY 12345-4700

FOR INSTRUCTIONAL USE ONLY

DATE	ITEM	AMOUNT

494

3-2
310

PAY _____ DOLLARS

PAY TO THE ORDER OF	DATE	GROSS	DISC.	CHECK AMOUNT
				$

NOT VALID

THE FIRST NATIONAL BANK – Princeton, NJ, 08540-2222
RB40BC-4-96

⑈"000000"⑈ ⑆1234567891⑉ ⑈876543 2⑈

PRACTON MEDICAL GROUP, INC.
4567 Broad Avenue
Woodland Hills, XY 12345-4700

FOR INSTRUCTIONAL USE ONLY

DATE	ITEM	AMOUNT

495

3-2
310

PAY _____ DOLLARS

PAY TO THE ORDER OF	DATE	GROSS	DISC.	CHECK AMOUNT
				$

NOT VALID

THE FIRST NATIONAL BANK – Princeton, NJ, 08540-2222
RB40BC-4-96

⑈"000000"⑈ ⑆1234567891⑉ ⑈876543 2⑈

PRACTON MEDICAL GROUP, INC.
4567 Broad Avenue
Woodland Hills, XY 12345-4700

FOR INSTRUCTIONAL USE ONLY

DATE	ITEM	AMOUNT

496

3-2
310

PAY _____ DOLLARS

PAY TO THE ORDER OF	DATE	GROSS	DISC.	CHECK AMOUNT
				$

NOT VALID

THE FIRST NATIONAL BANK – Princeton, NJ, 08540-2222
RB40BC-4-96

⑈"000000"⑈ ⑆1234567891⑉ ⑈876543 2⑈

Form 102

PRACTON MEDICAL GROUP, INC.
4567 Broad Avenue
Woodland Hills, XY 12345-4700

FOR INSTRUCTIONAL USE ONLY

DATE	ITEM	AMOUNT

497   3-2 / 310

PAY _____ DOLLARS

PAY TO THE ORDER OF	DATE	GROSS	DISC.		CHECK AMOUNT
				$	

NOT VALID

THE FIRST NATIONAL BANK – Princeton, NJ, 08540-2222
RB40BC-4-96

⑈⑈000000⑈⑈ ⑈:123456789⑈: ⑈⑈876543 2⑈⑈

PRACTON MEDICAL GROUP, INC.
4567 Broad Avenue
Woodland Hills, XY 12345-4700

FOR INSTRUCTIONAL USE ONLY

DATE	ITEM	AMOUNT

498   3-2 / 310

PAY _____ DOLLARS

PAY TO THE ORDER OF	DATE	GROSS	DISC.		CHECK AMOUNT
				$	

NOT VALID

THE FIRST NATIONAL BANK – Princeton, NJ, 08540-2222
RB40BC-4-96

⑈⑈000000⑈⑈ ⑈:123456789⑈: ⑈⑈876543 2⑈⑈

PRACTON MEDICAL GROUP, INC.
4567 Broad Avenue
Woodland Hills, XY 12345-4700

FOR INSTRUCTIONAL USE ONLY

DATE	ITEM	AMOUNT

499   3-2 / 310

PAY _____ DOLLARS

PAY TO THE ORDER OF	DATE	GROSS	DISC.		CHECK AMOUNT
				$	

NOT VALID

THE FIRST NATIONAL BANK – Princeton, NJ, 08540-2222
RB40BC-4-96

⑈⑈000000⑈⑈ ⑈:123456789⑈: ⑈⑈876543 2⑈⑈

Form 103

FOUR EASY STEPS TO HELP YOU BALANCE YOUR CHECKBOOK

1. UPDATE YOUR CHECKBOOK
- Compare and check-off each transaction recorded in your check register with those listed on this statement. These include checks, direct deposits, direct debits, deposits, ATM transactions, etc.
- Add interest and subtract service charges

2. DETERMINE OUTSTANDING ITEMS
- Use the charts below to list transactions shown in your check register but not included on this statement.
- Include any from previous months.

OUTSTANDING CHECKS OR OTHER WITHDRAWALS				DEPOSITS NOT CREDITED	
CHECK NO.	AMOUNT	CHECK NO.	AMOUNT	DATE	AMOUNT
	$		$		$
		TOTAL	$	TOTAL	$

3. BALANCE YOUR ACCOUNT
- Enter Ending Statement Balance shown on this statement. $ _____
- Add deposits listed in your register and not shown on this statement. + _____
- Subtract outstanding checks/withdrawals. - _____
- **ADJUSTED TOTAL** (should agree with your checkbook balance). $ _____

4. IF THE BALANCE IN YOUR CHECKBOOK DOES NOT AGREE WITH THE ADJUSTED TOTAL, THEN
- Check all addition and subtraction.
- Make sure all outstanding checks, withdrawals and deposits have been listed in the appropriate chart above.
- Compare the amount of each check, withdrawal and deposit in your checkbook with the amounts on this statement.
- Review the figures on last month's statement.

IN CASE OF ERRORS OR QUESTIONS ABOUT YOUR ELECTRONIC TRANSFERS, telephone us at the telephone number shown on this statement, or write us at: P.O. Box 30987, City of Industry, CA 91896-7987 as soon as you can if you think your statement or receipt is wrong or if you need more information about a transfer on the statement or receipt. We must hear from you no later than 60 days after we sent you the FIRST statement on which the error or problem appeared. Tell us your name and account number, and describe the error or the transfer you are unsure about. Please explain as clearly as you can why you believe there is an error or why you need more information. You must also tell us the exact dollar amount of the suspected error. If you tell us orally, we require that you send us your complaint or question in writing within 10 business days. If you do not put your complaint or questions in writing or we do not receive it within 10 business days, we may not recredit your account. If we decide that there was no error, we will send you a written explanation within 3 business days after we finish our investigation. You may ask for copies of the documents that we used in our investigation. For purposes of error resolution, our business days are Monday through Friday, 8:30 a.m. to 5:00 p.m., Pacific Time. We are closed Saturdays, Sundays and federal holidays.

All Non-POS, MasterMoney™ or Foreign Transactions
We will tell you the results of our investigation within 10 business days after we receive your written complaint and will correct any error promptly. If we need more time, however, we may take up to 45 days to investigate your complaint or questions. If we decide we need additional time, we will recredit your account within 10 business days for the amount you think is in error, so that you will have the use of the money during the time it takes us to complete our investigation.

POS, MasterMoney™ and Foreign Transactions
If the transfer results from a point-of-sale transaction, MasterMoney™ transaction or a transfer initiated outside the United States, we will still correct any error promptly. However, we may take up to 20 business days after we receive your written complaint to tell you the results of our investigation. If we need more time, we may use an additional 90 days. Should we take this additional time, we will recredit your account within 20 business days for the amount you think is in error. This will allow you to have the use of this money while we complete our investigation.

CF 5299F (5/96)

Form 104

PAYROLL REGISTER FOR PERIOD ENDING: _____

EMPLOYEE NAME	EARNINGS						DEDUCTIONS							
	No. of Exempts	Hours Worked	Hourly Rate	Reg. Pay	Over-time	Gross Pay	FICA	Fed. Inc. Tax	State Inc. Tax	SDI	Medicare	Other	TOTAL DEDUC.	Check No.	NET PAY

Form 105

EMPLOYEE EARNINGS RECORD FOR

Name_____

Address_____

_____

Telephone_____

Social Security Number_____

Date of Hire_____

Date of Birth_____

Position _____PT/FT

No. of Exemptions _____S/M

Rate of Pay_____ hr/wk/mo

Period Ended	Hours Worked	EARNINGS			DEDUCTIONS							NET PAY	Year to Date
		Reg. Pay	Over-time	Gross Pay	FICA	Fed. Inc. Tax	State Inc. Tax	SDI	Medicare	Other	TOTAL DEDUC.		

Form 106

------------------- **Cut here and give the certificate to your employer. Keep the top portion for your records.** -------------------

Form **W-4** Department of the Treasury Internal Revenue Service	**Employee's Withholding Allowance Certificate** ▶ **For Privacy Act and Paperwork Reduction Act Notice, see reverse.**	OMB No. 1545-0010 19**97**

1	Type or print your first name and middle initial	Last name	2	Your social security number

Home address (number and street or rural route)	3	☐ Single ☐ Married ☐ Married, but withhold at higher Single rate. **Note:** *If married, but legally separated, or spouse is a nonresident alien, check the Single box.*

City or town, state, and ZIP code	4	If your last name differs from that on your social security card, check here and call 1-800-772-1213 for a new card . . . . . . ▶ ☐

5   Total number of allowances you are claiming (from line G above or from the worksheets on page 2 if they apply) .   **5**

6   Additional amount, if any, you want withheld from each paycheck . . . .   **6** $

7   I claim exemption from withholding for 1997, and I certify that I meet **BOTH** of the following conditions for exemption:
  • Last year I had a right to a refund of **ALL** Federal income tax withheld because I had **NO** tax liability; **AND**
  • This year I expect a refund of **ALL** Federal income tax withheld because I expect to have **NO** tax liability.
  If you meet both conditions, enter "EXEMPT" here . . . . ▶ **7**

Under penalties of perjury, I certify that I am entitled to the number of withholding allowances claimed on this certificate or entitled to claim exempt status.

Employee's signature ▶   Date ▶   , 19

8	Employer's name and address (Employer: Complete 8 and 10 only if sending to the IRS)	9	Office code (optional)	10	Employer identification number

Cat. No. 10220Q

Form 107

BENEFIT	EMPLOYER PAYS	EMPLOYEE PAYS
Medical Insurance	$_____	$_____
Life Insurance	$_____	$_____
Accident Insurance	$_____	$_____
Disability Insurance	$_____	$_____
Worker's Compensation	$_____	$_____
Holiday # _____	$_____	$_____
Vacation # _____	$_____	$_____
Sick Leave # _____	$_____	$_____
Personal Leave	$_____	$_____
Education	$_____	$_____
Incentive Bonus	$_____	$_____
Retirement	$_____	$_____
Uniforms	$_____	$_____
Other	$_____	$_____
Totals	$_____	$_____

Total benefits employer/employee $_____

Gross wage for 199___ $_____

Total employment package $_____

Employee Name:_____   Date:_____

Form 108

OUTLINE FOR RESUME

PERSONAL DATA   Employment Objective:_____

Name_____ Date_____
          Last   First   Middle

Address_____
          Street   City   State   Zip Code

Phone Number_____ Social Security Number_____

Driver's License Number_____

Date of Birth_____Age_____Weight_____Height_____

Marital Status: Married___Single___Widowed___Divorced___Separated_____

Number of Children_____Dependents other than children_____

Citizen of the U. S. Yes_____No_____Nationality_____

Physical Defects_____Health_____
          Hearing, Vision, Speech   Illnesses in past 5 years

If married, name of spouse_____

Are you employed now?_____If yes, by whom?_____

EDUCATION

High School_____Year of Graduation_____
          Name   Street   City   State

College_____Degree_____
          Name   Street   City   State

          Number of years completed_____

Form 109

Trade, business or correspondence schools_____

                                     Name   Street   City   State

Number of years completed or year graduated_____

SPECIAL SKILLS

Typing Rate_____Shorthand and Transcription Rate_____

Transcribing Rate_____Other_____

Name business machines you are skilled in operating:_____

_____

SPECIAL INTERESTS, ACTIVITIES, AWARDS, VOLUNTEER SERVICES

_____

_____

_____

WORK EXPERIENCE (List last 4 employers, starting with most recent position first)

Name of Employer and Address	Position	Inclusive Dates	Reason for Leaving
1.			
2.			
3.			
4.			

REFERENCES: (List 3 persons not related to you that you have known well for at least one year)

Name	Address	Zip	Tel. No.	Business	Yrs. Acquainted
1.					
2.					
3.					

Form 110

PRACTON MEDICAL GROUP, INC.
4567 Broad Avenue
Woodland Hills, XY 12345-4700

Forwarding and Service Requested

Form 111

Form 112

Part III

Performance Evaluation Checklists

PERFORMANCE EVALUATION CHECKLIST
EXERCISE 1-1 SELF-ASSESSMENT

Name _____ Date _____ Score _____

PERFORMANCE OBJECTIVE

Task: Given access to all necessary materials, the student will honestly identify strengths and weaknesses by doing a self-assessment.
Scoring: One point for each step performed satisfactorily unless otherwise weighted. To obtain a percentage score, divide the total points earned by the number of points possible.
Standards: Time _____ minutes Note: Time element may be given by instructor.
NOTE TIME BEGAN _____   NOTE TIME COMPLETED _____

PROCEDURE STEPS	STEP PERFORMED SATISFACTORILY	COMMENTS
1. Assembled one sheet of plain paper and pen or pencil.	_____	
2. Answered 23 questions on plain paper.	_____	
3. Identified strengths.	_____	
4. Identified weaknesses.	_____	
5. Completed within time specified.	_____	

TOTAL POINTS EARNED: _____   TOTAL POINTS POSSIBLE: 5

Evaluator's Signature _____ NEED TO REPEAT: _____

PERFORMANCE EVALUATION CHECKLIST
EXERCISE 2-1 HOSPITAL REFERRALS

Name _____ Date _____ Score _____

PERFORMANCE OBJECTIVE

Task: Given access to all necessary information, the student will answer all questions directing the patient in the case scenario to the correct hospital department.

Scoring: One point for each step performed satisfactorily unless otherwise weighted. To obtain a percentage score, divide the number of points earned by the number of points possible.

Standards: Time _____ minutes   Note: Time element may be given by instructor.

NOTE TIME BEGAN _____   NOTE TIME COMPLETED _____

PROCEDURE STEPS	STEP PERFORMED SATISFACTORILY	COMMENTS
1. Assembled worksheet, pen or pencil.	_____	
2. Answered a.	_____	
3. Answered b.	_____	
4. Answered c.	_____	
5. Answered d.	_____	
6. Answered e.	_____	
7. Answered f.	_____	
8. Answered g.	_____	
9. Answered h.	_____	
10. Answered i.	_____	
11. Answered j.	_____	
12. Answered k.	_____	
13. Answered l.	_____	
14. Answered m.	_____	
15. Answered n.	_____	
16. Answered o.	_____	
17. Answered p.	_____	
18. Answered q.	_____	
19. Answered r.	_____	
20. Answered s.	_____	
21. Completed within time specified.	_____	

TOTAL POINTS EARNED: _____   TOTAL POINTS POSSIBLE: 21

Evaluator's Signature _____   NEED TO REPEAT: _____

PERFORMANCE EVALUATION CHECKLIST
EXERCISE 2-2 REFER PATIENTS TO THE CORRECT PHYSICIAN SPECIALIST

Name _____ Date _____ Score _____

PERFORMANCE OBJECTIVE

Task: Given access to all necessary information, the student will match the correct specialist with the patient's complaints.

Scoring: One point for each step performed satisfactorily unless otherwise weighted. To obtain a percentage score, divide the total points earned by the number of points possible.

Standards: Time _____ minutes Note: Time element may be given by instructor.

NOTE TIME BEGAN _____ NOTE TIME COMPLETED _____

PROCEDURE STEPS	STEP PERFORMED SATISFACTORILY	COMMENTS
1. Assembled worksheet, pen or pencil.	_____	
2. Matched specialist with patient complaint in question 1.	_____	
3. Matched specialist with patient complaint in question 2.	_____	
4. Matched specialist with patient complaint in question 3.	_____	
5. Matched specialist with patient complaint in question 4.	_____	
6. Matched specialist with patient complaint in question 5.	_____	
7. Matched specialist with patient complaint in question 6.	_____	
8. Matched specialist with patient complaint in question 7.	_____	
9. Matched specialist with patient complaint in question 8.	_____	
10. Matched specialist with patient complaint in question 9.	_____	
11. Matched specialist with patient complaint in question 10.	_____	
12. Matched specialist with patient complaint in question 11.	_____	
13. Matched specialist with patient complaint in question 12.	_____	
14. Matched specialist with patient complaint in question 13.	_____	
15. Matched specialist with patient complaint in question 14.	_____	
16. Matched specialist with patient complaint in question 15.	_____	
17. Matched specialist with patient complaint in question 16.	_____	
18. Matched specialist with patient complaint in question 17.	_____	
19. Completed within time specified.		

TOTAL POINTS EARNED: _____ TOTAL POINTS POSSIBLE: 19

Evaluator's Signature _____ NEED TO REPEAT: _____

PERFORMANCE EVALUATION CHECKLIST
EXERCISE 2-3 ABBREVIATIONS FOR HEALTH CARE PROFESSIONALS

Name _____ Date _____ Score _____

PERFORMANCE OBJECTIVE

Task: Given access to all necessary information, the student will write the correct terms for the abbreviations.

Scoring: One point for each step performed satisfactorily unless otherwise weighted. To obtain a percentage score, divide the total points earned by the number of points possible.

Standards: Time _____ minutes   Note: Time element may be given by instructor.

NOTE TIME BEGAN _____   NOTE TIME COMPLETED _____

PROCEDURE STEPS	STEP PERFORMED SATISFACTORILY	COMMENTS
1. Assembled worksheet, pen or pencil.	_____	
2. Wrote the term for EMT.	_____	
3. Wrote the term for DEM.	_____	
4. Wrote the term for MD.	_____	
5. Wrote the term for FACS.	_____	
6. Wrote the term for CMA.	_____	
7. Wrote the term for LVN.	_____	
8. Wrote the term for RNP.	_____	
9. Wrote the term for RPT.	_____	
10. Wrote the term for MT(ASCP).	_____	
11. Wrote the term for CMT.	_____	
12. Wrote the term for CPC.	_____	
13. Wrote the term for PA-C.	_____	
14. Wrote the term for VN.	_____	
15. Completed within time specified.	_____	

TOTAL POINTS EARNED: _____   TOTAL POINTS POSSIBLE: 15

Evaluator's Signature _____ NEED TO REPEAT: _____

PERFORMANCE EVALUATION CHECKLIST
EXERCISE 2-4 ADMINISTRATIVE JOB REQUIREMENTS

Name _____ Date _____ Score _____

PERFORMANCE OBJECTIVE

Task: Given access to all necessary equipment and information, the student will list eight basic skills the medical assistant needs. Answers may vary.

Scoring: One point for each step performed satisfactorily unless otherwise weighted. To obtain a percentage score, divide the total points earned by the number of points possible.

Standards: Time _____ minutes Note: Time element may be given by instructor.

NOTE TIME BEGAN _____   NOTE TIME COMPLETED _____

PROCEDURE STEPS	STEP PERFORMED SATISFACTORILY	COMMENTS
1. Assembled worksheet, pen or pencil.	_____	NOTE: Answers may vary for
2. Answered question a.	_____	questions a through h.
3. Answered question b.	_____	
4. Answered question c.	_____	
5. Answered question d.	_____	
6. Answered question e.	_____	
7. Answered question f.	_____	
8. Answered question g.	_____	
9. Answered question h.	_____	
10. Completed within time specified.	_____	

TOTAL POINTS EARNED: _____   TOTAL POINTS POSSIBLE: 10

Evaluator's Signature _____ NEED TO REPEAT: _____

PERFORMANCE EVALUATION CHECKLIST
EXERCISE 3-1 RELEASE OF INFORMATION

Name _____ Date _____ Score _____

PERFORMANCE OBJECTIVE

Task: Given access to all necessary equipment and information, the student will answer five multiple choice questions about releasing medical records.

Scoring: One point for each step performed satisfactorily unless otherwise weighted. To obtain a percentage score, divide the total points earned by the number of points possible.

Standards: Time _____ minutes Note: Time element may be given by instructor.

NOTE TIME BEGAN _____   NOTE TIME COMPLETED _____

PROCEDURE STEPS	STEP PERFORMED SATISFACTORILY	COMMENTS
1. Assembled multiple choice questions and pen or pencil.	_____	
2. Answered question No. 1.	_____	
3. Answered question No. 2.	_____	
4. Answered question No. 3.	_____	
5. Answered question No. 4.	_____	
6. Answered question No. 5.	_____	
7. Completed within time specified.	_____	

TOTAL POINTS EARNED: _____   TOTAL POINTS POSSIBLE: 7

Evaluator's Signature _____ NEED TO REPEAT: _____

PERFORMANCE EVALUATION CHECKLIST
EXERCISE 4-1 RESPONSES TO OFFICE SITUATIONS

Name _____ Date _____ Score _____

PERFORMANCE OBJECTIVE

Task: Given access to all necessary equipment and information, the student will study the situations, give responses, and key or handwrite them with tact and consideration for the patient's medical problem. Circle in red the numbers of situations you have difficulty handling and bring them to class for discussion.

Scoring: One point for each step performed satisfactorily unless otherwise weighted. To obtain a percentage score, divide the total points earned by the number of points possible.

Standards: Time _____ minutes Note: Time element may be given by instructor.

NOTE TIME BEGAN _____   NOTE TIME COMPLETED _____

PROCEDURE STEPS	STEP PERFORMED SATISFACTORILY	COMMENTS
1. Assembled two sheets of plain paper and a red pen.	_____	
2. Responded to question No. 1.	_____	
3. Responded to question No. 2.	_____	
4. Responded to question No. 3.	_____	
5. Responded to question No. 4.	_____	
6. Responded to question No. 5.	_____	
7. Responded to question No. 6.	_____	
8. Responded to question No. 7.	_____	
9. Responded to question No. 8.	_____	
10. Responded to question No. 9.	_____	
11. Responded to question No. 10.	_____	
12. Responded to question No. 11.	_____	
13. Responded to question No. 12.	_____	
14. Responded to question No. 13.	_____	
15. Responded to question No. 14.	_____	
16. Responded to question No. 15.	_____	
17. Responded to question No. 16.	_____	
18. Responded to question No. 17.	_____	
19. Responded to question No. 18.	_____	
20. Responded to question No. 19.	_____	
21. Responded to question No. 20.	_____	
22. Responded to question No. 21.	_____	
23. Responded to question No. 22.	_____	
24. Made note of difficult situations to bring up for class discussion.	_____	
25. Completed within time specified.	_____	

TOTAL POINTS EARNED: _____   TOTAL POINTS POSSIBLE: 25

Evaluator's Signature _____   NEED TO REPEAT: _____

PERFORMANCE EVALUATION CHECKLIST
EXERCISE 4-2 PREPARE A PATIENT REGISTRATION FORM

Name _____ Date _____ Score _____

PERFORMANCE OBJECTIVE

Task: Given access to all necessary equipment and information, the student will prepare a patient registration form by interviewing a classmate.

Scoring: One point for each step performed satisfactorily unless otherwise weighted. To obtain a percentage score, divide the total points earned by the number of points possible.

Standards: Time _____ minutes Note: Time element may be given by instructor.

NOTE TIME BEGAN _____   NOTE TIME COMPLETED _____

PROCEDURE STEPS	STEP PERFORMED SATISFACTORILY	COMMENTS
1. Assembled form 1 and pen.	_____	
2. Obtained a classmate to interview.	_____	
3. Obtained all insurance cards.	_____	
4. Photocopied insurance cards for the file.	_____	
5. Proofread form for legibility.	_____	
6. Verify patient's personal information section is completed or any blank not applicable is marked NA.	_____	
7. Verify patient's responsible party information section is completed or any blank not applicable is marked NA.	_____	
8. Verify patient's insurance information section is completed or any blank not applicable is marked NA.	_____	
9. Verify patient's referral information section is completed or any blank not applicable is marked NA.	_____	
10. Verify emergency contact section is completed or any blank not applicable is marked NA.	_____	
11. Verify the assignment of benefits/financial agreement is dated.	_____	
12. Verify the assignment of benefits/financial agreement is signed.	_____	
13. Completed within time specified.	_____	

TOTAL POINTS EARNED: _____   TOTAL POINTS POSSIBLE: 13

Evaluator's Signature _____ NEED TO REPEAT: _____

PERFORMANCE EVALUATION CHECKLIST
EXERCISE 4-3 PREPARE AN APPLICATION FORM FOR A DISABLED PERSON PLACARD

Name _____ Date _____ Score _____

PERFORMANCE OBJECTIVE

Task: Given access to all necessary equipment and information, the student will ask a student or friend to complete an application form for a disabled person placard and review the data.

Scoring: One point for each step performed satisfactorily unless otherwise weighted. To obtain a percentage score, divide the total points earned by the number of points possible.

Standards: Time _____ minutes Note: Time element may be given by instructor.

NOTE TIME BEGAN _____   NOTE TIME COMPLETED _____

PROCEDURE STEPS	STEP PERFORMED SATISFACTORILY	COMMENTS
1. Assembled form 2, pen, and license number reference.	_____	
2. Checked to see that correct box was marked at top of form.	_____	
3. Verify that section A was completed.	_____	
4. Verify that section B was completed.	_____	
5. Verify that section C was completed.	_____	
6. Verify that section D was completed.	_____	
7. Verify that section E was completed.	_____	
8. Completed section F.	_____	
9. Completed section G.	_____	
10. Completed section H.	_____	
11. Document ready for physician to review and sign.	_____	
12. Completed within time specified.	_____	

TOTAL POINTS EARNED: _____   TOTAL POINTS POSSIBLE: 12

Evaluator's Signature _____ NEED TO REPEAT: _____

PERFORMANCE EVALUATION CHECKLIST
EXERCISE 5-1 SCREEN TELEPHONE CALLS

Name _____ Date _____ Score _____

PERFORMANCE OBJECTIVE

Task: Given access to all necessary equipment and information, the student will study scenarios; screen incoming telephone calls to determine the person or persons who could take the calls; and indicate those that need message slips.

Scoring: One point for each step performed satisfactorily unless otherwise weighted. To obtain a percentage score, divide the total points earned by the number of points possible.

Standards: Time _____ minutes   Note: Time element may be given by instructor.

NOTE TIME BEGAN _____   NOTE TIME COMPLETED _____

PROCEDURE STEPS	STEP PERFORMED SATISFACTORILY	COMMENTS
1. Assembled scenarios and pen.	_____	
2. Screened call No. 1.	_____	
3. Screened call No. 2.	_____	
4. Screened call No. 3.	_____	
5. Screened call No. 4.	_____	
6. Screened call No. 5.	_____	
7. Screened call No. 6.	_____	
8. Screened call No. 7.	_____	
9. Screened call No. 8.	_____	
10. Screened call No. 9.	_____	
11. Screened call No. 10.	_____	
12. Screened call No. 11.	_____	
13. Screened call No. 12.	_____	
14. Screened call No. 13.	_____	
15. Screened call No. 14.	_____	
16. Screened call No. 15.	_____	
17. Screened call No. 16.	_____	
18. Screened call No. 17.	_____	
19. Screened call No. 18.	_____	
20. Screened call No. 19.	_____	
21. Screened call No. 20.	_____	
22. Screened call No. 21.	_____	
23. Screened call No. 22.	_____	
24. Screened call No. 23.	_____	
25. Screened call No. 24.	_____	
26. Screened call No. 25.	_____	
27. Put check mark by those needing message slips.	_____	
28. Completed within time specified.	_____	

TOTAL POINTS EARNED: _____   TOTAL POINTS POSSIBLE: 28

Evaluator's Signature _____ NEED TO REPEAT: _____

PERFORMANCE EVALUATION CHECKLIST
EXERCISE 5-2 TRIAGE APPOINTMENT SITUATIONS FOR APPROPRIATE SCHEDULING

Name _____ Date _____ Score _____

PERFORMANCE OBJECTIVE

Task: Given access to all necessary equipment and information, the student will triage appointment situations for appropriate scheduling.

Scoring: One point for each step performed satisfactorily unless otherwise weighted. To obtain a percentage score, divide the total points earned by the number of points possible.

Standards: Time _____ minutes Note: Time element may be given by instructor.

NOTE TIME BEGAN _____   NOTE TIME COMPLETED _____

PROCEDURE STEPS	STEP PERFORMED SATISFACTORILY	COMMENTS
1. Assembled appointment situations and pen.	_____	
2. Determined time element for situation 1.	_____	
3. Determined time element for situation 2.	_____	
4. Determined time element for situation 3.	_____	
5. Determined time element for situation 4.	_____	
6. Determined time element for situation 5.	_____	
7. Determined time element for situation 6.	_____	
8. Determined time element for situation 7.	_____	
9. Determined time element for situation 8.	_____	
10. Determined time element for situation 9.	_____	
11. Determined time element for situation 10.	_____	
12. Determined time element for situation 11.	_____	
13. Determined time element for situation 12.	_____	
14. Determined time element for situation 13.	_____	
15. Determined time element for situation 14.	_____	
16. Determined time element for situation 15.	_____	
17. Determined time element for situation 16.	_____	
18. Determined time element for situation 17.	_____	
19. Determined time element for situation 18.	_____	
20. Determined time element for situation 19.	_____	
21. Determined time element for situation 20.	_____	
22. Determined time element for situation 21.	_____	
23. Determined time element for situation 22.	_____	
24. Determined time element for situation 23.	_____	
25. Determined time element for situation 24.	_____	
26. Determined time element for situation 25.	_____	
27. Determined time element for situation 26.	_____	
28. Determined time element for situation 27.	_____	
29. Determined time element for situation 28.	_____	
30. Determined time element for situation 29.	_____	
31. Determined time element for situation 30.	_____	
32. Determined time element for situation 31.	_____	
33. Determined time element for situation 32.	_____	
34. Determined time element for situation 33.	_____	
35. Determined time element for situation 34.	_____	
36. Determined time element for situation 35.	_____	
37. Determined time element for situation 36.	_____	
38. Determined time element for situation 37.	_____	

39. Determined time element for situation 38. _____
40. Determined time element for situation 39. _____
41. Determined time element for situation 40. _____
42. Determined time element for situation 41. _____
43. Determined time element for situation 42. _____
44. Determined time element for situation 43. _____
45. Determined time element for situation 44. _____
46. Completed within time specified. _____

TOTAL POINTS EARNED: _____ TOTAL POINTS POSSIBLE: 46

Evaluator's Signature _____ NEED TO REPEAT: _____

PERFORMANCE EVALUATION CHECKLIST
EXERCISE 5-3 PREPARE MESSAGE FORMS

Name _____ Date _____ Score _____

PERFORMANCE OBJECTIVE

Task: Given access to all necessary equipment and information, the student will study incoming calls, determine those that require message forms, and complete the forms.

Scoring: One point for each step performed satisfactorily unless otherwise weighted. To obtain a percentage score, divide the total points earned by the number of points possible.

Standards: Time _____ minutes   Note: Time element may be given by instructor.

NOTE TIME BEGAN _____   NOTE TIME COMPLETED _____

PROCEDURE STEPS	STEP PERFORMED SATISFACTORILY	COMMENTS
1. Assembled forms 3-5, pen or pencil.	_____	
2. Completed message forms for call 1.	_____	
3. Completed message forms for call 2.	_____	
4. Completed message forms for call 3.	_____	
5. Completed message forms for call 4.	_____	
6. Completed message forms for call 5.	_____	
7. Completed message forms for call 6.	_____	
8. Completed message forms for call 7.	_____	
9. Completed message forms for call 8.	_____	
10. Completed message forms for call 9.	_____	
11. Completed message forms for call 10.	_____	
12. Completed message forms for call 11.	_____	
13. Completed message forms for call 12.	_____	
14. Completed message forms for call 13.	_____	
15. Completed message forms for call 14.	_____	
16. Completed message forms for call 15.	_____	
17. Wrote message forms legibly, including necessary information.	_____	
18. Took appropriate action in all situations requiring a response by the medical assistant.	_____	
19. Checked the priority box for situations that needed immediate attention.	_____	
20. Completed within time specified.	_____	

TOTAL POINTS EARNED: _____ TOTAL POINTS POSSIBLE: 20

Evaluator's Signature _____ NEED TO REPEAT: _____

PERFORMANCE EVALUATION CHECKLIST
EXERCISE 6-1 SCHEDULE APPOINTMENTS

Name _____ Date _____ Score _____

PERFORMANCE OBJECTIVE

Task: Given access to all necessary equipment and information, the student will schedule and record patient appointments using acceptable abbreviations; adjust to unexpected changes, write legible appointment cards, and make a photocopy for physician reference.

Scoring: One point for each step performed satisfactorily unless otherwise weighted. To obtain a percentage score, divide the total points earned by the number of points possible.

Standards: Time _____ minutes   Note: Time element may be given by instructor.

NOTE TIME BEGAN _____   NOTE TIME COMPLETED _____

PROCEDURE STEPS	STEP PERFORMED SATISFACTORILY	COMMENTS
1. Assembled forms 6, 7, 8, and 9 and pen or pencil.	_____	
2. Completed headings on three appointment record sheets 1, 2, and 3.	_____	
3. Blocked off appropriate times on appointment sheets 1, 2, and 3.	_____	
4. Determined the correct time allotment for all appointments.	_____	
5. Used abbreviations for procedures when known.	_____	
6. Used symbols to indicate reserved appointment times.	_____	
7. Wrote all dates for appointment sheet 1.	_____	
8. Wrote all dates for appointment sheet 2.	_____	
9. Wrote all dates for appointment sheet 3.	_____	
10. Made necessary remarks and notes in appropriate places for appointment sheets 1, 2, and 3.	_____	
11. Completed appointment card 1 legibly and completely.	_____	
12. Completed appointment card 2 legibly and completely.	_____	
13. Completed appointment card 3 legibly and completely.	_____	
14. Completed appointment card 4 legibly and completely.	_____	
15. Made appropriate appointment changes (times may vary) from dictated information.	_____	
14. Entered data for house call.	_____	
15. Made a photocopy (if copier is available).	_____	
16. Completed within time specified.	_____	

TOTAL POINTS EARNED: _____   TOTAL POINTS POSSIBLE: 16

Evaluator's Signature _____ NEED TO REPEAT: _____

PERFORMANCE EVALUATION CHECKLIST
EXERCISE 6-2 PREPARE AN APPOINTMENT SHEET

Name _____ Date _____ Score _____

PERFORMANCE OBJECTIVE

Task: Given access to all necessary equipment and information, the student will prepare a keyed or typed appointment reference sheet of patients on a given day or make a photocopy of the appointment sheet.

Scoring: One point for each step performed satisfactorily unless otherwise weighted. To obtain a percentage score, divide the total points earned by the number of points possible.

Standards: Time _____ minutes   Note: Time element may be given by instructor.

NOTE TIME BEGAN _____   NOTE TIME COMPLETED _____

PROCEDURE STEPS	STEP PERFORMED SATISFACTORILY	COMMENTS
1. Assembled one sheet of plain paper.	_____	
2. Keyed an appropriate and accurate heading.	_____	
3. Keyed patient information, appropriately spaced with centered columns.	_____	
4. Keyed and spelled patient names correctly with appointment times and procedure clearly indicated.	_____	
5. Indicated new patients.	_____	
6. Showed a house call if patient was to be seen before the lunch hour.	_____	
7. Made a photocopy of the appointment page and cut it in half vertically to give to designated physician.	_____	
8. Completed within time specified.	_____	

TOTAL POINTS EARNED: _____   TOTAL POINTS POSSIBLE: 8

Evaluator's Signature _____   NEED TO REPEAT: _____

PERFORMANCE EVALUATION CHECKLIST
EXERCISE 6-3 ABSTRACT INFORMATION FOR A HOSPITAL/SURGERY SCHEDULING FORM

Name _____ Date _____ Score _____

PERFORMANCE OBJECTIVE

Task: Given access to all necessary equipment and information, the student will review a patient's medical record and abstract and type or key the required information on the hospital/surgery scheduling form.

Scoring: One point for each step performed satisfactorily unless otherwise weighted. To obtain a percentage score, divide the total points earned by the number of points possible.

Standards: Time _____ minutes   Note: Time element may be given by instructor.

NOTE TIME BEGAN _____   NOTE TIME COMPLETED _____

PROCEDURE STEPS	STEP PERFORMED SATISFACTORILY	COMMENTS
1. Assembled form 10, pen or pencil, and correction fluid.	_____	
SECTION 1		
2. Keyed patient's name and procedure neatly above printed line.	_____	
3. Checked line 3.	_____	

4. Keyed diagnosis and hospital facility. _____
5. Checked lines 6, 7, and 8. _____
6. Keyed physicians' names. _____

SECTION 2

7. Checked lines 10, 11, and 14. _____
8. Keyed lines 10, 12, 13, and 15. _____
9. Made marks when information to be completed was not relevant. _____
10. Checked lines 16, 17, 19, and 20. _____
11. Indicated admission date on line 18. _____

SECTION 3

12. Keyed all information in lines 21 through 29. _____
13. Signed form. _____
14. Posted arrangements in the appointment book. _____

ALL SECTIONS

15. Proofread document for typographical and spelling errors. _____
16. Completed within time specified. _____

TOTAL POINTS EARNED: _____   TOTAL POINTS POSSIBLE: 16

Evaluator's Signature _____ NEED TO REPEAT: _____

PERFORMANCE EVALUATION CHECKLIST
EXERCISE 6-4 TRANSFER SURGERY SCHEDULING INFORMATION TO A LETTER

Name _____ Date _____ Score _____

PERFORMANCE OBJECTIVE

Task: Given access to all necessary equipment and information, the student will transfer surgery scheduling information to a letter.
Scoring: One point for each step performed satisfactorily unless otherwise weighted. To obtain a percentage score, divide the total points earned by the number of points possible.
Standards: Time _____ minutes Note: Time element may be given by instructor.
NOTE TIME BEGAN _____ NOTE TIME COMPLETED _____

PROCEDURE STEPS	STEP PERFORMED SATISFACTORILY	COMMENTS
1. Assembled form 10 for reference, form 11 with one copy, pen, and correction fluid.	_____	
2. Keyed date line.	_____	
3. Correctly typed inside address on the letter (above the designated line).	_____	
4. Entered accurate information in body of letter indicating specific dates and times.	_____	
5. Keyed the names of all physicians.	_____	
6. Signed the letter.	_____	
7. Keyed reference lines.	_____	
8. Proofread letter for typographical and spelling errors.	_____	
9. Completed within time specified.	_____	

TOTAL POINTS EARNED: _____   TOTAL POINTS POSSIBLE: 9

Evaluator's Signature _____ NEED TO REPEAT: _____

PERFORMANCE EVALUATION CHECKLIST
EXERCISE 6-5 REFER PATIENT FOR OUTSIDE SERVICES

Name _____ Date _____ Score _____

PERFORMANCE OBJECTIVE

Task: Given access to all necessary equipment and information, the student will handwrite information on forms to be given to the patient for outside services.

Scoring: One point for each step performed satisfactorily unless otherwise weighted. To obtain a percentage score, divide the total points earned by the number of points possible.

Standards: Time _____ minutes Note: Time element may be given by instructor.

NOTE TIME BEGAN _____   NOTE TIME COMPLETED _____

PROCEDURE STEPS	STEP PERFORMED SATISFACTORILY	COMMENTS
1. Assembled forms 12 and 13 and pen.	_____	
2. Entered patient's information on form 12.	_____	
3. Entered information for laboratory tests on form 12.	_____	
4. Entered diagnosis on form 12.	_____	
5. Entered billing information on form 12.	_____	
6. Entered patient's information on form 13.	_____	
7. Entered patient's complaint and findings on form 13.	_____	
8. Entered information for x-rays on form 13.	_____	
9. Completed within time specified.	_____	

TOTAL POINTS EARNED: _____   TOTAL POINTS POSSIBLE: 9

Evaluator's Signature _____   NEED TO REPEAT: _____

PERFORMANCE EVALUATION CHECKLIST
EXERCISE 7-1 COMPUTER FUNCTIONS

Name _____ Date _____ Score _____

PERFORMANCE OBJECTIVE

Task: Given access to all necessary equipment and information, the student will determine various functions the computer would be used for by health care professionals working in different positions in the medical office.

Scoring: One point for each step performed satisfactorily unless otherwise weighted. To obtain a percentage score, divide the total points earned by the number of points possible.

Standards: Time _____ minutes   Note: Time element may be given by instructor.

NOTE TIME BEGAN _____   NOTE TIME COMPLETED _____

PROCEDURE STEPS	STEP PERFORMED SATISFACTORILY	COMMENTS
1. Assembled worksheet, pen or pencil.	_____	
RECEPTIONIST:		
2. Answered a and b.	_____	(2 points)
TRANSCRIPTIONIST/MEDICAL RECORDS CLERK:		
3. Answered a and b.	_____	(2 points)
CLINICAL ASSISTANT:		
4. Answered a, b, c, and d.	_____	(4 points)
INSURANCE SPECIALIST:		
5. Answered a, b, and c.	_____	(3 points)
BOOKKEEPER:		
6. Answered, b, and c.	_____	(3 points)
ALL EMPLOYEES:		
7. Answered a and b.	_____	(2 points)
OFFICE MANAGER:		
8. Answered a.	_____	
9. Completed within time specified.	_____	
TOTAL POINTS EARNED:	_____	TOTAL POINTS POSSIBLE: 19

Evaluator's Signature _____ NEED TO REPEAT: _____

PERFORMANCE EVALUATION CHECKLIST
EXERCISE 7-2 COMPUTER TERMINOLOGY

Name _____ Date _____ Score _____

PERFORMANCE OBJECTIVE

Task: Given access to all necessary equipment and information, the student will determine the correct computer terminology.

Scoring: One point for each step performed satisfactorily unless otherwise weighted. To obtain a percentage score, divide the total points earned by the number of points possible.

Standards: Time _____ minutes Note: Time element may be given by instructor.

NOTE TIME BEGAN _____ NOTE TIME COMPLETED _____

PROCEDURE STEPS	STEP PERFORMED SATISFACTORILY	COMMENTS
1. Assembled worksheet, pen or pencil.	_____	
2. Answered clue #1.	_____	
3. Answered clue #2.	_____	
4. Answered clue #3.	_____	
5. Answered clue #4.	_____	
6. Answered clue #5.	_____	
7. Answered clue #6.	_____	
8. Answered clue #7.	_____	
9. Answered clue #8.	_____	
10. Answered clue #9.	_____	
11. Answered clue #10.	_____	
12. Answered clue #11.	_____	
13. Answered clue #12.	_____	
14. Answered clue #13.	_____	
15. Answered clue #14.	_____	
16. Answered clue #15.	_____	
17. Answered clue #16.	_____	
18. Completed within time specified.	_____	

TOTAL POINTS EARNED: _____   TOTAL POINTS POSSIBLE: 18

Evaluator's Signature _____ NEED TO REPEAT: _____

PERFORMANCE EVALUATION CHECKLIST
EXERCISE 7-3 CHANGE DOCUMENTS: SPELLING ERRORS

Name _____ Date _____ Score _____

PERFORMANCE OBJECTIVE

Task: Given access to all necessary equipment and information, the student will type the document making all necessary spelling corrections.

Scoring: One point for each step performed satisfactorily unless otherwise weighted. To obtain a percentage score, divide the total points earned by the number of points possible.

Standards: Time _____ minutes Note: Time element may be given by instructor.
NOTE TIME BEGAN _____ NOTE TIME COMPLETED _____

PROCEDURE STEPS	STEP PERFORMED SATISFACTORILY	COMMENTS
1. Assembled worksheet, red pen, and white typing or computer paper.		
2. Circled in red all spelling errors.	_____	
3. Corrected all spelling errors while typing, or by using the computer spell-check and search modes.	_____	
4. Proofread after keying or typing document for spelling errors while document remained on the computer screen or in the typewriter.	_____	
5. Produced two corrected copies using the printer, carbon paper, or photocopy machine.	_____	
6. Completed within time specified.	_____	

TOTAL POINTS EARNED: _____ TOTAL POINTS POSSIBLE: 6

Evaluator's Signature _____ NEED TO REPEAT: _____

PERFORMANCE EVALUATION CHECKLIST
EXERCISE 7-4 CHANGE DOCUMENTS: NAME

Name _____ Date _____ Score _____

PERFORMANCE OBJECTIVE

Task: Given access to all necessary equipment and information, the student will key or type the document making all necessary name changes.

Scoring: One point for each step performed satisfactorily unless otherwise weighted. To obtain a percentage score, divide the total points earned by the number of points possible.

Standards: Time _____ minutes Note: Time element may be given by instructor.
NOTE TIME BEGAN _____ NOTE TIME COMPLETED _____

PROCEDURE STEPS	STEP PERFORMED SATISFACTORILY	COMMENTS
1. Assembled red pen and white typing or computer paper.	_____	
2. Circled in red the name Thompsett.	_____	
3. Changed the name from Thompsett to Tompsett by keying it correctly, or by using the computer search mode.	_____	
4. Proofread after keying or typing document for name change and spelling errors while document remained on the computer screen or in the typewriter.	_____	
5. Produced two corrected copies using printer, carbon paper, or photocopy machine.	_____	
6. Completed within time specified.	_____	

TOTAL POINTS EARNED: _____ TOTAL POINTS POSSIBLE: 6

Evaluator's Signature _____ NEED TO REPEAT: _____

PERFORMANCE EVALUATION CHECKLIST
EXERCISE 7-5 CHANGE DOCUMENTS: PUNCTUATION

Name _____ Date _____ Score _____

PERFORMANCE OBJECTIVE

Task: Given access to all necessary equipment and information, the student will key or type the document making all necessary punctuation and capitalization corrections.

Scoring: One point for each step performed satisfactorily unless otherwise weighted. To obtain a percentage score, divide the total points earned by the number of points possible.

Standards: Time _____ minutes Note: Time element may be given by instructor.

NOTE TIME BEGAN _____ NOTE TIME COMPLETED _____

PROCEDURE STEPS	STEP PERFORMED SATISFACTORILY	COMMENTS
1. Assembled red pen and white typing or computer paper.	_____	
2. Circled all semicolons and letters needing to be capitalized.	_____	
3. Changed all semicolons to periods and capitalized all necessary letters by typing them correctly, or by using the computer search mode.	_____	
4. Proofread after keying or typing document for punctuation and spelling errors while document remained on the computer screen or in the typewriter.	_____	
5. Produced two corrected copies using a printer, carbon paper, or photocopy machine.	_____	
6. Completed within time specified.		

TOTAL POINTS EARNED: _____   TOTAL POINTS POSSIBLE: 6

Evaluator's Signature _____   NEED TO REPEAT: _____

PERFORMANCE EVALUATION CHECKLIST
EXERCISE 7-6 CHANGE DOCUMENTS: CAPITALIZATION

Name _____ Date _____ Score _____

PERFORMANCE OBJECTIVE

Task: Given access to all necessary equipment and information, the student will key or type the document making all necessary punctuation and capitalization corrections.

Scoring: One point for each step performed satisfactorily unless otherwise weighted. To obtain a percentage score, divide the total points earned by the number of points possible.

Standards: Time _____ minutes Note: Time element may be given by instructor.

NOTE TIME BEGAN _____ NOTE TIME COMPLETED _____

PROCEDURE STEPS	STEP PERFORMED SATISFACTORILY	COMMENTS
1. Assembled red pen and white typing or computer paper.	_____	
2. Circled in red the words *patient service*.	_____	
3. Capitalized the P in patient and the S in service each time it appeared; keying it correctly, or by using the computer search mode.	_____	
4. Proofread after keyboarding or typing document for capitalization and spelling errors while document remained on the computer screen or in the typewriter.	_____	
5. Produced two corrected copies using printer, carbon paper, or photocopy machine.	_____	
6. Completed within time specified.	_____	

TOTAL POINTS EARNED: _____   TOTAL POINTS POSSIBLE: 6

Evaluator's Signature _____   NEED TO REPEAT: _____

PERFORMANCE EVALUATION CHECKLIST
EXERCISE 8-1 PREPARE A PATIENT RECORD

Name _____ Date _____ Score _____

PERFORMANCE OBJECTIVE

Task: Given access to all necessary equipment and information, the student will complete a patient record form, label a file folder, and make a 3" x 5" file card.

Scoring: One point for each step performed satisfactorily unless otherwise weighted. To obtain a percentage score, divide the total points earned by the number of points possible.

Standards: Time _____ minutes Note: Time element may be given by instructor.

NOTE TIME BEGAN _____   NOTE TIME COMPLETED _____

PROCEDURE STEPS	STEP PERFORMED SATISFACTORILY	COMMENTS
1. Assembled form 14, file folder, and file card.	_____	
2. Keyed patient record information for Wayne G. Weather as supplied in workbook exercise 6-3.	_____	
3. Completed a file folder with label.	_____	
4. Completed a file card.	_____	
5. Inserted capitalization and abbreviations where appropriate.	_____	
6. Checked placement and spacing of all punctuation marks.	_____	
7. Keyed notation of office visit.	_____	
8. Keyed admission to the hospital.	_____	
9. Keyed notation of surgery.		
10. Proofread form for spelling and typographical errors while form remained in typewriter or on computer screen.	_____	
11. Ready for physician to read and sign.	_____	
12. Completed within time specified.	_____	

TOTAL POINTS EARNED: _____   TOTAL POINTS POSSIBLE: 12

Evaluator's Signature _____ NEED TO REPEAT: _____

PERFORMANCE EVALUATION CHECKLIST
EXERCISE 8-2 PREPARE A PATIENT RECORD FROM AN INTERVIEW

Name _____ Date _____ Score _____

PERFORMANCE OBJECTIVE

Task: Given access to all necessary equipment and information, the student will complete a patient record form, label a file folder, and make a 3" x 5" file card from an interview and from an October 25 office visit.

Scoring: One point for each step performed satisfactorily unless otherwise weighted. To obtain a percentage score, divide the total points earned by the number of points possible.

Standards: Time _____ minutes Note: Time element may be given by instructor.

NOTE TIME BEGAN _____   NOTE TIME COMPLETED _____

PROCEDURE STEPS	STEP PERFORMED SATISFACTORILY	COMMENTS
1. Assembled form 15, file folder, and file card.	_____	
2. Keyed patient record information.	_____	
3. Completed a file folder with label.	_____	

4. Completed a file card.   _____
5. Inserted capitalization and abbreviations where appropriate.   _____
6. Checked placement and spacing of all punctuation marks.   _____
7. Keyed notation of office visit.   _____
8. Proofread form for spelling and typographical errors while form remained in typewriter or on computer screen.   _____
9. Ready for physician to read and sign.   _____
10. Completed within time specified.   _____

TOTAL POINTS EARNED: _____   TOTAL POINTS POSSIBLE: 10

Evaluator's Signature _____ NEED TO REPEAT: _____

PERFORMANCE EVALUATION CHECKLIST
EXERCISE 8-3 PREPARE TELEPHONE MESSAGES

Name _____ Date _____ Score _____

PERFORMANCE OBJECTIVE

Task: Given access to all necessary equipment and information, the student will prepare telephone messages for a patient's medical record.

Scoring: One point for each step performed satisfactorily unless otherwise weighted. To obtain a percentage score, divide the total points earned by the number of points possible.

Standards: Time _____ minutes Note: Time element may be given by instructor.

NOTE TIME BEGAN _____ NOTE TIME COMPLETED _____

PROCEDURE STEPS	STEP PERFORMED SATISFACTORILY	COMMENTS
1. Assembled form 16, one sheet of colored paper, cellophane adhesive tape, scissors, and pen or pencil.	_____	
2. Keyed patient record information in upper right corner of colored sheet.	_____	
3. Keyed patient's name on each telephone message.	_____	
4. Proofread all keyed material.	_____	
5. Inserted four messages in the patient record.	_____	
6. Completed within time specified.	_____	

TOTAL POINTS EARNED: _____   TOTAL POINTS POSSIBLE: 6

Evaluator's Signature _____ NEED TO REPEAT: _____

PERFORMANCE EVALUATION CHECKLIST
EXERCISE 8-4 CORRECT A PATIENT RECORD

Name _____ Date _____ Score _____

PERFORMANCE OBJECTIVE

Task: Given access to all necessary equipment and information, the student will make a correction on a patient record.

Scoring: One point for each step performed satisfactorily unless otherwise weighted. To obtain a percentage score, divide the total points earned by the number of points possible.

Standards: Time _____ minutes   Note: Time element may be given by instructor.

NOTE TIME BEGAN _____   NOTE TIME COMPLETED _____

PROCEDURE STEPS	STEP PERFORMED SATISFACTORILY	COMMENTS
1. Assembled patient record number 1181 from exercise 8-2 and pen.	_____	
2. Made appropriate correction entries.	_____	
3. Handwrote and inserted or deleted information legibly.	_____	
4. Completed within time specified.	_____	
TOTAL POINTS EARNED:	_____	TOTAL POINTS POSSIBLE: 4

Evaluator's Signature _____ NEED TO REPEAT: _____

PERFORMANCE EVALUATION CHECKLIST
EXERCISE 8-5 ABSTRACT FROM MEDICAL RECORDS

Name _____ Date _____ Score _____

PERFORMANCE OBJECTIVE

Task: Given access to all necessary equipment and information, the student will abstract information from a patient record.

Scoring: One point for each step performed satisfactorily unless otherwise weighted. To obtain a percentage score, divide the total points earned by the number of points possible.

Standards: Time _____ minutes   Note: Time element may be given by instructor.

NOTE TIME BEGAN _____   NOTE TIME COMPLETED _____

PROCEDURE STEPS	STEP PERFORMED SATISFACTORILY	COMMENTS
1. Assembled patient record number 1181 from exercise 8-2, pencil or pen, and form 17.	_____	
2. Abstracted information from patient record number 1181.	_____	
3. Identified abbreviations from patient record.	_____	
4. Completed within time specified.	_____	
TOTAL POINTS EARNED:	_____	TOTAL POINTS POSSIBLE: 4

Evaluator's Signature _____ NEED TO REPEAT: _____

PERFORMANCE EVALUATION CHECKLIST
EXERCISE 8-6 PREPARE A HISTORY AND PHYSICAL (H&P)

Name _____ Date _____ Score _____

PERFORMANCE OBJECTIVE

Task: Given access to all necessary equipment and information, the student will prepare a patient record and file folder with label, make a 3" x 5" file card, prepare a history and physical, and make a photocopy of the report.

Scoring: One point for each step performed satisfactorily unless otherwise weighted. To obtain a percentage score, divide the total points earned by the number of points possible.

Standards: Time _____ minutes   Note: Time element may be given by instructor.

NOTE TIME BEGAN _____   NOTE TIME COMPLETED _____

PROCEDURE STEPS	STEP PERFORMED SATISFACTORILY	COMMENTS
1. Assembled form 18, file folder, label, file card, and plain paper.		
2. Completed a patient record on Sun Low Chung.	_____	
3. Completed a file folder with label.	_____	
4. Completed a file card.	_____	
5. Dated report.	_____	
6. Keyed in full-block report style.	_____	
7. Margins even, equal, and correct size.	_____	
8. Inserted main topic headings.	_____	
9. Inserted subtopic headings.	_____	
10. Inserted capitalization and abbreviations where appropriate.	_____	
11. Checked placement and spacing of all punctuation marks.	_____	
12. Inserted proper paragraphing.	_____	
13. Inserted a page 2 heading.	_____	
14. Placed a signature line at the end of the history and physical.	_____	
15. Inserted typist's identifying sign off data for the history and physical.	_____	
16. Proofread report for spelling and typographical errors while history and physical remained in typewriter, word processor, or on computer screen.	_____	
17. Document ready for physician to review and sign.	_____	
18. Made photocopy of report for patient's chart.	_____	
19. Completed within time specified.	_____	

TOTAL POINTS EARNED: _____   TOTAL POINTS POSSIBLE: 19

Evaluator's Signature _____ NEED TO REPEAT: _____

PERFORMANCE EVALUATION CHECKLIST
EXERCISE 9-1 TRANSLATE PRESCRIPTIONS

Name _____ Date _____ Score _____

PERFORMANCE OBJECTIVE

Task: Given access to all necessary equipment and information, the student will translate ten prescriptions from Latin into common English by referring to text Table 9-3 (Common Prescription Abbreviations and Symbols).

Scoring: One point for each step performed satisfactorily unless otherwise weighted. To obtain a percentage score, divide the total points earned by the number of points possible.

Standards: Time _____ minutes Note: Time element may be given by instructor.

NOTE TIME BEGAN _____ NOTE TIME COMPLETED _____

PROCEDURE STEPS	STEP PERFORMED SATISFACTORILY	COMMENTS
Note: each prescription should have: name of medication, dosage, amount, and directions.		
1. Assembled ten written prescriptions, plain paper, and pen or pencil.	_____	
2. Translated prescription 1.	_____	(4 points)
3. Translated prescription 2.	_____	(4 points)
4. Translated prescription 3.	_____	(4 points)
5. Translated prescription 4.	_____	(4 points)
6. Translated prescription 5.	_____	(4 points)
7. Translated prescription 6.	_____	(4 points)
8. Translated prescription 7.	_____	(4 points)
9. Translated prescription 8.	_____	(4 points)
10. Translated prescription 9.	_____	(4 points)
11. Translated prescription 10.	_____	(4 points)
12. Completed within time specified.	_____	

TOTAL POINTS EARNED: _____ TOTAL POINTS POSSIBLE: 42

Evaluator's Signature _____ NEED TO REPEAT: _____

PERFORMANCE EVALUATION CHECKLIST
EXERCISE 9-2 SPELL DRUG NAMES

Name _____ Date _____ Score _____

PERFORMANCE OBJECTIVE

Task: Given access to all necessary equipment and information, the student will spell ten brand or generic drug names.

Scoring: One point for each step performed satisfactorily unless otherwise weighted. To obtain a percentage score, divide the total points earned by the number of points possible.

Standards: Time _____ minutes Note: Time element may be given by instructor.

NOTE TIME BEGAN _____ NOTE TIME COMPLETED _____

PROCEDURE STEPS	STEP PERFORMED SATISFACTORILY	COMMENTS
1. Assembled list of ten drug names and a drug reference book.	_____	
2. Spelled drug name 1.	_____	
3. Spelled drug name 2.	_____	

4. Spelled drug name 3. _____
5. Spelled drug name 4. _____
6. Spelled drug name 5. _____
7. Spelled drug name 6. _____
8. Spelled drug name 7. _____
9. Spelled drug name 8. _____
10 Spelled drug name 9. _____
11. Spelled drug name 10. _____
12. Completed within time specified. _____

TOTAL POINTS EARNED: _____ TOTAL POINTS POSSIBLE: 12

Evaluator's Signature _____ NEED TO REPEAT: _____

PERFORMANCE EVALUATION CHECKLIST
EXERCISE 9-3 RECORD PRESCRIPTION REFILLS IN MEDICAL RECORDS

Name _____ Date _____ Score _____

PERFORMANCE OBJECTIVE

Task: Given access to all necessary equipment and information, the student will record four prescription refills on patients' medical records using pharmaceutical abbreviations and symbols.

Scoring: One point for each step performed satisfactorily unless otherwise weighted. To obtain a percentage score, divide the total points earned by the number of points possible.

Standards: Time _____ minutes Note: Time element may be given by instructor.

NOTE TIME BEGAN _____ NOTE TIME COMPLETED _____

PROCEDURE STEPS	STEP PERFORMED SATISFACTORILY	COMMENTS
1. Assembled four file folder labels, pen, and four patient's medical records.	_____	
2. Translated and recorded on patient's medical record prescription refill for problem 1 using pharmaceutical abbreviations and symbols.	_____	(7 points)
3. Translated and recorded on patient's medical record prescription refill for problem 2 using pharmaceutical abbreviations and symbols.	_____	(7 points)
4. Translated and recorded on patient's medical record prescription refill for problem 3 using pharmaceutical abbreviations and symbols.	_____	(7 points)
5. Translated and recorded on patient's medical record prescription refill for problem 4 using pharmaceutical abbreviations and symbols.	_____	(7 points)
6. Completed within time specified.	_____	

TOTAL POINTS EARNED: _____ TOTAL POINTS POSSIBLE: 30

Evaluator's Signature _____ NEED TO REPEAT: _____

PERFORMANCE EVALUATION CHECKLIST
EXERCISE 9-4 SPELL DRUG NAMES

Name _____ Date _____ Score _____

PERFORMANCE OBJECTIVE

Task: Given access to all necessary equipment and information, the student will choose the correct spelling for all generic, brand, and over-the-counter drug names.

Scoring: One point for each step performed satisfactorily unless otherwise weighted. To obtain a percentage score, divide the total points earned by the number of points possible.

Standards: Time _____ minutes   Note: Time element may be given by instructor.

NOTE TIME BEGAN _____   NOTE TIME COMPLETED _____

PROCEDURE STEPS	STEP PERFORMED SATISFACTORILY	COMMENTS
1. Assembled list of ten sentences and a drug reference book.	_____	
2. Spelled drug name 1.	_____	
3. Spelled drug name 2.	_____	
4. Spelled drug name 3.	_____	
5. Spelled drug name 4.	_____	
6. Spelled drug name 5.	_____	
7. Spelled drug name 6.	_____	
8. Spelled drug name 7.	_____	
9. Spelled drug name 8.	_____	
10. Spelled drug name 9.	_____	
11. Spelled drug name 10.	_____	
12. Completed within time specified.	_____	

TOTAL POINTS EARNED: _____   TOTAL POINTS POSSIBLE: 12

Evaluator's Signature _____ NEED TO REPEAT: _____

PERFORMANCE EVALUATION CHECKLIST
EXERCISE 9-5 WRITE A PRESCRIPTION

Name _____ Date _____ Score _____

PERFORMANCE OBJECTIVE

Task: Given access to all necessary equipment and information, the student will write a prescription using today's date and the prescription form by referring to text Table 9-3 (Common Prescription Abbreviations and Symbols).

Scoring: One point for each step performed satisfactorily unless otherwise weighted. To obtain a percentage score, divide the total points earned by the number of points possible.

Standards: Time _____ minutes Note: Time element may be given by instructor.

NOTE TIME BEGAN _____   NOTE TIME COMPLETED _____

PROCEDURE STEPS	STEP PERFORMED SATISFACTORILY	COMMENTS
1. Assembled the prescription form, abbreviation table, and a pen.	_____	
2. Entered the date, the patient's name, address, and refill information on the prescription form.	_____	
3. Entered the name of the medication and dosage.	_____	
4. Entered the amount of medication prescribed.	_____	
5. Entered the directions for taking the medication.	_____	
6. Completed within time specified.	_____	

TOTAL POINTS EARNED: _____   TOTAL POINTS POSSIBLE: 6

Evaluator's Signature _____ NEED TO REPEAT: _____

PERFORMANCE EVALUATION CHECKLIST
EXERCISE 9-6 USE *PHYSICIANS' DESK REFERENCE* (PDR)

Name _____ Date _____ Score _____

PERFORMANCE OBJECTIVE

Task: Given access to all necessary necessary equipment and information, the student will identify the correct medication dosage in the appropriate section of the *Physician's Desk Reference*.

Scoring: One point for each step performed satisfactorily unless otherwise weighted. To obtain a percentage score, divide the total points earned by the number of points possible.

Standards: Time _____ minutes Note: Time element may be given by instructor.

NOTE TIME BEGAN _____   NOTE TIME COMPLETED _____

PROCEDURE STEPS	STEP PERFORMED SATISFACTORILY	COMMENTS
1. Assembled *Physician's Desk Reference* and pen.	_____	
2. Entered dosage.	_____	
3. Entered section of *PDR* used.	_____	
4. Completed within time specified.	_____	

TOTAL POINTS EARNED: _____   TOTAL POINTS POSSIBLE: 4

Evaluator's Signature _____ NEED TO REPEAT: _____

PERFORMANCE EVALUATION CHECKLIST
EXERCISE 9-7 INTERPRET A MEDICATION LOG

Name _____ Date _____ Score _____

PERFORMANCE OBJECTIVE

Task: Given access to all necessary equipment and information, the student will study the medication log and determine the drug use habits of a patient.

Scoring: One point for each step performed satisfactorily unless otherwise weighted. To obtain a percentage score, divide the total points earned by the number of points possible.

Standards: Time _____ minutes Note: Time element may be given by instructor.
NOTE TIME BEGAN _____   NOTE TIME COMPLETED _____

PROCEDURE STEPS	STEP PERFORMED SATISFACTORILY	COMMENTS
1. Assembled the medication log and a pen.	_____	
2. Answered question a.	_____	
3. Answered question b.	_____	
4. Answered question c.	_____	
5. Answered question d.	_____	
6. Completed within time specified.	_____	
TOTAL POINTS EARNED:	_____	TOTAL POINTS POSSIBLE: 6

Evaluator's Signature _____ NEED TO REPEAT: _____

PERFORMANCE EVALUATION CHECKLIST
EXERCISE 9-8 RECORD ON A MEDICATION SCHEDULE

Name _____ Date _____ Score _____

PERFORMANCE OBJECTIVE

Task: Given access to all necessary equipment and information, the student will record the medication name, dosage, and instructins of three drugs on a medication schedule.

Scoring: One point for each step performed satisfactorily unless otherwise weighted. To obtain a percentage score, divide the total points earned by the number of points possible.

Standards: Time _____ minutes Note: Time element may be given by instructor.
NOTE TIME BEGAN _____   NOTE TIME COMPLETED _____

PROCEDURE STEPS	STEP PERFORMED SATISFACTORILY	COMMENTS
1. Assembled the medication schedule, and a pen or pencil.	_____	
2. Labeled medication schedule for Mr. Silva.	_____	
3. Entered information for Paxil medication.	_____	
4. Entered information for Sinemet medication.	_____	
5. Entered information for Lopressor medication.	_____	
6. Completed within time specified.	_____	
TOTAL POINTS EARNED:	_____	TOTAL POINTS POSSIBLE: 6

Evaluator's Signature _____ NEED TO REPEAT: _____

PERFORMANCE EVALUATION CHECKLIST
EXERCISE 10-1 DETERMINE FILING UNITS

Name _____ Date _____ Score _____

PERFORMANCE OBJECTIVE

Task: Given access to all necessary equipment and information, the student will designate first, second, third, and fourth filing units by underlining so that names can be filed alphabetically in the office file.

Scoring: One point for each step performed satisfactorily unless otherwise weighted. To obtain a percentage score, divide the total points earned by the number of points possible.

Standards: Time _____ minutes Note: Time element may be given by instructor.

NOTE TIME BEGAN _____   NOTE TIME COMPLETED _____

PROCEDURE STEPS	STEP PERFORMED SATISFACTORILY	COMMENTS
1. Assembled 50 names, pen or pencil.	_____	
2. Underlined each unit of the patient's name or business name.	_____	(50 points possible)
3. Completed within time specified.	_____	
TOTAL POINTS EARNED:	_____	TOTAL POINTS POSSIBLE: 52

Evaluator's Signature _____ NEED TO REPEAT: _____

PERFORMANCE EVALUATION CHECKLIST
EXERCISE 10-2 INDEX AND FILE NAMES ALPHABETICALLY

Name _____ Date _____ Score _____

PERFORMANCE OBJECTIVE

Task: Given access to all necessary equipment and information, the student will designate first, second, third, and fourth filing units by underlining so that names can be filed alphabetically in the office file and then alphabetize each group of three names.

Scoring: One point for each step performed satisfactorily unless otherwise weighted. To obtain a percentage score, divide the total points earned by the number of points possible.

Standards: Time _____ minutes Note: Time element may be given by instructor.

NOTE TIME BEGAN _____   NOTE TIME COMPLETED _____

PROCEDURE STEPS	STEP PERFORMED SATISFACTORILY	COMMENTS
1. Assembled 18 questions relating to file names and pen or pencil	_____	
2. Underlined each unit of the patient's name or business name for 18 questions.	_____	(18 points possible)
3. Answered question No. 1.	_____	
4. Answered question No. 2.	_____	
5. Answered question No. 3.	_____	
6. Answered question No. 4.	_____	
7. Answered question No. 5.	_____	
8. Answered question No. 6.	_____	
9. Answered question No. 7.	_____	
10. Answered question No. 8.	_____	
11. Answered question No. 9.	_____	
12. Answered question No. 10.	_____	
13. Answered question No. 11.	_____	

14. Answered question No. 12. _____
15. Answered question No. 13. _____
16. Answered question No. 14. _____
17. Answered question No. 15. _____
18. Answered question No. 16. _____
19. Answered question No. 17 _____
20. Answered question No. 18. _____
21. Completed within time specified. _____

TOTAL POINTS EARNED: _____ TOTAL POINTS POSSIBLE: 38

Evaluator's Signature _____ NEED TO REPEAT: _____

PERFORMANCE EVALUATION CHECKLIST
EXERCISE 10-3 FILE PATIENT NAMES AND BUSINESS NAMES ALPHABETICALLY

Name _____ Date _____ Score _____

PERFORMANCE OBJECTIVE

Task: Given access to all necessary equipment and information, the student will take each group of four names and arrange them alphabetically.

Scoring: One point for each step performed satisfactorily unless otherwise weighted. To obtain a percentage score, divide the total points earned by the number of points possible.

Standards: Time _____ minutes Note: Time element may be given by instructor.

NOTE TIME BEGAN _____ NOTE TIME COMPLETED _____

PROCEDURE STEPS	STEP PERFORMED SATISFACTORILY	COMMENTS
1. Assembled ten groups of names and pen or pencil.	_____	
2. Alphabetized group 1.	_____	
3. Alphabetized group 2.	_____	
4. Alphabetized group 3.	_____	
5. Alphabetized group 4.	_____	
6. Alphabetized group 5.	_____	
7. Alphabetized group 6.	_____	
8. Alphabetized group 7.	_____	
9. Alphabetized group 8.	_____	
10. Alphabetized group 9.	_____	
11. Alphabetized group 10.	_____	
12. Completed within time specified.	_____	

TOTAL POINTS EARNED: _____ TOTAL POINTS POSSIBLE: 12

Evaluator's Signature _____ NEED TO REPEAT: _____

PERFORMANCE EVALUATION CHECKLIST
EXERCISE 10-4 DETERMINE INDEXING ORDER AND COLOR TO BE USED FOR FOLDER LABELS AND ARRANGE NAMES IN ALPHABETICAL ORDER

Name _____ Date _____ Score _____

PERFORMANCE OBJECTIVE

Task: Given access to all necessary equipment and information, the student will index and key names on file labels uniformly in correct indexing arrangement for alphabetizing.

Scoring: One point for each step performed satisfactorily unless otherwise weighted. To obtain a percentage score, divide the total points earned by the number of points possible.

Standards: Time _____ minutes   Note: Time element may be given by instructor.

NOTE TIME BEGAN _____   NOTE TIME COMPLETED _____

PROCEDURE STEPS	STEP PERFORMED SATISFACTORILY	COMMENTS
1. Assembled forms 22, 23, and 24 and 60 3" by 5" cards or slips of paper and colored highlighter pens.	_____	
2. Indexed names by writing them on forms 22, 23, and 24.	_____	(60 points)
3. Proofread names for accuracy.	_____	
4. Keyed names uniformly on 60 cards with even margins and spacing.	_____	(60 points)
5. Alphabetized 60 cards with fewer than five errors.	_____	
6. Chose certain names to cross-reference and keyed them correctly.	_____	
7. Color-coded the second lettter of each patient's surname across the top of each card according to instructions.	_____	(60 points)
8. Alphabetized 60 cards a second time using colored top margin to facilitate arrangement and to speed filing time.	_____	
9. Completed within time specified.	_____	

TOTAL POINTS EARNED: _____   TOTAL POINTS POSSIBLE: 186

Evaluator's Signature _____ NEED TO REPEAT: _____

PERFORMANCE EVALUATION CHECKLIST
EXERCISE 11-1 ABSTRACT DATA FROM A CATALOG AND KEY A PURCHASE ORDER

Name _____ Date _____ Score _____

PERFORMANCE OBJECTIVE

Task: Given access to all necessary equipment and information, the student will abstract information from catalog data sheets, complete a purchase order form, and determine charges.

Scoring: One point for each step performed satisfactorily unless otherwise weighted. To obtain a percentage score, divide the total points earned by the number of points possible.

Standards: Time _____ minutes Note: Time element may be given by instructor.

NOTE TIME BEGAN _____   NOTE TIME COMPLETED _____

PROCEDURE STEPS	STEP PERFORMED SATISFACTORILY	COMMENTS
1. Assembled form 25, catalog data sheets, and pen or pencil.	_____	
2. Keyed shipped to data neatly, slightly above designated line, with no information missing.	_____	
3. Checked boxes.	_____	
4. Keyed order information neatly, slightly above designated line, with no information missing.	_____	
5. Determined price for item No. 1	_____	
6. Determined price for item No. 2	_____	
7. Determined price for item No. 3	_____	
8. Calculated sales tax.	_____	
9. Calculated total amount of order.	_____	
10. Keyed a sample of new heading to include the additional telephone and fax numbers.	_____	
11. Completed within time specified.	_____	

TOTAL POINTS EARNED: _____   TOTAL POINTS POSSIBLE: 11

Evaluator's Signature _____   NEED TO REPEAT: _____

PERFORMANCE EVALUATION CHECKLIST
EXERCISE 11-2 COMPLETE AN ORDER FORM FOR OFFICE SUPPLIES

Name _____ Date _____ Score _____

PERFORMANCE OBJECTIVE

Task: Given access to all necessary equipment and information, the student will complete an order form for office supplies and compute the total amount of the order.

Scoring: One point for each step performed satisfactorily unless otherwise weighted. To obtain a percentage score, divide the total points earned by the number of points possible.

Standards: Time _____ minutes Note: Time element may be given by instructor.

NOTE TIME BEGAN _____   NOTE TIME COMPLETED _____

PROCEDURE STEPS	STEP PERFORMED SATISFACTORILY	COMMENTS
1. Assembled form 26 and pen.	_____	
2. Inserted customer number.	_____	
3. Inserted shipped to data neatly, slightly above designated line, with no information missing.	_____	
4. Determined price for item No. 1	_____	
5. Determined price for item No. 2	_____	

6. Determined price for item No. 3 _____
7. Determined price for item No. 4 _____
8. Determined price for item No. 5 _____
9. Determined price for item No. 6 _____
10. Calculated sales tax. _____
11. Calculated total amount of order. _____
12. Completed within time specified. _____

TOTAL POINTS EARNED: _____ TOTAL POINTS POSSIBLE: 12

Evaluator's Signature _____ NEED TO REPEAT: _____

PERFORMANCE EVALUATION CHECKLIST
EXERCISE 11-3 PERFORM BASIC OFFICE MATHEMATICS

Name _____ Date _____ Score _____

PERFORMANCE OBJECTIVE

Task: Given access to all necessary equipment and information, the student will perform basic mathematic calculations on orders for supplies and determine the costs, taking advantage of any special discounts.

Scoring: One point for each step performed satisfactorily unless otherwise weighted. To obtain a percentage score, divide the total points earned by the number of points possible.

Standards: Time _____ minutes Note: Time element may be given by instructor.

NOTE TIME BEGAN _____ NOTE TIME COMPLETED _____

PROCEDURE STEPS	STEP PERFORMED SATISFACTORILY	COMMENTS
1. Assembled 10 problems, paper, and pencil.	_____	
2. Problem 1: Calculated the discount before computing total owed and total amount.	_____	
3. Problem 2: Calculated bill for office visits and gave patient adjustment.	_____	
4. Problem 3: Found amount of installment payments after subtracting down payment.	_____	
5. Problem 4: Compared invoice total, allowing for discount and sales tax to find total for check.	_____	
6. Problem 5: Calculated bill, allowing for discount and figuring sales tax.	_____	
7. Problem 6: Calculated total amount owed, allowing for discount and adding sales tax.	_____	
8. Problem 7: Calculated total amount of bill, taking advantage of discount and adding sales tax.	_____	
9. Problem 8: Determined amount owed by patient, including compounded monthly service charge.	_____	
10. Problem 9a: Calculated amount owed for needles.	_____	
11. Problem 9b: Calculated amount owed for needles.	_____	
12. Problem 10a: Calculated amount owed for needles less discount.	_____	
13. Problem 10b: Calculated amount owed for needles less discount.	_____	
14. Problem 10c: Determined the amount saved by ordering the supplies for one year.	_____	
15. Completed within time specified.	_____	

TOTAL POINTS EARNED: _____ TOTAL POINTS POSSIBLE: 15

Evaluator's Signature _____ NEED TO REPEAT: _____

PERFORMANCE EVALUATION CHECKLIST
EXERCISE 11-4 USE A CALCULATOR TO FIND TOTAL AMOUNTS

Name _____ Date _____ Score _____

PERFORMANCE OBJECTIVE

Task: Given access to all necessary equipment and information, the student will determine total amounts by operating a calculator using touch fingering.

Scoring: One point for each step performed satisfactorily unless otherwise weighted. To obtain a percentage score, divide the total points earned by the number of points possible.

Standards: Time _____ minutes Note: Time element may be given by instructor.

NOTE TIME BEGAN _____.   NOTE TIME COMPLETED _____

PROCEDURE STEPS	STEP PERFORMED SATISFACTORILY	COMMENTS
1. Assembled calculator, with or without tape, Figure 11-3, 7 problems, and pen or pencil.	_____	
2. Problem 1: Calculated total amount.	_____	
3. Problem 2: Calculated total amount.	_____	
4. Problem 3: Calculated total amount.	_____	
5. Problem 4: Calculated total amount.	_____	
6. Problem 5: Calculated total amount.	_____	
7. Properly placed decimals and dollar signs for problems 1 through 5.	_____	
8. Problem 6: Determined balance in checking account.	_____	
9. Problem 7: Found total of payment disbursed.	_____	
10. Attached tapes if data were printed.	_____	
12. Completed within time specified.	_____	

TOTAL POINTS EARNED: _____   TOTAL POINTS POSSIBLE: 12

Evaluator's Signature _____ NEED TO REPEAT: _____

PERFORMANCE EVALUATION CHECKLIST
EXERCISE 11-5 PREPARE PURCHASE ORDERS

Name _____ Date _____ Score _____

PERFORMANCE OBJECTIVE

Task: Given access to all necessary equipment and information, the student will type two purchase orders for medical supplies.

Scoring: One point for each step performed satisfactorily unless otherwise weighted. To obtain a percentage score, divide the total points earned by the number of points possible.

Standards: Time _____ minutes Note: Time element may be given by instructor.

NOTE TIME BEGAN _____   NOTE TIME COMPLETED _____

PROCEDURE STEPS	STEP PERFORMED SATISFACTORILY	COMMENTS
1. Assembled forms 27 and 28 and typewriter or computer.	_____	
2. Keyed company address completely and aligned for purchase order forms 235 and 236.	_____	(2 points)
3. Keyed identifying information in upper sections of purchase order forms 235 and 236.	_____	(2 points)

4. Keyed Quantity columns, with evenly aligned left margins for purchase order forms 235 and 236. _____ (2 points)

5. Keyed Description columns, with evenly aligned left margins for purchase order forms 235 and 236. _____ (2 points)

6. Keyed Unit Price in evenly aligned columns for purchase order forms 235 and 236. _____ (2 points)

7. Determined figures for Amount columns for purchase order forms 235 and 236. _____ (2 points)

8. Discounts are correct on each form. _____ (2 points)

9. Sales tax amounts are correct on each form. _____ (2 points)

10. Purchase order form totals are correct. _____ (2 points)

11. Each purchase order form is signed. _____ (2 points)

12. Completed within time specified. _____

TOTAL POINTS EARNED: _____ TOTAL POINTS POSSIBLE: 22

Evaluator's Signature _____ NEED TO REPEAT: _____

PERFORMANCE EVALUATION CHECKLIST
EXERCISE 11-6 PREPARE MATERIAL FOR AN OFFICE PROCEDURE MANUAL

Name _____ Date _____ Score _____

PERFORMANCE OBJECTIVE

Task: Given access to all necessary equipment and information, the student will type or key a reference sheet for an office procedures manual detailing appointment procedures.

Scoring: One point for each step performed satisfactorily unless otherwise weighted. To obtain a percentage score, divide the total points earned by the number of points possible.

Standards: Time _____ minutes Note: Time element may be given by instructor.

NOTE TIME BEGAN _____ NOTE TIME COMPLETED _____

PROCEDURE STEPS	STEP PERFORMED SATISFACTORILY	COMMENTS
1. Assembled one sheet of plain paper and reference material.	_____	
2. Keyed a centered heading for the reference sheet.	_____	
3. Keyed both physicians' names on sheet.	_____	
4. Office appointment hours clearly defined.	_____	
5. Noted time allotment for procedures and for work-ins and emergency appointments.	_____	
6. Indicated surgery days for both physicians.	_____	
7. Keyed page is neatly centered.	_____	
8. Proofread for typographical and spelling errors.	_____	
9. Completed within time specified.	_____	

TOTAL POINTS EARNED: _____ TOTAL POINTS POSSIBLE: 9

Evaluator's Signature _____ NEED TO REPEAT: _____

PERFORMANCE EVALUATION CHECKLIST
EXERCISE 11-7 WRITE AN AGENDA FOR AN OFFICE MEETING

Name _____ Date _____ Score _____

PERFORMANCE OBJECTIVE

Task: Given access to all necessary equipment and information, the student will assemble information and prepare an agenda for an office meeting in outline form.

Scoring: One point for each step performed satisfactorily unless otherwise weighted. To obtain a percentage score, divide the total points earned by the number of points possible.

Standards: Time _____ minutes   Note: Time element may be given by instructor.

NOTE TIME BEGAN _____   NOTE TIME COMPLETED _____

PROCEDURE STEPS	STEP PERFORMED SATISFACTORILY	COMMENTS
1. Assembled Figure 11-4, plain paper, and if necessary, correction materials.	_____	
2. Keyed a centered heading.	_____	
3. Named person calling meeting to order.	_____	
4. Noted reading of minutes.	_____	
5. Recorded attendance.	_____	
6. Outlined committee reports.	_____	
7. Noted unfinished business.	_____	
8. Noted new business.	_____	
9. Indicated closing remarks with date and time of next meeting.	_____	
10. Keyed in outline format.	_____	
11. Proofread agenda for typographical, spacing, and spelling errors.	_____	
12. Neatly centered agenda on sheet.	_____	
13. Completed within time specified.	_____	

TOTAL POINTS EARNED: _____   TOTAL POINTS POSSIBLE: 13

Evaluator's Signature _____ NEED TO REPEAT: _____

PERFORMANCE EVALUATION CHECKLIST
EXERCISE 12-1 SPELL MEDICAL WORDS

Name _____ Date _____ Score _____

PERFORMANCE OBJECTIVE

Task: Given access to all necessary equipment and information, the student will select the correctly spelled medical word from the choices given.

Scoring: One point for each step performed satisfactorily unless otherwise weighted. To obtain a percentage score, divide the total points earned by the number of points possible.

Standards: Time _____ minutes   Note: Time element may be given by instructor.

NOTE TIME BEGAN _____   NOTE TIME COMPLETED _____

PROCEDURE STEPS	STEP PERFORMED SATISFACTORILY	COMMENTS
1. Assembled list of words and pen or pencil.	_____	
2. Circled the word from question No. 1.	_____	
3. Circled the word from question No. 2.	_____	
4. Circled the word from question No. 3.	_____	
5. Circled the word from question No. 4.	_____	
6. Circled the word from question No. 5.	_____	
7. Circled the word from question No. 6.	_____	
8. Circled the word from question No. 7.	_____	
9. Circled the word from question No. 8.	_____	
10. Circled the word from question No. 9.	_____	
11. Circled the word from question No. 10.	_____	
12. Circled the word from question No. 11.	_____	
13. Circled the word from question No. 12.	_____	
14. Circled the word from question No. 13.	_____	
15. Circled the word from question No. 14.	_____	
16. Circled the word from question No. 15.	_____	
17. Circled the word from question No. 16.	_____	
18. Circled the word from question No. 17.	_____	
19. Circled the word from question No. 18.	_____	
20. Circled the word from question No. 19.	_____	
21. Circled the word from question No. 20.	_____	
22. Circled the word from question No. 21.	_____	
23. Circled the word from question No. 22.	_____	
24. Circled the word from question No. 23.	_____	
25. Circled the word from question No. 24.	_____	
26. Circled the word from question No. 25	_____	
27. Completed within time specified.	_____	

TOTAL POINTS EARNED: _____   TOTAL POINTS POSSIBLE: 27

Evaluator's Signature _____ NEED TO REPEAT: _____

PERFORMANCE EVALUATION CHECKLIST
EXERCISE 12-2 KEY A LETTER OF WITHDRAWAL

Name _____ Date _____ Score _____

PERFORMANCE OBJECTIVE

Task: Given access to all necessary equipment and information, the student will key a letter of withdrawal for the physician's signature.

Scoring: One point for each step performed satisfactorily unless otherwise weighted. To obtain a percentage score, divide the total points earned by the number of points possible.

Standards: Time _____ minutes   Note: Time element may be given by instructor.

NOTE TIME BEGAN _____   NOTE TIME COMPLETED _____

PROCEDURE STEPS	STEP PERFORMED SATISFACTORILY	COMMENTS
1. Assembled form 29, guide form 29A, and keying accessories.	_____	
2. Used letterhead.	_____	
3. Dated letter.	_____	
4. Keyed in full-block style.	_____	
5. Used mixed punctuation.	_____	
6. Attractive placement of letter on stationery.	_____	
7. Margins even and equal.	_____	
8. Wrote appropriate letter with wording that is legally correct.	_____	
9. Correctly placed signature line.	_____	
10. Checked placement and spacing of all punctuation marks.	_____	
11. Keyed reference initials.	_____	
12. Proofread for spelling and typographical errors while letter remained on computer screen.	_____	
13. Letter ready for physician to read and sign.	_____	
14. Completed within time specified.	_____	

TOTAL POINTS EARNED: _____   TOTAL POINTS POSSIBLE: 14

Evaluator's Signature _____   NEED TO REPEAT: _____

PERFORMANCE EVALUATION CHECKLIST
EXERCISE 12-3 EDIT—REVIEW OF FUNDAMENTALS

Name _____ Date _____ Score _____

PERFORMANCE OBJECTIVE

Task: Given access to all necessary equipment and information, the student will edit sentences to eliminate words, to change the sequence of words, and to eliminate redundant phrases to improve writing.

Scoring: One point for each step performed satisfactorily unless otherwise weighted. To obtain a percentage score, divide the total points earned by the number of points possible.

Standards: Time _____ minutes Note: Time element may be given by instructor.

NOTE TIME BEGAN _____   NOTE TIME COMPLETED _____

PROCEDURE STEPS	STEP PERFORMED SATISFACTORILY	COMMENTS
1. Assembled 20 sentences and pen or pencil.	_____	
2. Edited, rewrote, and read sentence No. 1 to determine whether the meaning was clear and the sentence structure improved.	_____	
3. Edited, rewrote, and read sentence No. 2 to determine whether the meaning was clear and the sentence structure improved.	_____	
4. Edited, rewrote, and read sentence No. 3 to determine whether the meaning was clear and the sentence structure improved.	_____	
5. Edited, rewrote, and read sentence No. 4 to determine whether the meaning was clear and the sentence structure improved.	_____	
6. Edited, rewrote, and read sentence No. 5 to determine whether the meaning was clear and the sentence structure improved.	_____	
7. Edited, rewrote, and read sentence No. 6 to determine whether the meaning was clear and the sentence structure improved.	_____	
8. Edited, rewrote, and read sentence No. 7 to determine whether the meaning was clear and the sentence structure improved.	_____	
9. Edited, rewrote, and read sentence No. 8 to determine whether the meaning was clear and the sentence structure improved.	_____	
10. Edited, rewrote, and read sentence No. 9 to determine whether the meaning was clear and the sentence structure improved.	_____	
11. Edited, rewrote, and read sentence No. 10 to determine whether the meaning was clear and the sentence structure improved.	_____	
12. Edited, rewrote, and read sentence No. 11 to determine whether the meaning was clear and the sentence structure improved.	_____	
13. Edited, rewrote, and read sentence No. 12 to determine whether the meaning was clear and the sentence structure improved.	_____	
14. Edited, rewrote, and read sentence No. 13 to determine whether the meaning was clear and the sentence structure improved.	_____	
15. Edited, rewrote, and read sentence No. 14 to determine whether the meaning was clear and the sentence structure improved.	_____	
16. Edited, rewrote, and read sentence No. 15 to determine whether the meaning was clear and the sentence structure improved.	_____	
17. Edited, rewrote, and read sentence No. 16 to determine whether the meaning was clear and the sentence structure improved.	_____	
18. Edited, rewrote, and read sentence No. 17 to determine whether the meaning was clear and the sentence structure improved.	_____	
19. Edited, rewrote, and read sentence No. 18 to determine whether the meaning was clear and the sentence structure improved.	_____	
20. Edited, rewrote, and read sentence No. 19 to determine whether the meaning was clear and the sentence structure improved.	_____	
21. Edited, rewrote, and read sentence No. 20 to determine whether the meaning was clear and the sentence structure improved.	_____	
22. Completed within time specified.	_____	

TOTAL POINTS EARNED: _____   _____ TOTAL POINTS POSSIBLE: 22

Evaluator's Signature _____ NEED TO REPEAT: _____

PERFORMANCE EVALUATION CHECKLIST
EXERCISE 12-4 COMPOSE AND KEY A MAILABLE LETTER

Name _____ Date _____ Score _____

PERFORMANCE OBJECTIVE

Task: Given access to all necessary equipment and information, the student will compose and key an original letter dealing with a failed appointment.

Scoring: One point for each step performed satisfactorily unless otherwise weighted. To obtain a percentage score, divide the total points earned by the number of points possible.

Standards: Time _____ minutes Note: Time element may be given by instructor.

NOTE TIME BEGAN _____   NOTE TIME COMPLETED _____

PROCEDURE STEPS	STEP PERFORMED SATISFACTORILY	COMMENTS
1. Assembled form 30, guide form 29A, and reference materials.	_____	
2. Used letterhead.	_____	
3. Dated letter.	_____	
4. Keyed in full-block style.	_____	
5. Used mixed punctuation.	_____	
6. Letter is centered on stationery with even margins.	_____	
7. Keyed inside address.	_____	
8. Keyed appropriate salutation.	_____	
9. Keyed reference or subject line.	_____	
10. Mentioned failed appointment with date and time in body of letter in clear, concise manner.	_____	
11. Inserted proper paragraphing.	_____	
12. Keyed appropriate closing lines.	_____	
13. Letter ready for physician to read and sign.	_____	
14. Inserted reference data.	_____	
15. Proofread letter for typographical, spelling, punctuation, and capitalization errors while letter remained in typewriter or on computer screen.	_____	
16. Completed within time specified.	_____	

TOTAL POINTS EARNED: _____   TOTAL POINTS POSSIBLE: 16

Evaluator's Signature _____ NEED TO REPEAT: _____

PERFORMANCE EVALUATION CHECKLIST
EXERCISE 12-5 COMPOSE AND KEY A MAILABLE LETTER

Name _____ Date _____ Score _____

PERFORMANCE OBJECTIVE

Task: Given access to all necessary equipment and information, the student will compose and key an original letter explaining procedures for the first visit and suggesting insurance information needed.

Scoring: One point for each step performed satisfactorily unless otherwise weighted. To obtain a percentage score, divide the total points earned by the number of points possible.

Standards: Time _____ minutes Note: Time element may be given by instructor.

NOTE TIME BEGAN _____   NOTE TIME COMPLETED _____

PROCEDURE STEPS	STEP PERFORMED SATISFACTORILY	COMMENTS
1. Assembled form 31, guide form 29A, and reference materials.	_____	
2. Used letterhead.	_____	
3. Dated letter.	_____	
4. Keyed in full-block style.	_____	
5. Used mixed punctuation.	_____	
6. Letter is centered on stationery with even margins.	_____	
7. Keyed inside address.	_____	
8. Keyed appropriate salutation.	_____	
9. Mentioned appointment time, date, fee, and insurance coverage information in body of letter.	_____	
10. Inserted proper paragraphing.	_____	
11. Keyed appropriate closing lines.	_____	
12. Letter signed by medical assistant/student.	_____	
13. Inserted reference initials.	_____	
14. Proofread letter for typographical, spelling, punctuation, and capitalization errors while letter remained in typewriter or on computer screen.	_____	
15. Completed within time specified.	_____	

TOTAL POINTS EARNED: _____   TOTAL POINTS POSSIBLE: 15

Evaluator's Signature _____ NEED TO REPEAT: _____

PERFORMANCE EVALUATION CHECKLIST
EXERCISE 12-6 COMPOSE AND KEY A MAILABLE LETTER

Name _____ Date _____ Score _____

PERFORMANCE OBJECTIVE

Task: Given access to all necessary equipment and information, the student will compose and key an original letter to a physician, stating that Dr. Fran Practon's patient may need medical attention while on a visit to Mexico. Make a copy to mail to the patient.

Scoring: One point for each step performed satisfactorily unless otherwise weighted. To obtain a percentage score, divide the total points earned by the number of points possible.

Standards: Time _____ minutes   Note: Time element may be given by instructor.

NOTE TIME BEGAN _____   NOTE TIME COMPLETED _____

PROCEDURE STEPS	STEP PERFORMED SATISFACTORILY	COMMENTS
1. Assembled form 32, guide form 29A, and reference materials.	_____	
2. Used letterhead.	_____	
3. Dated letter.	_____	
4. Keyed in modified-block style.	_____	
5. Used open punctuation.	_____	
6. Letter is centered on stationery with even margins.	_____	
7. Keyed inside address.	_____	
8. Keyed appropriate salutation.	_____	
9. Mentioned enclosed clinical evaluation in body of letter.	_____	
10. Inserted proper paragraphing.	_____	
11. Keyed appropriate closing lines.	_____	
12. Keyed reference or subject line.	_____	
13. Letter ready for physician to read and sign.	_____	
14. Keyed enclosure notation.	_____	
15. Keyed copy notation.	_____	
16. Keyed reference initials.	_____	
17. Proofread letter for typographical, spelling, punctuation, and capitalization errors while letter remained in typewriter or on computer screen.	_____	
18. Made a copy to mail to the patient.	_____	
19. Completed within time specified.	_____	

TOTAL POINTS EARNED: _____   TOTAL POINTS POSSIBLE: 19

Evaluator's Signature _____   NEED TO REPEAT: _____

PERFORMANCE EVALUATION CHECKLIST
EXERCISE 12-7 COMPOSE AND KEY A MAILABLE LETTER

Name _____ Date _____ Score _____

PERFORMANCE OBJECTIVE

Task: Given access to all necessary equipment and information, the student will compose and key an original letter over physician's signature, requesting payment on a bill.

Scoring: One point for each step performed satisfactorily unless otherwise weighted. To obtain a percentage score, divide the total points earned by the number of points possible.

Standards: Time _____ minutes Note: Time element may be given by instructor.

NOTE TIME BEGAN _____ NOTE TIME COMPLETED _____

PROCEDURE STEPS	STEP PERFORMED SATISFACTORILY	COMMENTS
1. Assembled form 33, guide form 29A, and reference materials.	_____	
2. Used letterhead.	_____	
3. Dated letter.	_____	
4. Keyed in modified-block style.	_____	
5. Used open punctuation.	_____	
6. Letter is centered on stationery with even margins.	_____	
7. Keyed inside address.	_____	
8. Keyed appropriate salutation.	_____	
9. Requested payment, stating amount owed in body of letter.	_____	
10. Inserted proper paragraphing.	_____	
11. Keyed appropriate closing lines.	_____	
12. Keyed reference line.	_____	
13. Letter ready for physician to read and sign.	_____	
14. Enclosure notation correct.	_____	
15. Proofread letter for typographical, spelling, punctuation, and capitalization errors while letter remained in typewriter or on computer screen.	_____	
16. Completed within time specified.	_____	

TOTAL POINTS EARNED: _____ TOTAL POINTS POSSIBLE: 16

Evaluator's Signature _____ NEED TO REPEAT: _____

PERFORMANCE EVALUATION CHECKLIST
EXERCISE 12-8 KEY MEMORANDA FROM HANDWRITTEN NOTES

Name _____ Date _____ Score _____

PERFORMANCE OBJECTIVE

Task: Given access to all necessary equipment and information, the student will abstract information from a handwritten note and key the message onto an interoffice memo form.

Scoring: One point for each step performed satisfactorily unless otherwise weighted. To obtain a percentage score, divide the total points earned by the number of points possible.

Standards: Time _____ minutes Note: Time element may be given by instructor.

NOTE TIME BEGAN _____   NOTE TIME COMPLETED _____

PROCEDURE STEPS	STEP PERFORMED SATISFACTORILY	COMMENTS
1. Assembled form 34 and handwritten note.	_____	
2. Read note before beginning to compose memo.	_____	
3. Prepared a rough draft of memo.	_____	
4. Aligned memo headings evenly with added information.	_____	
5. Completed fill-in spaces after each guide word with appropriate information.	_____	
6. Chose appropriate information for subject heading.	_____	
7. Wrote concise message using appropriate sentence structure.	_____	
8. Included all relevant information related to note.	_____	
9. Proofread memo for typographical, spelling, punctuation, and capitalization errors while memo remained in typewriter or on computer screen.	_____	
10. Completed within time specified.	_____	

TOTAL POINTS EARNED: _____   _____ TOTAL POINTS POSSIBLE: 10

Evaluator's Signature _____ NEED TO REPEAT: _____

PERFORMANCE EVALUATION CHECKLIST
EXERCISE 12-9 KEY MEMORANDA FROM HANDWRITTEN NOTES

Name _____ Date _____ Score _____

PERFORMANCE OBJECTIVE

Task: Given access to all necessary equipment and information, the student will abstract information from a handwritten note and transfer the message onto an interoffice memo form.

Scoring: One point for each step performed satisfactorily unless otherwise weighted. To obtain a percentage score, divide the total points earned by the number of points possible.

Standards: Time _____ minutes Note: Time element may be given by instructor.

NOTE TIME BEGAN _____   NOTE TIME COMPLETED _____

PROCEDURE STEPS	STEP PERFORMED SATISFACTORILY	COMMENTS
1. Assembled form 35 and handwritten note.	_____	
2. Read note before beginning to compose memo.	_____	
3. Prepared a rough draft of memo.	_____	
4. Aligned memo headings evenly with added information.		
5. Completed fill-in spaces after each guide word with appropriate information.	_____	

6. Chose appropriate information for subject heading. _____
7. Wrote concise message using appropriate sentence structure. _____
8. Included all relevant information related to note. _____
9. Proofread memo for typographical, spelling, punctuation, and capitalization errors while memo remained in typewriter or on computer screen. _____
10. Completed within time specified. _____

TOTAL POINTS EARNED: _____ TOTAL POINTS POSSIBLE: 10

Evaluator's Signature _____ NEED TO REPEAT: _____

PERFORMANCE EVALUATION CHECKLIST
EXERCISE 12-10 ABSTRACT PATIENT INFORMATION FOR A LETTER

Name _____ Date _____ Score _____

PERFORMANCE OBJECTIVE

Task: Given access to all necessary equipment and information, the student will abstract patient information from a chart and then key a mailable letter to a referring physician.

Scoring: One point for each step performed satisfactorily unless otherwise weighted. To obtain a percentage score, divide the total points earned by the number of points possible.

Standards: Time _____ minutes Note: Time element may be given by instructor.

NOTE TIME BEGAN _____ NOTE TIME COMPLETED _____

PROCEDURE STEPS	STEP PERFORMED SATISFACTORILY	COMMENTS
1. Assembled form 36, guide form 29A, and reference materials.	_____	
2. Used letterhead.	_____	
3. Dated letter.	_____	
4. Keyed in full-block style.	_____	
5. Used mixed punctuation.	_____	
6. Letter is centered on stationery with even margins.	_____	
7. Keyed inside address.	_____	
8. Keyed appropriate salutation.	_____	
9. Included reference or subject line.	_____	
10. Patient's name and purpose of letter are mentioned at the beginning of the letter.	_____	
11. Included all dates and medical information in body of letter with nothing missing.	_____	
12. Inserted proper paragraphing.	_____	
13. Keyed appropriate concluding sentence.	_____	
14. Keyed reference initials.	_____	
15. Letter ready for physician to read and sign.	_____	
16. Proofread letter for typographical, spelling, punctuation, and capitalization errors while letter remained in typewriter or on computer screen.	_____	
17. Completed within time specified.	_____	

TOTAL POINTS EARNED: _____ TOTAL POINTS POSSIBLE: 17

Evaluator's Signature _____ NEED TO REPEAT: _____

PERFORMANCE EVALUATION CHECKLIST
EXERCISE 12-11 KEY A TWO-PAGE LETTER

Name _____ Date _____ Score _____

PERFORMANCE OBJECTIVE

Task: Given access to all necessary equipment and information, the student will key a two-page letter on letterhead with subject and attention lines, proper paragraphing and capitalization, and an appropriate second-page heading.

Scoring: One point for each step performed satisfactorily unless otherwise weighted. To obtain a percentage score, divide the total points earned by the number of points possible.

Standards: Time _____ minutes Note: Time element may be given by instructor.

NOTE TIME BEGAN _____ NOTE TIME COMPLETED _____

PROCEDURE STEPS	STEP PERFORMED SATISFACTORILY	COMMENTS
1. Assembled form 37, guide form 29A, one sheet of plain paper for page 2, and reference materials.	_____	
2. Used letterhead.	_____	
3. Dated letter.	_____	
4. Included reference or subject and attention lines.	_____	
5. Keyed in full-block style.	_____	
6. Used open punctuation.	_____	
7. Letter is centered on stationery with 1 1/2 inch margins.	_____	
8. Keyed inside address.	_____	
9. Keyed appropriate salutation.	_____	
10. Inserted proper paragraphing.	_____	
11. Made necessary capitalization corrections.	_____	
12. Chose appropriate line to end page 1.	_____	
13. Inserted second page heading.	_____	
14. Keyed appropriate concluding sentence.	_____	
15. Inserted closing and signature lines.	_____	
16. Keyed reference initials.	_____	
17. Letter ready for physician to read and sign.	_____	
18. Proofread letter for typographical, spelling, punctuation, and capitalization errors while letter remained in typewriter or on computer screen.	_____	
19. Completed within time specified.	_____	

TOTAL POINTS EARNED: _____   TOTAL POINTS POSSIBLE: 19

Evaluator's Signature _____ NEED TO REPEAT: _____

PERFORMANCE EVALUATION CHECKLIST
EXERCISE 13-1 PROCESS INCOMING MAIL

Name _____ Date _____ Score _____

PERFORMANCE OBJECTIVE

Task: Given access to all necessary equipment and information, the student will sort and process incoming mail and determine disbursement of each communication. Circle in red pen the introductory number of any situations you have difficulty processing for class discussion.

Scoring: One point for each step performed satisfactorily unless otherwise weighted. To obtain a percentage score, divide the total points earned by the number of points possible.

Standards: Time _____ minutes Note: Time element may be given by instructor.

NOTE TIME BEGAN _____   NOTE TIME COMPLETED _____

PROCEDURE STEPS	STEP PERFORMED SATISFACTORILY	COMMENTS
1. Assembled list of 35 pieces of incoming mail, pen or pencil and red pen.	_____	
2. Read and determined disbursement of mail No. 1.	_____	
3. Read and determined disbursement of mail No. 2.	_____	
4. Read and determined disbursement of mail No. 3.	_____	
5. Read and determined disbursement of mail No. 4.	_____	
6. Read and determined disbursement of mail No. 5.	_____	
7. Read and determined disbursement of mail No. 6.	_____	
8. Read and determined disbursement of mail No. 7.	_____	
9. Read and determined disbursement of mail No. 8.	_____	
10. Read and determined disbursement of mail No. 9.	_____	
11. Read and determined disbursement of mail No.10.	_____	
12. Read and determined disbursement of mail No.11.	_____	
13. Read and determined disbursement of mail No.12.	_____	
14. Read and determined disbursement of mail No.13.	_____	
15. Read and determined disbursement of mail No.14.	_____	
16. Read and determined disbursement of mail No.15.	_____	
17. Read and determined disbursement of mail No.16.	_____	
18. Read and determined disbursement of mail No.17.	_____	
19. Read and determined disbursement of mail No.18.	_____	
20. Read and determined disbursement of mail No.19.	_____	
21. Read and determined disbursement of mail No.20	_____	
22. Read and determined disbursement of mail No.21.	_____	
23. Read and determined disbursement of mail No.22.	_____	
24. Read and determined disbursement of mail No.23.	_____	
25. Read and determined disbursement of mail No.24.	_____	
26. Read and determined disbursement of mail No.25.	_____	
27. Read and determined disbursement of mail No.26.	_____	
28. Read and determined disbursement of mail No.27.	_____	
29. Read and determined disbursement of mail No.28.	_____	
30. Read and determined disbursement of mail No.29.	_____	
31. Read and determined disbursement of mail No.30.	_____	
32. Read and determined disbursement of mail No.31.	_____	
33. Read and determined disbursement of mail No.32.	_____	
34. Read and determined disbursement of mail No.33.	_____	
35. Read and determined disbursement of mail No.34.	_____	
36. Read and determined disbursement of mail No.35.	_____	

37. Circled introductory number of any piece of mail
    if uncertain of its destination.   _____

38. Discussed with class or instructor problem
    situations about mail distribution.   _____

39. Completed within time specified.   _____

TOTAL POINTS EARNED: _____   TOTAL POINTS POSSIBLE: 39

Evaluator's Signature _____ NEED TO REPEAT: _____

PERFORMANCE EVALUATION CHECKLIST
EXERCISE 13-2 CLASSIFY OUTGOING MAIL

Name _____ Date _____ Score _____

PERFORMANCE OBJECTIVE

Task: Given access to all necessary equipment and information, the student will identify classes of mail.

Scoring: One point for each step performed satisfactorily unless otherwise weighted. To obtain a percentage score, divide the total points earned by the number of points possible.

Standards: Time _____ minutes   Note: Time element may be given by instructor.

NOTE TIME BEGAN _____   NOTE TIME COMPLETED _____

PROCEDURE STEPS	STEP PERFORMED SATISFACTORILY	COMMENTS
1. Assembled list of 23 pieces of outgoing mail and pen or pencil.	_____	
2. Identified class for outgoing piece of mail No. 1.	_____	
3. Identified class for outgoing piece of mail No. 2.	_____	
4. Identified class for outgoing piece of mail No. 3.	_____	
5. Identified class for outgoing piece of mail No. 4.	_____	
6. Identified class for outgoing piece of mail No. 5.	_____	
7. Identified class for outgoing piece of mail No. 6.	_____	
8. Identified class for outgoing piece of mail No. 7.	_____	
9. Identified class for outgoing piece of mail No. 8.	_____	
10. Identified class for outgoing piece of mail No. 9.	_____	
11. Identified class for outgoing piece of mail No. 10.	_____	
12. Identified class for outgoing piece of mail No. 11.	_____	
13. Identified class for outgoing piece of mail No. 12.	_____	
14. Identified class for outgoing piece of mail No. 13.	_____	
15. Identified class for outgoing piece of mail No. 14.	_____	
16. Identified class for outgoing piece of mail No. 15.	_____	
17. Identified class for outgoing piece of mail No. 16.	_____	
18. Identified class for outgoing piece of mail No. 17.	_____	
19. Identified class for outgoing piece of mail No. 18.	_____	
20. Identified class for outgoing piece of mail No. 19.	_____	
21. Identified class for outgoing piece of mail No. 20.	_____	
22. Identified class for outgoing piece of mail No. 21.	_____	
23. Identified class for outgoing piece of mail No. 22.	_____	
24. Identified class for outgoing piece of mail No. 23.	_____	
25. Completed within time specified.	_____	

TOTAL POINTS EARNED: _____   TOTAL POINTS POSSIBLE: 25

Evaluator's Signature _____ NEED TO REPEAT: _____

PERFORMANCE EVALUATION CHECKLIST
EXERCISE 13-3 ANNOTATE MAIL

Name _____ Date _____ Score _____

PERFORMANCE OBJECTIVE

Task: Given access to all necessary equipment and information, the student will read a letter, annotate significant words or phrases, and make comments in the margins concerning the action to be taken.

Scoring: One point for each step performed satisfactorily unless otherwise weighted. To obtain a percentage score, divide the total points earned by the number of points possible.

Standards: Time _____ minutes Note: Time element may be given by instructor.

NOTE TIME BEGAN _____   NOTE TIME COMPLETED _____

PROCEDURE STEPS	STEP PERFORMED SATISFACTORILY	COMMENTS
1. Assembled letter, highlighter or colored pen.	_____	
2. Read letter.	_____	
3. Highlighted or underlined significant words or phrases.	_____	
4. Made comments about a reply in margin.	_____	
5. Completed within time specified.	_____	
TOTAL POINTS EARNED:	_____	TOTAL POINTS POSSIBLE: 5

Evaluator's Signature _____ NEED TO REPEAT: _____

PERFORMANCE EVALUATION CHECKLIST
EXERCISE 13-4 COMPOSE A LETTER AND CERTIFY THE MAIL

Name _____ Date _____ Score _____

PERFORMANCE OBJECTIVE

Task: Given access to all necessary equipment and information, the student will compose and key an important letter in a specified format; address and prepare a large envelope for OCR processing as certified mail.

Scoring: One point for each step performed satisfactorily unless otherwise weighted. To obtain a percentage score, divide the total points earned by the number of points possible.

Standards: Time _____ minutes Note: Time element may be given by instructor.

NOTE TIME BEGAN _____   NOTE TIME COMPLETED _____

PROCEDURE STEPS	STEP PERFORMED SATISFACTORILY	COMMENTS
1. Assembled forms 38, 39, and 40, guide form 29A, and reference materials.	_____	
2. Used letterhead.	_____	
3. Dated letter.	_____	
4. Keyed in modified-block style.	_____	
5. Used mixed punctuation.	_____	
6. Letter is centered on stationery with even margins.	_____	
7. Keyed inside address.	_____	
8. Keyed appropriate salutation.	_____	
9. Wrote appropriate letter with wording that is legally correct.	_____	
10. Patient's name and purpose of letter are mentioned at the beginning of the letter.	_____	
11. Inserted proper paragraphing.	_____	

12. Keyed closing lines in correct position with proper punctuation.   _____

13. Keyed reference initials.   _____

14. Letter ready for physician to read and sign.   _____

15. Proofread letter for typographical, spelling, punctuation, and capitalization errors while letter remained in typewriter or on computer screen.   _____

16. Keyed large envelope in OCR format with no errors.   _____

17. Completed necessary data on certified mail slip.   _____

18. Folded letter and inserted it into envelope.   _____

17. Completed within time specified.   _____

TOTAL POINTS EARNED: _____   TOTAL POINTS POSSIBLE: 17

Evaluator's Signature _____ NEED TO REPEAT: _____

PERFORMANCE EVALUATION CHECKLIST
EXERCISE 13-5 COMPLETE A MAIL-ORDER FORM FOR POSTAL SUPPLIES

Name _____ Date _____ Score _____

PERFORMANCE OBJECTIVE

Task: Given access to all necessary equipment and information, the student will complete a mail-order form for postal supplies and compute the total amount owed.

Scoring: One point for each step performed satisfactorily unless otherwise weighted. To obtain a percentage score, divide the total points earned by the number of points possible.

Standards: Time _____ minutes Note: Time element may be given by instructor.

NOTE TIME BEGAN _____   NOTE TIME COMPLETED _____

PROCEDURE STEPS	STEP PERFORMED SATISFACTORILY	COMMENTS
1. Assembled form 41 and pen.	_____	
2. Printed the telephone number and address.	_____	
3. Computed and recorded the quantity.	_____	
4. Computed the cost column.	_____	
5. Completed within time specified.	_____	

TOTAL POINTS EARNED: _____   TOTAL POINTS POSSIBLE: 5

Evaluator's Signature _____ NEED TO REPEAT: _____

PERFORMANCE EVALUATION CHECKLIST
EXERCISE 13-6 PREPARE A COVER SHEET FOR FAX TRANSMISSION

Name _____ Date _____ Score _____

PERFORMANCE OBJECTIVE

Task: Given access to all necessary equipment and information, the student will prepare a transmission slip to accompany a message for fax communication.

Scoring: One point for each step performed satisfactorily unless otherwise weighted. To obtain a percentage score, divide the total points earned by the number of points possible.

Standards: Time _____ minutes   Note: Time element may be given by instructor.

NOTE TIME BEGAN _____   NOTE TIME COMPLETED _____

PROCEDURE STEPS	STEP PERFORMED SATISFACTORILY	COMMENTS
1. Assembled form 42 and typewriter or computer.	_____	
2. Keyed all information slightly above designated lines.	_____	
3. Indicated number of pages to be sent.	_____	
4. Information in remarks section was clear and concise.	_____	
5. Completed within time specified.	_____	
TOTAL POINTS EARNED:	_____	TOTAL POINTS POSSIBLE: 5

Evaluator's Signature _____ NEED TO REPEAT: _____

PERFORMANCE EVALUATION CHECKLIST
EXERCISE 13-7 ADDRESS ENVELOPES FOR OCR PROCESSING

Name _____ Date _____ Score _____

PERFORMANCE OBJECTIVE

Task: Given access to all necessary equipment and information, the student will address small envelopes for OCR processing using acceptable abbreviations and ZIP codes.

Scoring: One point for each step performed satisfactorily unless otherwise weighted. To obtain a percentage score, divide the total points earned by the number of points possible.

Standards: Time _____ minutes   Note: Time element may be given by instructor.

NOTE TIME BEGAN _____   NOTE TIME COMPLETED _____

PROCEDURE STEPS	STEP PERFORMED SATISFACTORILY	COMMENTS
1. Assembled forms 43 and 44.	_____	
ENVELOPE NO. 1:		
2. Keyed address.	_____	
3. Used OCR abbreviations.	_____	
4. Keyed ZIP code.	_____	
5. Proofread for typographical, spelling, and spacing errors.	_____	
6. Completed within time specified.	_____	
ENVELOPE NO. 2:		
7. Keyed address.	_____	
8. Used OCR abbreviations.	_____	
9. Keyed ZIP code.	_____	
10. Proofread for typographical, spelling, and spacing errors.	_____	
11. Completed within time specified.	_____	

ENVELOPE NO. 3:

12. Keyed address.	_____	
13. Used OCR abbreviations.	_____	
14. Keyed ZIP code.	_____	
15. Proofread for typographical, spelling, and spacing errors.	_____	
16. Completed within time specified.	_____	

TOTAL POINTS EARNED: _____ TOTAL POINTS POSSIBLE: 16

Evaluator's Signature _____ NEED TO REPEAT: _____

PERFORMANCE EVALUATION CHECKLIST
EXERCISE 13-8 KEY AND FOLD AN ORIGINAL LETTER FOR A SMALL ENVELOPE; ADDRESS AN ENVELOPE FOR OCR PROCESSING; COMPLETE AND ATTACH CERTIFIED MAIL AND RETURN-RECEIPT-REQUESTED FORMS

Name _____ Date _____ Score _____

PERFORMANCE OBJECTIVE

Task: Given access to all necessary equipment and information, the student will key a letter, prepare a small envelope for OCR processing, fold and insert the letter into the envelope, and attach special mailing forms.

Scoring: One point for each step performed satisfactorily unless otherwise weighted. To obtain a percentage score, divide the total points earned by the number of points possible.

Standards: Time _____ minutes Note: Time element may be given by instructor.

NOTE TIME BEGAN _____ NOTE TIME COMPLETED _____

PROCEDURE STEPS	STEP PERFORMED SATISFACTORILY	COMMENTS
1. Assembled forms 45, 46, and 47, guide form 29A, reference materials, and pen.		
2. Used letterhead.	_____	
3. Dated letter.	_____	
4. Keyed in full-block style.	_____	
5. Used mixed punctuation.	_____	
6. Letter is centered on stationery with even margins.	_____	
7. Keyed inside address.	_____	
8. Keyed appropriate salutation.	_____	
9. Wrote letter of withdrawal with wording that is legally correct.	_____	
10. Inserted proper paragraphing.	_____	
11. Keyed closing lines in correct position with proper punctuation.	_____	
12. Keyed reference initials.	_____	
13. Letter ready for physician to read and sign.	_____	
14. Proofread letter for typographical, spelling, punctuation, and capitalization errors while letter remained in typewriter or on computer screen.	_____	
15. Keyed small envelope in OCR format with no errors.	_____	
16. Completed necessary data on certified mail slip.	_____	
17. Folded letter and inserted it into envelope.	_____	
18. Completed within time specified.	_____	

TOTAL POINTS EARNED: _____ TOTAL POINTS POSSIBLE: 18

Evaluator's Signature _____ NEED TO REPEAT: _____

PERFORMANCE EVALUATION CHECKLIST
EXERCISE 13-9 KEY AND FOLD AN ORIGINAL LETTER FOR A LARGE ENVELOPE; ADDRESS AN ENVELOPE FOR OCR PROCESSING; COMPLETE AND ATTACH CERTIFIED MAIL AND RETURN-RECEIPT-REQUESTED FORMS

Name _____ Date _____ Score _____

PERFORMANCE OBJECTIVE

Task: Given access to all necessary equipment and information, the student will key a letter, prepare an envelope for OCR processing, fold and insert the letter into the envelope, and attach special mailing forms.

Scoring: One point for each step performed satisfactorily unless otherwise weighted. To obtain a percentage score, divide the total points earned by the number of points possible.

Standards: Time _____ minutes Note: Time element may be given by instructor.

NOTE TIME BEGAN _____   NOTE TIME COMPLETED _____

PROCEDURE STEPS	STEP PERFORMED SATISFACTORILY	COMMENTS
1. Assembled forms 48, 49, and 50, guide form 29A, reference materials, and pen.		
2. Used letterhead.	_____	
3. Dated letter.	_____	
4. Keyed in modified-block style.	_____	
5. Used open punctuation.	_____	
6. Letter is centered on stationery with even margins.	_____	
7. Mentioned confirmation of discharge by patient in letter.	_____	
8. Keyed inside address.	_____	
9. Keyed appropriate salutation.	_____	
10. Wrote appropriate letter with wording that is legally correct.	_____	
11. Inserted proper paragraphing.	_____	
12. Keyed closing lines in correct position with proper punctuation.	_____	
13. Keyed reference initials.	_____	
14. Letter ready for physician to read and sign.	_____	
15. Proofread letter for typographical, spelling, punctuation, and capitalization errors while letter remained in typewriter or on computer screen.	_____	
16. Keyed large envelope in OCR format with no errors.	_____	
17. Completed necessary data on certified mail slip.	_____	
18. Folded letter and inserted it into envelope.	_____	
19. Completed within time specified.	_____	

TOTAL POINTS EARNED: _____   TOTAL POINTS POSSIBLE: 19

Evaluator's Signature _____ NEED TO REPEAT: _____

PERFORMANCE EVALUATION CHECKLIST
EXERCISE 14-1 KEY A CURRICULUM VITAE

Name _____ Date _____ Score _____

PERFORMANCE OBJECTIVE

Task: Given access to all necessary equipment and information, the student will key a curriculum vitae in outline form after abstracting information from a memorandum.

Scoring: One point for each step performed satisfactorily unless otherwise weighted. To obtain a percentage score, divide the total points earned by the number of points possible.

Standards: Time _____ minutes Note: Time element may be given by instructor.

NOTE TIME BEGAN _____   NOTE TIME COMPLETED _____

PROCEDURE STEPS	STEP PERFORMED SATISFACTORILY	COMMENTS
1. Assembled memo and plain paper.	_____	
2. Heading includes physician's name with address centered.	_____	
3. Margins well balanced.	_____	
4. Line spacing consistent.	_____	
5. Educational background organized by years.	_____	
6. Experience includes years 1968-70 and 1971-81.	_____	
7. Named professional activities.	_____	
8. Inserted abbreviations where appropriate.	_____	
9. Attractive format.	_____	
10. Proofread for typographical, spelling, spacing, abbreviation and capitalization errors.	_____	
11. Attached second copy.	_____	
12. Completed within time specified.	_____	

TOTAL POINTS EARNED: _____   TOTAL POINTS POSSIBLE: 12

Evaluator's Signature _____ NEED TO REPEAT: _____

PERFORMANCE EVALUATION CHECKLIST
EXERCISE 14-2 KEY A MANUSCRIPT FOR PUBLICATION

Name _____ Date _____ Score _____

PERFORMANCE OBJECTIVE

Task: Given access to all necessary equipment and information, the student will key a title page and a manuscript page from a corrected rough draft in acceptable form for publication; prepare manuscript for mailing by writing a cover letter and preparing a No. 10 envelope for OCR processing.

Scoring: One point for each step performed satisfactorily unless otherwise weighted. To obtain a percentage score, divide the total points earned by the number of points possible.

Standards: Time _____ minutes   Note: Time element may be given by instructor.

NOTE TIME BEGAN _____   NOTE TIME COMPLETED _____

PROCEDURE STEPS	STEP PERFORMED SATISFACTORILY	COMMENTS
1. Assembled several sheets of plain paper and form 51.	_____	
2. Keyed and centered title page.	_____	
3. Studied proofreading marks and read manuscript before beginning to key a final draft.	_____	
4. Keyed final draft of manuscript.	_____	
5. Keyed main heading, centered and all caps.	_____	
6. Double-spaced the copy and indented paragraphs.	_____	
7. Keyed numbered sentences in body of manuscript in appropriate position for emphasis.	_____	
8. Proofread manuscript on computer screen for typographical, spelling, spacing, capitalization, with no words or phrases missing.	_____	
9. Keyed transmittal letter including pertinent data related to manuscript.	_____	
10. Proofread letter on computer screen for typographical, spelling, spacing, capitalization, with no words or phrases missing.	_____	
11. Keyed a large envelope for OCR processing.	_____	
12. Proofread envelope for typographical, spelling, spacing, capitalization, with no words or phrases missing.	_____	
13. Completed within time specified.	_____	

TOTAL POINTS EARNED: _____   TOTAL POINTS POSSIBLE: 13

Evaluator's Signature _____ NEED TO REPEAT: _____

PERFORMANCE EVALUATION CHECKLIST
EXERCISE 14-3 PROOFREAD AND KEY A LEGAL FORM

Name _____ Date _____ Score _____

PERFORMANCE OBJECTIVE

Task: Given access to all necessary equipment and information, the student will use proofreading marks and symbols to correct a rough draft of a legal form and key the corrected master for the printer.

Scoring: One point for each step performed satisfactorily unless otherwise weighted. To obtain a percentage score, divide the total points earned by the number of points possible.

Standards: Time _____ minutes Note: Time element may be given by instructor.

NOTE TIME BEGAN _____   NOTE TIME COMPLETED _____

PROCEDURE STEPS	STEP PERFORMED SATISFACTORILY	COMMENTS
1. Assembled form 52, plain paper, and pen or pencil.	_____	
2. Proofread legal form, marking errors before beginning to key.	_____	
3. Inserted proofreading symbols in column and corrected copy.	_____	
4. Keyed form double-spaced with balanced margins.	_____	
5. Keyed the heading centered in all caps with appropriate spacing.	_____	
6. Keyed the corrected material.	_____	
7. Keyed balanced signature and date lines, allowing sufficient space for handwritten names.	_____	
8. Proofread final copy on screen for spacing, spelling, or typographical errors to produce error-free copy.	_____	
9. Completed within time specified.	_____	

TOTAL POINTS EARNED: _____   TOTAL POINTS POSSIBLE: 9

Evaluator's Signature _____ NEED TO REPEAT: _____

PERFORMANCE EVALUATION CHECKLIST
EXERCISE 14-4 PROOFREAD TRANSCRIPTION

Name _____ Date _____ Score _____

PERFORMANCE OBJECTIVE

Task: Given access to all necessary equipment and information, the student will proofread medical transcription and prepare copy for transfer to patient's chart.

Scoring: One point for each step performed satisfactorily unless otherwise weighted. To obtain a percentage score, divide the total points earned by the number of points possible.

Standards: Time _____ minutes Note: Time element may be given by instructor.

NOTE TIME BEGAN _____   NOTE TIME COMPLETED _____

PROCEDURE STEPS	STEP PERFORMED SATISFACTORILY	COMMENTS
1. Assembled four example transcripts, pen, glossary, dictionary, textbook Figure 14-1, typewriter or computer.	_____	
2. Inserted proofreading marks to indicate errors for four example transcripts.	_____	(4 points)

3. Determined correct spelling of all words.   _____   (4 points)
4. Keyed patient note No. 1.   _____
5. Proofread patient note No. 1   _____
6. Keyed patient note No. 2.   _____
7. Proofread patient note No. 2.   _____
8. Keyed patient note No. 3.   _____
9. Proofread patient note No. 3.   _____
10. Keyed patient note No. 4.   _____
11. Proofread patient note No. 4.   _____
12. Completed within time specified.   _____

TOTAL POINTS EARNED: _____   TOTAL POINTS POSSIBLE: 18

Evaluator's Signature _____ NEED TO REPEAT: _____

PERFORMANCE EVALUATION CHECKLIST
EXERCISE 14-5 PREPARE A TRAVEL EXPENSE REPORT

Name _____ Date _____ Score _____

PERFORMANCE OBJECTIVE

Task: Given access to all necessary equipment and information, the student will complete a travel expense report for the accountant using figures from a detailed record of expenses.

Scoring: One point for each step performed satisfactorily unless otherwise weighted. To obtain a percentage score, divide the total points earned by the number of points possible.

Standards: Time _____ minutes Note: Time element may be given by instructor.

NOTE TIME BEGAN _____ NOTE TIME COMPLETED _____

PROCEDURE STEPS	STEP PERFORMED SATISFACTORILY	COMMENTS
1. Assembled form 53 and pen or pencil.	_____	
2. Inserted dates of trip.	_____	
3. Inserted dates in columns.	_____	
4. Transferred figures to expense report form.	_____	
5. Placed figures in appropriate columns.	_____	
6. Totaled horizontal column.	_____	
7. Totaled vertical column.	_____	
8. Horizontal and vertical columns are equal.	_____	
9. Total amount is shown in lower right corner of form.	_____	
10. Purpose of trip stated on lines provided.	_____	
11. Completed within time specified.	_____	

TOTAL POINTS EARNED: _____   TOTAL POINTS POSSIBLE: 11

Evaluator's Signature _____ NEED TO REPEAT: _____

PERFORMANCE EVALUATION CHECKLIST
EXERCISE 15-1 COLLECTION ROLE PLAYING

Name _____ Date _____ Score _____

PERFORMANCE OBJECTIVE

Task: Given access to all necessary equipment and information, the student will write how he or she would handle fee collection in the twelve situations of this exercise.

Scoring: One point for each step performed satisfactorily unless otherwise weighted. To obtain a percentage score, divide the total points earned by the number of points possible.

Standards: Time _____ minutes Note: Time element may be given by instructor.

NOTE TIME BEGAN _____   NOTE TIME COMPLETED _____

PROCEDURE STEPS	STEP PERFORMED SATISFACTORILY	COMMENTS
1. Assembled two sheets of plain typing paper, pen or pencil, and twelve role playing situations.	_____	
2. Answered scenario 1.	_____	(3 points)
3. Answered scenario 2.	_____	(3 points)
4. Answered scenario 3.	_____	(3 points)
5. Answered scenario 4.	_____	(3 points)
6. Answered scenario 5.	_____	(3 points)
7. Answered scenario 6.	_____	(3 points)
8. Answered scenario 7.	_____	(3 points)
9. Answered scenario 8.	_____	(3 points)
10. Answered scenario 9.	_____	(3 points)
11. Answered scenario 10.	_____	(3 points)
12. Answered scenario 11.	_____	(3 points)
13. Answered scenario 12.	_____	(3 points)
14. Completed within time specified.	_____	

TOTAL POINTS EARNED: _____   TOTAL POINTS POSSIBLE: 38

Evaluator's Signature _____ NEED TO REPEAT: _____

ADDITIONAL COLLECTION SCENARIOS

15. Answered scenario 13.	_____	(2 points)
16. Answered scenario 14.	_____	(2 points)
17. Answered scenario 15.	_____	(2 points)
18. Answered scenario 16.	_____	(2 points)
19. Answered scenario 17.	_____	(2 points)
20. Answered scenario 18.	_____	(2 points)
21. Answered scenario 19.	_____	(2 points)
22. Answered scenario 20.	_____	(2 points)
23. Completed within time specified.	_____	

TOTAL POINTS EARNED: _____   TOTAL POINTS POSSIBLE: (17) 55

Evaluator's Signature _____ NEED TO REPEAT: _____

PERFORMANCE EVALUATION CHECKLIST
EXERCISE 15-2 COMPLETE CASH RECEIPTS

Name _____ Date _____ Score _____

PERFORMANCE OBJECTIVE

Task: Given access to all necessary equipment and information, the student will complete four cash receipt forms.
Scoring: One point for each step performed satisfactorily unless otherwise weighted. To obtain a percentage score, divide the total points earned by the number of points possible.
Standards: Time _____ minutes Note: Time element may be given by instructor.
NOTE TIME BEGAN _____ NOTE TIME COMPLETED _____

PROCEDURE STEPS	STEP PERFORMED SATISFACTORILY	COMMENTS
1. Assembled four cash receipts forms, typing paper, pen and carbon paper.	_____	
2. Calculated charges and completed cash receipt for Ms. Beth Hobson.	_____	(3 points)
3. Calculated charges and completed cash receipt for Henry P. Moran.	_____	(2 points)
4. Calculated charges and completed cash receipt for Mrs. Harriet F. Garber.	_____	(2 points)
5. Calculated charges and completed receipt for Miss Carole V. Putnam.	_____	(3 points)
6. Made carbon copies or photocopies of all receipts.	_____	
7. Completed within time specified.	_____	

TOTAL POINTS EARNED: _____   TOTAL POINTS POSSIBLE: 13

Evaluator's Signature _____ NEED TO REPEAT: _____

PERFORMANCE EVALUATION CHECKLIST
EXERCISE 15-3 TYPE A COLLECTION LETTER, ENVELOPE, AND LEDGER CARD

Name _____ Date _____ Score _____

PERFORMANCE OBJECTIVE

Task: Given access to all necessary equipment and information, the student will type a collection letter, envelope, and ledger card, and make a photocopy of the letter.
Scoring: One point for each step performed satisfactorily unless otherwise weighted. To obtain a percentage score, divide the total points earned by the number of points possible.
Standards: Time _____ minutes Note: Time element may be given by instructor.
NOTE TIME BEGAN _____ NOTE TIME COMPLETED _____

PROCEDURE STEPS	STEP PERFORMED SATISFACTORILY	COMMENTS
1. Assembled letterhead form, No. 10 envelope (or form), ledger card form, references, and typing accessories.	_____	
2. Composed a rough draft.	_____	
3. Identified person to whom letter is being written.	_____	
4. Stated reason for letter.	_____	
5. Indicated expected response.	_____	

6. Used letterhead. _____
7. Dated letter. _____
8. Typed in full-block form. _____
9. Centered letter on page. _____
10. Placed margins even and equal. _____
11. Used proper address format for inside address. _____
12. Placed salutation. _____
13. Placed reference line. _____
14. Used consistent punctuation. _____
15. Inserted capitalization and abbreviations where appropriate in body of letter. _____
16. Inserted proper paragraphing in body of letter. _____
17. Placed complimentary close and signature line. _____
18. Inserted proper enclosure notation. _____
19. Proofread after typing for spelling and typographical errors while letter remained in typewriter, or on computer screen. _____
20. Prepared envelope using United States Postal Service's approved format. _____
21. Prepared patient's ledger card and made a photocopy for enclosure. _____
22. Attached envelope to letter and enclosure in presentation format ready for signature. _____
23. Completed within time specified. _____

TOTAL POINTS EARNED: _____   _____ TOTAL POINTS POSSIBLE: 23

Evaluator's Signature _____ NEED TO REPEAT: _____

PERFORMANCE EVALUATION CHECKLIST
EXERCISE 15-4 USE A CALCULATOR

Name _____ Date _____ Score _____

PERFORMANCE OBJECTIVE

Task: Given access to all necessary equipment and information, the student will total charges, payments, and adjustments on a ledger card using a calculator, adding machine, or computer calculator.

Scoring: One point for each step performed satisfactorily unless otherwise weighted. To obtain a percentage score, divide the total points earned by the number of points possible.

Standards: Time _____ minutes   Note: Time element may be given by instructor.

NOTE TIME BEGAN _____   NOTE TIME COMPLETED _____

PROCEDURE STEPS	STEP PERFORMED SATISFACTORILY	COMMENTS
1. Assembled ledger card; calculator, adding machine, or computer calculator; and pen or pencil.	_____	
2. Turned calculator on and cleared machine.	_____	
3. Keyed balance from right hand column.	_____	
4. Keyed all figures from ledger.	_____	
5. Calculated all charges, payments and adjustments.	_____	(13 points)
6. Circled ending balance and kept tape.	_____	
7. Completed within time specified.	_____	

TOTAL POINTS EARNED: _____   _____ TOTAL POINTS POSSIBLE: 19

Evaluator's Signature _____ NEED TO REPEAT: _____

PERFORMANCE EVALUATION CHECKLIST
EXERCISE 15-5 COMPLETE A CREDIT CARD AUTHORIZATION FORM

Name _____ Date _____ Score _____

PERFORMANCE OBJECTIVE

Task: Given access to all necessary equipment and information, the student will fill in authorization to charge credit card form with correct information.

Scoring: One point for each step performed satisfactorily unless otherwise weighted. To obtain a percentage score, divide the total points earned by the number of points possible.

Standards: Time _____ minutes Note: Time element may be given by instructor.

NOTE TIME BEGAN _____   NOTE TIME COMPLETED _____

PROCEDURE STEPS	STEP PERFORMED SATISFACTORILY	COMMENTS
1. Assembled authorization to charge credit card form, case scenario, and pen or pencil.	_____	
2. Entered name and address.	_____	
3. Entered all items on the authorization form.	_____	(11 points)
4. Completed within time specified.	_____	
TOTAL POINTS EARNED:	_____	TOTAL POINTS POSSIBLE: 14

Evaluator's Signature _____ NEED TO REPEAT: _____

PERFORMANCE EVALUATION CHECKLIST
EXERCISE 15-6 COMPLETE A PATIENT COMPLAINT DOCUMENT

Name _____ Date _____ Score _____

PERFORMANCE OBJECTIVE

Task: Given access to all necessary equipment and information, the student will fill in a patient complaint document.

Scoring: One point for each step performed satisfactorily unless otherwise weighted. To obtain a percentage score, divide the total points earned by the number of points possible.

Standards: Time _____ minutes Note: Time element may be given by instructor.

NOTE TIME BEGAN _____   NOTE TIME COMPLETED _____

PROCEDURE STEPS	STEP PERFORMED SATISFACTORILY	COMMENTS
1. Assembled patient complaint document form, case scenario, and pen or pencil.	_____	
2. Recorded today's date, the patient's name, account number, and account balance.	_____	(4 points)
3. Described the patient's complaint accurately and briefly.	_____	(2 points)
4. Completed within time specified.	_____	
TOTAL POINTS EARNED:	_____	TOTAL POINTS POSSIBLE: 8

Evaluator's Signature _____ NEED TO REPEAT: _____

PERFORMANCE EVALUATION CHECKLIST
EXERCISE 15-7 COMPLETE A FINANCIAL AGREEMENT

Name _____ Date _____ Score _____

PERFORMANCE OBJECTIVE

Task: Given access to all necessary equipment and information, the student will fill in the financial agreement form with a schedule of payments.

Scoring: One point for each step performed satisfactorily unless otherwise weighted. To obtain a percentage score, divide the total points earned by the number of points possible.

Standards: Time _____ minutes Note: Time element may be given by instructor.

NOTE TIME BEGAN _____   NOTE TIME COMPLETED _____

PROCEDURE STEPS	STEP PERFORMED SATISFACTORILY	COMMENTS
1. Assembled financial agreement form, case scenario, calculator, and pen or pencil.	_____	
2. Entered patient's name and telephone number.	_____	
3. Entered information in sections 1 through 9.	_____	(9 points)
4. Calculated amounts for monthly payments and entered information in 7 areas on the bottom section of the form.	_____	(7 points)
5. Entered balance owed and filled in schedule of payments.	_____	(2 points)
6. Completed within time specified.	_____	

TOTAL POINTS EARNED: _____   TOTAL POINTS POSSIBLE: 21

Evaluator's Signature _____ NEED TO REPEAT: _____

PERFORMANCE EVALUATION CHECKLIST
EXERCISE 16-1 CODE EVALUATION AND MANAGEMENT

Name _____ Date _____ Score _____

PERFORMANCE OBJECTIVE

Task: Given access to all necessary equipment and information, the student will locate the correct procedure code for each question and/or case scenario.

Scoring: One point for each step performed satisfactorily unless otherwise weighted. To obtain a percentage score, divide the total points earned by the number of points possible.

Standards: Time _____ minutes Note: Time element may be given by instructor.

NOTE TIME BEGAN _____   NOTE TIME COMPLETED _____

PROCEDURE STEPS	STEP PERFORMED SATISFACTORILY	COMMENTS
1. Assembled questions and/or case scenarios, pen or pencil, and *Current Procedural Terminology* code book.	_____	
2. Completed question No. 1	_____	(6 points)
3. Completed question No. 2	_____	(6 points)
4. Obtained CPT code numbers for question No. 3	_____	(3 points)
5. Obtained CPT code numbers for question No. 4	_____	(3 points)
6. Obtained CPT code numbers for question No. 5	_____	(5 points)
7. Obtained CPT code numbers for question No. 6	_____	(5 points)
8. Obtained CPT code numbers for question No. 7	_____	(5 points)
9. Completed within time specified.	_____	

TOTAL POINTS EARNED: _____   TOTAL POINTS POSSIBLE: 35

Evaluator's Signature _____ NEED TO REPEAT: _____

PERFORMANCE EVALUATION CHECKLIST
EXERCISE 16-2 CODE SURGICAL PROCEDURES AND SERVICES

Name _____ Date _____ Score _____

PERFORMANCE OBJECTIVE

Task: Given access to all necessary equipment and information, the student will locate the correct procedure code for each question and/or case scenario.

Scoring: One point for each step performed satisfactorily unless otherwise weighted. To obtain a percentage score, divide the total points earned by the number of points possible.

Standards: Time _____ minutes Note: Time element may be given by instructor.

NOTE TIME BEGAN _____   NOTE TIME COMPLETED _____

PROCEDURE STEPS	STEP PERFORMED SATISFACTORILY	COMMENTS
1. Assembled questions and/or case scenarios, pen or pencil, and *Current Procedural Terminology* code book.	_____	
2. Obtained CPT code number for problem No. 1.	_____	
3. Obtained CPT code number for problem No. 2.	_____	
4. Obtained CPT code number for problem No. 3.	_____	
5. Obtained CPT code number for problem No. 4.	_____	
6. Obtained CPT code number for problem No. 5.	_____	

7. Obtained CPT code number for problem No. 6. _____

8. Obtained CPT code number for problem No. 7. _____

9. Obtained CPT code number for problem No. 8. _____

10. Obtained CPT code number for problem No. 9. _____

11. Obtained CPT code number for problem No. 10. _____

12. Obtained CPT code number for problem No. 11. _____

13. Obtained CPT code number for problem No. 12. _____

14. Obtained CPT code number for problem No. 13. _____

15. Obtained CPT code number for problem No. 14. _____

16. Obtained CPT code number for problem No. 15. _____

17. Obtained CPT code number for problem No. 16. _____

18. Completed within time specified. _____

TOTAL POINTS EARNED: _____   TOTAL POINTS POSSIBLE: 18

Evaluator's Signature _____ NEED TO REPEAT: _____

PERFORMANCE EVALUATION CHECKLIST
EXERCISE 16-3 CODE RADIOLOGY AND PATHOLOGY PROCEDURES AND SERVICES

Name _____ Date _____ Score _____

PERFORMANCE OBJECTIVE

Task: Given access to all necessary equipment and information, the student will locate the correct procedure code for each question and/or case scenario.

Scoring: One point for each step performed satisfactorily unless otherwise weighted. To obtain a percentage score, divide the total points earned by the number of points possible.

Standards: Time _____ minutes Note: Time element may be given by instructor.

NOTE TIME BEGAN _____   NOTE TIME COMPLETED _____

PROCEDURE STEPS	STEP PERFORMED SATISFACTORILY	COMMENTS
1. Assembled questions and/or case scenarios, pen or pencil, and *Current Procedural Terminology* code book.	_____	
2. Obtained CPT code number for problem No. 1.	_____	
3. Obtained CPT code number for problem No. 2.	_____	
4. Obtained CPT code number for problem No. 3.	_____	
5. Obtained CPT code number for problem No. 4.	_____	
6. Completed within time specified.	_____	

TOTAL POINTS EARNED: _____   TOTAL POINTS POSSIBLE: 6

Evaluator's Signature _____ NEED TO REPEAT: _____

PERFORMANCE EVALUATION CHECKLIST
EXERCISE 16-4 CODE PROCEDURES AND SERVICES

Name _____ Date _____ Score _____

PERFORMANCE OBJECTIVE

Task: Given access to all necessary equipment and information, the student will locate the correct procedure code for each question and/or case scenario.

Scoring: One point for each step performed satisfactorily unless otherwise weighted. To obtain a percentage score, divide the total points earned by the number of points possible.

Standards: Time _____ minutes   Note: Time element may be given by instructor.

NOTE TIME BEGAN _____   NOTE TIME COMPLETED _____

PROCEDURE STEPS	STEP PERFORMED SATISFACTORILY	COMMENTS
1. Assembled questions and/or case scenarios, pen or pencil, and *Current Procedural Terminology* code book.	_____	
2. Obtained CPT code numbers for problem No. 1.	_____	(9 points)
3. Obtained CPT code numbers for problem No. 2.	_____	(9 points)
4. Completed within time specified.	_____	
TOTAL POINTS EARNED:	_____	TOTAL POINTS POSSIBLE: 20

Evaluator's Signature _____ NEED TO REPEAT: _____

PERFORMANCE EVALUATION CHECKLIST
EXERCISE 16-5 CODE PROCEDURES AND SERVICES

Name _____ Date _____ Score _____

PERFORMANCE OBJECTIVE

Task: Given access to all necessary equipment and information, the student will locate the correct procedure code for each question and/or case scenario.

Scoring: One point for each step performed satisfactorily unless otherwise weighted. To obtain a percentage score, divide the total points earned by the number of points possible.

Standards: Time _____ minutes   Note: Time element may be given by instructor.

NOTE TIME BEGAN _____   NOTE TIME COMPLETED _____

PROCEDURE STEPS	STEP PERFORMED SATISFACTORILY	COMMENTS
1. Assembled questions and/or case scenarios, pen or pencil, and *Current Procedural Terminology* code book.	_____	
2. Obtained CPT code number for problem No. 1.	_____	
3. Obtained CPT code number for problem No. 2.	_____	
4. Obtained HCPCS code numbers for problem No. 3	_____	(4 points)
5. Completed within time specified.	_____	
TOTAL POINTS EARNED:	_____	TOTAL POINTS POSSIBLE: 8

Evaluator's Signature _____ NEED TO REPEAT: _____

PERFORMANCE EVALUATION CHECKLIST
EXERCISE 16-6 COMPLETE A MANAGED CARE AUTHORIZATION FORM

Name _____ Date _____ Score _____

PERFORMANCE OBJECTIVE

Task: Given access to all necessary equipment and information, the student will complete a managed care authorization form.
Scoring: One point for each step performed satisfactorily unless otherwise weighted. To obtain a percentage score, divide the total points earned by the number of points possible.
Standards: Time _____ minutes Note: Time element may be given by instructor.
NOTE TIME BEGAN _____   NOTE TIME COMPLETED _____

PROCEDURE STEPS	STEP PERFORMED SATISFACTORILY	COMMENTS
1. Assembled form 62, typewriter or computer, and pen or pencil.	_____	
2. Listed patient's vital data.	_____	
3. Listed physician's name and ID number.	_____	
4. Inserted diagnosis and diagnosis code.	_____	
5. Stated treatment plan.	_____	
6. Inserted description of procedure and code.	_____	
7. Listed hospital data.	_____	
8. Proofread form for spelling and typographical errors while form remained in typewriter or on computer screen.	_____	
9. Ready for physician to read and sign.	_____	
10. Completed within time specified.	_____	

TOTAL POINTS EARNED: _____   TOTAL POINTS POSSIBLE: 10

Evaluator's Signature _____ NEED TO REPEAT: _____

PERFORMANCE EVALUATION CHECKLIST
EXERCISE 16-7 COMPLETE A HEALTH INSURANCE CLAIM FORM

Name _____ Date _____ Score _____

PERFORMANCE OBJECTIVE

Task: Given access to all necessary equipment and information, the student will complete a health insurance claim form (HCFA-1500).
Scoring: One point for each step performed satisfactorily unless otherwise weighted. To obtain a percentage score, divide the total points earned by the number of points possible.
Standards: Time _____ minutes Note: Time element may be given by instructor.
NOTE TIME BEGAN _____   NOTE TIME COMPLETED _____

PROCEDURE STEPS	STEP PERFORMED SATISFACTORILY	COMMENTS
1. Assembled form 63, patient record, E/M code checklist, ledger card, typewriter or computer, and pen or pencil.	_____	
2. Proofread form for spelling and typographical errors while form remained in typewriter or on computer screen.	_____	
3. Recorded information on the patient's ledger card.	_____	

4. Ready for physician to read and sign.　　　　_____

5. Completed within time specified.　　　　_____

HCFA 1500 INSURANCE CLAIM FORM SCORING AND COMMENT SHEET

BLOCK	INCORRECT	MISSING	NOT NEEDED	REMARKS	BLOCK	INCORRECT	MISSING	NOT NEEDED	REMARKS
					18				
1A					19				
2					20				
3					21				
4									
5					22				
6					23				
7					24A				
8					24B				
					24C				
9					24D				
9A									
9B									
9C					24E				
9D									
					24F				
10A					24G				
10B					24H, 24I				
10C					24J				
10D					24K				
11					25, 26				
11A			✓		27				
11B					28				
11C					29				
11D									
12					30				
13									
14					31				
15									
16					32				
17									
17A					33				
					Reference Initials				

TOTAL POINTS EARNED:　　　　_____　　　　TOTAL POINTS POSSIBLE: 38

Evaluator's Signature　_____　NEED TO REPEAT: _____

PERFORMANCE EVALUATION CHECKLIST
EXERCISE 16-8 COMPLETE A MEDICARE CLAIM FORM

Name _____ Date _____ Score _____

PERFORMANCE OBJECTIVE

Task: Given access to all necessary equipment and information, the student will complete a health insurance claim form (HCFA-1500).

Scoring: One point for each step performed satisfactorily unless otherwise weighted. To obtain a percentage score, divide the total points earned by the number of points possible.

Standards: Time _____ minutes   Note: Time element may be given by instructor.

NOTE TIME BEGAN _____   NOTE TIME COMPLETED _____

PROCEDURE STEPS	STEP PERFORMED SATISFACTORILY	COMMENTS
1. Assembled form 64, patient record, E/M code checklist, ledger card, typewriter or computer, and pen or pencil.	_____	
2. Proofread form for spelling and typographical errors while form remained in typewriter or on computer screen.	_____	
3. Recorded information on the patient's ledger card.	_____	
4. Ready for physician to read and sign.	_____	
5. Completed within time specified.	_____	

HCFA 1500 INSURANCE CLAIM FORM SCORING AND COMMENT SHEET

BLOCK	INCORRECT	MISSING	NOT NEEDED	REMARKS	BLOCK	INCORRECT	MISSING	NOT NEEDED	REMARKS
					18				
1A					19				
2					20				
3					21				
4									
5					22				
6					23				
7					24A				
8					24B				
					24C				
9					24D				
9A									
9B									
9C					24E				
9D									
					24F				
10A					24G				
10B					24H, 24I				
10C					24J				
10D					24K				
11					25, 26				
11A					27				
11B					28				
11C					29				
11D									
12					30				
13									
14					31				
15									
16					32				
17									
17A					33				
					Reference Initials				

TOTAL POINTS EARNED: _____ TOTAL POINTS POSSIBLE: 38

Evaluator's Signature _____ NEED TO REPEAT: _____

PERFORMANCE EVALUATION CHECKLIST
EXERCISE 16-9 COMPLETE A TRICARE/CHAMPUS CLAIM FORM

Name _____ Date _____ Score _____

PERFORMANCE OBJECTIVE

Task: Given access to all necessary equipment and information, the student will complete a health insurance claim form (HCFA-1500).

Scoring: One point for each step performed satisfactorily unless otherwise weighted. To obtain a percentage score, divide the total points earned by the number of points possible.

Standards: Time _____ minutes   Note: Time element may be given by instructor.

NOTE TIME BEGAN _____   NOTE TIME COMPLETED _____

PROCEDURE STEPS	STEP PERFORMED SATISFACTORILY	COMMENTS
1. Assembled form 65, patient record, E/M code checklist, ledger card, typewriter or computer, and pen or pencil.	_____	
2. Proofread form for spelling and typographical errors while form remained in typewriter or on computer screen.	_____	
3. Recorded information on the patient's ledger card.	_____	
4. Ready for physician to read and sign.	_____	
5. Completed within time specified.	_____	

HCFA 1500 INSURANCE CLAIM FORM SCORING AND COMMENT SHEET

BLOCK	INCORRECT	MISSING	NOT NEEDED	REMARKS	BLOCK	INCORRECT	MISSING	NOT NEEDED	REMARKS
					18				
1A					19				
2					20				
3					21				
4									
5					22				
6					23				
7					24A				
8					24B				
					24C				
9					24D				
9A									
9B									
9C					24E				
9D									
					24F				
10A					24G				
10B					24H, 24I				
10C					24J				
10D					24K				
11					25, 26				
11A					27				
11B					28				
11C					29				
11D									
12					30				
13									
14					31				
15									
16					32				
17									
17A					33				
					Reference Initials				

TOTAL POINTS EARNED: _____ TOTAL POINTS POSSIBLE: 38

Evaluator's Signature _____

PERFORMANCE EVALUATION CHECKLIST
EXERCISE 17-1 WRITE CHECKS

Name _____ Date _____ Score _____

PERFORMANCE OBJECTIVE

Task: Given access to all necessary equipment and information, the student will handwrite or type two checks.

Scoring: One point for each step performed satisfactorily unless otherwise weighted. To obtain a percentage score, divide the total points earned by the number of points possible.

Standards: Time _____ minutes   Note: Time element may be given by instructor.

NOTE TIME BEGAN _____   NOTE TIME COMPLETED _____

PROCEDURE STEPS	STEP PERFORMED SATISFACTORILY	COMMENTS
1. Assembled form 66 (blank checks and invoices) and pen.	_____	
CHECK REGISTER FOR CHECK NO. 1:		
2. Entered amount.	_____	
3. Entered date.	_____	
4. Entered payee information.	_____	
5. Listed previous balance.	_____	
6. Entered new balance.	_____	
CHECK NO. 1:		
7. Entered date on check.	_____	
8. Entered payee.	_____	
9. Entered numerical amount of check.	_____	
10. Wrote out amount as far left as possible.	_____	
11. Made straight line to fill space.	_____	
CHECK REGISTER FOR CHECK NO. 2:		
12. Entered amount.	_____	
13. Entered date.	_____	
14. Entered payee information.	_____	
15. Listed previous balance.	_____	
16. Entered new balance.	_____	
CHECK NO. 2:		
17. Entered date on check.	_____	
18. Entered payee.	_____	
19. Entered numerical amount of check.	_____	
20. Wrote out amount as far left as possible.	_____	
21. Made straight line to fill space.	_____	
22. Recorded remit information on invoices.	_____	
23. Proofread form 66 for spelling and typographical errors while checks remained in typewriter.	_____	
24. Ready for physician to read and sign.	_____	
25. Completed within time specified.	_____	

TOTAL POINTS EARNED: _____   TOTAL POINTS POSSIBLE: 25

Evaluator's Signature _____   NEED TO REPEAT: _____

PERFORMANCE EVALUATION CHECKLIST
EXERCISE 17-2 ENDORSE A CHECK

Name _____ Date _____ Score _____

PERFORMANCE OBJECTIVE

Task: Given access to all necessary equipment and information, the student will enter a restrictive endorsement on the back of a patient's check.

Scoring: One point for each step performed satisfactorily unless otherwise weighted. To obtain a percentage score, divide the total points earned by the number of points possible.

Standards: Time _____ minutes Note: Time element may be given by instructor.

NOTE TIME BEGAN _____   NOTE TIME COMPLETED _____

PROCEDURE STEPS	**STEP PERFORMED SATISFACTORILY**	**COMMENTS**
1. Assembled check from patient and pen.	_____	
2. Entered a restrictive endorsement on the back of the patient's check.	_____	
3. Placed restrictive endorsement in proper location.	_____	
4. Completed within time specified.	_____	
TOTAL POINTS EARNED:	_____	TOTAL POINTS POSSIBLE: 4

Evaluator's Signature _____ NEED TO REPEAT: _____

PERFORMANCE EVALUATION CHECKLIST
EXERCISE 17-3 POST TO A LEDGER CARD

Name _____ Date _____ Score _____

PERFORMANCE OBJECTIVE

Task: Given access to all necessary equipment and information, the student will post a check to a patient's ledger card.

Scoring: One point for each step performed satisfactorily unless otherwise weighted. To obtain a percentage score, divide the total points earned by the number of points possible.

Standards: Time _____ minutes Note: Time element may be given by instructor.

NOTE TIME BEGAN _____   NOTE TIME COMPLETED _____

PROCEDURE STEPS	**STEP PERFORMED SATISFACTORILY**	**COMMENTS**
1. Assembled patient's ledger card, check, and pen.	_____	
2. Posted check received on patient's ledger card.	_____	
3. Posted payment in credit column.	_____	
4. Subtracted payments from balance due.	_____	
5. Entered new balance due.	_____	
6. Completed within time specified.	_____	
TOTAL POINTS EARNED:	_____	TOTAL POINTS POSSIBLE: 6

Evaluator's Signature _____ NEED TO REPEAT: _____

PERFORMANCE EVALUATION CHECKLIST
EXERCISE 17-4 POST TO LEDGER CARDS

Name _____ Date _____ Score _____

PERFORMANCE OBJECTIVE

Task: Given access to all necessary equipment and information, the student will post entries to patients' ledger cards.
Scoring: One point for each step performed satisfactorily unless otherwise weighted. To obtain a percentage score, divide the total points earned by the number of points possible.
Standards: Time _____ minutes Note: Time element may be given by instructor.
NOTE TIME BEGAN _____ NOTE TIME COMPLETED _____

PROCEDURE STEPS	STEP PERFORMED SATISFACTORILY	COMMENTS
1. Assembled patients' ledger cards and pen.	_____	
2. Posted entry/entries to Elizabeth Hooper's ledger card.	_____	
3. Posted entry/entries to Maria Sanchez's ledger card.	_____	
4. Posted entry/entries to Brett Walker's ledger card.	_____	
5. Posted entry/entries to Edna Holgrove's ledger card.	_____	
6. Posted entry/entries to Beth Jones's ledger card.	_____	
7. Added or subtracted charges, payments, or adjustments and entered new balance due on five ledgers.	_____	(5 points)
8. Completed within time specified.	_____	

TOTAL POINTS EARNED: _____ TOTAL POINTS POSSIBLE: 12

Evaluator's Signature _____ NEED TO REPEAT: _____

PERFORMANCE EVALUATION CHECKLIST
EXERCISE 17-5 RECONCILE A BANK STATEMENT

Name _____ Date _____ Score _____

PERFORMANCE OBJECTIVE

Task: Given access to all necessary equipment and information, the student will reconcile a bank statement.
Scoring: One point for each step performed satisfactorily unless otherwise weighted. To obtain a percentage score, divide the total points earned by the number of points possible.
Standards: Time _____ minutes Note: Time element may be given by instructor.
NOTE TIME BEGAN _____ NOTE TIME COMPLETED _____

PROCEDURE STEPS	STEP PERFORMED SATISFACTORILY	COMMENTS
1. Assembled form 67, bank statement, pen or pencil.	_____	
2. Listed the bank balance in the appropriate space on the reconciliation worksheet.	_____	
3. Listed outstanding checks.	_____	
4. Totaled outstanding checks.	_____	
5. Added to the bank statement balance any deposits not shown on the bank statement.	_____	
6. Subtracted from checkbook balance items such as withdrawals, automatic payments, or service charges that appeared on the statement but not in the checkbook.	_____	

7. Checkbook balance and adjusted total on bank statement agree. _____

8. Completed within time specified. _____

TOTAL POINTS EARNED: _____ TOTAL POINTS POSSIBLE: 8

Evaluator's Signature _____ NEED TO REPEAT: _____

PERFORMANCE EVALUATION CHECKLIST
EXERCISE 17-6 SCAN A CHECK

Name _____ Date _____ Score _____

PERFORMANCE OBJECTIVE

Task: Given access to all necessary equipment and information, the student will scan a patient's check and answer nine questions.

Scoring: One point for each step performed satisfactorily unless otherwise weighted. To obtain a percentage score, divide the total points earned by the number of points possible.

Standards: Time _____ minutes Note: Time element may be given by instructor.

NOTE TIME BEGAN _____ NOTE TIME COMPLETED _____

PROCEDURE STEPS	STEP PERFORMED SATISFACTORILY	COMMENTS
1. Assembled questions and pen or pencil.	_____	
2. Answered question No. 1a and 1b.	_____	
3. Answered question No. 2.	_____	
4. Answered question No. 3.	_____	
5. Answered question No. 4.	_____	
6. Answered question No. 5.	_____	
7. Answered question No. 6.	_____	
8. Answered question No. 7.	_____	
9. Answered question No. 8.	_____	
10. Answered question No. 9.	_____	
11. Completed within time specified.	_____	

TOTAL POINTS EARNED: _____ TOTAL POINTS POSSIBLE: 6

Evaluator's Signature _____ NEED TO REPEAT: _____

PERFORMANCE EVALUATION CHECKLIST
EXERCISE 18-1 COMPLETE LEDGER CARDS

Name _____ Date _____ Score _____

PERFORMANCE OBJECTIVE

Task: Given access to all necessary equipment and information, the student will complete 28 ledger cards and arrange them in alphabetical sequence.

Scoring: One point for each step performed satisfactorily unless otherwise weighted. To obtain a percentage score, divide the total points earned by the number of points possible.

Standards: Time _____ minutes   Note: Time element may be given by instructor.

NOTE TIME BEGAN _____   NOTE TIME COMPLETED _____

PROCEDURE STEPS	STEP PERFORMED SATISFACTORILY	COMMENTS
1. Assembled forms 68 through 82, typewriter or pen. LEDGER CARDS: Inserted name of patient, address, ZIP code, telephone number, name of insurance company, policy number, birthdate, and balance forward.	_____	
2. Completed ledger on Maria Bargioni	_____	
3. Completed ledger on Charlotte J. Brown	_____	
4. Completed ledger on Adrienne Cane	_____	
5. Completed ledger on Howard S. Chan	_____	
6. Completed ledger on Mary Lou Chaney	_____	
7. Completed ledger on Lois A. Conrad	_____	
8. Completed ledger on Marylou Conrad	_____	
9. Completed ledger on Joan Gomez	_____	
10. Completed ledger on Mark B. Hanson	_____	
11. Completed ledger on J. B. Haupman	_____	
12. Completed ledger on Kathryn L. Hope	_____	
13. Completed ledger on Margaret Jenkins	_____	
14. Completed ledger on Robert T. Jenner	_____	
15. Completed ledger on Jack J. Johnson	_____	
16. Completed ledger on Betty K. Lawson	_____	
17. Completed ledger on Harold B. Mason	_____	
18. Completed ledger on Rachel T. O'Brien	_____	
19. Completed ledger on Rosa K. Okida	_____	
20. Completed ledger on Martin P. Owens	_____	
21. Completed ledger on Hannah F. Riley	_____	
22. Completed ledger on Stephen B. Riley, Jr.	_____	
23. Completed ledger on Roger T. Simpson	_____	
24. Completed ledger on Joseph C. Smith	_____	
25. Completed ledger on Russell O. Smith	_____	
26. Completed ledger on Russell P. Smith	_____	
27. Completed ledger on Jody F. Swinney	_____	
28. Completed ledger on Carol M. Wolf	_____	
29. Completed ledger entitled "Miscellaneous"	_____	
30. Arranged the ledger cards in alphabetical sequence.	_____	
31. Completed within time specified.	_____	

TOTAL POINTS EARNED: _____   TOTAL POINTS POSSIBLE: 31

Evaluator's Signature _____   NEED TO REPEAT: _____

PERFORMANCE EVALUATION CHECKLIST
EXERCISE 18-2 BOOKKEEPING PART I GRADE SHEET

Name _____ Date _____ Score _____

PERFORMANCE OBJECTIVE

Task: Given access to all necessary equipment and information, the student will post to ledger cards, prepare a deposit slip and checks, prepare the daily journal, and complete cash receipts.

Scoring: One point for each step performed satisfactorily unless otherwise weighted. To obtain a percentage score, divide the total points earned by the number of points possible.

Standards: Time _____ minutes Note: Time element may be given by instructor.

NOTE TIME BEGAN _____   NOTE TIME COMPLETED _____

PROCEDURE STEPS	STEP PERFORMED SATISFACTORILY	COMMENTS
1. Assembled forms 83, 84, 85, 88, and 89 and pen.	_____	
JOURNAL OF DAILY CHARGES, PAYMENTS, AND DEPOSITS:		
2. Total of payments equals $ _____ .	_____	
3. Total of balance-services rendered- equals $ _____ .	_____	
LEDGER CARDS:		
4. Posted to ledgers: Adrienne Cane, Mary Lou Chaney Mark B. Hanson, J. B. Haupman, Robert T. Jenner Betty K. Lawson, Harold B. Mason, Russell O. Smith Jody F. Swinney, Carol M. Wolf, Miscellaneous Ledger **Note:** Deduct points for failure to post (3 points), failure to extend or extension incorrect (3 points), any other error (1 point).	_____	(11 points)
ACCOUNTS RECEIVABLE:		
5. June 28 accounts receivable total: $ _____ .	_____	
BANKING:		
6. June 28 bank deposit: $ _____ .	_____	
7. Deposit slip completed.	_____	
8. Restrictive endorsement on back of checks.	_____	(5 points)
9. Cash receipts completed.	_____	(2 points)
10. Completed within time specified.	_____	

TOTAL POINTS EARNED: _____   TOTAL POINTS POSSIBLE: 24

Evaluator's Signature _____ NEED TO REPEAT: _____

PERFORMANCE EVALUATION CHECKLIST
EXERCISE 18-2 (CONTINUED) BOOKKEEPING PART II GRADE SHEET

Name _____ Date _____ Score _____

PERFORMANCE OBJECTIVE

Task: Given access to all necessary equipment and information, the student will post to ledger cards, prepare a deposit slip and checks, prepare the daily journal, complete cash receipts, and complete petty cash transactions.

Scoring: One point for each step performed satisfactorily unless otherwise weighted. To obtain a percentage score, divide the total points earned by the number of points possible.

Standards: Time _____ minutes   Note: Time element may be given by instructor.

NOTE TIME BEGAN _____   NOTE TIME COMPLETED _____

PROCEDURE STEPS	STEP PERFORMED SATISFACTORILY	COMMENTS
1. Assembled forms 86, 87, 88, 95, and 96 and pen.	_____	
JOURNAL OF DAILY CHARGES, PAYMENTS, AND DEPOSITS:		
2. Total of payments equals $ _____ .	_____	
3. Total of balance-services rendered- equals $ _____ .	_____	
LEDGER CARDS:		
4. Posted to ledgers: Maria Bargioni, Howard S. Chan, Lois A. Conrad, Marylou Conrad, Joan Gomez, Margaret Jenkins, Robert T. Jenner, Jack J. Johnson, Harold B. Mason, Rosa K. Okida, Hannah F. Riley, Stephen B. Riley, Jr., Rogert T. Simpson, Miscellaneous Ledger	_____	(14 points)
Note: Deduct points for failure to post (3 points), failure to extend or extension incorrect (3 points), any other error (1 point).		
ACCOUNTS RECEIVABLE:		
5. June 29 accounts receivable total: $ _____ .	_____	
BANKING:		
6. June 29 bank deposit: $ _____ .	_____	
7. Deposit slip completed.	_____	
8. Restrictive endorsement on back of checks.	_____	(3 points)
9. Cash receipt completed.	_____	
PETTY CASH:		
10. Completed receipts for expenditures.	_____	
11. Completed within time specified.	_____	
TOTAL POINTS EARNED:	_____	TOTAL POINTS POSSIBLE: 25

Evaluator's Signature _____ NEED TO REPEAT: _____

PERFORMANCE EVALUATION CHECKLIST
EXERCISE 18-2 (CONTINUED) BOOKKEEPING PART III GRADE SHEET

Name _____ Date _____ Score _____

PERFORMANCE OBJECTIVE

Task: Given access to all necessary equipment and information, the student will post to ledger cards, prepare a deposit slip and checks, prepare the daily journal, complete cash receipts, and complete petty cash transactions.

Scoring: One point for each step performed satisfactorily unless otherwise weighted. To obtain a percentage score, divide the total points earned by the number of points possible.

Standards: Time _____ minutes Note: Time element may be given by instructor.

NOTE TIME BEGAN _____   NOTE TIME COMPLETED _____

PROCEDURE STEPS	STEP PERFORMED SATISFACTORILY	COMMENTS
1. Assembled forms 88, 91, 92, 95, and 96 and pen.	_____	
JOURNAL OF DAILY CHARGES, PAYMENTS, *AND DEPOSITS:*		
2. Total of payments equals $ _____ .	_____	
3. Total of balance-services rendered- equals $ _____ .	_____	
LEDGER CARDS:		
4. Posted to ledgers: Charlotte J. Brown, Howard S. Chan Joan Gomez, J. B. Haupman, Kathryn L. Hope Robert T. Jenner, Rachel T. O'Brien, Martin P. Owens Stephen B. Riley, Jr., Joseph C. Smith, Russell P. Smith **Note:** Deduct points for failure to post (3 points), failure to extend or extension incorrect (3 points), any other error (1 point).	_____	(11 points)
ACCOUNTS RECEIVABLE:		
5. June 30 accounts receivable total: $ _____ .	_____	
BANKING:		
6. June 30 bank deposit: $ _____ .	_____	
7. Deposit slip completed.	_____	
8. Restrictive endorsement on back of checks.	_____	(2 points)
9. Cash receipt completed.	_____	
PETTY CASH:		
10. Completed receipt for expenditures.	_____	
11. Completed within time specified.	_____	
TOTAL POINTS EARNED:	_____	TOTAL POINTS POSSIBLE: 20

Evaluator's Signature _____ NEED TO REPEAT: _____

PERFORMANCE EVALUATION CHECKLIST
EXERCISE 18-3 DISBURSEMENTS

Name _____ Date _____ Score _____

PERFORMANCE OBJECTIVE

Task: Given access to all necessary equipment and information, the student will write checks for disbursement, enter transactions on the check register, and post deposits.

Scoring: One point for each step performed satisfactorily unless otherwise weighted. To obtain a percentage score, divide the total points earned by the number of points possible.

Standards: Time _____ minutes Note: Time element may be given by instructor.

NOTE TIME BEGAN _____   NOTE TIME COMPLETED _____

PROCEDURE STEPS	STEP PERFORMED SATISFACTORILY	COMMENTS
1. Assembled forms 93, 94, 98 through 103, and blue or black and red pens.	_____	
BILLS AND CHECKING:		
2. Checks completed for disbursements.	_____	(12 points)
3. Checkbook balance correct.	_____	
4. Deposits written in red ink.	_____	(8 points)
5. Checks entered in disbursement columns on check register.	_____	(12 points)
6. Completed within time specified.	_____	
TOTAL POINTS EARNED:	_____	TOTAL POINTS POSSIBLE: 35

Evaluator's Signature _____ NEED TO REPEAT: _____

PERFORMANCE EVALUATION CHECKLIST
EXERCISE 18-4 PAY BILLS AND REPLENISH PETTY CASH

Name _____ Date _____ Score _____

PERFORMANCE OBJECTIVE

Task: Given access to all necessary equipment and information, the student will write checks for invoices received, complete the check register, enter deposit, and replenish petty cash.

Scoring: One point for each step performed satisfactorily unless otherwise weighted. To obtain a percentage score, divide the total points earned by the number of points possible.

Standards: Time _____ minutes Note: Time element may be given by instructor.

NOTE TIME BEGAN _____   NOTE TIME COMPLETED _____

PROCEDURE STEPS	STEP PERFORMED SATISFACTORILY	COMMENTS
1. Assembled forms 93, 94, 96, 102, and 103, and blue or black and red pens.	_____	
BILLS AND CHECKING:		
2. Bills paid.	_____	(4 points)
3. Bills marked "paid, dated, and check #"	_____	(4 points)
4. Checks completed.	_____	(4 points)
5. Checkbook balance correct.	_____	
6. Deposit written in red ink.	_____	
7. Checks entered in disbursement columns on check register.	_____	(4 points)

PETTY CASH:

8. Replenished petty cash and prepared a check. _____

9. Entered petty cash transaction on check register. _____

10. Disbursed under the proper column. _____

11. Entered expenditures on office fund voucher envelope for
    June 29 and 30. _____ (4 points)

CHECK REGISTER:

12. Totaled all columns of the check register. _____ (14 points)

13. Balanced check register by using proof formulas shown
    at bottom of register. _____

14. Completed within time specified. _____

TOTAL POINTS EARNED: _____   TOTAL POINTS POSSIBLE: 42

Evaluator's Signature _____ NEED TO REPEAT: _____

PERFORMANCE EVALUATION CHECKLIST
EXERCISE 18-5 BANK RECONCILIATION

Name _____ Date _____ Score _____

PERFORMANCE OBJECTIVE

Task: Given access to all necessary equipment and information, the student will reconcile a bank statement.

Scoring: One point for each step performed satisfactorily unless otherwise weighted. To obtain a percentage score, divide the total points earned by the number of points possible.

Standards: Time _____ minutes Note: Time element may be given by instructor.

NOTE TIME BEGAN _____   NOTE TIME COMPLETED _____

PROCEDURE STEPS	STEP PERFORMED SATISFACTORILY	COMMENTS
1. Assembled form 104, checkbook stubs completed in Exercises 18-3 and 18-4, bank statement, and pen or pencil.	_____	
2. Listed the bank balance in the appropriate space on the reconciliation worksheet.	_____	
3. Listed outstanding checks.	_____	
4. Totaled outstanding checks.	_____	
5. Added to the bank statement balance any deposits not shown on the bank statement.	_____	
6. Subtracted from checkbook balance items such as withdrawals, automatic payments, or service charges that appeared on the statement but not in the checkbook.	_____	
7. Checkbook balance and adjusted total on bank statement agree.	_____	
8. Completed within time specified.	_____	

TOTAL POINTS EARNED: _____   TOTAL POINTS POSSIBLE: 20

Evaluator's Signature _____ NEED TO REPEAT: _____

PERFORMANCE EVALUATION CHECKLIST
EXERCISE 19-1 PREPARE PAYROLL

Name _____ Date _____ Score _____

PERFORMANCE OBJECTIVE

Task: Given access to all necessary equipment and information, the student will prepare payroll for seven employees by calculating their gross pay, FICA deductions, Federal income tax deductions, state income tax deductions, state disability insurance deductions, Medicare deductions, and any other deductions. The student will total all deductions and calculate each employee's net pay.

Scoring: One point for each step performed satisfactorily unless otherwise weighted. To obtain a percentage score, divide the total points earned by the number of points possible.

Standards: Time _____ minutes Note: Time element may be given by instructor.

NOTE TIME BEGAN _____ NOTE TIME COMPLETED _____

PROCEDURE STEPS	STEP PERFORMED SATISFACTORILY	COMMENTS
1. Assembled case scenarios, income tax tables, pencil or pen, and calculator.	_____	
2. Calculated payroll deductions, gross, and net pay for problem 1.	_____	(9 points)
3. Calculated payroll deductions, gross, and net pay for problem 2.	_____	(9 points)
4. Calculated payroll deductions, gross, and net pay for problem 3.	_____	(9 points)
5. Calculated payroll deductions, gross, and net pay for problem 4.	_____	(9 points)
6. Calculated payroll deductions, gross, and net pay for problem 5.	_____	(9 points)
7. Calculated payroll deductions, gross, and net pay for problem 6.	_____	(9 points)
8. Calculated payroll deductions, gross, and net pay for problem 7.	_____	(9 points)
9. Completed within time specified.	_____	

TOTAL POINTS EARNED: _____   TOTAL POINTS POSSIBLE: 65

Evaluator's Signature _____ NEED TO REPEAT: _____

PERFORMANCE EVALUATION CHECKLIST
EXERCISE 19-2 COMPLETE A PAYROLL REGISTER

Name _____ Date _____ Score _____

PERFORMANCE OBJECTIVE

Task: Given access to all necessary equipment and information, the student will complete a payroll register.

Scoring: One point for each step performed satisfactorily unless otherwise weighted. To obtain a percentage score, divide the total points earned by the number of points possible.

Standards: Time _____ minutes Note: Time element may be given by instructor.

NOTE TIME BEGAN _____ NOTE TIME COMPLETED _____

PROCEDURE STEPS	STEP PERFORMED SATISFACTORILY	COMMENTS
1. Assembled payroll information from Exercise 19-1, payroll register form, typewriter, pen or pencil.	_____	
2. Entered payroll period and entered names in alphabetical order.	_____	

4. Completed payroll register for Hillary Sheehan.   _____

5. Completed payroll register for Roger Young.   _____

6. Completed payroll register for Kelly Jones.   _____

7. Completed payroll register for Maryjane Moran.   _____

8. Completed payroll register for Carla O'Hare.   _____

9. Completed payroll register for Amy Seaforth.   _____

10. Completed payroll register for Lisa Adams.   _____

11. Completed within time specified.   _____

TOTAL POINTS EARNED: _____   _____   TOTAL POINTS POSSIBLE: 11

Evaluator's Signature _____   NEED TO REPEAT: _____

PERFORMANCE EVALUATION CHECKLIST
EXERCISE 19-3 COMPLETE AN EMPLOYEE EARNING RECORD

Name _____   Date _____   Score _____

PERFORMANCE OBJECTIVE

Task: Given access to all necessary equipment and information, the student will complete an employee earnings record card.

Scoring: One point for each step performed satisfactorily unless otherwise weighted. To obtain a percentage score, divide the total points earned by the number of points possible.

Standards: Time _____ minutes   Note: Time element may be given by instructor.

NOTE TIME BEGAN _____   NOTE TIME COMPLETED _____

PROCEDURE STEPS	STEP PERFORMED SATISFACTORILY	COMMENTS
1. Assembled employee earning record form, typewriter, and pen or pencil.	_____	
2. Completed the name, address, telephone number, and social security number.	_____	
3. Completed the date of hire, date of birth, position, number of exemptions, and rate of pay.	_____	
4. Circled the working status, marital status, and frequency of each pay period.	_____	
5. Completed the earnings and deductions sections of the form.	_____	
6. Completed within time specified.	_____	

TOTAL POINTS EARNED: _____   _____   TOTAL POINTS POSSIBLE: 6

Evaluator's Signature _____   NEED TO REPEAT: _____

PERFORMANCE EVALUATION CHECKLIST
EXERCISE 19-4 COMPLETE AN EMPLOYEE'S WITHHOLDING ALLOWANCE CERTIFICATE

Name _____ Date _____ Score _____

PERFORMANCE OBJECTIVE

Task: Given access to all necessary equipment and information, the student will complete an employee's withholding allowance certificate.

Scoring: One point for each step performed satisfactorily unless otherwise weighted. To obtain a percentage score, divide the total points earned by the number of points possible.

Standards: Time _____ minutes   Note: Time element may be given by instructor.

NOTE TIME BEGAN _____   NOTE TIME COMPLETED _____

PROCEDURE STEPS	STEP PERFORMED SATISFACTORILY	COMMENTS
1. Assembled employee's withholding allowance certificate form, typewriter, and pen or pencil.	_____	
2. Filled in name, social security number, address, and marital status.	_____	
3. Filled in the total number of allowances being claimed.	_____	
4. Signed and dated the form.	_____	
5. Completed within time specified.	_____	

TOTAL POINTS EARNED: _____   TOTAL POINTS POSSIBLE: 5

Evaluator's Signature _____ NEED TO REPEAT: _____

PERFORMANCE EVALUATION CHECKLIST
EXERCISE 19-5 COMPLETE AN EMPLOYEE BENEFIT FORM

Name _____ Date _____ Score _____

PERFORMANCE OBJECTIVE

Task: Given access to all necessary equipment and information, the student will extract information from the case scenario, calculate employee benefits, and complete an employee benefit form.

Scoring: One point for each step performed satisfactorily unless otherwise weighted. To obtain a percentage score, divide the total points earned by the number of points possible.

Standards: Time _____ minutes Note: Time element may be given by instructor.

NOTE TIME BEGAN _____ NOTE TIME COMPLETED _____

PROCEDURE STEPS	STEP PERFORMED SATISFACTORILY	COMMENTS
1. Assembled case scenario, employee benefit form, calculator, typewriter, and pen or pencil.	_____	
2. Calculated gross wage income for one year.	_____	
3. Calculated holiday pay for one year.	_____	
4. Calculated vacation pay for one year.	_____	
5. Calculated sick pay for one year.	_____	
6. Calculated medical insurance premiums for one year.	_____	
7. Calculated life insurance premiums for one year.	_____	
8. Calculated accident insurance premiums for one year.	_____	
9. Calculated workers' compensation premiums form one year.	_____	
10. Calculated disability insurance premiums for one year.	_____	
11. Extracted figures for uniform allowance and AAMA dues for one year.	_____	
12. Totaled both columns.	_____	
13. Calculated total benefits employer and employee pays.	_____	
14. Calculated the total employment package benefits	_____	
15. Entered name and current date.	_____	
16. Completed within time specified.	_____	

TOTAL POINTS EARNED: _____ TOTAL POINTS POSSIBLE: 16

Evaluator's Signature _____ NEED TO REPEAT: _____

PERFORMANCE EVALUATION CHECKLIST
EXERCISE 20-1 OUTLINE A RESUME

Name _____ Date _____ Score _____

PERFORMANCE OBJECTIVE

Task: Given access to all necessary equipment and information, the student will research information and complete worksheets in preparation for keying a resumé.

Scoring: One point for each step performed satisfactorily unless otherwise weighted. To obtain a percentage score, divide the total points earned by the number of points possible.

Standards: Time _____ minutes Note: Time element may be given by instructor.

NOTE TIME BEGAN _____ NOTE TIME COMPLETED _____

PROCEDURE STEPS	STEP PERFORMED SATISFACTORILY	COMMENTS
1. Assembled worksheet forms 109 and 110 and pen or pencil.	_____	
2. Completed all spaces on worksheet where applicable.	_____	
3. Gathered information dealing with work experience.	_____	
4. Researched information to complete reference details.	_____	
5. Completed within time specified.	_____	

TOTAL POINTS EARNED: _____   TOTAL POINTS POSSIBLE: 5

Evaluator's Signature _____ NEED TO REPEAT: _____

PERFORMANCE EVALUATION CHECKLIST
EXERCISE 20-2 KEY A RESUME

Name _____ Date _____ Score _____

PERFORMANCE OBJECTIVE

Task: Given access to all necessary equipment and information, the student will key a resumé in attractive format.

Scoring: One point for each step performed satisfactorily unless otherwise weighted. To obtain a percentage score, divide the total points earned by the number of points possible.

Standards: Time _____ minutes Note: Time element may be given by instructor.

NOTE TIME BEGAN _____ NOTE TIME COMPLETED _____

PROCEDURE STEPS	STEP PERFORMED SATISFACTORILY	COMMENTS
1. Assembled two sheets of plain paper.	_____	
2. Keyed rough draft of resume for instructor's comments.	_____	
3. Attractive format.	_____	
4. Heading centered.	_____	
5. Margins balanced.	_____	
6. Copy is easy to read and attracts attention.	_____	
7. Page is clean and neat.	_____	
8. Proofread resume for typographical, spelling and spacing errors.	_____	
9. Completed within time specified.	_____	

TOTAL POINTS EARNED: _____   TOTAL POINTS POSSIBLE: 9

Evaluator's Signature _____ NEED TO REPEAT: _____

PERFORMANCE EVALUATION CHECKLIST
EXERCISE 20-3 COMPOSE A COVER LETTER OF INTRODUCTION

Name _____ Date _____ Score _____

PERFORMANCE OBJECTIVE

Task: Given access to all necessary equipment and information, the student will compose and key a letter of introduction to accompany the resumé and place in a prepared envelope.

Scoring: One point for each step performed satisfactorily unless otherwise weighted. To obtain a percentage score, divide the total points earned by the number of points possible.

Standards: Time _____ minutes Note: Time element may be given by instructor.

NOTE TIME BEGAN _____   NOTE TIME COMPLETED _____

PROCEDURE STEPS	STEP PERFORMED SATISFACTORILY	COMMENTS
1. Assembled two sheets of plain paper and form 111.	_____	
2. Composed cover letter of introduction.	_____	
3. Keyed rough draft of letter and had it checked by instructor.	_____	
4. Keyed final draft of letter.	_____	
5. Dated letter.	_____	
6. Letter is centered with even margins.	_____	
7. Keyed inside address.	_____	
8. Keyed appropriate salutation.	_____	
9. Inserted proper paragraphing.	_____	
10. Keyed closing lines in correct position with proper punctuation.	_____	
11. Included enclosure notation.	_____	
12. Proofread letter for typographical, spelling, punctuation, and capitalization errors while letter remained in typewriter or on computer screen.	_____	
13. Signed letter.	_____	
14. Keyed large envelope.	_____	
15. Letter and resumé folded neatly and placed in envelope.	_____	
16. Completed within time specified.	_____	

TOTAL POINTS EARNED: _____   TOTAL POINTS POSSIBLE: 16

Evaluator's Signature _____ NEED TO REPEAT: _____

PERFORMANCE EVALUATION CHECKLIST
EXERCISE 20-4 PREPARE A FOLLOW-UP THANK-YOU LETTER

Name _____ Date _____ Score _____

PERFORMANCE OBJECTIVE

Task: Given access to all necessary equipment and information, the student will compose and key a follow-up thank-you letter and address a No. 6 envelope.

Scoring: One point for each step performed satisfactorily unless otherwise weighted. To obtain a percentage score, divide the total points earned by the number of points possible.

Standards: Time _____ minutes   Note: Time element may be given by instructor.

NOTE TIME BEGAN _____   NOTE TIME COMPLETED _____

PROCEDURE STEPS	STEP PERFORMED SATISFACTORILY	COMMENTS
1. Assembled a sheet of plain paper and form 112.	_____	
2. Composed a thank-you letter.	_____	
3. Keyed rough draft of letter for instructor's comments.	_____	
4. Keyed final draft of letter.	_____	
5. Dated letter.	_____	
6. Letter is centered with even margins.	_____	
7. Keyed inside address.	_____	
8. Keyed appropriate salutation.	_____	
9. Inserted proper paragraphing.	_____	
10. Keyed closing lines in correct position with proper punctuation.	_____	
11. Proofread letter for typographical, spelling, punctuation, and capitalization errors while letter remained in typewriter or on computer screen.	_____	
12. Signed letter.	_____	
13. Keyed small envelope.	_____	
14. Letter folded neatly and placed in envelope.	_____	
15. Completed within time specified.	_____	

TOTAL POINTS EARNED: _____   TOTAL POINTS POSSIBLE: 15

Evaluator's Signature _____ NEED TO REPEAT: _____

Part IV | Appendix

INTRODUCTION

To gain practical experience and put theory to work, assume that you have been hired to work as an administrative medical assistant for a husband-and-wife team and perform the tasks in the exercises presented in this workbook as if you were on the job. Dr. Fran T. Practon is a family practitioner (FP) and Dr. Gerald M. Practon is a general practitioner (GP). They are on the staff of a nearby hospital, College Hospital. Use this reference sheet for data required in many of the exercises.

MEDICAL PRACTICE REFERENCE SHEET

Practon Medical Group, Inc.
4567 Broad Avenue
Woodland Hills, XY 12345-4700
Telephone No. 013-486-9002
Fax No. 013-488-7815
Group tax identification number: 95-3664021
Medicare Durable Medical Equipment supplier number: 3342098567

Fran T. Practon, MD
Federal Tax Identification Number: 73-4031321
State license number C 15038
Medicare NPI number 6549994780

Gerald M. Practon, MD
Federal Tax Identification Number: 78-5134298
State license number C14021
Medicare NPI number 4627889700

College Hospital
500 Broad Avenue
Woodland Hills, XY 12345-4700
Telephone No. 013-487-6789
Provider number: 5437860120

OFFICE POLICIES

The office policies set down by Drs. Fran and Gerald Practon appear on the next several pages. Refer to them for office hours, appointment scheduling, telephone procedures, daily routine, and filing practices as you complete the workbook exercises.

Office Hours

The physicians' office hours are 9A.M. to 5P.M. on Monday through Friday of each week except Wednesdays, when both physicians leave the office at 3P.M. Both physicians reserve one morning each week for surgery and additional hospital responsibilities; Gerald reserves Tuesday mornings and Fran, Thursday mornings. An asterisk (*) distinguishes Fran's patients from Gerald's when physician verification is necessary. Each physician covers the office while the other is at the hospital on those two mornings. The lunch hour is from noon to 1P.M. No elective appointments are scheduled after 11:30A.M. and after 4P.M. daily. This free time allows for callbacks, work-ins, emergencies, and dictation.

Appointments

Of necessity, both physicians must work by appointment. Patients should be specific in outlining the nature of their medical problem so appropriate time is allowed. If multiple problems exist and are made known by the patient, additional time will be allotted. Brief office visits for injections and removal of sutures are scheduled for 15-minute appointments. When treating a patient for the first time and giving a complete physical examination and/or consultation, 1-hour appointments are set up. All other appointments are scheduled for 1/2 hour. The first day after a holiday may require slots for emergency workins. Try to schedule light during the first hour of the day and then heavier toward the late afternoon. Try to schedule sales or pharmaceutical representatives mid-week around the noon hour. Also, if a patient is known to be habitually late, schedule him or her 15 minutes before the real appointment. There is no charge if appointments are canceled 24 hours in advance; uncancelled appointments are billed at one-half the usual fee. Appointments should be scheduled consecutively when possible. House calls are discouraged but, if absolutely necessary, are made for after 5 P.M.

Telephone Calls

The medical assistant answers most inquiries so the physicians need not leave patients being examined to answer the telephone. When the assistant is unable to give a complete answer to a patient question, the physician reviews the chart and either calls back the same day or has a member of the staff make the call-back. Calls that the physicians personally return are made during lunch hour or after 4 P.M.

Daily Routine

The physicians prefer that the medical assistant call the answering service for messages and handle the incoming mail before the patients begin to arrive. Correspondence is to be mailed the same day it is dictated. Each patient's medical record is to be completed as soon as possible after he or she is seen in the office or hospital.

Filing

Correspondence in reference to a patient is filed under the patient's name. Folders are filed alphabetically, and material is filed chronologically within file folders. Medical histories belong in the front of the folders; all other material, such as reports and correspondence, follow chronologically. Ledger cards are kept in a special file box (but in our mock situation, you put them in front of the history in the file folder).

Billing and Insurance

The Practon Medical Group, Inc. is submitting bills as a group rather than as individual practicing physicians. When completing the HCFA-1500 insurance claim form, follow these instructions.

Block 17A: When services are ordered or referred by another physician, enter the referring physician's *national provider identifier* (NPI).

Block 24J: Enter the first two digits of the NPI as there is insufficient room in Block 24K.

Block 24K: Enter the last eight digits of the performing physician's NPI for each service rendered.

Block 25: Enter the physician's *federal tax identification number* also known as *employer identification number* (EIN) issued by the Internal Revenue Service.

Block 33: Enter the *group's tax identification number*.

For CHAMPUS claims: Block 24K: Enter the physician's *state license number* for each service rendered.

ACCOUNTS

After a patient is seen, the fee is entered on the day sheet. Figure A-1 is the fee schedule for the Practon Medical Group, Inc. All figures listed are for example only. Fees can vary with the region of the United States (West, Midwest, South, and East), the specialty of the practitioner, the type of community, (urban, suburban, or rural), the type of practice (incorporated or unincorporated—solo, partners, or shareholders), the overhead, and a number of other factors.
The four columns to the right indicate the following:

- Column 1 is the physician's regular fee
- Column 2 is the Medicare payment for a participating physician
- Column 3 is the Medicare payment for nonparticipating physicians
- Column 4 is the Medicare limiting charge for nonparticipating physicians

In regard to Medicare patients, the physicians charge their regular fees. If the physician is participating, an adjustment fee must be entered on the patient's ledger card. (NOTE: A nonparticipating physician cannot charge more than his or her limiting charge.)
In regard to the fee schedule, the first-column figures are the physicians' standard fees and should always be used when billing private patients as well as those patients on state or federal

programs (Medicare, Medicaid, CHAMPUS). The second column of figures is what the Medicare program pays to the participating physician for the service rendered. The third column of figures is what the Medicare program pays to the nonparticipating physician. The fourth column of figures is the highest amount that a nonparticipating physician is allowed to bill for the service rendered.

Payments, if made at the time of the visit, are entered on the day sheet. Charges, payments, and adjustments are transferred to the patient's ledger card. If a payment is received by mail, it is entered on the day sheet. Patients are expected to pay copayments at the time professional services are rendered.

When the physician services others in the medical profession who have insurance—such as physicians, members of their immediate families, dentists, pharmacists, nurses, medical assistants, parents of physicians, and clergy—a claim is sent listing the standard fee for each service. The physician accepts what the insurance pays as payment in full, adjusting off the balance.

FRAN T. PRACTON, M.D.
Family Practice

GERALD M. PRACTON, M.D.
General Practice

PRACTON MEDICAL GROUP, INC.
4567 Broad Avenue
Woodland Hills, XY 12345-0001

FEE SCHEDULE

CPT Code No. and Description		Mock Fees	Medicare		
			Participating	Non-Participating	Limiting Charge
EVALUATION AND MANAGEMENT*					
OFFICE New Patient					
99201	Level I	33.25	30.43	28.91	33.25
99202	Level II	51.91	47.52	45.14	51.91
99203	Level III	70.92	64.92	61.67	70.92
99204	Level IV	106.11	97.13	92.27	106.11
99205	Level V	132.28	121.08	115.03	132.38
Established Patient					
99211	Level I	16.07	14.70	13.97	16.07
99212	Level II	28.55	26.14	24.83	28.55
99213	Level III	40.20	36.80	34.96	40.20
99214	Level IV	61.51	56.31	53.49	61.51
99215	Level V	96.97	88.76	84.32	96.97
HOSPITAL Observation Services (new or est pt)					
99217	Discharge	66.88	61.22	58.16	66.88
99218	D hx/exam SF/LC DM	74.22	67.91	64.54	74.22
99219	C hx/exam MC DM	117.75	107.78	102.39	117.75
99220	C hx/exam HC DM	147.48	134.99	128.24	147.48
Inpatient Services (new or est pt)					
99221	30 min	73.00	66.82	63.48	73.00
99222	50 min	120.80	110.57	105.04	120.80
99223	70 min	152.98	140.03	133.03	152.98
Subsequent Hospital Care					
99231	15 min	37.74	34.55	32.82	37.74
99232	25 min	55.56	50.85	48.31	55.56
99233	35 min	76.97	70.45	66.93	76.97
99238	Discharge	65.26	59.74	56.75	65.26

Table continued on following page

*See Tables 16-6 and 16-7 in the textbook for more descriptions on E/M codes 99201 through 99499.

Figure A-1 A fee schedule for reference when doing the workbook exercises.

FEE SCHEDULE (Continued)

CPT Code No. and Description		Mock Fees	Medicare		
			Participating	Non-Participating	Limiting Charge
CONSULTATIONS office (new/est pt)					
99241	Level I	51.93	47.54	45.16	51.93
99242	Level II	80.24	73.44	69.77	80.24
99243	Level III	103.51	94.75	90.01	103.51
99244	Level VI	145.05	132.77	126.13	14.05
99245	Level V	195.48	178.93	169.98	195.48
Inpatient (new/est pt)					
99251	Level I	53.29	48.78	46.34	53.29
99252	Level II	80.56	73.74	70.05	80.56
99253	Level III	106.10	97.12	92.26	106.10
99254	Level VI	145.26	132.96	126.31	145.26
99255	Level V	196.55	179.91	170.91	196.55
Follow-up Inpatient (new/est pt)					
99261	Focused	29.66	27.15	25.79	29.66
99262	Expanded	50.57	46.28	43.97	50.57
99263	Detailed	76.36	69.90	66.40	76.36
Confirmatory 2nd-3rd opinion (new/est pt)					
99271	Focused	45.47	41.62	39.54	45.47
99272	Expanded	67.02	61.35	58.28	67.02
99273	Detailed	95.14	87.08	82.73	95.14
99274	Comprehensive	125.15	114.56	108.83	125.15
99275	Comprehensive	172.73	158.10	150.20	172.73
EMERGENCY DEPARTMENT (new/est pt)					
99281	PF hx/exam SF DM	24.32	22.26	21.15	24.32
99282	EPF hx/exam LC DM	37.02	33.88	32.19	37.02
99283	EPF hx/exam MC DM	66.23	60.62	57.59	66.23
99284	D hx/exam MC DM	100.71	92.18	87.57	100.71
99285	C hx/exam HC DM	158.86	145.41	138.14	158.86
CRITICAL CARE SERVICES					
99291	First hour	208.91	191.22	181.66	208.91
99292	Each addl. 30 min	102.02	92.46	87.84	102.02
NEONATAL INTENSIVE CARE					
99295	Initial	892.74	817.16	776.30	892.74
99296	Subsequent unstable case	418.73	383.27	364.11	418.73
99297	Subsequent stable case	214.68	196.50	i86.68	214.68
NURSING FACILITY					
99301	30 min	64.11	58.68	55.75	64.11
99302	40 min	90.55	82.88	78.74	90.55
99303	50 min	136.76	125.18	118.92	136.76
Subsequent (new/est pt)					
99311	15 min	37.95	34.74	33.00	37.95
99312	25 min	55.11	50.44	47.92	55.11
99313	35 min	69.61	63.72	60.53	69.61
DOMICILIARY, REST HOME, CUSTODIAL CARE New patient					
99321	PF hx/exam LC DM	46.10	42.20	40.09	46.10
99322	EPF hx/exam MC DM	65.02	59.52	56.54	65.02
99323	D hx/exam HC DM	86.18	78.88	74.94	86.18
Established patient					
99331	Pf hx/exam LC DM	37.31	34.15	32.44	37.31
99332	EPF hx/exam MC DM	49.22	45.05	42.80	49.22
99333	D hx/exam HC DM	60.61	55.47	52.70	60.61
HOME SERVICES New patient					
99341	PF hx/exam LC DM	70.32	64.37	61.15	70.32
99342	EPF hx/exam LC DM	91.85	84.07	79.87	91.85
99343	D hx/exam HC DM	120.24	110.06	104.56	120.24

Table continued on following page

FEE SCHEDULE (Continued)

CPT Code No. and Description		Mock Fees	Medicare		
			Participating	Non-Participating	Limiting Charge
Established patient					
99351	PF hx/exam LC DM	54.83	50.19	47.68	54.83
99352	EPF hx/exam LC DM	70.06	64.13	60.92	70.06
99353	D hx/exam HC DM	88.33	80.85	76.81	88.33
PROLONGED SERVICES WITH CONTACT Outpatient					
99354	First hour	96.67	88.76	84.32	96.97
99355	Each addl. 30 min	96.97	88.76	84.32	96.97
Inpatient					
99356	First hour	96.42	88.25	83.84	96.42
99357	Each addl. 30 min	96.42	88.25	83.84	96.42
PROLONGED SERVICES WITHOUT DIRECT CONTACT					
99358	First hour	90.00			
99359	Each addl. 30 min	90.00			
PHYSICIAN STANDBY SERVICE					
99360	Each 30 min	95.00			
CASE MANAGEMENT SERVICES Team Conferences					
99361	30 min	85.00			
99362	60 min	105.00			
Telephone Calls					
99371	Simple or brief	30.00			
99372	Intermediate	40.00			
99373	Complex	60.00			
CARE PLAN OVERSIGHT SERVICES					
99375	30-60 min	93.40	85.49	81.22	93.40
99376	Greater than 60 min	118.00			
PREVENTIVE MEDICINE New Patient					
99381	Infant under age 1 year	50.00			
99382	1-4 years	50.00			
99383	5-11 years	45.00			
99384	12-17 years	45.00			
99385	18-30 years	50.00			
99386	40-64	50.00			
99387	65 yrs and over	55.00			
Established Patient					
99391	Infant under age 1 year	35.00			
99392	1-4 years	35.00			
99393	5-11 years	30.00			
99394	12-17 years	30.00			
99395	18-39 years	35.00			
99396	40-64 years	35.00			
99397	65 yrs & over	40.00			
COUNSELING (new/est pt)					
Individual					
99401	15 min	35.00			
99402	30 min	50.00			
99403	45 min	65.00			
99404	60 min	80.00			
Group					
99411	30 min	30.00			
99412	60 min	50.00			
Other preventive medicine services					
99420	Health hazard appraisal	50.00			
99429	Unlisted preventive med serv	variable			
NEWBORN CARE					
99431	Birthing room delivery	102.15	93.50	88.83	102.15

Table continued on following page

---

* Some services and procedures may not be considered a benefit under the Medicare program, and when listed on a claim form, no reimbursement may be received. However, it is important to include these codes when billing because Medicare policies may change without an individual knowing of a new benefit. For this reason, some of the services shown in this mock fee schedule do not have any amounts listed under the three Medicare columns.

FEE SCHEDULE (Continued)

CPT Code No. and Description	Mock Fees	Medicare Participating	Non-Participating	Limiting Charge
99432 Other than birthing room	110.16	100.83	95.79	110.16
99433 Subsequent hospital care	54.02	49.44	46.97	54.02
99440 Newborn resuscitation	255.98	234.30	222.59	255.98
99499 Unlisted E/m service	variable			

ANESTHESIOLOGY

Anesthesiology fees are presented here for CPT codes. However, each case would require a fee for time, e.g., every 15 minutes would be worth $55. Some anesthetists may list a surgical code on a subsequent line for carriers that do not acknowledge anesthesia codes.

99100	Anes for pt under 1 yr/over 70	55.00
99116	Anes complicated use total hypothermia	275.00
99135	Anes complicated use hypotension	275.00
99140	Anes complicated emer cond	110.00

PHYSICIAN STATUS MODIFIER CODES

P-1	Normal healthy patient	00.00
P-2	Patient with mild systemic disease	00.00
P-3	Patient with severe systemic disease	55.00
P-4	Patient with severe systemic disease (constant threat to life)	110.00
P-5	Moribund pt not expected to survive for 24 hr with or without operation	165.00
P-6	Declared brain-dead pt. organs being removed for donor	00.00

HEAD

00160	Anes for proc nose & accessory sinuses: NOS	275.00
00172	Anes repair cleft palate	165.00

THORAX

00400	Anes for proc ant integumentary system of chest, include SC tissue	165.00
00402	Anes breast reconstruction	275.00
00546	Anes pulmonary resection with thoracoplasty	275.00
00600	Anes cervical spine and cord	550.00

LOWER ABDOMEN

00800	Anes for proc lower ant abdominal wall	165.00
00840	Anes intraperitoneal proc lower abdomen: NOS	330.00
00842	Amniocentesis	220.00
00914	Anes TURP	275.00
00942	Anes colporrhaphy, colpotomy, colpectomy	220.00

UPPER LEG

01210	Anes open proc hip joint: NOS	330.00
01214	Total hip replacement	440.00

UPPER ARM AND ELBOW

01740	Anes open proc humerus/elbow; NOS	220.00
01758	Exc cyst/tumor humerus	275.00

RADIOLOGIC PROCEDURES

01922	Anes CAT scan	385.00

MISCELLANEOUS PROCEDURE(S)

01999	Unlisted anes proc	variable

Table continued on following page

FEE SCHEDULE (Continued)

CPT Code No. and Description	Mock Fees	Medicare			
		Participating	Non-Participating	Limiting Charge	Follow-Up Days[1]
10060* I & D furuncle, onchia, paronychia; single	75.92	69.49	66.02	75.92	10
11040* Debridement; skin, partial thickness	79.32	75.60	68.97	79.32	10
11044 Debridement; skin, subcu. muscle, bone	269.28	246.48	234.16	269.28	
11100 Biopsy of skin, SC tissue &/or mucous membrane; 1 lesion	65.43	59.89	56.90	65.43	10
11200* Exc. skin tags; up to 15	55.68	50.97	48.42	55.68	10
11401 Exc. benign lesion, 0.6-1.0 cm trunk, arms, legs	95.62	87.53	83.15	96.62	10
11402 1.1-2.0 cm	121.52	111.23	105.67	121.52	10
11403 2.1-3.0 cm	151.82	138.97	132.02	151.82	10
11420 Exc. benign lesion. 0.5 cm or less scalp, neck, hands, feet, genitalia	75.44	69.05	65.60	75.44	10
11422 Exc. benign lesion scalp, neck, hands, feet, or genitalia; 1.1-2.0 cm	131.35	120.23	114.22	131.35	10
11441 Exc. benign lesion face, ears, eyelids, nose, lips, or mucous membrane; 0.6-1.0 cm dia or less	119.08	109.00	103.55	119.08	10
11602 Exc. malignant lesion, trunk, arms, or legs; 1.1-2.0 cm dia	195.06	178.55	169.62	195.06	10
11700* Debridement of nails, manual	32.58	29.82	28.33	32.58	0
11710* Debridement of nails, electric	32.58	29.82	28.33	32.58	0
11730* Avulsion nail plate, partial or complete, simple repair; single	76.91	70.40	66.88	76.91	0
11750 Exc. nail or nail matrix, partial or complete	193.45	177.07	168.22	193.45	10
12001* Simple repair (scalp, neck, axillae, ext genitalia, trunk, or extremities incl hands & feet): 2.5 cm or less	91.17	83.45	79.82	91.17	10
12011* Simple repair (face, ears, eyelids, nose, lips or mucous membranes); 2.5 cm or less	101.44	92.85	88.21	101.44	10

Table continued on following page

---

[1] Data for the surgical follow-up days from St. Anthony's CPT '96 Companion: a Guide to Medicare Billing

* Codes marked with an asterisk appear in CPT marked as shown.

FEE SCHEDULE (Continued)

CPT Code No. and Description	Mock Fees	Medicare			
		Participating	Non-Participating	Limiting Charge	Follow-Up Days[1]
12013* 2.6-5.0 cm	123.98	113.48	107.81	123.98	10
12032 Repair, scapl axillae, trunk (intermediate)	169.73	155.36	147.59	169.73	10
12034 Repair, intermediate, layer closure of wounds (scalp, axillae, trunk, or extremities) excl hands or feet; 7.6-12.5 cm	214.20	196.06	186.26	214.20	10
12051* Repair, intermediate, layer closure of wounds (face, ears, eyelids, nose, lips, or mucous membranes); 2.5 cm	167.60	153.41	145.74	167.60	10
17000* Cauterization of wart; 2 lesions or less	52.56	48.11	45.70	52.56	10
17001 Caut. second and third lesions, each	19.41	17.77	16.88	19.41	10
17100* Destruction, any method, skin lesion (benign) any area except face–one	44.86	41.06	39.01	44.86	10
17101 Second lesion	15.21	13.93	13.23	15.21	10
17102 Over two lesions, ea. additional up to fifteen	9.59	8.78	8.34	9.59	10
19020 Mastotomy, drainage/exploration deep abscess	237.36	217.26	206.40	237.36	90
19100* Biopsy, breast, needle	96.17	88.03	83.63	96.17	0
19101 Biopsy, breast, incisional	281.51	257.67	244.79	281.51	10
20610* Arthrocentesis, aspiration or injection joint (should, hip, knee) or bursa	52.33	47.89	45.50	52.33	0
21330 Nasal fracture, open treatment complicated	599.46	548.71	521.27	599.46	90
24066 Biopsy, deep, soft tissue, upper arm, elbow	383.34	350.88	333.34	383.34	90
27455 Osteotomy, proximal tibia	1248.03	1142.36	1085.24	1248.03	90
27500 Treatment closed femoral shaft fracture without manipulation	554.90	507.92	482.52	554.90	90
27530 Treatment closed tibial fracture, proximal, without manipulation	344.24	315.90	299.34	344.24	90
27750 Treatment closed tibial shaft fracture without manipulation	400.94	366.99	348.64	400.94	90
27752 With manipulation	531.63	486.62	462.29	531.63	90
29345 Appl long leg cast (thigh to toes)	123.23	112.80	107.16	123.23	0
29355 Walker or ambulatory type	133.75	122.42	116.30	133.75	0
29425 Appl short leg walking cast	102.10	93.45	88.78	102.10	0
30110 Excision, simple nasal polyp	145.21	132.92	126.27	145.21	10
30520 Septoplasty	660.88	604.93	574.68	660.88	90
30903* Control nasal hemorrhage; unilateral	118.17	108.17	102.76	118.17	0
30905* Control nasal hemorrhage, posterior with posterior nasal packs; initial	190.57	174.43	165.71	190.57	0

Table continued on following page

FEE SCHEDULE (Continued)

CPT Code No. and Description		Mock Fees	Medicare			
			Participating	Non-Participating	Limiting Charge	Follow-Up Days[1]
30906*	Subsequent	173.01	158.36	150.44	173.01	
31625	Bronchoscopy with biopsy	312.87	286.38	272.06	312.87	0
32310	Pleurectomy	1234.79	1130.24	1073.73	1234.79	90
32440	Pneumonectomy, total	1972.10	1805.13	1714.87	1972.10	90
33020	Pericardiotomy	1289.25	1180.09	1121.09	1289.25	90
33206	Insertion of pacemaker; atrial	728.42	666.75	633.41	728.42	90
33208	AV sequential	751.57	687.89	653.50	751.57	90
35301	Thromboendarterectomy with or without patch graft; carotid, vertebral, subclavian by neck incision	1585.02	1450.82	1378.28	1585.02	90
36005	Intravenous injection for contrast venography	59.18	54.17	51.46	59.18	0
36248	Catheter placement (selective) arterial system, 2nd, 3rd and beyond	68.54	62.74	59.60	68.54	0
36415*	Routine venipuncture for collection of specimen(s)	10.00	—	—	—	XXX
38101	Splenectomy, partial	994.44	910.24	864.73	994.44	90
38510	Biopsy/excision deep cervied node/s	327.42	299.69	284.71	327.42	90
39520	Excision tumor, mediastinal	1436.50	1314.87	1249.13	1436.50	90
42820	T & A under age 12 years	341.63	312.71	297.07	341.63	90
42821	T & A over age 12 years	410.73	375.96	357.16	410.73	90
43234	Upper GI endoscopy, simple primary exam	201.86	184.77	175.53	201.86	0
43235	Upper GI endoscopy incl esophagus, stomach, duodenum, or jejunum; complex	238.92	218.69	207.76	238.92	0
43456	Dilation esophagus	254.52	232.97	221.32	254.52	0
43820	Gastrojejunostomy	971.86	889.58	845.10	971.86	90
44150	Colectomy, total, abdominal	1757.81	1608.98	1528.53	1757.81	90
44320	Colostomy or skin cecostomy	966.25	884.44	840.22	966.25	90
44950	Appendectomy	568.36	520.24	494.23	568.36	90
45308	Proctosigmoidoscopy for removal of polyp	135.34	123.88	117.69	135.34	0
45315	Multiple polyps	185.12	169.44	160.97	185.12	0
45330	Sigmoidoscopy, diagnostic (for biopsy or collection of specimen by brushing or washing)	95.92	87.80	83.41	95.92	0
45380	Colonoscopy with biopsy	382.35	349.98	332.48	382.35	0
46255	Hemorrhoidectomy int & ext, simple	503.57	460.94	437.89	503.57	90
46258	Hemorrhoidectomy with fistulectomy	636.02	582.17	553.06	636.02	90

Table continued on following page

[1] Data for the surgical follow-up days from St. Anthony's CPT '96 Companion: a Guide to Medicare Billing
* Codes marked with an asterisk appear in CPT marked as shown.

FEE SCHEDULE (Continued)

CPT Code No. and Description		Mock Fees	Medicare			
			Participating	Non-Participating	Limiting Charge	Follow-Up Days[1]
46600	Anoscopy; diagnostic	32.86	30.07	28.57	32.86	0
46614	With coagulation for control of hemorrhage	182.10	166.68	158.35	182.10	0
46700	Anoplastic, for stricture, adult	657.39	601.73	571.64	657.39	90
47600	Cholecystectomy	937.74	858.35	815.43	937.74	90
49505	Inguinal hernia repair, age 5 or over	551.07	504.41	479.19	551.07	90
49520	Repair, inguinal hernia, any age; recurrent	671.89	615.00	584.25	671.89	90
50080	Nephrostolithotomy, percutaneous	1323.93	1211.83	1151.24	1323.93	90
50780	Ureteronecystostomy	1561.23	1429.84	1357.59	1561.23	90
51900	Closure of vesicovaginal fistula abdominal approach	1196.32	1095.48	1040.71	1196.82	90
52000	Cystourethroscopy	167.05	152.90	145.26	167.05	0
52601	Transurethral resection of prostate	1193.53	1092.47	1037.85	1193.53	90
53040	Drainage of deep periurethral abscess	520.11	476.07	452.27	520.11	90
53230	Excision, female diverticutum (urethral)	859.69	786.91	747.56	859.69	90
53240	Marsupialization of urethral diverticulum, M or F	520.11	476.07	452.27	520.11	90
53620*	Dilation, urethra, male	100.73	92.20	87.59	100.73	0
53660*	Dilation, urethra, female	48.32	44.23	42.02	48.32	0
54150	Circumcision–newborn	111.78	102.32	97.20	111.78	10
54520	Orchiectomy, simple	523.92	479.56	455.58	523.92	90
55700	Biopsy of prostate, needle or punch	156.22	142.99	135.84	156.22	0
55801	Prostatectomy, perineal subtotal	1466.56	1342.39	1275.27	1466.56	90
57265	Colporrhaphy AP with enterocele repair	902.24	825.85	784.56	902.24	90
57452*	Colposcopy	84.18	77.05	73.20	84.18	0
57510	Cauterization of cervix, electro or thermal	115.15	105.40	100.13	115.15	10
57520	Circumferential (cone) of cervix with or without D & C, with or without Sturmdorff-type repair	387.08	354.30	336.59	387.08	90
58100*	Endometrial biopsy	71.88	65.79	62.50	71.88	8
58120	D & C diagnostic and/or therapeutic (nonOB)	272.83	249.73	237.24	272.83	10
58150	TAH w/without salpingo-oophorectomy	1167.72	1068.85	1015.41	1167.72	90
58200	Total hysterectomy, extended, corpus cancer, including partial vaginectomy	1707.24	1562.69	1484.56	1707.24	90

Table continued on following page

FEE SCHEDULE (Continued)

CPT Code No. and Description	Mock Fees	Medicare Participating	Non-Participating	Limiting Charge	Follow-Up Days[1]
58210 With bilateral radical pelvic lymphadenectomy	2160.78	1977.83	1878.94	2160.78	90
58300* Insertion of intrauterine device	100.00	—	—	—	0
58340* Hysterosalpingography with inj proc	73.06	66.87	63.53	73.06	0
58720 Salpingo-oophorectomy, complete or partial, unilateral or bilateral Surgical treatment of ectopic pregnancy	732.40	670.39	636.87	732.40	90
59120 Salpinectomy and/or oophorectomy	789.26	722.43	686.31	789.26	90
59121 without salpingectomy and/or oophorectomy	638.84	584.75	555.51	638.84	90
59130 abdominal pregnancy	699.12	639.93	607.93	699.12	90
59135 Total hysterectomy, interstitial, uterine pregnancy	1154.16	1056.44	1003.62	1154.16	90
59136 Partial uterine resection, interstitial uterine pregnancy	772.69	707.26	671.90	772.69	90
59140 cervical, with evacuation	489.68	448.22	425.81	489.68	90
59160 D & C postpartum hemorrhage (separate proc)	293.46	268.61	255.18	293.46	10
59400 OB Care-routine, inc. antepartum/postpartum care	1864.30	1706.45	1621.13	1864.30	N/A
59515 C-section, low cervical, include in-hosp postpartum care (separate proc)	1469.80	1345.36	1278.09	1469.80	N/A
59510 Including antepartum and postpartum care	2102.33	1924.33	1828.11	2102.33	N/A
59812 Treatment of incompl abortion, any trimester; completed surgically	357.39	327.13	310.77	357.39	90
61314 Craniotomy infratentorial	2548.09	2332.35	2215.73	2548.09	90
62270* Spinal puncture, lumbar; diagnostic	77.52	70.96	67.41	77.52	0
65091 Excision of eye, without implant	708.22	648.25	615.84	708.22	90
65205* Removal of foreign body, ext eye	56.02	51.27	48.71	56.02	0
65222* Corneal, with slit lamp	73.81	67.56	64.18	73.81	0
69420* Myringotomy	97.76	89.48	85.01	97.76	10

Table continued on following page

[1] Data for the surgical follow-up days from St. Anthony's CPT '96 Companion: a Guide to Medicare Billing
* Codes marked with an asterisk appear in CPT marked as shown.

FEE SCHEDULE (Continued)

CPT Code No. and Description		Mock Fees	Medicare		
			Participating	Non-Participating	Limiting Charge
RADIOLOGY, NUCLEAR MEDICINE, AND DIAGNOSTIC ULTRASOUND					
70120	X-ray mastoids, 2 views	38.96	35.66	33.88	38.96
70130	X-ray mastoids, 3 views	56.07	51.33	48.76	56.07
71010	X-ray chest, 1 view	31.95	29.24	27.78	31.95
71020	Chest x-ray, 2 views	40.97	37.50	35.63	40.97
71030	Chest x-ray, compl. 4 views	54.02	49.44	46.97	54.02
71060	Bronchogram, bilateral	143.75	131.58	125.00	143.75
72100	X-ray spine, LS; AP & lat views	43.23	39.57	37.59	43.23
72114	Complete, incl bending views	74.97	68.62	65.19	74.97
73100	X-ray wrist, 2 views	31.61	28.94	27.49	31.61
73500	X-ray hip, 1 view	31.56	28.88	27.44	31.56
73540	X-ray pelvis & hips, infant or child, 2 views	37.94	34.73	32.99	37.94
73590	X-ray tibia & fibula, 2 views	33.35	30.53	29.00	33.35
73620	Radiologic exam, foot; AP & lat views	31.61	28.94	27.49	31.61
73650	X-ray calcaneus, 2 views	30.71	28.11	26.70	30.71
74241	Radiologic exam, upper gastrointestinal tract, with/without delayed films with KUB	108.93	99.71	94.72	108.93
74245	Upper GI tract with small bowel	161.70	148.01	140.61	161.70
74270	Barium enema	118.47	108.44	103.02	118.47
74290	Oral cholecystography	52.59	48.14	45.73	52.59
74400	Urography (pyelography), intravenous, with or without KUB	104.78	95.90	91.11	104.78
74405	Urography (pyelography) intravenous with spec hypertensive contrast	118.36	108.34	102.92	118.36
74410	Urography, infusion	116.76	106.87	101.53	116.76
74420	Urography, retrograde	138.89	127.13	120.77	138.89
75982	Percutaneous placement of drainage catheter	359.08	328.67	312.24	359.08
76090	Mammography, unilateral	62.57	57.27	54.51	62.57
76091	Mammography, bilateral	82.83	75.82	72.03	82.83
76805	Echography, pregnant uterus, B-scan or real time; complete	154.18	141.13	134.07	154.18
76810	Echography, pregnant uterus, complete: multiple gestation, after first trimester	306.54	280.59	266.56	306.54
76946	Ultrasonic guidance for amniocentesis	91.22	83.49	79.32	91.22
77300	Radiation dosimetry	97.58	89.32	84.85	97.58
77315	Teletherapy, isodose plan, complex	213.59	195.51	185.73	213.59
78104	Bone marrow imaging, whole body	230.56	211.04	200.49	230.56
78215	Liver and spleen imaging	160.44	146.85	139.51	160.44
78800	Tumor localization, limited area	191.53	175.32	166.55	191.53

PATHOLOGY AND LABORATORY[1]

Laboratory tests done as groups or combination "profiles" performed on multichannel equipment should be billed using the appropriate code number (80002 through 80019). Following is a list of the tests. The subsequent listing illustrates how to find the correct code.

Alanine aminotransferase (ALT, SGPT)	Carbon dioxide content	Phosphorus (inorganic phosphate)
Albumin	Chloride	Potassium
Aspartate aminotransferase (AST, SGOT)	Cholesterol	Protein, total
	Creatinine	Sodium
Bilirubin, direct	Glucose (sugar)	Urea nitrogen (BUN)
Billirubin, total	Lactate dehydrogenase (LD)	Uric acid
Calcium	Phosphatase, alkaline	

[1] Mock fees for laboratory test presented in this schedule may not be representative of fees in your region due to the variety of capitation and managed care contracts as well as discount policies made by laboratories. At the time of this edition, Medicare guidelines may or may not pat for automatic multichannel tests where a large number of tests are performed per panel. Some cases require documentation and a related diagnostic code for each test performed. Provider must have the CLIA level of licensure to bill for tests and test results must be documented.

FEE SCHEDULE (Continued)

CPT Code No. and Description	Mock Fees	Medicare		
		Participating	Non-Participating	Limiting Charge
AUTOMATIC MULTICHANNEL TEST				
80002 1 or 2 clinical chemistry tests	10.00	9.80	8.88	12.03
80003 3 clinical chemistry tests	15.00	14.60	13.87	16.64
80004 4 clinical chemistry tests	20.00	19.20	15.99	21.87
80005 5 clinical chemistry tests	20.00	19.20	15.99	21.87
80006 6 clinical chemistry tests	25.00	20.99	19.94	23.93
80007 7 clinical chemistry tests	25.00	20.99	19.94	23.93
80008 8 clinical chemistry tests	27.00	25.00	20.88	24.98
80009 9 clinical chemistry tests	27.00	25.00	20.88	24.98
80010 10 clinical chemistry tests	30.00	28.60	25.97	32.16
80011 11 clinical chemistry tests	30.00	28.60	25.97	32.16
80012 12 clinical chemistry tests	32.00	30.70	27.54	34.15
80016 13-16 clinical chemistry tests	32.00	30.70	27.54	34.15
80018 17-18 clinical chemistry tests	35.00	33.55	31.87	38.24
80019 19 or more clinical chemistry tests	35.00	33.55	31.87	38.24
81000 Urinalysis, non-automated, with microscopy	8.00	7.44	5.98	8.84
81001 Urinalysis, automated, with microscopy	8.00	7.44	5.98	8.84
81002 Urinalysis, non-automated without microscopy	8.00	7.44	5.98	8.84
81015 Urinalysis, microscopy only	8.00	7.44	5.98	8.84
82565 Creatinine; blood	10.00	9.80	8.88	12.03
82951 Glucose tol test, 3 spec	40.00	41.00	36.80	45.16
82952 Each add spec beyond 3	30.00	28.60	25.97	32.16
83020 Hemoglobin, electrophoresis	25.00	20.00	19.94	23.93
83715 Lipoprotein, blood; electrophoretic separation	25.00	20.00	19.94	23.93
84478 Triglycerides, blood	20.00	19.20	15.99	21.87
84479 Tribodothyronine (T-3)	20.00	19.20	15.99	21.87
84520 Urea nitrogen, blood (BUN); quantitative	25.00	20.99	19.94	23.93
84550 Uric acid, blood chemical	20.00	19.20	15.99	21.87
84702 Gonadotropin, chorionic; quantitative	20.00	19.20	15.99	21.87
84703 Qualitative	20.00	19.20	15.99	21.87
85022 Complete blood count, manual, diff with WBC count	20.00	19.20	15.99	21.87
85025 Complete blood count (hemogram), platelet count, automated, differential WBC count	25.00	20.00	19.94	23.93
85031 Complete blood count, manual	25.00	20.00	19.94	23.93
85095 Bone marrow, aspiration only	73.52	67.29	63.93	73.52
85102 Bone marrow aspiration (biopsy)	90.65	82.98	78.83	90.65
85345 Coagulation time; Lee & White	20.00	19.20	15.99	21.87
85590 Platelet count (Rees-Ecker)	20.00	19.20	15.99	21.87
86038 Antinuclear antibodies	25.00	20.00	19.94	23.93
87081 Culture, bacterial, screening for single organisms	25.00	20.00	19.94	23.93
87181 Sensitivity studies, antibiotic; per antibiotic	20.00	19.20	15.99	21.87
87184 Disk method, per plate (12 disks or less)	20.00	19.20	15.99	21.87
87210 Smear, primary source, wet mount with simple stain, for bacteria, fungi, ova, and/or parasites	35.00	48.35	45.93	55.12
88150 Papanicolaou cytopath	35.00	48.35	45.93	55.12
88302 Surgical pathology, gross & micro exam (skin, fingers, nerve, testis)	24.14	22.09	20.99	24.14
88305 Bone marrow, interpret	77.69	71.12	67.56	77.69

NOTE: Drs. Practon and Practon perform some laboratory tests under a waived test certificate that complies with the rules of the Clinical Laboratory Improvement Amendments (CLIA) of 1988, implemented in September, 1992.

FEE SCHEDULE (Continued)

CPT Code No. and Description		Mock Fees	Medicare* Participating	Medicare* Non-Participating	Medicare* Limiting Charge
MEDICINE PROCEDURES					
Immunization Injections					
90701	Diphtheria, tetanus, pertussis	34.00			
90703	Tetanus toxoid	28.00			
90712	Poliovirus vaccine, oral	28.00			
Therapeutic injections					
90782	IM or SC medication	4.77	4.37	4.15	4.77
90784	IV	21.33	19.53	18.55	21.33
90788	IM antibiotic	5.22	4.78	4.54	5.22
Psychiatry					
90825	Psychiatric consult, psychometric tests	175.00			
90843	Psychotherapy 20-30 min	60.25	55.15	52.39	60.25
90844	Psychotherapy 45-50 min	93.71	85.78	81.49	93.71
90853	Group therapy	29.22	26.75	25.41	29.22
Hemodialysis					
90935	Single phys evaluation	117.23	107.31	101.94	117.23
900937	Repeat evaluation	206.24	188.78	179.34	206.24
Gastroenterology					
91000	Esophageal intubation	69.82	63.91	60.71	69.82
91055	Gastric intubation	87.41	80.01	16.01	87.41
Opthalmologic Services					
92004	Comprehensive eye exam	90.86	83.17	79.01	90.86
92100	Tonometry	47.31	43.31	41.14	47.31
92230	Fluorescein angloscopy	55.49	50.79	48.25	55.49
82275	Electroretinography	81.17	74.29	70.58	81.17
95231	Spontaneous nystagmus	26.00			
Audiologic Function Tests					
92557	Basic comprehensive audiometry	54.33	49.73	47.24	54.33
95296	Ear measurements	26.81	24.54	23.31	26.31
Cardiovascular Therapeutic Services					
93000	Electrocardiogram (ECG)	34.26	31.36	29.79	34.26
93015	Treadmill ECG	140.71	128.80	122.36	140.71
93040	Rhythm ECG; 1-3 leads	18.47	16.90	16.06	18.47
Pulmonary					
94010	Spirometry	38.57	35.31	33.54	38.57
94060	Spirometry before and after bronchodilator	71.67	65.60	62.32	71.67
94150	Vital capacity, total	13.82	12.65	12.02	13.82
Allergy and Clinical Immunology					
95024	Intradermal tests	6.58	6.02	5.72	6.58
95044	Patch tests	8.83	8.08	7.68	8.83
95115	Treatment for allergy, corticosteroids, single inj.	17.20	15.75	14.96	17.20
95117	Treatment for allergy, two or more inj.	22.17	20.29	19.28	22.17
95165	Allergen immunotherapy, single or multiple antigens, multiple-dose vials		6.50	6.18	7.11

* Some services and procedures may not be considered a benefit under the Medicare program, and when listed on a claim form, no reimbursement may be received. However, it is important to include these codes when billing because Medicare policies may change without an individual knowing of a new benefit. For this reason, some of the services shown in this mock fee schedule do not have any amounts under the three Medicare columns.

FEE SCHEDULE (Continued)

CPT Code No. and Description		Mock Fees	Medicare*		
			Participating	Non-Participating	Limiting Charge
Neurology					
95812	Electroencephalogram, Up to one hr.	129.32	118.37	112.45	129.32
95819	Electroencephalogram– awake and asleep	126.81	116.07	110.27	126.81
95860	Electromyography, 1 extremity	88.83	81.31	77.24	88.83
95864	Electromyography, 4 extremities	239.99	219.67	208.69	239.99
96100	Psychological testing (per hour)	80.95	74.10	70.39	80.95
Physical Medicine					
97024	Diathermy	14.27	13.06	12.41	14.27
97036	Hubbard tank, each 15 min	24.77	22.67	21.54	24.77
97110	Physical therapy, initial 30 min	23.89	21.86	20.77	23.89
97260	Manipulation (cervical, thoracic, lumbosacral, sacro-iliac, hand, wrist), one area	16.93	15.49	14.72	16.93
Special Services and Reports					
99000	Handling of specimen (transfer from Dr.'s office to lab)	5.00			
99025	Initial surg eval (new pt) with starred procedure	50.00			
99050	Services requested after office hours in addition to basic service	25.00			
99052	Services between 10 p.m and 8 a.m. in addition to basic service	35.00			
99054	Services on Sundays and holidays in addition to basic service	35.00			
99056	Services normally provided in office requested by pt in location other than office	20.00			
99058	Office services provided on an emergency basis	65.00			
99070	Supplies and materials (itemize drugs and materials provided)	25.00			
99080	Special reports:				
	Insurance forms	10.00			
	Review of data to clarify pt's status	20.00			
	WC reports	50.00			
	WC extensive review report	250.00			

CPT MODIFIERS

-20	Microsurgery (attach report to claim)	Variable
-21	Prolonged evaluation and management services (attach report to claim)	Variable
-22	Unusual procedural services (attach report to claim)	Variable
-23	Unusual anesthesia (pt requires general anesthetic when procedure done usually requires no anesthesia or local anesthesia)	Variable
-24	Unrelated evaluation and management service to the original service by the same physician during a postoperative period	Variable
-25	Significant, separate identifiable evaluation and management service by the same physician on the day of a procedure	Variable

* Some services and procedures may not be considered a benefit under the Medicare program, and when listed on a claim form, no reimbursement may be received. However, it is important to include these codes when billing because Medicare policies may change without an individual knowing of a new benefit. For this reason, some of the services shown in this mock fee schedule do not have any amounts under the three Medicare columns.

FEE SCHEDULE (Continued)

CPT MODIFIERS (continued)

-26	Professional component (physician component only not technical component)	Variable
-32	Mandated services (i.e., consult by a third party payor)	Variable
-47	Anesthesia by surgeon	Variable
-50	Bilateral procedure	Variable
-51	Multiple procedures performed on the same day or at the same session	Variable
-52	Reduced services	Variable
-54	Surgical care only	Variable
-55	Postoperative care only	Variable
-56	Preoperative care only	Variable
-57	Decision for surgery	Variable
-58	Staged or related procedure or service by the same physician during the postoperative period	Variable
-62	Two surgeons (usually with different skills)	Variable
-66	Surgical team	Variable
-76	Repeat procedure by the same physician	Variable
-77	Repeat procedure by another physician	Variable
-78	Return to the operating room for a related procedure during the postoperative period	Variable
-79	Unrelated procedure or service by the same physician during the postoperative period	Variable
-80	Assistant surgeon	Variable
-81	Minimum assistant surgeon	Variable
-82	Assistant surgeon (when qualified resident surgeon not available)	Variable
-90	Reference (outside) laboratory procedures performed by a lab other than the treating physician	Variable
-99	Multiple modifiers (use of two or more modifiers for a service)	Variable

MEDICARE HCPCS CODES

These codes have been selected from many HCPCS codes as examples. The fees stated are only examples.

			FEES
A	0010	Ambulance service, base rate, emergency	$300
A	2000	Manipulation of spine by chiropractor	$50
A	4460	Elastic bandage, per roll	$15
A	5051	Ostomy pouch	$15
A	9150	Nonprescription drugs	$10
B	4034	Enteral feeding supply kit	$25
E	0100	Cane	$60
E	0110	Crutches	$100
H	5300	Occupational therapy	$45
J	0110	Administration of injection, including cost of drug	$35
J	0120	Injection, tetracycline	$25
J	0170	Injection, adrenalin	$25
J	0540	Injection, penicillin G	$25
J	1460	Injection, gamma globulin, intramuscular, 1cc	$20
J	1470	Injection, gamma globulin, intramuscular, 2cc	$25
L	0180	Cervical, multiple post collar	$50
L	3209	Surgical boot, child	$50
M	0005	Office visit with 2 or more modalities to the same area	$70
P	3001	Papanicolaou smear, interpretation by physician	$25